TEACHING SOCIAL STUDIES IN THE ELEMENTARY SCHOOL

TEACHING SOCIAL STUDIES IN THE ELEMENTARY SCHOOL

TEACHING SOCIAL STUDIES
IN THE ELEMENTARY SCHOOL

Third Edition

52328

RALPH C. PRESTON
University of Pennsylvania

HOLT, RINEHART AND WINSTON, INC.
New York   Chicago   San Francisco   Atlanta   Dallas
Montreal   Toronto   London

PREFACE

The field of social studies has been transformed in many ways since the publication in 1958 of the second edition of *Teaching Social Studies in the Elementary School*. The infusion of new ideas has driven social studies off dead center where it had seemed lodged for so long. Old assumptions are being challenged; new curriculums are being experimented with. Never before has the elementary school teacher enjoyed a wider range of competing ideas, methods, and materials to choose from.

One of my major purposes in the present revision is to describe the newer developments in functional terms so that they may have maximum significance for teachers. These developments include the sharp attention being given to the structure of subject matter; the rediscovery of "discovery" as an element in learning; applications of the momentous work of Piaget; the pioneering of inventive minds such as Senesh and Bloom; the growing awareness of the educational needs of disadvantaged children; the renewed interest in the pedagogical system of Montessori; and new applications of media such as programmed materials and television, with their potentially revolutionary effect upon the future role of the teacher. To a considerable extent, the impact of these and other current developments upon social studies is the *raison d'être* for this third edition.

Another purpose of this revision is to clear up foggy areas of social studies. Periods of change are frequently periods of confusion, and the present period is no exception. While we badly need the stimulation of zealots and the progressive ideas which they promulgate, we cannot afford to overlook the perplexity and insecurity among teachers which rapid innovation leaves in its wake. I have attempted to clarify the relationship of the new ideas to ways of classroom teaching, and to differentiate probable fad aspects of the new ideas from their more solid contributions.

The thoughts of many persons have influenced this revision. I owe a great deal to countless teachers for the generous opportunity to observe their work in the classroom and to discuss their work with them. Informal conversations with social studies specialists have widened my perspective. I am grateful to the social scientists whose works I have read or with whom I have consulted. Some of them have read relevant chapters of the manuscript from the points of view of their respective fields. I am particularly indebted to Professor James John Flannery, Department of Geography, University of Wisconsin at Milwaukee, for his careful and helpful review of Chapters 5 and 10; and to Professor Celia Stendler Lavatelli, Associate Director of the National Laboratory on Early Childhood Education, University of Illinois, who gave the entire manuscript a critical reading and whose penetrating observations and suggestions have in most instances resulted in changes and additions. Perhaps I should have acted on all her suggestions. Needless to say, the foregoing persons should be spared responsibility for the final product. I wish to record my thanks to Mrs. Janet B. Kuenne who helped with the bibliographies. I am deeply grateful to my wife, Madeline, who cheerfully worked her way through the various drafts of the manuscript, giving them the benefit of her keen language sense and editorial skill.

R.C.P.

Philadelphia, Pennsylvania
February 1968

CONTENTS

TEACHING SOCIAL STUDIES IN THE ELEMENTARY SCHOOL

PART
ONE

SOCIAL STUDIES
IN THE
ELEMENTARY SCHOOL

THE SOCIAL STUDIES: NATURE, PURPOSE, AND SIGNS OF CHANGE

Know then thyself, presume not to God to scan;
The proper study of mankind is man.
ALEXANDER POPE

Exploring the world and its people—that is the alluring opportunity afforded by the social studies. How can the opportunity most fully be realized in the elementary school?[1] To begin with, the nature, importance, and purpose of social studies must be clarified. This chapter will attempt to penetrate the obscurity which frequently surrounds social studies and to identify some of the forces which are making for change.

IMPORTANCE OF SOCIAL STUDIES

The foremost problems of today are social problems. They include a wide range of areas, from the maintenance of peace to the elimination of poverty; from conservation of resources to control of crime; from making government more efficient and less corrupt to maintaining security; from the provision of civil rights for all to employment for all. Obviously, the school cannot take responsibility for attempting to develop in the elementary-school child the knowledge and mature insights required in the solution of such problems. He is too young to attain these attributes, even if he were able to grasp the magnitude and complexity of the problems. However, he needs to begin to understand society and the conditions which give rise to social problems. This will help him, later on, as an adult citizen, to contribute to the solution of both the still unsolved, old problems and the new ones which society then will be facing.

---

[1] The term "elementary school," as used in this book, consists of the primary grades (kindergarten and Grades 1, 2, and 3) and the intermediate grades (Grades 4, 5, and 6). Occasional references are made to Grades 7 and 8, classified as elementary grades in some schools.

3

If the child is to grasp the importance of what he learns in social studies, he must see how it relates to the rapidly changing world of today. This does not mean that we should exclude study of the past and remote places. It simply means that social studies should form obvious links between those societies studied and the humming world which the child observes about him. For example, the study of transportation should give children much more than a bland picture of progress from the raft to the airplane; it should focus attention upon such current problems as mass transportation in urban centers, mounting highway accidents, increasing loss to newly constructed highways of open spaces, creek valleys, and long-established settled areas, and possible effects of mass air transportation upon trade barriers and cultural differences. By way of further example, the study of the conflict between the white pioneer and the American Indian should not be left as a bloody, far-off situation happily past. It should raise searching questions about the situation of the Indians today—where they are and why, the present status of Indian reservations, and the continuing conflict over treaties and land rights between surviving Indian tribes and the government.

The children in today's classrooms will live out a good part of their lives in difficult times. Their generation will have to struggle toward solutions of such pressing problems as those occasioned by the population explosion which brings, more than ever into sharp relief, the menace of hunger and shortages of water and other resources including wilderness and other recreation areas. Problems of war and race relations show no signs of immediate solution. It is not proposed here that teachers should set children the task of tackling such difficult problems in the classroom. That would be inappropriate and unwise. But social studies instruction can and should make children aware of such problems, of why they are not easily solved, of values that should be taken into account in searching for solutions, and of the fact that rational solutions are possible.

It should be added that social studies are important not just because they deal with problems. They contain the information, the ideas, and the methods of inquiry which make possible a satisfying and creative intellectual life. They also give a basis for tolerance of the dissimilarities that differentiate social groups.

WHAT THE SOCIAL STUDIES ARE

The social studies are those portions of social sciences that are selected for use in teaching in elementary and secondary schools. The question then arises: What are the social sciences? The social sciences are the fields of knowledge which deal with man's social behavior and his social institutions. The six social sciences which are most frequently drawn upon by elementary-school social studies are the following:

GEOGRAPHY   Geography is the study of the regions of the earth, with special emphasis upon man's relations to his habitat (its land, climate, and other physical features), and how these relationships are influenced by his energy, imagination, technical skill, aesthetic instincts, traditions, and beliefs. The trend among geographers, for purposes of introductory courses in school and college, is to define and classify regions in terms of areas which are relatively homogeneous with respect to cultural features.[2] Geography, as a field of scholarship, has been subdivided into subareas including economic geography, political geography, human geography, physical geography, and cartography. In his specialized teaching and research, a geographer will naturally classify a region according to the demands of his specialty. Thus, a political geographer must deal with political boundaries even when they cut across regions where there is a commonality of cultural features or of economic activity. Physical geography was once dominant and led teachers to look for physical causes of human behavior. For example, the motivation for human migration was oversimplified, explained almost purely in such terms as the presence of features (such as rivers) which facilitated movement, coupled with the presence of features (such as a desert) which discouraged movement. The swing away from this "environmental determinism" led to a sounder balance between physical and cultural features. The teaching of studies emphasizing geography is taken up in Chapter 5.

HISTORY   History is "the totality of what has transpired,"[3] only a small portion of which, of course, has been recorded. Even the recorded portion is too vast to be mastered by a single historian, and the portion to be incorporated in the social studies of the elementary school necessarily is quite restricted. It should be centered upon those episodes of the past which will supply guidelines for intelligent reaction to new problems.[4] For the study of American history, authoritative opinion among historians holds that the period of exploration and the colonial period should receive the heaviest emphasis;[5] for the study of man's history elsewhere, the background of several other cultures should be studied.[6] Some historians, on the other hand, think that schools overemphasize the period of exploration

[2] Ross N. Pearson, "Progress in Regional Geography," in *New Viewpoints in Geography*; Twenty-ninth Yearbook. Washington, D.C.: National Council for the Social Studies, 1959. Chap. 6.

[3] Thomas Woody, "Of History and Its Method," *Journal of Experimental Education*, 15 (March 1947), 175–201.

[4] Joseph R. Strayer, "History," in Bernard Berelson, *et al.*, *The Social Studies and the Social Sciences*. New York: Harcourt, 1962. Pp. 20–41.

[5] Strayer. P. 28. That historians have been consistent in this position for many years, may be seen by referring to the Report of the Committee on American History in Schools and Colleges of the American Historical Association, *et al.*, *American History in Schools and Colleges*. New York: Crowell-Collier and Macmillan, 1944.

[6] Strayer. P. 34.

in the study of American history, believing that the topic is more properly an aspect of European history. The colonial period is recommended by historians largely because of its impact upon the origin and growth of democratic institutions. While this impact is dealt with in elementary schools, the schools also give much attention (some educators think too much) to the picturesque colonial way of life—details of home, religious worship, agricultural methods, and the like. The teaching of studies emphasizing history is taken up in Chapter 6.

ECONOMICS   Economics is the study of man's use of his resources. It deals with the production, distribution, and consumption of *commodities*, and with the utilization of *services* of all types, ranging from unskilled services to professional services. It deals with "the ways in which, as a people, we manage our productive human and natural resources and the goods and services which result from the employment and use of these resources."[7] It is quite feasible in the elementary school to introduce children to such economic concepts as the specialization among producers, the interdependence of producers, the role of savings in production, the influence of consumer choice upon production, and the interaction of supply and demand.[8] The teaching of studies emphasizing economics is taken up in Chapter 7.

GOVERNMENT   Government (sometimes called "civics" at the lower-school levels and "political science" at the college level) focuses upon the structure, functions, and administration of political institutions. Elementary schools commonly give attention to the structure of local government, the political units of "state" and "province," and governmental services, including services which are local (fire, police, health, and so on), national (postal, national park, agricultural, and others), and international (like the World Health Organization or the Universal Postal Union). Chapter 8 is devoted to the teaching of studies emphasizing government.

ANTHROPOLOGY   Anthropology is a diversified field which includes the study of cultures and social systems, the study of language, the study of man's past existence, and the study of human races, evolution, and biological maturation.[9] It is a fruitful source of elementary school subject matter, making obvious contributions to studies of primitive groups and of both

[7] Ben W. Lewis, "Economics," in Berelson, *et al.*, *The Social Studies and the Social Sciences*. P. 108.

[8] Lawrence Senesh, "The Organic Curriculum: A New Experiment in Economic Education," *The Councilor*, **21** (March 1960), 43–56.

[9] George D. Spindler, "New Trends and Applications in Anthropology," in *New Viewpoints in the Social Sciences*; Twenty-eighth Yearbook, Washington, D.C.: National Council for the Social Sciences, 1958. Chap. 7.

native and foreign cultures. Applications will be found in the treatment of culture studies in Chapter 5 and of American Indian studies in Chapter 6.

SOCIOLOGY   Sociology is the study of societies and of associations within societies, including both their structures and the processes of socialization. There is scarcely a social studies topic which does not draw upon content and concepts of the sociologist, as will be observed in examining Chapters 5 through 8.

Thus, it is evident that social studies are derived directly from recognized academic disciplines. The term "social studies" does not always (or even necessarily) imply a unified (sometimes called "fused") treatment of social sciences, as is sometimes mistakenly believed. A *unified* social studies topic contains generalizations which cut across the boundaries separating geography, history, and other social sciences. Thus, a unified third-grade study of the American Indian might contain such generalizations as the following:

> The Indians' food, clothing, and homes were quite different from ours, since the Indians were not as advanced technologically nor as independent of their physical environment as modern man (Economics)
> What nature provides differs from one section of the country to the other (Geography)
> There was not just one kind of Indian culture; Indian cultures were different in different parts of the country (Anthropology)
> The white settlers who first came to America learned many things about how to live in this country from the Indians (History)

"Why, those generalizations add up to straight history as taught by any conscientious history teacher!" some readers may exclaim. "Why call programs 'unified social studies' simply because they are comprehensively taught?" That is a good point: To a certain extent, the distinction between the teaching of unified social studies and a separate subject has been overdrawn and is artificial. The chief difference lies in the fact that a plan of unified social studies usually results in *a greater degree of emphasis* upon related subjects than when the topic is pursued as part of a separate subject. Unified social studies programs are described in greater detail in Chapter 2.

Kidd presented an impressive argument for the logic of using "social science" in preference to "social studies,"[10] and Keller proposed, as a substitute, the term "history and the social sciences" as more precise and

---

[10] John W. Kidd, "Social Science or Social Studies," *Social Education*, 17 (May 1953), 207–208.

meaningful.[11] The fact remains that the term "social studies" continues to be more widely used than any other, not only by schoolmen, but also by scholars, when referring collectively to social sciences (however organized) as taught in elementary and secondary schools.

OBJECTIVES OF THE SOCIAL STUDIES

George Santayana declared that "Fanaticism consists in redoubling your efforts when you have forgotten your aim." Teachers who lose sight of their objectives often react similarly—they work all the harder, but their efforts are wastefully expended and erratic. In teaching, as in other fields of human endeavor, the slighting of objectives is a calamity. Exertion of extra "effort," however conscientious, fails to compensate for lack of purpose and direction.

The reader will find it helpful, in studying this section, to consult the classification of objectives as given in the two volumes of *Taxonomy of Educational Objectives* (see Chapter 13, Footnote 1) or its summary as given in Chapter 13 of this book. The classification scheme of each of these works consists of a series of categories arranged in an increasing order of complexity, each category corresponding to a separate learning situation described in terms of the intended behaviors of the learners.

Those who are in the most authoritative position to indicate social studies objectives are the social scientists themselves. The objectives discussed below are based upon ideas furnished by them.[12]

Knowledge and Understanding

One of the functions of the elementary school is to transmit knowledge and understanding—to pass on to each succeeding generation important facts and ideas that have been received from past generations. Children need to know what adults have learned, and believe to be true, about society. The social studies, by transmitting knowledge and understanding of our society, promote in children some sense of continuity and stability, and provide the kind of information and techniques upon which the perpetuation of civilization is dependent. Needless to say, man does not merely conserve present institutions and beliefs—he is also concerned with improving them. Otherwise, there would be no social progress. However,

---

[11] Charles R. Keller, "Needed: Revolution in the Social Studies," *Saturday Review*, 44 (September 16, 1961), 60–62.

[12] The author is particularly indebted to the discussion contained in Berelson, *et al.*, *The Social Studies and the Social Sciences*. The contributors wrote with the secondary school in mind, but most of their discussion of goals applies to the elementary school as well.

sound progress has its roots in the present; it is essential, therefore, that the child be grounded in the knowledge and understandings that prevail in society today.

Knowledge and understanding, which constitute major learning objectives for children in social studies classes and agreed upon by social scientists as desirable, include:

1. The cultural history, traditions, and values of the child's own society,
2. The cultural history, traditions, and values of selected societies, representing varying beliefs and practices,
3. Man's culture in varying environments and its influence upon his relation to his habitat,
4. The extent to which the nations of the world have moved and are moving toward interdependence,
5. Society's management and use of its economic resources, both natural and human,
6. The methods employed by social scientists in their respective fields.

Attitudes toward Learning

As important as the acquisition of content is the acquisition of a spirit of inquiry. Intellectual curiosity and imagination play as vital a role in the child's development as does knowledge. It must be remembered that many of the ideas and the items of information which the child learns in the classroom are ephemeral. They represent the present condition of knowledge, but may not be appropriate ten years from now. New discoveries are continually requiring revision of subject matter (new data uncovered by geologists and archeologists play havoc with textbook figures on man's tenancy of the earth); industrial processes are overhauled with changes in technology (the utilization of nuclear power, new chemical processes, and the computer are transforming today's manufacturing); the perspective of time yields certain historical interpretations, often including revisions of historical judgments (historians evaluate more generously today than a generation ago the contributions to the American economy of Carnegie, Rockefeller, and other aggressive entrepreneurs of their day); place names and symbols change (Siam, Persia, Madagascar, and Formosa have been officially replaced). The shifting nature of ideas, processes, and names brings to the fore the teacher's crucial job of stimulating the more stable outcomes of teaching: broad generalizations, study habits and skills, methods of inquiry, and *attitudes toward learning*. The teacher is properly charged with bringing about a number of attitudes:

1. Toward the subjects and topics under study—curiosity about, and interest in, their subject matter,
2. Toward questions and problems—inclination to formulate hunches or hypotheses about their possible answers and solutions,
3. Toward the entire social studies area—desire to continue exploring it outside of the classroom,
4. Toward hackneyed stereotypes—a desire to reject them and to make a fresh examination of phenomena and desire to form conclusions directly from raw data.

Social Values and Attitudes

Knowledge and understanding of society are not essentially ends in themselves. Their larger importance lies in the contribution they make to the child's perspective and to his equipment for citizenship. Children, as developing citizens, require considerable guidance in interpreting what they learn about their complex world and in acquiring a scale of values on which to base their interpretations. For social sciences contain *value elements*. Social scientists, in their writings, frequently make it obvious that they assume human personality, for example, to be of worth in itself. Writes a historian:

> When we seek to know the facts, the questions which we ask, and therefore the answers which we obtain, are prompted by our system of values. Our picture of the facts of our environment is moulded by our values. . . . Values enter into the facts and are an essential part of them. . . . It is through our values that we have the capacity to adapt ourselves to our environment, and to adapt our environment to ourselves. . . .[13]

Thus, we find in the writings of professional social scientists such value statements as the following:

> Man achieves his fullest potential in an atmosphere of freedom.
> Facts are established by evidence, not by intuition or authority.
> The policy of embracing evil in the name of appeasement is cowardly and bankrupt.

Most American adults accept a republican form of government; they jealously guard the voice they have in selecting their representatives; they deplore corruption; they believe in peaceful negotiation to settle disputes between nations and between labor and management; and they

[13] Edward Hallett Carr, *What Is History?* New York: Knopf, 1962. P. 174.

have faith in the ultimate justice of the American legal system, disapproving the exercise of mob action. Such attitudes, when passed on to our children, give them a point of reference by which to judge their own behavior and *by which* to chart changes in the social order.

What is likely to happen when the fostering of attitudes is neglected? An illustration was furnished in a study of community workers by a certain third-grade class. The children had gained an understanding of the following two generalizations:

Most occupations in modern industrial society are specialized.

Workers in modern industrial society are interdependent.

However, some of the children whose fathers were white-collar workers felt that their fathers were superior to fathers who wore overalls. They had failed to develop respect for the dignity of useful work *per se.* Home and community factors beyond the teacher's control had obviously exerted a heavy influence upon those children's attitudes. The teacher's role here is not to teach that one job is as important as another, or that all kinds of work contribute equally to society, or that truck drivers do as significant work as cancer researchers. That would be misleading. But the teacher *should* emphasize that the truck driver's work, too, is essential and respectable.

The teacher can contribute to desirable attitudes by furnishing a worthy model in his own behavior. Some examples of things he might do at appropriate times are to insist on a fair examination of evidence by the class concerning the merits of a controversial bill before Congress, supply opportunities for children to assume responsibilities, supply an informational base for responsible attitudes—such as underscoring the industry and sacrifices of pioneers (as detailed in writings of Hamlin Garland,[14] John Muir,[15] and others) or of public servants as illustrated by George Washington's selflessness in the face of duty.

Teachers realistically can hope to cultivate general attitudes as follows:

1. Toward evidence—respect for it and acceptance of the rules which govern it,
2. Toward man—appreciation of human dignity and sensitivity to the feelings of others,
3. Toward community and country—devotion to their welfare and development of a sense of responsibility with regard to them,

---

[14] Hamlin Garland, *Boy Life on the Prairie.* Lincoln, Neb.: University of Nebraska Press, 1961.
[15] John Muir, *The Story of My Boyhood and Youth.* Boston: Houghton Mifflin, 1925.

4. Toward scarce natural resources—recognition of the need for their conservation and wise use,

5. Toward generalizations about human behavior—critical, discriminating analysis of generalizations.

Before leaving the subject of attitudes, it is necessary to consider briefly the doubts held by some as to whether the school can shape the attitudes of children. In reviewing three studies of efforts to influence children's attitudes, Mayer gloomily wrote: "It is more than doubtful that the schools can successfully teach values other than those of the child's home, or those of the larger community."[16] He personally observed attempts at teaching democratic values in many classrooms and concluded that such teaching was a "waste of time" and induced "dreadful boredom."[17]

On the other hand, one summary of research on the effects of classroom instruction on attitudes toward racial groups reports that about twice as many studies cited significant favorable changes in attitude as cite insignificant changes or no changes.[18] Whether or not shifts in attitude take place, according to the authors of the summary, seems to be due to the nature of the information (that is, how favorable it is toward the group which is being studied by the children), the teacher's attitude toward the group, and the relationship between the pupils and the teacher (that is, the pupils' readiness to accept the teacher's feelings as well as his information). The last two factors have been neglected by research, and this probably accounts for the puzzling inconsistency in the findings.[19]

Skills

As the child studies society, he should learn to use the skills and tools of social studies.

He should learn how to look for evidence and how to weigh it; how to compare sources, and how to check discrepancies against still other sources. He should learn the elements of scientific thinking in a spirit of free inquiry, rejecting attitudes of either unquestioning acceptance or debunking. He should learn and practice the study skills, including the reading and interpreting of sources of information—textbooks, reference books, charts, time

---

[16] Martin Mayer, *The Schools*. New York: Harper & Row, 1961. P. 344.

[17] Mayer. P. 346.

[18] John Harding, *et al.*, "Prejudice and Ethnic Relations," in Gardner Lindzey (Ed.), *Handbook of Social Psychology*. Reading, Mass.: Addison-Wesley, 1954. P. 1047. See also Robert E. Mainer's conclusion that "intergroup education programs are successful in producing greater opposition to social discrimination." H. H. Remmers (Ed.), *Anti-Democratic Attitudes in American Schools*. Evanston, Ill.: Northwestern University Press, 1963. P. 144.

[19] Muzafer Sherif and Carl I. Hovland, *Social Judgment*. New Haven, Conn.: Yale University Press, 1961. Pp. 146–147.

lines, graphs, and tables. He should learn how to locate pertinent data in these and other sources.

Almost every undertaking in social studies classes should provide opportunity for practice and improvement of the following skills:

1. Examination of data about society, with objectivity,
2. Judging the validity and relevancy of data,
3. Compilation and classification of data,
4. Interpretation of maps, globes, and graphic material which present social data,
5. Formation of generalizations and hypotheses from raw data,
6. Using some of the social scientists' methods in collecting firsthand data.

A Final Word about Objectives

Objectives are useful as checklists for teachers to refer to from time to time in order to test the adequacy and comprehensiveness of the generalizations and skills which they are stressing in their teaching. Children will move toward the achievement of the foregoing broad objectives—acquiring knowledge and understanding of our society and its relationship to other societies, learning study and research skills, and adopting conscientious attitudes toward society—with a high degree of probability if their teachers, in addition to being intuitively (not self-consciously) aware of the objectives, are steeped in the subject matter which they are teaching.

THE SOCIAL STUDIES IN TRANSITION

Dissatisfaction with various aspects of the social studies program has been smoldering for a long time. Several years ago, the writer stated:

> A body without a spirit is a corpse; a spirit without a body is a spook; the social studies curriculum in today's elementary school is both corpse and spook. It is a corpse in those schools where "covering ground" is an obsession and where the psychology of introducing children to social concepts is unknown. It is a spook where a sentimental cult of educators has rendered the social studies thin and chaotic. . . .[20]

More recently, Keller wrote that "the social studies are in the doldrums,"[21] and Mayer declared: "No force now apparent anywhere seems strong enough to lift the social studies from today's slough of careless

[20] Ralph C. Preston, *Teaching Social Studies in the Elementary School.* New York: Holt, Rinehart and Winston, 1950. "Preface," p. v.

[21] Keller. Pp. 60–62. Subsequently, Keller has been an active force in driving social studies from the doldrums.

boredom."[22] Nevertheless, changes are taking place, and forces are at work which will, in all probability, bring about still greater changes. Revolutionary forces are sweeping the entire field of education, and social studies are as exposed as any other area.

One of the important agents of change has been the emergence of an aggressively critical public mood toward education. The feverish competition over outer space, popularly heralded by the launching of the Soviet Union's first Sputnik, in 1957, jolted the American public's complacent, casual attitude toward education. Invidious comparisons were drawn between the United States and the Soviet Union with respect to expenditures for education, the intensity and quality of the education of children and youth, and the training, pay, and prestige of teachers and other intellectual workers.

The uneasiness promoted by Sputnik also provided a wider hearing for the criticisms and proposals of such groups in the United States as the Council for Basic Education, which had been airing their highly critical views with only limited effectiveness. Many citizens became persuaded that our schools were in need of fundamental curriculum changes. Certain journalists and commentators reflected the new mood by repeating the charges and keeping them in the forefront. Although some of the criticisms were groundless and unfair,[23] few school officials escaped the resultant pressure. Many educators bristled defensively, but most conceded, at least tacitly, that weaknesses existed in their schools. They took up the byword, "Excellence," and sought to establish higher standards.

The greatest concern, at first, was to improve the teaching of mathematics and science, but social studies, too, soon began receiving a share of the public's new interest in, and attention to, education.

NATURE OF THE CHANGES

Change 1: Increased Emphasis on Scholarship

There is greater recognition of the value content *per se* and greater stress upon it. New curriculum plans reveal more firmly structured content.

[22] Keller. Pp. 359–360. Mayer has expressed greater hope in a subsequent book, *Where, When, and Why: Social Studies in American Schools.* New York: Harper & Row, 1963.

[23] Discussion of the criticisms will be found in the following publications: Harry D. Gideonse, *On the Educational Statesmanship of a Free Society.* Pamphlet. New York: The Woodrow Wilson Foundation, 1959; Byron S. Hollinshead, "Is European Education Better?" *Educational Record,* **39** (April 1958), 89–96; Sydney Hook, "Modern Education and Its Critics," in *The American Association of Colleges for Teacher Education: Seventh Yearbook.* Oneonta, N.Y.: The Association, 1954; George L. Newsome, Jr. and Albert J. Kingston, Jr., "A Critique of Criticisms of Education," *Educational Theory,* **12** (October 1962), 218–226; C. Winfield Scott, *et al., The Great Debate: Our Schools in Crisis.* Englewood Cliffs, N.J.: Prentice-Hall, 1959.

The content of the primary grades, while still including community institutions, workers, and processes, is beginning to extend beyond the community; it is slowly divorcing itself from platitudes and sentimentality. In the intermediate grades, the unified programs are giving greater identity to the content of geography, history, economics, government, and other social sciences.

Recent events "are tending rapidly to close the gap" between the curriculum and available scholarly knowledge.[24] Those new concepts that scholars believe to be of primary significance in their fields are beginning to find their way into the classrooms. For example, better materials on other cultures are being used, and the archaic and misleading stereotypes often associated with them are giving ground to more realistic portrayals, reflecting recent reappraisals and revised attitudes. Some schools have moved from studies of tropical rain forests to studies of particular African nations, such as Nigeria, and their struggles to enter the twentieth century.

Various forms of departmentalization in the elementary school (mostly in Grades 4–6) are finding favor in a number of school systems. Under departmentalization, a teacher is responsible for teaching only one academic subject, or a limited number of academic subjects, as opposed to the self-contained classroom scheme, under which a single teacher is given total responsibility for the instruction of a group of children in a variety of subjects throughout the day. (The term "departmentalization" is usually not used to describe the assignment of special subject teachers in music, art, and physical education.) According to one report: "Departmentalization at the elementary level is still relatively rare, and most of the plans which *do* exist are limited and experimental."[25] Yet, the report points out further, there are 40 large school systems in which each academic subject (English, social studies, mathematics, and science) is taught by a separate teacher, and 34 in which one teacher is responsible for language arts and social studies, with the remaining subjects taught by specialists; more than a score of other patterns exist.[26]

The advantage of departmentalization is threefold. In the first place, it facilitates increased teacher specialization and understanding of subject matter by limiting the total range of subject matter to be handled by any one teacher; "the deeper the teacher's understanding of his subject, the greater the likelihood of excellent instruction."[27] Second, not all children

---

[24] Michael B. Petrovich, "Teaching about Russia and Eastern Europe," in Berelson, et al., *The Social Studies and the Social Sciences*. P. 241.

[25] National Education Association, Research Division, and American Association of School Administrators, *Departmentalization in Elementary Schools*. Educational Research Service Circular No. 7. Washington, D.C.: The Association, 1965. P. 1.

[26] National Education Association, Research Division, "Departmentalization in Elementary Schools," *NEA Research Bulletin*, 44 (February 1966), 27–28.

[27] Richard C. Anderson, "The Case for Teacher Specialization in the Elementary School," *Elementary School Journal*, 62 (February 1962), 253–260.

respond equally to the instruction of a single teacher; the rapport in some instances may be poor. If a class has two or three academic teachers, a child's chances of responding favorably to a teacher are increased. Third, departmentalization makes it possible for the teacher to spend more time on preparation if he so desires. Departmentalization or semidepartmentalization with young children has certain questionable features. A young child needs closer personal guidance from a teacher who knows him well, and such guidance is often not received from a group of coldly objective, subject-minded specialists.

In any case, the present experimentation with departmentalization is giving a fresh emphasis to the importance of the quality of teacher scholarship and teacher preparation. It is probably sounding the death knell of the hardy, but senseless and maudlin, slogan of "teach the child and not the subject." In its vigorous advocacy of solid content and careful preparation of lessons, it is influencing salubriously the teaching of social studies.

A major factor in the increased emphasis on scholarship is the widespread participation of social scientists in curriculum programs. The traditional aloofness of scholars to curriculum problems of the lower schools has given way to expressions of active interest. The participation of scholars in California's social studies program, although limited, is an indication of the promising possibilities.[28]

Reference has already been made (footnotes 4–7, 12, 13, and 25) to the notable volume by Berelson and other social scientists, who joined six professors of education in its preparation. Other examples are a Working Seminar on the Improvement of the Social Studies Curriculum, meeting at Stanford University in July 1963, which consisted of ten social scientists and ten social studies specialists; and a Conference on Needed Research in the Teaching of the Social Studies held at Syracuse University in October 1963, attended by approximately 40 social scientists, social studies specialists, and psychologists. Various scholarly associations (such as the American Anthropological Association, American Economic Association, Association of American Geographers, and American Sociological Association) have task forces at work on specialized aspects of social studies. The Anthropology Curriculum Study Project, for example, sponsored by the first of the foregoing organizations, is publishing materials for use in high schools. Its publications are setting a standard for curriculum work in their emphasis upon primary sources (eye-witness reports and the like) and studies in depth. They should be studied by elementary school workers who wish to see how these features may be developed. Other examples of collaboration by scholars in curriculum projects are taking place in experimental undertakings. There can be little doubt that the attention of scholars

---

[28] *Report of the State Central Committee on Social Studies to the California State Curriculum Commission.* Sacramento: California State Department of Education, 1961.

to the work of the lower schools will result in a clarification of the objectives, and in improvement of the content, of the social studies.

Change 2: New Applications of Old Insights

Recent psychological research has brought to the fore the importance to learning of *subject-matter structure, pupil discovery,* and *reinforcement.* The principles underlying these concepts are not new, but they have received fresh emphasis, and their applications to classroom teaching have been actively explored.

The importance of *subject-matter structure* has been vigorously brought out by Jerome S. Bruner.[29] Bruner tells us, "Grasping the structure of a subject is understanding it in a way that permits many other things to be related to it."[30] This is done by seeing to it that the curriculum reflects the basic ideas (generalizations) in the field being studied. For example, transportation (which is often approached in the elementary school chiefly as a geographical study) may be organized so that the study of it is built around generalizations which give structure to the subject of transportation. They are centers around which details of the study can be grouped. One of the major generalizations may be stated thus:

Topographic features have played a role in the development of transportation.

Two items of information which illustrate this generalization are:

The Baltimore and Ohio Railroad, in laying its first westward rails, had to overcome serious technical problems in order to cope with the hills of the Potomac Valley and the mountains of West Virginia.

Before steel bridges were introduced, it was necessary to ferry railroad passengers across wide rivers, such as the Delaware.

The two illustrative items of information draw their significance from the major generalization cited. If the teacher stresses the major generalization and makes sure that the child recognizes it as one of the pegs on which to hang relevant details, then the subject becomes more comprehensible to the child. If the subject ends, on the other hand, as a jumble of isolated items of information, comprehension will be poor. Furthermore, if the structure is mastered by the child, he will remember the detail better because it fits into a structured pattern. The major generalization about the relationship between physical geography and transportation is remembered because it

[29] Jerome S. Bruner, *The Process of Education,* 1961; *Toward a Theory of Instruction,* 1966. Cambridge, Mass.: Harvard University Press.
[30] Bruner, *The Process of Education.* P. 7.

is one of the pillars of the structure; when recalling this generalization, the detail about the Baltimore and Ohio's engineering difficulties in laying its tracks westward is likely to be brought to mind because it vividly illustrates the generalization.

But, just because certain generalizations are important does not justify teaching which consists largely of the teacher's "unloading" the generalizations upon a child and asking him to memorize them. The pupil also needs opportunity to *discover* generalizations for himself.

Pupil discovery was another concept effectively promoted by Bruner.[31] Traditionally, subject matter has been taught by having teachers and textbooks "tell" pupils the facts and generalizations to be learned. Bruner's theory is that an attitude on the part of a pupil to want to formulate a generalization or solve a problem, is part of mastering a field. The children begin with facts which are already known to them, which they themselves collected, or which are presented to them.

Bruner cites a vivid example from a study by a group of children of the geography of the North Central States.[32] The children were given blank maps of the region which showed only rivers, lakes, and various natural resources. They were asked to show on their maps where the main cities, railroads, and highways would be located without looking up this information in books or maps. A class discussion followed in which individual children explained their reasons for locating cities at particular points and arteries of transportation between various points. After an hour of heated discussion, the children excitedly compared their own maps with a wall map.

There are various approaches to discovery. In a third-grade class, the children learned that, within a given unit of time (1) fewer men are required to milk a given number of cows by machine than by hand; (2) fewer men are required to prepare a given quantity of hay with a power mower and a power baler than with hand tools; and (3) fewer men are required to weave a given amount of cloth on power looms than on hand looms. The teacher asked the class to think what these three facts mean. One child replied: "Every new labor-saving machine seems to cut down the number of workers needed for that job." This was a reasonably adequate generalization; the teacher repeated it and had other children restate it. If a wrong generalization had been given, the class would have been encouraged to think further about the facts. Other illustrations of the discovery method appear in subsequent chapters.

[31] Bruner, *The Process of Education*. Pp. 20–22.
[32] Richard C. Anderson and David P. Ausubel, *Readings in the Psychology of Cognition*. New York: Holt, Rinehart and Winston, 1965. Pp. 80–81. Examples of "discovery" as applied to high school teaching will be found in Edwin Fenton, *Teaching the New Social Studies in Secondary Schools: An Inductive Approach*. New York: Holt, Rinehart and Winston, 1966.

Of course, Bruner's belief in the importance of pupil discovery is not new, nor has it been untried. It was advocated by Jean Jacques Rousseau, John Dewey, and others. A generation ago, Lucy Sprague Mitchell expressed the view that children can learn satisfactorily only "by the active process of discovering relationships" and that the school, therefore, should operate "essentially as a laboratory where such discoveries may be made."[33]

A word of caution is in order. Aspects of the "discovery" method are faddish, and too much has been claimed for it. Some studies have shown that giving students a rule for solving problems was just as effective as withholding the rule to encourage discovery, whether judged in terms of learning the rule, satisfaction on the part of the student with the method, or carrying on independent work on the use of the rule after the learning period.[34] A leading psychologist writes:

> The evidence is not particularly one-sided that this (pupil-discovery) is the better method. After all, one should not forget that man is a verbal animal, and there are marvelous shortcuts in learning to be achieved by the use of language. The chances are that . . . telling the learner the principle verbally is much quicker than any other method, and may well be as effective.[35]

The psychological advantage of discovery experiences probably lies in their success in promoting motivation through inviting the pupil to put the final touches on a learning task.

But, obviously not all learning can be of this order. No sensible person would propose that *all* relationships and generalizations be discovered by children; obviously, there would not be time even in a long life to rediscover all that man has learned over the ages. The need is simply for children to have some opportunity every day to put facts together, to try to see what generalizations or conclusions the facts seem to suggest, and to apply old generalizations in tackling new questions. In this way, a larger proportion of children than heretofore may become self-propelled thinkers, able to learn on their own after they leave school.

The principle that efficient learning requires *reinforcement* (a reward, for example, may for certain pupils and in certain circumstances constitute

[33] Lucy Sprague Mitchell, *Young Geographers*. New York: Basic Books, 1963 (original printing, 1934). P. 11.

[34] Robert C. Craig, "Discovery, Task Completion, and the Assignment as Factors in Motivation," *American Educational Research Journal*, 2 (November 1965), 217–222; John D. Krumboltz and William W. Yabroff, "The Comparative Effects of Inductive and Deductive Sequences in Programed Instruction," *American Educational Research Journal*, 2 (November 1965), 223–235.

[35] Robert M. Gagné, *The Conditions of Learning*. New York: Holt, Rinehart and Winston, 1965. P. 53. See also the detailed, careful critique by David P. Ausubel, *The Psychology of Meaningful Verbal Learning*. New York: Grune & Stratton, 1963.

a reinforcement) has been applied by Skinner[36] and others in their development of programmed instruction. Programmed instruction, implemented in the form of a teaching machine or a programmed textbook, consists of subject matter which has been arranged in a carefully developed sequence of steps. The pupil is called upon to make an active response to a question or problem at each step. He punches his response into a machine, or he writes it out, or he marks one of several alternative answers. In the case of a teaching machine, he receives a prompt "feedback" (a correction or a confirmation of his response). In the case of a textbook, he is told where he will be able to check the correctness of his response. Whether programmed instruction is presented by means of a machine or a textbook, the pupil proceeds at his own rate from step to step—as rapidly as he is able, or as slowly as he must. He masters each step before attempting the next step.

Programmed instruction provides a practical means for systematically taking care of individual differences in the pacing of material and in assuring, at each step, reinforcement of the correct response (through immediate confirmation of a correct response). There are, to be sure, limitations to programmed instruction (see Chapter 11), and only a few of the programmed materials now available deal with social studies.[37] Nevertheless, programming has influenced teachers by making them acutely aware of the signal role of reinforcement in learning.

Change 3: Expanded Curriculum Experimentation

A variety of new curriculum designs is being tried, and still others are being formulated. Grants from the United States Office of Education under "Project Social Studies" are supporting a number of applied research projects and curriculum study centers designed to reexamine the nature and aims of the social studies curriculum and to improve teaching methods and materials.[38] For example:

> A new curriculum, kindergarten–sophomore year of college (University of Minnesota, Edith West, Director). A new curriculum for Grades K–14 is being developed by a team of specialists from each of the social science disciplines and education. For the primary grades,

[36] B. F. Skinner, "The Science of Learning and the Art of Teaching"; "Teaching Machines," in A. A. Lumsdaine and Robert Glaser (Eds.), *Teaching Machines and Programmed Learning: A Source Book.* Washington, D.C.: National Education Association, Department of Audio-visual Instruction, 1960. Pp. 99–113; 137–158.

[37] Leonard W. Ingraham, "Programmed Instructional Materials in Social Studies: 1963," *Social Education,* 28 (January 1964), 15–17, 26.

[38] Edwin Fenton and John M. Good, "Project Social Studies: A Progress Report," *Social Education,* 29 (April 1965), 206–208.

the staff will draw heavily on concepts from anthropology, sociology, and geography. In the middle grades, "the tentative curriculum calls for greater focus upon the separate disciplines of geography and history. However, key concepts from the other disciplines are crucial to the study of these courses.[39]

Instructional materials based on a fresh identification of concepts and methods of the social scientist (Syracuse University, Roy A. Price, Director). A group of social scientists and social studies specialists are identifying the major concepts from social sciences and allied disciplines that appear to be appropriate for programs in selected elementary and secondary grades. The study will include identification of the methods of social scientists, including attitudes (objectivity, respect for evidence, and the like) and techniques (interview, experimentation, and so on). Finally, the group will construct instructional materials for classroom use.[40]

Instructional materials for a new approach to American history (Northwestern University, John R. Lee, Director). A group of social scientists and school personnel are developing materials for a new approach to the study of American history. They are drawing upon concepts from American history, economics, geography, and political science. The end product will be a program in which much of the duplication that occurs in the teaching of American history in Grades 5, 8, and 11 will be eliminated.[41]

Curriculum guides and materials for Asiatic studies (University of California at Berkeley, John U. Michaelis, Director). Specialists on Asia, other social scientists, classroom teachers, and curriculum specialists will develop teaching guides and instructional materials for elementary and secondary schools, based on the work of scholars. Annotated bibliographies of selected topics will also be prepared.[42]

Other groups, with support from other sources, have been at work. Educational Services Incorporated (ESI), producers of the revolutionary physics program of the Physical Science Study Committee, has been giving attention to social studies.[43] ESI's emerging sequence is of special signifi-

[39] Edith West, "University of Minnesota: An Articulated Curriculum for Grades K-14," *Social Education*, 29 (April 1965), 209–211.

[40] Roy A. Price, "Syracuse University: Social Science Concepts and Workways as the Basis for Curriculum Revision," *Social Education*, 29 (April 1965), 218–220.

[41] John R. Lee, "Northwestern University: Materials for a New Approach in American History," *Social Education*, 29 (April 1965), 223.

[42] John U. Michaelis, "University of California at Berkeley" (under "Centers Established in 1964: A Brief Report"), *Social Education*, 29 (April 1965), 225.

[43] Educational Services Incorporated, "A Statement of the Aims of the Course of Study Being Developed by the Social Studies Program." Mimeographed. Cambridge, Mass.: ESI, 1964; Bruner, *Toward a Theory of Instruction*. Chap. 4.

cance by virtue of its efforts to create educational materials and methods which allow children to work as social scientists would work, using such methods as evaluating data according to the rules of evidence, and formulating and testing hypotheses.

The schools of Glens Falls, N.Y., in collaboration with the National Council for the Social Studies, have been experimenting, since 1957, with the teaching of world affairs. Elementary school teachers in Lexington, Mass., have been experimenting with new materials and methods under the direction of Joseph Grannis of Harvard. Teachers in Elkhart, Ind., under the direction of Lawrence Senesh of Purdue University, have been experimenting with an economics-oriented elementary school curriculum. These will be described further in subsequent chapters. Such varied experimentation is new in social studies. While its final evaluation is probably years away, the experimentation is creating a climate in which improvement of the social studies curriculum and social studies teaching can be expected.

In Conclusion

A warning should be issued. Periods of change are not only periods of challenge. They are also periods of danger. They are exploited by sloganeers and faddists. If the social studies are to emerge sound and strong from the current ferment, it will be necessary for each new proposition to be scrutinized carefully and experimented with critically—particularly those propositions which are largely organizational in nature. Otherwise, we may find in 15 years that, instead of having made progress, we have simply experienced another ride on a pendulum.

RELATION OF SOCIAL STUDIES TO SOCIAL EDUCATION

Social education embraces much more than social studies. It comprises all those educational activities which seek the formation in children of desired attitudes, skills, knowledge, and behavior.[44] These range from the profound to the trivial. Social education takes place, for example, under the following conditions:

1. When the class learns the necessity of order and quiet for the accomplishment of most school learning activities,
2. When the class formulates rules for keeping the cloakroom clean and neat,
3. When the teacher sees to it that the attention-seeker is gratified only when he makes positive contributions to the class.

[44] Henry J. Otto, *Social Education in Elementary Schools.* New York: Holt, Rinehart and Winston, 1956. P. 34.

4. When the teacher gives the timid child responsibility for performing a task through which he can build self-assurance.
5. When loquacious children learn they may not monopolize class discussions.

Social education requires the organization of each classroom as a miniature society, disciplined and democratic. Children's attitudes toward themselves, their classmates, their teachers, and society at large are in a continuous process of modification as a result of *all* their school experiences, whether these take place during periods set aside for mathematics, for preparing for dismissal at the end of the school day, or for any other purpose. For this reason, teachers are continually in positions of responsibility for the kinds of social attitudes and habits which their pupils are forming.

Some educators have taken the position that if a teacher is carrying out social education, he is simultaneously teaching social studies. Such is not the case. Social studies are an organized body of learning, with objectives as described earlier in this chapter. Social studies do not treat the entire range of social education. The social studies program obviously contributes to social education, but it does not do so more than the programs in mathematics, reading, and other subjects. However, social studies have the more explicit purpose of widening children's knowledge and understanding of man in his environment and society.

FOR REVIEW AND REFLECTION

1. Define the term "social studies."
2. What are the objections of Bestor, Keller, and Kidd (see "Supplementary Reading" below) to the term "social studies?" To what extent are their objections solid? To what extent are their objections merely semantic?
3. Give examples of generalizations derived from lists of objectives which you believe children should learn in their study of a selected social studies topic.
4. Give a concrete illustration of how orderly thinking can be developed through social studies.
5. Draw up a list of criteria by which changes in social studies might be evaluated.

ASSIGNMENTS

1. List two or three social sciences which are not mentioned in this chapter. What is the nature and scope of each? What aspects of their content appear appropriate for study by children?
2. Bruner writes: ". . . there is no reason to believe that any subject matter cannot be taught to any child at virtually any age in some form" (see "Supplementary Reading"). Discuss implications and applications of his statement.

3. Visit a social studies class in an elementary school and draw conclusions concerning the probable purposes which were being sought by the teacher through the observed activities.

4. Select one of the "agents of change" described in this chapter, read about it, and speculate on its ultimate impact upon the social studies curriculum and social studies teaching.

SUPPLEMENTARY READING

Bauer, Nancy W. (Ed.), *Revolution and Reaction: The Impact of the New Social Studies.* Cranbrook Curriculum Conference Proceedings. Bloomfield Hills, Mich.: Cranbrook School, 1966. Statements by Keller and others who want fundamental changes in social studies.

Berelson, Bernard, *et al., The Social Studies and the Social Sciences.* New York: Harcourt, 1962. Representatives of various social sciences discuss objectives and scope of the social studies program from the point of view of their respective disciplines.

Bestor, Arthur, *The Restoration of Learning.* New York: Knopf, 1955. Chap. 10. Criticizes the term "social studies," finding it unnecessary and objectionable because it espouses teaching which focuses too narrowly on contemporary questions.

Bloom, Benjamin S. (Ed.), *Taxonomy of Educational Objectives: Handbook I: Cognitive Domain.* New York: McKay, 1956. A valuable classification of cognitive objectives arranged in a hierarchy of categories in terms of complexity.

Bruner, Jerome S., *The Process of Education.* Cambridge, Mass.: Harvard University Press, 1961. Points out, among other things, the importance of having the curriculum reflect a subject's "structure" to promote understanding, permanence of learning, and transfer.

Ford, G. W., and Lawrence Pugno (Eds.), *The Structure of Knowledge and the Curriculum.* Skokie, Ill.: Rand McNally, 1964. Contains a contribution by Scriven which presents the structure of knowledge in the social sciences.

Heath, Robert W. (Ed.), *New Curricula: A Report on the Methods and Programs for Teaching Science and the Humanities Which Promise to Revolutionize American Education.* New York: Harper & Row, 1964. Pp. 197–206. Reviews new thinking about the social studies curriculum and certain new projects which are under way.

Henry, Nelson B. (Ed.), *Social Studies in the Elementary School;* Fifty-sixth Yearbook of the National Society for the Study of Education. Pt. II. Chicago: University of Chicago Press, 1957. Contains chapters by Hanna, Dimond, Ojemann, Preston, and others on objectives, child development, curriculum, reading, evaluation, citizenship, and other topics as they relate to social studies.

Horn, Ernest, *Methods of Instruction in the Social Studies.* New York: Scribner, 1937. A classic—one of the more penetrating books written about teaching social studies—and still applicable.

Hunnicut, C. W. (Ed.), *Social Studies for the Middle Grades.* Washington,

D.C.: National Council for the Social Studies, 1960. A collection of articles on a number of aspects of social studies teaching.

Keller, Charles R., "Needed: Revolution in the Social Studies," *Saturday Review*, **44** (September 16, 1961), 60–62. Calls for fundamental revision of the social studies curriculum.

Kidd, John W., "Social Science or Social Studies," *Social Education*, **17** (May 1953), 207–208. Suggests substitution of social science" for "social studies."

Krathwohl, David R., *et al.*, *Taxonomy of Educational Objectives: Handbook II: Affective Domain*. New York: McKay, 1964. Classifies objectives which deal with interests, attitudes, values, and other aspects of affective behavior.

Mayer, Martin, *The Schools*. New York: Harper & Row, 1961. Chapter 16 is a searching scrutiny of social studies instruction by a critical journalist.

————, *Where, When, and Why: Social Studies in American Schools*. New York: Harper & Row, 1963. A journalistic examination of practices in social studies theory and practice; extravagant judgments mixed with incisive observations.

Michaelis, John U. (Ed.), *Social Studies in Elementary Schools*; Thirty-second Yearbook. Washington, D.C.: National Council for the Social Studies, 1962. The contribution of Paul R. Hanna and John R. Lee, "Generalizations from the Social Sciences" (pp. 62–89), reviews studies which have produced generalizations which can be useful in checking the comprehensiveness and the objectives of a social studies program.

————, and A. Montgomery Johnston (Eds.), *The Social Sciences*: Foundation of the Social Studies. Boston: Allyn & Bacon, 1965. Discusses the respective ways of thinking and working in eight social sciences and considers implications for planning the social studies program.

Phenix, Philip M., *Realms of Meaning: A Philosophy of the Curriculum for General Education*. New York: McGraw-Hill, 1964. Chap. 11. Presents a thumbnail sketch of the structure of knowledge in the separate disciplines which constitute social sciences.

President's Commission on National Goals, *Goals for Americans*. Englewood Cliffs, N.J.: Prentice-Hall, 1960. Sets forth goals in foreign policy, education, economic life, and other areas, with recommendations of steps to take in reaching them.

Preston, Ralph C., "Introduction," "The Role of Social Studies in Elementary Education," "The Yearbook's Proposals in Relation to Certain Realities Facing the Elementary School," in *Social Studies in the Elementary School;* Fifty-sixth Yearbook of the National Society for the Study of Education, Pt. II. Chicago: University of Chicago Press, 1957. Pp. 1–3, Chaps. 1, 13. Discusses issues and strategies in social studies education.

Price, Roy A. (Ed.), *Needed Research in the Teaching of the Social Studies*. Research Bulletin No. 1. Washington, D.C.: National Council for the Social Studies, 1964. A collection of analytical and provocative papers by a distinguished panel (including the philosopher Frankel, the sociologist Tumin, the political scientist Odegard, the educators Havighurst and Haefner, and the psychologist McKeachie) which illuminate central issues of the social studies.

Smith, B. Othanel, and Robert H. Ennis (Eds.), *Language and Concepts in Education*. Skokie, Ill.: Rand McNally, 1961. Clarifies ambiguous terms often used as cliches ("learning by experience," "pupil needs," "neutrality in teaching is impossible," and so on) which have contributed to needless confusion in teaching, not least in teaching of social studies.

"Social Studies Projects, Directory of," *Social Education*, **31** (October 1967), 509–511. A list of research and curriculum projects.

Whipple, Guy Montrose (Ed.), *The Social Studies in the Elementary and Secondary School*; Twenty-second Yearbook of the National Society for the Study of Education. Bloomington, Ill.: Public School Publishing Co., 1923 (now available from University of Chicago Press, Chicago). Describes issues and problems besetting social studies education almost fifty years ago.

2

ORGANIZATION OF THE
SOCIAL STUDIES CURRICULUM

*Order and simplification are the first steps toward the
mastery of a subject.*

THOMAS MANN

THE SELECTION OF CONTENT

The first task in curriculum organization is to select the information
and ideas which are to be taught. Who should make this selection? Three
groups of professionals have contributions to make toward it: (1) social
scientists (geographers, historians, economists, and so on); (2) curriculum
specialists with training in child psychology and learning theory (preferably
with some experience in teaching social studies); and (3) classroom
teachers.

The chief role of social scientists is to identify the central generalizations
to be taught. Not all social scientists are equally qualified—some are too
narrowly specialized or find it tedious and unrewarding to analyze their
fields in terms of their contribution to the learning experience of children.
There are social scientists, on the other hand, who do qualify, because they
have maintained a broad orientation to their respective fields and are interested in identifying the central concepts, the unifying ideas, of their respective disciplines.[1] Writers of curriculum guides should not attempt to
make such a selection without first becoming familiar with the points of
view of social scientists. Unfortunately, this has not been standard practice
in curriculum work.

The kinds of generalizations that have come from an analysis of social
sciences by social scientists appear in subsequent chapters devoted to the
respective subject areas. It is from such lists that the scope of the social
studies curriculum is best determined.

[1] Examples of writings in which social scientists have attempted such treatment of
their disciplines appear in Bernard Berelson, *et al.*, *The Social Studies and the Social
Sciences*. New York: Harcourt, 1962.

Specialists in curriculum who have had appropriate training in principles of child growth and learning are needed to help decide, on the basis of present knowledge of children's learning capacities, what aspects of each generalization will have greatest meaning at successive grade or age levels. In collaboration with social scientists and classroom teachers, they have the responsibility of determining a sequence of topics which is not only consistent with an orderly structure of the subject matter, but which is also in harmony with sequences in child development. Because of conflicting interpretations currently given to data on the intellectual growth of children and because of disagreement among social scientists about the structure of their fields, several competing schemes of grade placement are found in practice. Some of them will be described in the next section of this chapter.

The classroom teacher also has a vital part to play in designing a curriculum. His chief contribution is made through his daily decisions concerning which aspects of a subject to emphasize. No matter what curriculum scheme or what textbook in social studies he follows, the possible specifics of content which he could teach in a given grade in conformity with that scheme are so numerous that seldom can he "cover" everything. If the teacher's preparation in social sciences is adequate, he can be expected to use sound judgment in making his selections. If, on the other hand, his preparation is meager, the school system which employs him should designate a social scientist, perhaps a social studies teacher in the high school, with whom he may consult for help with problems of subject-matter selection and emphasis.

CURRICULUM PLANS

Prevailing Offerings
and Their Grade Placement

Surveys by Adams[2] and Bush,[3] when combined, suggest the following "central tendencies" of topics offered in elementary schools:

Grade 1—Home; school; pets; farm life; holidays.
Grade 2—Community services and community workers.
Grade 3—The local community and its relationship to other com-

---

[2] Fay Adams, "National Survey: Curriculum Content and Basic Materials in the Social Studies." Unpublished report, June 1962. Adams obtained information from 45 state departments of education, the District of Columbia, and Canal Zone, and from 158 cities of varying size.
[3] Byron O. Bush, Bedford Hills, N.Y., conducted a series of surveys of curriculum guides from states, counties, cities, and towns throughout the United States from 1958 to 1964. The number of guides Bush studied in the various samples ranged from 39 to 127.

munities; food, clothing, and shelter; transportation and communication; Indians.

Grade 4—Contrasting regions and cultures of the world; contrasting regions of the United States; the local state.

Grade 5—Geography and history of the United States; geography and history of Canada and Latin America.[4]

Grade 6—Geography and history of the Eastern Hemisphere;[5] Geography and history of Canada and Latin America (see Footnote 4).

Grade 7—Geography and history of the Eastern Hemisphere (see Footnote 5); history of the United States;[6] geography of the United States; geography of the world.

Grade 8—History of the United States (see Footnote 6); local state; civics.

Evaluation of Prevailing Offerings

The reader is reminded that a "central tendency" is merely what *tends* to be practiced. It does not indicate the full range of practice, nor does it necessarily indicate what *ought* to be practiced.

The prevailing plan—sometimes the plan is called "design" of "framework"—is based roughly on the expanding-environment principle. According to this principle, the first-grade child is taught about his immediate environment (for example, home, school, and neighborhood); then, as he advances in school, he studies consecutively larger segments of the world: the city or town, the state, the country, the hemisphere, and finally, the world as a whole.

The principle of the expanding environment provides a logical scheme for introducing the child to his world. Paul R. Hanna, a leading promoter of the scheme, explains it as follows:

> In the elementary schools, by following the holistic and coordinated approach to the study of men living in societies, we design our program as follows: The sequence of themes or emphases is drawn from the fact that each of us lives within a system or set of expanding communities that starts with the oldest, smallest, and most crucial community—the family, placed in the center of the concentric circles—and progresses outward in ever widening bands through the child's neighborhood com-

---

[4] Geography and history of Canada and Latin America were taught with almost equal frequency in Grade 5 and in Grade 6.

[5] Geography and history of the Eastern Hemisphere were taught with almost equal frequency in Grade 6 and in Grade 7.

[6] History of the United States was taught in a minority of schools in Grade 7.

munity; the child's local communities of city, county, etc.; the state community; the regions-of-states community; and the national community.[7]

The principle of the expanding environment has the merit of providing for the school beginner an interpretation of the environment in which he lives—the environment about which he can form generalizations which are relevant to his life and which he can verify.

On the other hand, rigid adherence to the principle of the expanding environment has been found wanting in its failure to keep pace with the child's expanding intellectual horizons. The pace at which children advance beyond the narrow confines of their communities is much more rapid today than before the advent of television and before the increase in family travel. The need to aid children in the interpretation of the distant, as well as the immediate, world is thus evident. This has long been recognized; and hence, the principle is almost nowhere strictly adhered to in its pure form. For example, the farm is customarily taught in Grade 1 before the systematic survey of work patterns in the local community, which commonly occurs in Grade 2, even though for most children in industrialized countries, the farm is part of the outside world. By way of further example, contrasting regions of the world are commonly taught in Grade 4 before the systematic study of regions of the United States, which is deferred until Grade 5. Such adaptations are desirable. They do not deny the general soundness of the principle of the expanding environment as a preliminary scheme for roughing out sequence. But the principle must be modified to meet the need of today's children for early exposure to various components of the world.[8]

Another criticism of the prevailing emphasis upon the familiar "here and now" in the primary grades is directed toward its tendency to end in the teaching of banalities about the familiar such as "the policeman is our friend." Bruner offers the alternative pedagogical principle of contrast.[9] This principle involves comparison of the form of social organization familiar to the child with those of strangely different forms. Probably, most curriculum workers accept the reasonableness of the principle of contrast. There is a lack of evidence, however, to indicate how sharp the contrast should be, and how the contrasting elements should be organized and presented. It is not surprising, therefore, that there is a lack of agreement

[7] Paul R. Hanna, "Revising the Social Studies: What Is Needed?" *Social Education*, **27** (April 1963), 192.

[8] Examples of appropriate modification will be found in the *Heath Social Studies Series*. Boston: Heath, 1964, 1965; and in the National Council for Geographic Education's *Curriculum Guide for Geographic Education*. Chicago, Ill. 60602.: The Council, 1963.

[9] Jerome S. Bruner, *Toward a Theory of Instruction*. Cambridge, Mass.: Harvard University Press, 1966. Pp. 64, 84, 93.

CURRICULUM PLANS · 31

on these matters. Bruner's application of the principle of contrast will be seen in the next section, which describes the ESI curriculum with which Bruner has been associated.

Newer Programs

ANTHROPOLOGICALLY-ORIENTED PROGRAMS Educational Services Incorporated (ESI) is constructing a social studies curriculum for the elementary school dominated by anthropological concepts.[10] Studies for the primary grades deal with "hunters and gatherers" (Eskimos, African bushmen, and Australian aborigines) and with human evolution. Studies for the intermediate grades take up the origins of settled life, the domestication of plants and animals, the origins of urban life, and the beginnings of the Western tradition. A more recent report[11] describes in detail an intermediate-grade course entitled "Man." It is divided into various topics —tool making, language, and other "humanizing forces" which can be used to explain essential characteristics of humans and how they have developed. The principle of contrast operates throughout. For example, the child contrasts how humans and animals send and receive messages, and he compares his own social organization with the organizations found among baboons and primitive peoples.

Units in anthropology are being tried out in a number of schools in Georgia.[12] Based on the belief that the cognitive abilities and interests of elementary school children have been underestimated, the Georgia project provides units for specified grade levels. Unit titles include "Concept of Culture," "Development of Man and His Culture," and "Cultural Dynamics." The nature of the units can be illustrated by a description of two of them on "Concept of Culture," one designed for Grade 1, and the other for Grade 4.[13] In the first grade, a comparative study is made of three cultures, the Arunta of Australia, the Kazak of Central Asia, and the American. The children are supplied with information which leads to the conclusions that all people have to meet the problems of survival and social intercourse, and that the three peoples under study meet them in their

[10] Educational Services Incorporated, "A Statement of the Aims of the Course of Study Being Developed by the Social Studies Program." Mimeographed. Cambridge, Mass.: Educational Services Incorporated, July 1964.

[11] Jerome S. Bruner, "Man: A Course of Study," *ESI Quarterly Report,* 3 (Summer-Fall 1965), 92; reprinted with a few deletions in Bruner, *Toward a Theory of Instruction.* Chap. 4.

[12] Marion J. Rice and Wilfred C. Bailey, "University of Georgia: A Sequential Curriculum in Anthropology for Grades 1–7," *Social Education,* **29** (April 1965), 211–212.

[13] Wilfred C. Bailey, "The Role of the Anthropologist." Mimeographed. Athens, Ga.: Anthropology Curriculum Project, University of Georgia, November 27, 1965.

respective ways. At the fourth-grade level, the children, studying the same topic, learn further of the universality of human problems, of how each culture develops its own solutions, of how people learn the traits of their culture, and of how cultures change and grow. Children's learning from these units have been evaluated. The findings show that children can learn substantial amounts of anthropology.

A CHRONOLOGICAL, THEME-CENTERED PROGRAM   Joseph C. Grannis has worked with teachers in the public schools of Lexington, Mass., in developing a curriculum organized around a series of themes.[14] Both the chronological principle and the expanding-environment principle are followed, but not rigidly. The plan's chronology resembles somewhat the curricula adopted by many elementary schools over a generation ago in which a study of primitive peoples was assigned to the third grade, and in subsequent grades, successive historical periods were presented chronologically.[15]

At the risk of oversimplifying Grannis' complex and carefully thought-out plan, the author presents the following condensed and paraphrased version, for kindergarten to Grade eight:

Kindergarten—Comparison of human and animal life (to discover the superior flexibility and inventiveness of man).

Grade 1—Home and neighborhood life in one or two foreign places compared with life in the children's own community (to discover the diversity of ways in which similar problems are met).

Grade 2—Life in one or two foreign places compared with life in the children's own community (to discover the variety of patterns and institutions).

Grade 3—The relationships between the cultures and environments of selected, contrasting, primitive peoples (to discover simple adaptation to a variety of habitats).

Grade 4—Primitive and modern ways of managing the environment in various regions of the world compared (to discover modern man's inventiveness).

Grade 5—The continuing industrial revolution in selected countries, and its historical origins (to discover the new opportunities and problems created by the industrial revolution).

Grade 6—Aspects of culture in selected ancient, medieval, and Renaissance societies (to discover how man's creativity is the product

[14] For a full account, see Joseph C. Grannis, "The Framework of the Social Studies Curriculum," *National Elementary Principal*, 14 (April 1963), 20–26.

[15] New Orleans Public Schools, *Course of Study*. New Orleans, La.: The Public Schools, 1927; School District of Philadelphia, *History: Grades One to Six*. Philadelphia: The School District, 1929; State of Maine, *Elementary School Curriculum*. Augusta, Me.: State Department of Education, 1931.

of his society and to explore problems created by the Industrial Revolution).

Grade 7—England and her American colonies (to discover how political institutions have their roots in man's need for law, order, and freedom).

Grade 8—Topics from United States history (to discover interrelationships of political and economic developments).

Plans of this type, in which the content for an entire school year is determined by a single theme, often result in overly specialized content for a given grade. On the other hand, they have the advantage of making unmistakably clear the major goal for each grade.

EXPERIMENT IN ECONOMIC EDUCATION   A program in economic education was developed in the schools of Elkhart, Ind., by Lawrence Senesh. The experiment

> . . . rests on the hypothesis that children on every grade level, with proper motivation, can become excited about the abstract ideas underlying their experiences, and that these ideas can be presented in such a way as to reflect the basic structure of the body of economic knowledge.[16]

The intent of the program is not to alter the arrangement of topics in the curriculum, but rather to unify the prevailing curriculum through the presentation of ideas which "reflect the basic structure of the body of economic knowledge." Senesh lists five ideas (which he terms "the basic contours of the economic world") as follows:

> 1. All people and all nations are confronted with the conflict between their unlimited wants and limited resources. . . .
> 2. From the beginning, men have tried new ways and means to lessen the gap between unlimited wants and limited resources. . . .
> 3. In all countries the basic questions to be answered are: what goods and services will be produced; how much of these will be produced; how will they be produced . . . ; and who will rereceive the goods and services?
> 4. In the United States what and how much will be produced, how it will be produced, and for whom are largely determined by the free choices of the American people. . . .
> 5. Through their political process the American people sometimes limit their individual free choices in order to increase the general welfare.[17]

---

[16] Lawrence Senesh, "The Organic Curriculum: A New Experiment in Economic Education," *The Councilor*, **21** (March 1960), 45. Another account of the experiment is by Anne Reid McAllister, "Economic Education: A New Horizon," *The Instructor*, **73** (January 1964), 7–15. For an illustration of Senesh's approach, see Figure 7.1.

[17] Senesh. P. 55.

The program has demonstrated the challenging nature of carefully selected abstract ideas from economics, even at the first-grade level. Following such instruction, children in one group of first-graders were able to explain orally, for example, what impact the decisions both of consumers and investors have upon the total level of our economy.[18]

The Senesh program provides for the teaching of each of these "contours" at successively expanded and successively complex levels, grade by grade. It shows that economic ideas and relationships, long neglected in the elementary school, are well within the grasp of even primary-grade children. An example of Senesh's approach appears in Figure 7.1.

GLENS FALLS WORLD AFFAIRS EXPERIMENT While an experiment on world affairs in Glens Falls, N.Y., was not involved with curriculum reorganization *per se*, it deserves mention because (1) it illustrates how curriculum change can come about without conscious redesign, and (2) it influenced curriculum redesigning elsewhere.

It came about through the initiation, in 1957, by the National Council for the Social Studies, of a three-year project entitled "Improving the Teaching of World Affairs," and it was carried out by the personnel of the public schools of Glens Falls, N.Y.[19] The project sought to give instruction about other peoples and their cultures at every grade level and in every subject. Although this project was established within the framework of the existing curriculum, it brought about modification of the curriculum by emphasizing and adding content not normally included—as in the kindergarten class which studied about "Our Chinese Friends," and the first-grade class which studied about homes and foods of children in other lands.

"Our Chinese Friends" illustrates a potential danger in world affairs studies. They often result in a sentimental and unrealistic approach, particularly in the primary grades. At this writing, our little "friends" in China are singing songs of hatred for their little "friends" in America. While a study of such aspects of life in contemporary China is not suitable for primary children, neither is a romanticized version. This is an example of how a good idea may yield absurd social studies content.

Nevertheless, Glens Falls' effort to raise the level of world consciousness in its schools is worthy of emulation. The question of human survival is balanced, because of the threat of thermonuclear war, on the razor's edge of toleration, understanding, and cooperation among nations. Schools should not turn aside from responsibility in this area. It is significant that the Glens Falls experiment, developed at this present time, when curricu-

---

[18] Senesh. P. 45.
[19] Harold M. Long and Robert N. King, *Improving the Teaching of World Affairs: The Glens Falls Story*. Washington, D.C.: National Council for the Social Studies, 1963.

lum revision is popular, has demonstrated how concepts of other cultures and peoples can be acquired within the framework of a traditional curriculum has been modified, not by deliberately restructuring it, but by placing upon each teacher the job of developing in the pupils a larger awareness and keener sense of responsibility for world affairs. Community support accorded the program is impressive: following the three-year experiment, the Board of Education of Glens Falls agreed unanimously to continue the project as an integral part of the school system's educational program.

OTHER PROGRAMS PROVIDING STUDY OF FOREIGN CULTURES IN PRIMARY GRADES   The Glens Falls experiment has been one influence, albeit generally an indirect one, upon curriculum innovation in other school systems. Curriculum guides from Nashville, Denver, San Diego County (Calif.), and elsewhere now provide for the study of foreign cultures in the primary grades. Among the topics introduced into the primary curriculum are "Living in England and France," "Traveling in Other Lands," and "Interdependence of People: Latin America and the Orient." It is difficult to evaluate such innovations without exploring pertinent questions like the following, the answers to which are presently not known:

1. Are primary-grade children sufficiently grounded in the use of the techniques of the social scientist (such as they gain by exploring and surveying their own locale, and by comparing experiences and analyzing selected problems in connection with their own homes, school, and neighborhoods) to be able to understand that information about foreign cultures which they learn at second hand is similarly gathered?
2. What opportunities can be provided for primary-grade children in the study of foreign cultures to gather and examine data, discover generalizations, and consider applications of the generalizations?
3. What material can be given teachers and children to replace the quantity of material currently available which is a mixture of romance, fancy, and anachronism?
4. What are the quality and content of a primary-grade child's concepts which are gained from the study of a miscellany of foreign cultures?
5. Is there a tendency for these studies of other cultures, including studies which take the typical anthropological approach, to select the wrong generalizations for teaching? They teach: "Man everywhere must have food for life but solves the problem differently." Ought not children to know that the world is developing into a world of haves and have-nots, that half the world may go to bed hungry, that overpopulation and underdevelopment of technology are responsible, and that cultural mores make change difficult?

Nevertheless, because of the pressing need to build a world view in all children and to block the development of provincial attitudes, those undertaking these programs should be commended for their vision. They should be encouraged to observe and evaluate them critically for the purpose of discovering answers to the foregoing questions. It may well be that the goals can best be achieved either by comparative community studies or by one really adequate study during each of the primary-grade years to the end of attaining depth and avoiding the superficiality that comes when children are "run" through a series of cultures too early and too rapidly.

CRITERIA FOR JUDGING CURRICULUM PLANS

In planning a social studies curriculum, it is necessary to observe the principles of *continuity, balance, relevance,* and *contrast* in order to insure psychological soundness. The principle of continuity recognizes psychological growth and the child's need for challenge at successively higher levels of maturity. The principle of balance rests on studies of children's exploratory behavior which reveal their search for orientation to varied aspects of the world. The principle of relevance recognizes the importance, for the child, of finding meaning and value in his studies, of finding implications of personal significance. The principal of contrast recognizes the need for breadth and depth.

Continuity

Continuity in a social studies curriculum is provided by seeing to it that the major generalizations of social sciences are systematically taught, year by year. When continuity is provided, children encounter each generalization repeatedly, at successively higher levels of complexity and depth, as they advance from one grade to the next. As an illustration, let us take the generalization that man's way of life is influenced by a combination of environmental and cultural factors. One way to illustrate this for young children is through a study of a farmer's adaptation to weather and climate and his use of scientific weather forecasting; the next year, the same children could enlarge the generalization through a study of the effect of a desert environment upon the way of life of a desert society, in which they learn of the changes wrought in the lives of desert people by man's discovery of how to drill for oil and how to extract the salt from sea water. Each subsequent year, the generalization could be broadened and deepened through study of new and successively more complex applications of the generalization. It probably is clear that an adequate scheme of continuity must be based on those generalizations which are central to the social sciences.

Balance

Balance is achieved by insuring at each grade level that the child has contact with the major ideas of at least two or three of the social sciences. By this standard, many social studies programs have little balance. Some provide an exclusive diet of community studies in the primary grades, mainly sociological in nature, and confine the intermediate grades to geography or history. On the other hand, a fifth-grade program adhering to the principle of balance might have studies in three social sciences—one emphasizing the history of the United States, one emphasizing its geography, and a third emphasizing conservation—the economics of natural resources in the United States. Chart 2.1 shows an open framework which a school system could use for determining the degree of balance in its social studies program.

Chart 2.1. Open Framework for Determining Degree of Balance in the Social Studies Curriculum

	GEOG-RAPHY	HISTORY	ECO-NOMICS	GOVERN-MENT	SOCIOLOGY-ANTHROPOLOGY
Kindergarten					
Grade 1					
Grade 2					
Grade 3					
Grade 4					
Grade 5					
Grade 6					
Grade 7					
Grade 8					

Personal Relevance

The principle of relevance is also important. This principle states that the curriculum should provide content relevant to the child's life—which dovetails in some significant manner with concepts, values, and interests which he has already acquired. Bruner refers to it as "the personalization of knowledge."[20] The principle of relevance does not necessarily limit the child to the "here and now" world as is sometimes believed, although during the early school years, there is usually a close correspondence between that which is personally relevant and that which is familiar and at hand.

At the primary-grade level, the child may study about the supermarket, for example, because it is a familiar institution, but the study must launch him to the examination of central relationships. For example, the familiar supermarket is related to the unfamiliar wholesale outlets, warehouses, processing plants, producers, and together, they are presented as a web of interrelated activity. The supermarket has a place in the curriculum to the extent that it leads the child to discover this economic network. Similarly, the child studies his town or city, not only because it is close at hand and is a microcosm of society in general, but because he learns how it is part of a hierarchy of political units (city, county, state) which relate it to the nation.

There are those who are suspicious of familiar subject matter in the primary grades. They believe that its advocates ignore "how difficult it is for human beings to see generality in what has become familiar."[21] It must be acknowledged that it is difficult indeed to see "generality" (to see relationships and then to form generalizations) in familiar material. Whether it is easier for a child to see generality in remote material has yet to be established. One disadvantage of familiar material is that it may contain emotional associations for the child which make objectivity difficult. Or its very commonplaceness may smother curiosity. On the other hand, there is evidence that familiarity is an element to be deliberately incorporated in the curriculum.[22] Familiar things are learned more easily than unfamiliar things, they tend to be more meaningful, and they provide richer opportunities to learn how the social scientist collects and verifies information and how such information is used in making generalizations.

For the older child, the principle of relevance is still important, but it operates in a different way. The study may be quite foreign on the surface, but before it is concluded, its content ties in with the child's present knowledge and interests. For example, a fourth-grade pupil studies the moder-

[20] Bruner, *Toward a Theory of Instruction.* Pp. 160 ff.
[21] Bruner, *Toward a Theory of Instruction.* P. 92.
[22] Evidence is cited by Ralph C. Preston, "Familiarity and Contrast as Curriculum Principles," *Social Education,* **31** (October 1967), 491–493.

ating effect of the North Atlantic drift on the climate of northwestern Europe. The subject may strike both pupil and teacher as unrelated to the child's existence. When properly developed, the topic adds a new dimension to the child's concept of already familiar forces such as water currents and wind, and a familiar factor such as temperature. By keeping personal relevance in mind, the teacher helps the pupil form new generalizations which, while opening up new ideas, give significance to familiar concepts.

Contrast

Teaching the familiar without providing the child with the experience to make contrasts with the unfamiliar runs the risk of being trite and shallow. Thus, teaching the child about the institutions of his own community (stores, homes, transportation facilities, and so on) without acquainting him with the same institutions as they are organized and operated elsewhere may result in a distorted view of the institutions. It is important for the teacher to offer his class systematic opportunities for making contrasts so that he has more instances of fact upon which to formulate generalizations. To alter a Kipling passage slightly: "And what can they know of England who only England know?" The study of the remote in conjunction with the present enables the child to make a more meaningful analysis of close-at-hand elements of his own society. Thus, contrast enhances the meaningfulness of the here-and-now. And study of the here-and-now gives a concrete basis for comprehending parallel processes and institutions elsewhere.

Applications of the Criteria

It is recommended that directors of curriculum refer to the criteria of continuity, balance, relevance, and contrast as a means of evaluating programs currently in use and new programs which come under consideration. The teacher, by keeping the criteria in mind, will be reminded of the role which his daily teaching plays in the continuous education of the child, the need for a distribution of emphasis among the various social sciences, and the need for content which has a personal ring to the child, as well as for content which offers contrast.

It must be acknowledged, however, that there is a tendency today for curriculum arrangements to be overemphasized. Because curriculum organization is central in determining the sequence, breadth, and relevance of the child's learning, some educators jump to the conclusion that changing from one curriculum plan to an "ideal" one will give vitality to uninspired teaching. The fact is, vital teaching is almost independent of curriculum organization. Furthermore, there is no "ideal" organization. As Clinchy expressed it: "Any order we or the world's greatest social scientists impose on this field is going to be arbitrary and to some extent personal."[23]

DIVERSITY AND UNIFORMITY OF CURRICULUM PLANS

Practices Contributing to Diversity

Probably in no curricular field is there such *laissez-faire* teaching as in social studies. Even in schools that have officially developed a curriculum framework or have adopted a textbook series, one often finds teachers who package their own brand of social studies. Sometimes, such a teacher explains his teaching on the basis of children's interests; sometimes, on the basis of a new interest of his own; and other times, on the basis of its having proved teachable elsewhere. Some programs appear so thin and casual as hardly to constitute a social studies program at all. Such teaching is probably practiced by only a small and declining percentage of elementary school teachers, yet it persists and is considered by some teachers a sort of birthright.

While some teachers, being both more thoughtful and more capable than the average might be able to plan a truly balanced social studies program, most would not be qualified. As we have seen, it requires a combination of experts in a variety of fields.

Diversity stems also from the traditional American practice whereby the school systems of regional and local political units (states, counties, cities, and towns) develop their own individual curriculum plans. The assumption underlying this practice is that local initiative in such matters increases teachers' understanding of their curricula and their interest in them. Furthermore, it is argued, local planning results in a curriculum which is adapted to local conditions and local needs. While local planning has encouraged diversity, the fact is that the myriad plans or designs thus developed (sometimes called "courses of study" or "curriculum guides") are remarkably similar. Teachers have wasted countless hours on such planning, only to come up with a curriculum guide like one hundred others. This strange phenomenon will be understood upon exploring the factors which make for uniformity.

Practices Contributing to Uniformity

Why has the practice of local curriculum work produced so little originality? The method of work of local curriculum committees supplies part

[23] Evans R. Clinchy, "Magic, Social Studies and the New Progressivism," in Nancy W. Bauer (Ed.), *Revolution and Reaction: The Impact of the New Social Studies,* Cranbrook Curriculum Conference. Bloomfield Hills, Mich.: Cranbrook School, 1966. P. 30.

of the answer. Local curriculum committees of teachers often start their work by collecting curriculum plans from other school systems. These plans tend to become models in the development of the new program, particularly those which are detailed and are attractively printed and bound. Such printed plans are typically the products of relatively wealthy school districts which use consultants in developing their plans. Neighboring districts sometimes employ the same consultants. Curriculum committees also have been influenced by the various textbook series. Textbook publishers, seeking the largest possible market, tend to turn out books which conform, more or less, to the curricular "central tendency."

A National Curriculum Plan

A number of educators wish to reduce differences in content, and are in favor of stronger leadership at the national level. Paul Hanna stirred the attention of educators by his assertion that our traditional local curriculum-building ". . . may not be providing sufficient common understanding of, loyalty to, and competence in our democratic way of life." Through nonpolitical and voluntary agencies, he would hope "that a [national] curriculum design would emerge that would give greatest assurance of the survival and progress of the values, laws, and institutions of free peoples."[24] A report of a commission of the National Council for the Social Studies suggests that:

> . . . carefully selected committees of social scientists and educators can provide leadership at the national level by developing a basic pattern within which local curriculum workers may organize programs which will be appropriate for their own situations.[25]

Others have pointed out that a national curriculum design would meet the need for providing continuity for the many children whose families move from one school district to another. Writes Stratemeyer:

> We have approximately six million pupils who transfer from one school to another annually. When, due to our custom of local curriculum-making, each new move means adjustment to a new social studies program, the effect on interest, continuity, and sequence in learning can be disastrous.[26]

[24] Paul R. Hanna, "Design for a National Curriculum," *Nation's Schools,* **62** (September 1958), 43–45.

[25] National Council for the Social Studies, National Commission on the Social Studies, *Curriculum Planning in American Schools: The Social Studies.* Washington, D.C.: The Council, 1958. P. 21. See also its revised edition *Social Studies in Transition: Guidelines for Change,* 1965. P. 5.

[26] Clara G. Stratemeyer, "Guidelines for Social Studies Revision," *Curriculum Letter No. 50.* Middletown, Conn.: Dept. School Services and Publications, Wesleyan University, 1962.

The advantages of a national social studies curriculum are clear. We need also to be aware of the arguments against it. There are those who feel that a national commission to create a national curriculum design is not the best means to the end of feeding into the curriculum the most significant generalizations. Thus, one social scientist states: "I should think that a sustained effort to improve the subject-matter training of teachers would be a more suitable approach."[27] It is indeed true that at least the urgency of the need for a national curriculum would be removed if all elementary school teachers knew a lot more about social sciences than they do. Better mastery of social sciences would enable them to know and to recognize "the values, laws, and institutions of free peoples." To direct major emphasis upon, and confine it to, curriculum "design" may cause educators and the public to place unjustified faith in paper curriculum plans *per se*. Better paper plans are important, but the education of teachers in social sciences is a greater need. The best plan in the hands of a teacher who is only superficially grounded in social sciences will fail in its purpose. Not only is such a teacher poorly informed; he is apt also to be insecure, uninspired, and uninspiring to his pupils.

Another objection is that a national curriculum might stifle initiative. Calvin E. Gross, former Superintendent of Schools, New York City, said in an interview: "The quickest way to stultify progress is to impose a national curriculum. You put a ceiling on those who want to fly, even while you are raising up those at the bottom."[28]

There are those who fear a commission would "freeze" social studies curriculum at a time when equally defensible strategies are possible and are being experimented with. They assert that fashioning a single framework is unwarranted, because social studies represent such an enormous volume of potential content, divided among so many disciplines, and because they lend themselves to more than one defensible organizational scheme. These critics feel that there will probably never be much unanimity of opinion, among either scholars or schoolmen, concerning the best plan.

The fact remains that present methods of curriculum building, with each school system developing its own plan, are wasteful of the time and energy of the teachers who are drafted to help. The products are often shocking in their inadequacy, to both the discriminating social scientist and the discriminating schoolman. Haefner states the dilemma as follows:

I am convinced that the present system of curricular change is wholly inadequate to the needs of the time. However, the whole idea is fraught

[27] V. O. Key, Jr., quoted in *Nation's Schools*, **62** (November 1958), 55.
[28] Quoted in Terry Ferrer, *Classroom Revolution.* Pamphlet. New York: The New York Herald Tribune, 1963. Unpaged.

with risks. Safeguards are needed to maintain the rights of local authorities.[29]

Most, if not all, the objections and fears would be dispelled if Hanna's specifications for the roster, work, and status of the proposed national commission could be assured. Hanna would have the commission represent:

> . . . the scholarly community, the lay community, and the professional education community. This commission would be composed of men of integrity, intelligence, and prestige who would give their full and undivided attention to curricular problems. They would continuously assess national goals in a world setting, translate them into educational techniques with priorities of content and with due consideration of method and technique. Out of such a commission should come a continuous flow of curriculum proposals, providing alternatives from which the states and localities might choose. The commission would be kept independent of the federal government, and care would be exercised to keep it from becoming a federal agency.[30]

CHILDREN'S INTERESTS
AND CURRICULUM ORGANIZATION

There are still those who believe that social studies topics should be selected by asking children what they would like to study. Their argument runs as follows: If education is a process of taking the child "from where he is to where he ain't," the crucial activity for the teacher is to discover the points of contact between the child and his culture. The teacher learns a few of these points of contact by taking note when a child stirs his classmates with an account of a personal adventure or when children describe in class some version of events of general interest. These are matters the child apparently has set his teeth into, runs the contention, and they, therefore, should form the core of social studies content. Thus, the content cannot be planned ahead of time; it must be improvised. Whether the child is talking with his friends about war or the circus, let the topic be studied until the educational content (consistent with his stage of development) is extracted, the argument continues. If children are excited by a wild west show on television, let them pursue a study of the American frontier until the interest runs its course, say these people. If an impending national election has aroused a group in the classroom, its members should be helped to extend their knowledge of campaign issues or election machinery.

[29] John H. Haefner, "Discussion Summary," in Roy A. Price (Ed.), *Needed Research in the Teaching of the Social Studies*, Washington, D.C.: National Council for the Social Studies, 1964. P. 102.
[30] Paul R. Hanna, "A National Commission for Curriculum Research and Development," *Phi Delta Kappan*, **42** (May 1961), 331–338.

This is the way adults learn, we are told. Adults lack time to systematize content, to arrange a logical sequence, and to drill themselves on factual information; yet, it is obvious that they continue to learn and keep abreast of the world through day-by-day experience which they utilize on the spot. Improvised learning thus is alleged to be the natural learning. This shallow argument has won many adherents—although their number seems to be declining.

A little thought shows that it would be hazardous to permit school experience to be charted by the ebb and flow of chance experience. For normal growth, children require an ever-increasing understanding of society. While they doubtless assimilate some of this in the course of daily living and learning, they can scarcely be adequately enlightened for either present or future living through such a hit-or-miss process.

Intelligent living in society places many demands upon the individual and requires a greater volume of systematic knowledge than would be acquired through allegedly "natural" learning. The analogy of how adults learn is weak. Most adults have a background of learning, in addition to having learned the fundamentals in school as children. Even so, if adults took the trouble to explore their world more systematically, they would be better masters of it. Society demands greater knowledge than possibly can be acquired merely through affable living. Successful, effective living depends, in part, on informed maturity.

It would seem obvious that a child's choice of what to study must often fail to contribute to significant concepts or to curriculum-balance. In following a systematic program, the teacher does not violate the learner's personality as is sometimes contended, nor is he conspiring to bring about the downfall of democracy! In fact, the teacher needs to project his own plans for the very purpose of furthering the child's personality development and protecting the rights of all the children. For a question of statement of interest from one pupil or a few pupils does not necessarily represent an interest of a majority of the group. It may not even represent a deep and sound interest of the child expressing it. Since children's expressed interests are socially determined and reflect past experiences, they often lead up blind alleys. Also, in the case of the disadvantaged child, his interests and experiences may be severely limited, narrow, and even asocial.

Another question, sometimes overlooked in discussions of this point, relates to whether any topic or activity can ever be said to characterize the interests of "the" children, if, by that, the teacher means 100 percent of his pupils, or even 80 percent, for that matter. For often one child or a few children determine, through subtle forms of domination, the expressed interests of their classmates.

It should be emphasized that scarcely a handful of educators would deny the teacher's responsibility in dealing with pupil-expressed interests as they arise and in helping children interpret them so that they may see their deeper significance. But there can be no justification for "show-and-tell" periods which in kindergarten and Grade 1 often become the core of social studies.

UNIFIED SOCIAL STUDIES

The most favored form of organization of content through Grade 6 is the system of unified social studies, a form of organization in which the content from various social sciences is blended. (The unified concept was introduced and illustrated in the preceding chapter.)

The blending may be extreme, wherein the ingredients of the blend (geography, history, economics, and the like) are almost impossible to identify, or the blend may be quite moderate, with only rather obvious and natural relationships between the social sciences being developed. Perhaps, the chief common characteristic of unified social studies is that the content is presented under the label of "social studies" rather than of "geography," or "history," or "civics," or some other subject category.

Table 2.1. Prevalence of Unified Social Studies

INVESTIGATOR	YEAR	NUMBER OF CITY AND STATE SCHOOL SYSTEMS SURVEYED	PERCENT OF PROGRAMS WHICH WERE UNIFIED Grades 1–3	Grades 4–6	Grades 7–8
Adams[a]	1962	205	94%	79%	48%
Adams[b]	1962	205	90%	69%	34%
Preston and Bush[c]	1962	88	89%	73%	41%
Duffey[d]	1967	—	81%	82%	——

[a] See Footnote 2. These figures describe preference for unified organization.
[b] See Footnote 2. These figures describe basal textbooks in use.
[c] Ralph C. Preston and Byron O. Bush. Unpublished survey.
[d] Robert V. Duffey, "Practices Reported by Teachers in Elementary School Social Studies." Mimeographed report. College Park, Md.: University of Maryland, 1967. Data supplied by 1,141 Maryland teachers.

Prevalence of Unified Social Studies

Table 2.1 summarizes information concerning the prevalence of unified social studies. It shows that the majority of schools prefer unified social studies for Grades 1–6 to organization in terms of separate subjects. The reverse is true with respect to Grades 7 and 8. In 1957, Fraser wrote that the trend toward a unified approach had been gradual but persistent "for at least two decades."[31] Adams, in her report, notes a slight increase in the proportion of schools which prefer a unified program over a separate-subject program since her survey of 20 years ago. On the other hand, upon comparing the data in Table 2.1 with Hodgson's figures of 1954,[32] a slight relative decrease appears in the teaching of unified social studies; McAulay presents evidence suggesting a possible trend away from unified social studies.[33]

Rationale

The point of view which gave rise to unified social studies appears in the writings of many social scientists and educators. Two social scientists wrote:

> The problems of living in society do not range themselves so as to fit the artificial isolation forced upon the social sciences by differences of specific subject and method. . . .[34]

Another social scientist wrote:

> . . . the boundaries between them [the social sciences] in the world of today have little or no existence outside the covers of a university catalogue.[35]

A philosopher stated:

> There is no subject that does not, when the life of reflection gets into it, begin to stir uneasily in its hard little academic pot and send feelers out over its sides.[36]

A teacher wrote:

> No condition, custom, relationship or problem of contemporary life can be truly understood by the immature except as we bring together at one time the geographical influences, historical antecedents, and civic

[31] Dorothy McClure Fraser in Nelson B. Henry (Ed.), *Social Studies in the Elementary School*; Fifty-sixth Yearbook of the National Society for the Study of Education. Pt. II. Chicago: University of Chicago Press, 1957. P. 134.

[32] Frank M. Hodgson, "Trend in Social Studies in the Elementary School," *School and Society*, **80** (September 18, 1954), 85–87.

[33] J. D. McAulay, "Brush Fires in the Social Studies," *Education*, **84** (January 1964), 266–270.

[34] William F. Ogburn and Alexander Goldenwasser (Eds.), *The Social Sciences and Their Interrelations*. Boston: Houghton Mifflin, 1927. P. 7.

[35] W. B. Munro, "Clio and Her Cousins: Some Reflections upon the Place of History among the Social Sciences," *Pacific Historical Review*, **10** (December 1941), 403–410.

[36] Brand Blanshard, "Education as Philosophy." *Swarthmore College Bulletin*. Vol. 42. No. 4, 1945.

implications that are pertinent to it. Organization of material must promote integration of experiences and thought, *not* artificially restrict it.[37]

An illustration of the foregoing views was presented by Boutwell:

> Knowing the *geography* of Soviet Russia isn't enough. You must know the *philosophy* that guides Russian actions. Knowing the *history* of Europe is not enough. You must know how the actions of the European Common Market countries will affect the economics of fruit exports from California. . . . Wisdom from all eight [social science] disciplines must somehow be woven into a battery of courses for children from 6 to 18.[38]

Paul Hanna develops the rationale in psychological terms:

> We believe there is a growing mass of evidence from the medical sciences that supports the idea that the learner needs in the beginning to have access to the over-all structure of the field that he is to enter. Bruner, Galanter, Hebb, Miller, and Pribram are among those who point out the basic relation of plans, structures, and organizations to effective learning. Those who propose to start the separate courses in history, geography, sociology, anthropology, economics, and political science in the elementary grades seem to us to violate the psychological principle that experiences with holistic plans and structures for the field should precede experiences with partial plans and structures of the components.[39]

Unified Social Studies
versus Scrambled Social Studies

It is regrettable that some unified social studies programs have been more "scrambled" than "unified." In one such program, the fifth-grader:

> will find no marked clarity of outline. . . . The "blend" of everything will be so creamy that the student will have the impression that he has feasted on homogenized richness. But if he were to be drafted for an unrehearsed and unfixed quiz program it is doubtful that he could analyze the blend for what went into it.[40]

Some programs actually ". . . fragment what is naturally related and integrate what doesn't fit."[41]

---

[37] Sister Carmella, "The Social Studies: Their Challenge," *Catholic School Journal*, **50** (June 1950), 173–175.

[38] William D. Boutwell, "What's Happening in Education?" *PTA Magazine*, **55** (March 1963), 13–14.

[39] Hanna, "Revising the Social Studies: What Is Needed?" P. 192.

[40] John Chamberlain, "Comeback for Clarity," *Wall Street Journal* (February 12, 1960), 8.

[41] Edward Coleson, "The Elementary Social Studies: Sense and Nonsense in Integration," *Journal of Geography*, **57** (April 1958), 202.

There has been a marked revolt against scrambled social studies. The better-unified programs, far from being scrambled, are arranged so that, as the child advances through the elementary school, he becomes increasingly aware of the different academic subjects (geography, history, and so on) which contribute to social studies, just as in his study of science he becomes increasingly aware of the separate fields of chemistry and astronomy. He learns more each year about how social studies fields are differentiated, their respective emphases, and the methods of work peculiar to each.

Even in Grade 1, it is desirable for the teacher to think in terms of the disciplines which contribute most directly to social studies topics which are being studied. Such a practice will sharpen organization of content and will insure its solidity and richness. Thus, in a study of the farm, the teacher may divide the study into economic aspects and geographic aspects. When thinking of it as a topic of economics, he will emphasize the division of labor on the farm, the role of the farm in our interdependent economic system, and economic risks in farming due to the weather variable and the unpredictable market. When thinking of the farm as a topic of geography, the teacher will emphasize types of land and their utilization, types of the farm's natural resources (soil, woods, water, and so forth), the relation between crop and climate, and the like. There is obviously an overlap between the economic and geographic aspects of farming, but by thinking in terms of economics and geography in this study, the teacher's presentations will be crisper and meatier, and the tendency for sprawling content and confused notions will be kept in check. In the intermediate grades, the academic subjects which contribute to each study should be even more marked, and the child himself should be able to separate from the descriptive material of, say, Mexico, those principles which are geographic, those which are historical, those which are economic, and those which are political. By the time the child reaches Grade 7 or 8, having already learned of the relatedness of life, he should be able profitably to undertake straightforward, specialized courses in geography, history, economics, and government.

Research on Unified Social Studies

To the author's knowledge, no significant research concerning the merits of unified social studies has been reported in recent years. Practically all such research was conducted between 1923 and 1943. The earlier studies have been reviewed by the author elsewhere.[42] Three of the more influential will be cited.

An experiment by Oberholtzer, utilizing 73 teachers and more than 2,000 pupils in Grades 4 and 5, compared the achievements of classes having one

---

[42] Ralph C. Preston, "An Appraisal of Fusion of Social Studies in the Elementary School," *Elementary School Journal*, 44 (December 1943), 205–207.

daily period of unified social studies (the control group) with classes devoting half or more of their school time to unified social studies (the experimental group).[43] The experimental classes maintained as high a standard of achievement in the fundamental skills as did the classes with single, daily social studies periods, and they demonstrated greater knowledge of social studies and greater interest and enthusiasm in school work. One finding was that unified social studies fared best with teachers of high ability and superior training.

A comparison of the outcomes of a unified and a nonunified social studies curriculum was made by Farthing with two sixth-grade classes containing children of superior ability.[44] The investigator concluded that children in the unified program generally made better progress.

Integration of the curriculum of Long Beach, Calif., appeared to have no deleterious effect upon the maintenance of the fundamental skills in Grades 3–6.[45] Even slow-moving groups were nearly up to standard, as judged by performance on standardized tests.

These and other studies, when judged by today's standards, show a lack of precision and rigor. They indicate little more than that unified social studies did not handicap the pupils in their learning.

What is known of differentiation in mental development suggests that most individuals will, at some time, reach a point where the need for specialization by subjects is strong. Even at the elementary school level, no educator rightly can be dogmatic about how much or what kind of unification should be adopted, owing to the small amount of evidence on the matter.

From a practical point of view, there is much to be said in favor of unified social studies. Today, each of various scholarly disciplines is seeking its rightful place in the curriculum. Social scientists as well as curriculum specialists recognize the unfeasibility of having the elementary school offer separate courses in geography, history, economics, government, anthropology, and sociology. The alternative, long accepted in the natural sciences through a program of "general" science, is a program of general social science (unified social studies).

Whatever the advantages of unified social studies, the task of unification is, unquestionably, a most difficult one. The French historian, De Coulanges, is credited with the remark: "Years of analysis are required for one day of synthesis." He was referring to the synthesis within the single field of history. How much more difficult it will then be, and how much longer it will take, to work out a satisfactory synthesis of all social sciences!

[43] E. E. Oberholtzer, *An Integrated Curriculum in Practice.* New York: Teachers College, 1937.

[44] D. K. Farthing, *Techniques for the Appraisal of Elementary School Instructional Programs.* Jefferson City, Mo.: State Superintendent of Public Schools, 1940.

[45] Etta Howell, *et al.,* "Measuring the Skills in an Integrated Program," *Journal of Experimental Education,* 1 (June 1933), 316–319.

THE PROBLEM OF TIME ALLOTMENT

Present Time Allotment for Social Studies

Table 2.2 summarizes results of a nationwide survey, by the author, of the daily amount of time devoted to social studies. In examining the Table, the reader should bear in mind that in some of the school systems which were sampled, the social studies were not taught every day; the figures are average lengths of periods for only those days on which the social studies were scheduled. Robert V. Duffey, in a mimeographed publication (1967), reported that Maryland teachers were devoting an average of 40 minutes per day to social studies in the primary grades and 55 minutes per day in the intermediate grades. (See Footnote d, Table 2.1.)

Table 2.2. Average Length of Social Studies Periods per Day in 84 School Systems

	GRADES 1–3 (N=84)		GRADES 4–8 (N=85)	
	N	%	N	%
30 minutes or less	58	69	2	2
31–45 minutes	25	30	29	34
46–60 minutes	—	—	50	59
Over 60 minutes	1	1	4	5

Competing Demands for Time

The elementary school program lays the foundation of learnings which may be classified as follows:

1. *Communication skills and arts*, which consist of reading, writing, spelling, written composition, oral expression, and listening,
2. *Social Studies*, which consist of content drawn from social sciences,
3. *Natural sciences*, which consist of content drawn from the physical, biological, and earth sciences,
4. *Mathematics*, which consists of the study of numbers and counting, equality and inequality, numeration, and the other unifying ideas of quantitative relationship,
5. The *arts*, which consist of study of, and creative experimentation in, music, drawing, painting, and other fine arts,
6. *Health and physical education*, which consist of the study of the rules of health and safety and the development of physical fitness through participation in physical exercises and games.

By fairly general agreement among educators, the first of the above areas—the communication skills and arts—receives a larger proportion of school instruction than any of the other areas. In writing of the objectives of formal education, the geographer Preston E. James says that ". . . perhaps the most important of all . . . is to polish and enrich the techniques of communication, to develop an appreciation of the beauty of the sentence, to gain a reverence for the precise meaning of words."[46] The established difficulty in learning to read and spell in the English language gives further justification to a generous time allotment for the communications area, especially in the primary grades.

Science, on the other hand, was a sort of stepchild in the elementary school curriculum until fairly recent years. Many schools had ignored it, and others had merely merged scraps of it with social studies. The importance of science to the individual and to society is recognized today, with the result that it now commands a generous share of the day in schools— 15 years ago, it was scarcely taught.

The new mathematics requires more time in the school program than formerly, since it emphasizes mathematical ideas (in addition to the computational skills and simple problem-solving of traditional arithmetic) and provides for pupil-discovery of mathematical principles. Thus, it goes beyond the old arithmetic which emphasized processes of computation, fragmented from the science of mathematics.

Social studies, too, are bidding for more time. Their importance was discussed in the previous chapter.

Partial Solutions

The problem is where to find the extra time demanded by these expanding subjects. Obviously, "something has to give." Aside from the controversial possibilities of lengthening the school day or the school year, there are other practices which may be followed to solve the dilemma.

One method is for the teacher to use topics or units in both social studies and in science as integrating centers for systematic application of reading and writing skills. For example, the supplementary reading expected of children in reading classes, instead of being of a miscellaneous or random nature, relates to social studies and science topics under study. The writing of compositions and oral reports also uses material from social studies and science programs.

The meager time allotment for social studies in the primary grades— averaging 30 or 40 minutes—may be due to the widely held view that most of the child's time in these grades should be spent learning the three R's, and that social studies (and science, too) are of secondary importance

[46] James in Berelson, *et al.*, *The Social Studies and the Social Sciences*. P. 43.

during these years. Without denying the justifiable priority for the skills program, it needs to be recognized that the teaching of reading is, not uncommonly, taught to the point of diminishing returns.

It is pertinent to note that slow-learning children in one school, with reduced instruction in reading *per se* and increased social studies projects:

> . . . apparently acquired as much reading ability as equivalent pupils in the conventional school and established the habits of reading more widely . . . [and] enjoyed reading more. . . . [The] writers of this report feel that in many cases the . . . teacher [who taught the experimental class] has turned out more satisfied and well-rounded learners than would have been secured had the pressure upon reading been more insistent.[47]

Beyond a certain point, additional drill and practice of any skill, mental or motor, yield meager results and poor attitudes toward learning. A well-planned social studies program proves an ally of the basic-skills program by providing incentive and opportunity for practicing reading and writing. A social studies lesson should last long enough so that, virtually daily, the child has an opportunity to apply reading-and-writing skills to the acquisition and reporting of the content. Some teachers of exceptional ability may accomplish a great deal of teaching within 30 minutes, but it is hard to imagine how learning in reasonable depth can take place within such a brief period.

FOR REVIEW AND REFLECTION

1. Evaluate the following rejoinder to Hanna's proposal for a national commission to construct a national curriculum design: "Hasn't our experience convinced us that we don't change the curriculum without changing teachers?"
2. What are the strengths and weaknesses of the expanding-environment principles? Of the ESI program? Of the Elkhart program in economic education?
3. What criteria other than, or in place of, continuity, balance, relevance, and contrast would you propose?
4. What is the essence of the issue of unified social studies versus the separate-subjects approach?
5. What considerations should determine the distribution of time among the various subject fields of the elementary school?

ASSIGNMENTS

1. Obtain a social studies curriculum guide or course of study from a nearby school district (or from a library or a curriculum center), and study it to

---

[47] Arthur I. Gates and Miriam C. Pritchard, *Teaching Reading to Slow-Learning Children.* New York: Teachers College, 1942. P. 62.

determine how it deviates from the "prevailing offerings"; whether social scientists are mentioned as having contributed in any way to the formulation of content; and the extent to which it appears to satisfy the criteria of continuity, balance, relevance, and contrast.
2. Analyze Grannis' criticism of the expanding-environment principle (cited in "Supplementary Reading").
3. Construct an "ideal" curriculum plan for a specified grade for one year's study of social studies. Justify your selection of topics and the order in which you think they should be taken up.
4. Analyze an elementary-school social studies textbook and a geography or history textbook designed for the same grade. Compare them in terms of depth of content, logic, and clarity of organization.

SUPPLEMENTARY READING

Fraser, Dorothy McClure, "Status and Expectations of Current Research and Development Projects," *Social Education,* **29** (November 1965), 421–434. Indicates trends as revealed by over 40 current projects.

Grannis, Joseph C., "The Framework of the Social Studies Curriculum," *National Elementary Principal,* **42** (April 1963), 20–26. Describes the ESI and Harvard-Lexington programs.

Haefner, John H., "Needed Research on Selection and Organization of Content for Teaching Purposes," in *Needed Research in the Teaching of Social Studies,* Roy A. Price (Ed.), Washington, D.C.: National Council for the Social Studies, 1964. Pp. 93–106.

Hanna, Paul R., "Design for a National Curriculum," *Nation's Schools,* **62** (September 1958), 54–56. This article cogently brought the issue of a national curriculum design to the attention of the profession.

————, "Revising the Social Studies: What Is Needed?" *Social Education,* **27** (April 1963), 190–196. Presents the foundation for a curriculum design based on the expanding-horizon principle.

Heath, Robert W. (Ed.), *New Curricula: A Report on the Methods and Programs for Teaching Science and the Humanities Which Promise to Revolutionize American Education.* New York: Harper & Row, 1964. Contains descriptions of new curricula in several fields, including social studies, and a discussion of their implications.

Heffernan, Helen, "Social Studies in Relation to the Total School Program," in *Social Studies in the Elementary School,* Nelson B. Henry, (Ed.); Fifty-sixth Yearbook of the National Society for the Study of Education, Pt. II. Chicago: University of Chicago Press, 1957. Chap. 5. Approaches social studies as an integrating center of the curriculum.

Kaltsounis, Theodore, "A Modification of the 'Expanding Environment' Approach," *Social Studies,* **55** (March 1964), 99–102. Contains practical suggestions for meeting the situation in which children in the primary grades know more of the social studies content than is assumed.

Keller, Charles R., "Needed: Revolution in the Social Studies," *Saturday Review,* **44** (September 16, 1961), 60–62. An oft-cited critical appraisal of the traditional social studies curriculum.

Lunstrum, John P., "A Proposed Social Studies Curriculum, Grades Kinder-garten–12," *Indiana Social Studies Quarterly,* **14** (Spring 1961), 11–18. A proposal "based upon a careful examination of varying points of view" containing "many of the suggestions or ideas . . . used successfully by competent teachers for a number of years."

Martin, Clyde Inez, *An Elementary School Social Studies Program.* Austin, Tex.: University of Texas, 1963. Appears in two volumes. Pt. I ("Components of the Program") presents a design for kindergarten–Grade 6 developed by the author and the faculties of two elementary schools. The content is based on eight generalizations and certain social problems, stated as a series of problems aimed to stimulate inquiry on the part of the children. Pt. II ("The Children's Program") describes the program in detail and describes "depth studies" to illustrate the teaching of certain of the generalizations.

Martin, William Oliver, "The Structure of Knowledge in the Social Sciences," in *Education and the Structure of Knowledge,* Stanley Elam, (Ed.). Skokie, Ill.: Rand-McNally, 1965. Chap. 6. Presents a structure and suggests criteria for selecting content for a curriculum.

Michaelis, John U., and A. Montgomery Johnston (Eds.), *The Social Sciences: Foundation of the Social Studies.* Boston: Allyn & Bacon, 1965. Discusses the respective ways of thinking and working in eight social sciences and considers implications for planning the social studies program.

National Council for the Social Studies, National Commission on the Social Studies. Washington, D.C.: The Council, 1958. A searching critique and a proposal for improving the social studies curriculum.

National Elementary Principal **42** (April and May 1963). These two issues carry a series of provocative and important articles on elementary school social studies.

Senesh, Lawrence, "The Pattern of the Economic Curriculum," *Social Education,* **32** (January 1968), 47–50, 59. Presents a sensible 8-point structure, not only for the economic curriculum, but also for any social studies curriculum.

"Social Studies Projects, Directory of," *Social Education,* **31** (October 1967), 509–511. A list of research and curriculum projects, complete through June 1967.

State (California) Curriculum Commission, *Social Studies Framework for the Public Schools of California.* Sacramento: California State Department of Education, 1962. Describes content which, for the elementary program, follows, more or less, the expanding-environment principle.

Volberding, Eleanor, and Woodson W. Fishback (Eds.), *Teaching the Social Studies in Grades K–9.* Illinois Curriculum Program, Subject Field Series, Bulletin C-7. Springfield, Ill.: Office of the Superintendent of Public Instruction, 1962. Proposes experimentation by teachers in search of a new curriculum framework.

3

THE CHILD AND HOW HE LEARNS
SOCIAL STUDIES

The important thing is not so much that every child should be taught, as that every child should be given the wish to learn.

JOHN LUBBOCK

A teacher can help his pupils find pleasure and satisfaction in learning social studies. Obviously, the greater the child's interest and satisfaction, the greater his application to the subject, and the more fruitful the results. It behooves the teacher to learn what makes children tick. He will then know what strategies for social studies teaching to employ. Successful teaching of social studies also demands familiarity, on the part of the teacher, with basic principles of learning. This chapter brings together that information about children and about learning which seems especially applicable to social studies instruction.

CHILDHOOD TRAITS AND SOCIAL STUDIES

In presenting the generalizations about children which follow, the writer assumes that the teacher already knows that each child, while sharing some traits with other children, is a unique learner, possessing a singular personality, a distinctive background of experience, and a preferred mode of learning. It is the purpose of this section not to labor the obvious point—the uniqueness of each child—but to describe characteristics shared widely by children.

The Child Responds to Varied Aspects
of the World

Children quite spontaneously seek orientation to many aspects of the world. Their curiosity is diverse and shifting. During a stage in a child's development, when he is seemingly totally preoccupied by some specialized interest (caring for a pet, playing at war, or collecting stamps), he normally has a host of simultaneous, subsidiary interests. The spread of children's interests is well known. One indication of it was shown in Rudman's investigation of children in Grades 4–8.[1] Rudman found, for example, that many children whose chief *reading* interests resided in literature (stories of adventure, for example) reported active curiosity (unassociated with reading) in machines, maps, and a variety of other things. A similarly wide spread was found by Bresnehan.[2] Her subjects, in Grades 2–8, revealed interests rather evenly distributed among nine categories of social studies topics.

Such evidence supports the kind of curriculum balance proposed in Chapter 2—a distribution of social studies topics among several areas during any given school year. Such balance is not for the sake of catering to alleged child interests (see section on this in Chapter 2 for refutation of selection of content on that basis). It is because, if the topics for a single grade were all drawn from the same category (say, geography), we could not satisfy what appears to be the pressing intellectual need of young children for broad orientation.

The Child Is an Investigator

A desire to find out how things work is one of the strongest drives of children. Although children's most active investigations are directed toward objects and ideas found in their environment, it should be noted that they also are curious to explore the remote, the unfamiliar, and the antiquated.

The intellectual curiosity and zest for inquiry of many children declines as they advance to the intermediate grades and to high school. A number of reasons have been cited to account for this decline. Jersild believes it ". . . springs from the fact that the content of the curriculum seems academic, arbitrary, and remote from their concerns."[3] Lack of apparent relevance of the curriculum to the pupil reminds us again of the third criterion for judging a curriculum, discussed in Chapter 2: the curriculum content should relate to the child's life.

In addition to making sure that the content has relevance, teachers should provide outlets for investigation—collection of data through observation, surveys, reference work, and similar means.

---

[1] Herbert C. Rudman, "The Informational Needs and Reading Interests of Children in Grades IV through VIII," *Elementary School Journal*, **55** (May 1955), 502–512.

[2] Virginia W. Bresnehan, *et al.*, "Preferences of Children in Grades Two through Eight in Social Studies Areas" Unpublished Masters thesis, Boston University. Summarized by W. Linwood Chase and Gilbert M. Wilson, "Preference Studies in Elementary School Social Studies," *Journal of Education*, **140** (April 1958), 19–21.

[3] Arthur T. Jersild, *Child Psychology* (5th ed.). Englewood Cliffs, N.J.: Prentice-Hall, 1960. P. 431.

The Child Is a Doer

The child is characterized by action, and this creates a problem in teaching him social studies. For, as Abt points out, social studies by their very nature fail to provide, in themselves, much opportunity for children to learn by doing. A child cannot make history or solve social problems.[4] Abt proposes formal games for learning which, as realistically as possible, simulate events or situations to be learned, and through which children have an opportunity to become personally involved in situations and in devising strategies. He gives examples of games of hunting, empire building, adventuring, and so on, which have fascinating possibilities—at least, for the brighter child. The games were designed for Educational Services, Inc., Cambridge, Mass.

Other activities which enable children to identify with the thinking, decision-making, and strategy-planning employed by communities of men in other times and places are:

INDUSTRIAL ARTS ACTIVITIES   By experimenting with making pottery or baskets or with weaving mats, children can gain substantial insight into, and confirmation of, verbally transmitted information they receive about the resourcefulness of the American Indian, his dependence on nearby raw materials, and the relatively large amount of time required for constructing simple utensils and accessories. Details of industrial arts activities appear throughout this book.

DRAMATIZATION   Children may seek identification with a worker, a historical figure, or a period of time by reenacting through dramatic play the work of an airplane pilot, an episode such as Washington's trip to Fort Le Boeuf, or the regimen of a frontier family. The role of dramatics is treated later in this book.

COLLECTING   By collecting, sorting, and exhibiting objects (stalks of different kinds of grain, samples of varieties of timber, leather, or textiles), children are not only engaged in "action," but they also are classifying and organizing some of the components of their studies.

Such learning activities enlarge children's understanding by capitalizing on their apparent need for overt activity.

The Child Has Strong Interest in Detail

Students of child development have remarked on children's concern with detail. Havighurst points out their "preference for details rather than

[4] Clark C. Abt, *Games for Learning*. Occasional Paper No. 7. Cambridge, Mass.: Educational Services Incorporated, 1966.

wholes," their interest in "sidelines, oddities, minor details," and their "avidness for detail."[5] By way of illustration, a third-grade class, in a study of transportation, asked questions such as these about railroads:

Why are engines black?
How is the whistle hooked on the engine?
Is there a special car for a king?
How many people can a passenger train carry?
Why is a caboose red?

The point is not that such questions often lack significance; nor need we be concerned whether a teacher can answer, or assist the class in answering, such questions. (Let us hope the teacher will answer when he can or, better, help the child find the answer.) The important point is that children, while engaged in learning designed to lead to significant generalizations, do become captivated by such "sidelines and oddities," sometimes trivial, sometimes based on misconceptions, sometimes profound. It is desirable that the teacher know what these side interests are, but since the children will not always express them, he should supply large quantities of verbal and pictorial illustrations to insure details which will explain and document the factual generalizations and the values which he is teaching.

The Child Has a Rich Imaginative Life

Imaginative play and make-believe are prominent in the life of a young child. They decline in outward expression during the elementary school years, but in revised form, they continue to play a significant role in his development. Their more obvious expressions are drawing, painting, creative writing, and creative dramatics. Such art experiences can be executed legitimately during social studies periods when they are means to a closer understanding of a people or a period, through identification with them, or by representing details of their life and work. These possibilities are taken up in Chapter 11.

Another channel for children's imaginative impulses is the formulation of hypotheses or hunches in seeking to explain events and processes. Teachers can stimulate children in this activity by having them tackle such questions as the following, which call upon imaginative thought and the discovery of new relationships:

Stone lasts longer than wood. Why, then, are more houses in our community made of wood than stone?

[5] Robert J. Havighurst, *Human Development and Education.* New York: McKay, 1953. Chap. 7.

Why does lace made by hand cost more than lace made by machine?

Why could corn and rice not be grown on the same farm land?

How can natural resources be used without destroying them?

How do the mountain ranges of the Far West cause desert areas in western United States?

Why did the Industrial Revolution come to England before other countries?

The children's hypotheses, in answer to such questions, should be considered critically by the teacher and the class, checking, when necessary, with the textbook and other sources. Children thus are encouraged to work over familiar facts in order to discover new ideas. A regular diet of such experiences helps lay the basis of a thoughtful, creative intellectual life.

STAGES AND AGES

It has long been the practice of writers of texts in elementary education to list descriptions of child behavior at various stages of development. The six-year-old might be described as an active, energetic child, needing much physical activity and opportunities to satisfy intellectual curiosity. Unfortunately, such descriptions were often impressionistic rather than founded on research findings, and were of only limited help to the classroom teacher.

Today we have better descriptions, at least of the intellectual development of the child. Piaget, a Swiss psychologist, has provided us with a picture of the stages of development of logical reasoning typical of children in the Western world. These stages are age-related, but not age-determined. That is, there is a probability that a child of six or seven years is likely to reason about a problem in a particular way, and the young adolescent will employ very different thought processes.[6]

Piaget has described the characteristics of thought at different stages for us. However, there will be individual differences within an age group, with some children being more advanced than others, because of such factors as heredity and opportunities for learning. The first stage in the development of intelligence is the *sensorimotor* lasting from birth to about 18 months. During this period, the infant is carrying on countless transactions with the physical world, as he looks, sucks, grasps, and experiments with objects in his environment. He assimilates information from these transactions—that an object continues to exist even when it is out of sight, for example—and his developing mental structures change to accommodate the new information. "Thinking," however, is action-oriented; the infant does not

[6] A few of Piaget's writings are cited in Footnote 13 and in "Supplementary Reading" under Inhelder. See also Tuddenham's article listed in "Supplementary Reading."

have the capability for representational thought and so can only *act out* what is going on in his mind. If asked "Where is your teddy bear?", he can look at the teddy and lift up the teddy, but he cannot visualize or think about the action before carrying it out.

The next stage, that of preoperational thought, is of concern to the primary teacher, for most children in kindergarten and first grade are to be found in this stage. Thought is "preoperational," for the child lacks the ability to perform operations of thought upon data. Instead, the following characteristics describe his thinking processes:

1. The child is perceptually oriented; he makes judgments in terms of how things look to him. If he has made a map on the classroom floor and is looking north on the map, he cannot answer a question from the point of view of an observer looking south. He will answer as things look to him, for he cannot turn the map around in his mind.
2. The child centers on one variable only, usually the variable that stands out visually; he lacks the ability to coordinate variables. For example, a kindergarten child is pouring juice into paper cups. The standard-size cups run out, and the teacher substitutes some that are much higher but are also smaller in diameter. As the children drink their juice, several comment on the fact that Jimmy, Eddie, and Danny have more juice. Why? Because those children have cups that are taller. The dimension of height, not width, stands out. The child's thinking is rigid; he does not perform operations on what he sees. Later, he will reason that "higher than" is compensated for by "skinnier than," and that both kinds of cups may hold the same amount of juice. This ability to see reciprocal changes in two sets of data is an important logical tool available to older children, but not to the preoperational child.
3. The child has difficulty in realizing that an object can possess more than one property, and that multiple classifications are possible. It is hard for the child to see that one can live in Los Angeles and in California at the same time, that the city is contained in the state, and that, since there are cities in the state in addition to Los Angeles, there are logically *more* people in the state than in any one city in that state. The operation of combining elements to form a whole and then seeing a part in relation to the whole has not yet developed, and so hierarchical relationships cannot be mastered.

So far, this consideration of preoperational thinking has been largely negative. We have seen that the child lacks the ability to combine parts into a whole, to put parts together in different ways, and to reverse processes. What, then, can the child do? The development of logical processes is not at a standstill during this period; there are some positive accomplishments. We see, for example, the rudiments of classification: the child can make collections of things on the basis of some criterion; he can also shift that criterion. Thus, if we present a kindergarten child with a collection of pink and blue squares and circles, some large and some small, and ask him to sort them into two piles with those in each pile being alike in some way, he can usually make two different collections on the basis of color and shape (a few children discover the third criterion of size). Such an ability, of course, is essential to the formation of classes, and eventually, of a hierarchy of classes.

The child is also beginning to arrange things in a series. He can compare two members of a set when they are in a consecutive order; he knows that Tuesday comes after Monday. But since Friday comes after Tuesday, which is after Monday, does Friday also come after Monday? This operation, involving seeing logical relations among things or events that are arranged in a series, is not yet possible to the preoperational child, but experiences with seriation (the calendar, for example) are preparatory to the development of such operations. The "inching up" that an older pupil does in trying to establish equilibrium between two parts of a physical system (add a little to one side; then, add a little to the other) is an example of a more sophisticated use of seriation.

Between 7 and 11 years of age, on the average, as the child assimilates information from his actions and accommodates mental structures to the new information, thinking processes change. The child abandons his perceptual judgments, and thought takes on certain logical properties. Piaget calls this the stage of *concrete operations*, because, while the child uses logical operations, the content of his thinking is concrete rather than abstract. One of the mental operations that develops is that of combining elements; the child begins to put two and two together figuratively as well as literally. He uses this combining operation to discover (although not until toward the end of this stage) the concept of a hierarchy, and so the relations involved in city, county, state, nation, hemisphere begin to become clear.

Another property of logical thought is that elements of a whole can be associated in various ways without changing the total. The political map of Europe may change many times, but the total area of Europe remains the same, or is conserved.

A third property of logical thought is that of identity. The identity operation is basically a null operation; the child can mentally cancel out the effects of any operation by combining it with its opposite. An extension of the identity operation is the one-to-one correspondence a pupil carries on to establish identity between two sets. Is Sweden an archipelago? The pupil must compare each characteristic in the set of archipelagoes with each in the Sweden set, on a one-to-one basis, to answer the question.

Of all of the properties of logical thinking, one of the most critical to develop is that of reversibility. Every change that the mind makes upon sensory data is reversible. The child can mentally rearrange sticks in a zigzag line, putting them into a straight one, to see that length is conserved, even after the transformation. Similarly, a pupil can solve the problem of whether matter in a total system is conserved, when a river carries away soil and deposits it in the river delta, by reversing the depositing process.

The fourth stage in the development of logical thinking, the stage of formal thinking, begins roughly at 12 years of age. According to Piaget, most adolescents are capable of doing a "if this happens, then that is likely to happen" kind of thinking. They can identify variables in a problem and examine them critically. It is possible, for example, for a student at the formal level to analyze the absurdity of a state legislature castigating a Big Ten Conference Committee that ordered suspension of university football players and coaches caught violating the rules of the Conference, as if the Conference Committee had performed the misdeed and not the violators.

The teacher who is aware of stage characteristics is in a better position to diagnose pupil thought and ask the kinds of questions that will help children to think more logically. The teacher also can plan learning activities suited to the developmental characteristics of his class. Many examples of these will be found in the chapters to follow.

THE PROBLEM OF "READINESS"

In recent years, the "readiness" problem in social studies has focused upon the question: Are average children ready to study, formally and systematically, remote places and remote times (as opposed to the here-and-now) at an earlier age than a generation ago? Are children, in short, more precocious?

Evidence of the Precocity of Today's Children

Those who answer affirmatively point to studies which report that many children today, as a probable consequence of the advent of television, of expanded family travel, and of increased availability of children's books, have wider frames of reference than did children of a generation ago.[7] They point also to studies which are believed to show that children are sometimes taught in school what they already know. In one such study, Lowry tested and interviewed 287 second-grade children concerning con-

---

[7] Typical of these studies are William W. Crowder, "A Study of the Out-of-School Experiences of Selected Second Grade Children with Implications for Revision of the Social Studies Course of Study." Ph.D. thesis, Indiana University, 1958; and Kenneth D. Wann, "Children Want to Know," *Childhood Education*, **37** (September 1960), 8–12.

cepts they were about to be taught.[8] She concluded that they knew on the average from 64 to 85 percent of the concepts! In an earlier study of second-grade children, McAulay interviewed 70 pupils during the first month of school and felt that they then knew much of what most second-grade children are taught in social studies.[9] One teacher in Illinois is reported to have given a pretest and found that pupils knew about 51 percent of the material which he was planning to teach.[10] Kaltsounis reported that third-grade children knew about 37 percent of typical third-grade content prior to its formal instruction.[11]

These investigations properly call our attention to the ever-present danger of underchallenging our children. It is amazingly easy to belabor the familiar! Although teachers should begin with what children already know, they should move on quickly to what their pupils do not know.

Possible Exaggeration
of Children's Precocity

On the other hand, is it not possible that we are exaggerating the sophistication of today's children? Are we, perhaps, mistaking their verbal glibness on Topic A as a sign of readiness for Topic B?

These questions were investigated by Mugge with 180 second-grade pupils whose mean intelligence and socioeconomic status were above average.[12] She found that they lacked precision of knowledge with respect to important aspects of the community, the farm, and other topics normally studied in Grades 1 and 2. In regard to the post office, for example, very few children could tell how much it costs to send a letter or why a stamp is canceled. Also, they had difficulty in keeping cities, states, and countries in their proper hierarchical relationship. Those children who traveled did not know significantly more than those who had not traveled. The disparity between Mugge's results and those of investigators who have found modern children well informed is probably attributable to the fact that Mugge, when asking children for a definition, was not satisfied with

[8] Betty C. Lowry, "A Survey of the Knowledge of Social Studies Concepts Possessed by Second-Grade Children Previous to the Time These Concepts Are Taught in the Social Studies Lessons." Ph.D. thesis, State University of Iowa, *Dissertation Abstracts*, **24** (1963), 2324–2325.

[9] J. D. McAulay, "Social Studies in the Primary Grades," *Social Education*, **18** (December 1954), 357–358.

[10] Eleanor Volberding and Woodson W. Fishback (Eds.), *Teaching the Social Studies in Grades K–9*. Springfield, Ill.: Illinois Curriculum Program, Office of the Superintendent of Public Instruction, 1962. P. 86.

[11] Theodore Kaltsounis, "A Study Concerning Third Graders' Knowledge of Social Studies Content Prior to Instruction," *Journal of Educational Research*, **57** (March 1964), 345–357. See also Kaltsounis' "A Modification of the 'Expanding Environment' Approach," *Social Studies*, **55** (March 1964), 99–102.

[12] Dorothy J. Mugge, "Precocity of Today's Young Children: Real or Wishful?" *Social Education*, **27** (December 1963), 436–439.

vague synonyms, minor usage, or trivial attributes; when children offered her these, she probed further and often found a sea of empty concepts beneath a facile surface. Further reason for caution against precipitating children too early into studies of remote places and times is found in the literature of child development. What is known about children's thought structures at various age levels? Piaget, previously mentioned, whose importance is now being belatedly acknowledged by his American colleagues, found that seven-year-olds, in structuring ideas, were tied to concrete content, still bound to the here and now.[13] Data consistent with Piaget's findings have been reported by various investigators.[14] To be sure, Piaget is more concerned with cognitive operations than with content, and the subjects of Piaget and most other investigators whose conclusions are generally in accord with his, were not reared in a television-saturated culture. Nevertheless, there are indications in the studies cited that the successive stages by which children structure their thoughts while growing up is independent to a surprising degree of the information and ideas to which they are exposed.

Reconciliation of Diverse Theories of Readiness

How does Piaget's view relate to the view that, in Bruner's words, ". . . there is no reason to believe that any subject cannot be taught to any child at virtually any age in some form?"[15] The views are complementary. As Bruner himself points out:

> . . . It is only when we are equipped with such knowledge [as produced by Piaget in the study of physical causality, of morality, of number, and the rest] that we will be in a position to know how the child will translate whatever we present to him into his own subjective terms.[16]

[13] Jean Piaget, *The Language and Thought of the Child* (3d ed.). London: Routledge, 1959. *The Child's Conception of Space* (with Bärbel Inhelder). London: Routledge, 1963. *The Growth of Logical Thinking from Childhood to Adolescence* (with Bärbel Inhelder). New York: Basic Books, 1958.

[14] Harold V. Baker, *Children's Contributions in Elementary School General Discussion.* Child Development Monographs, No. 29. New York: Teachers College, 1942; Franziska Baumgarten-Tramer, "Was ist ein Soldat?" *Schweitzer Erziehungs-Rundschau,* 12 (March 1940), 217–222; Ralph C. Preston, *Children's Reactions to a Contemporary War Situation.* Child Development Monographs, No. 28. New York: Teachers College, 1942; Laurance F. Shaffer, *Children's Interpretation of Cartoons.* New York: Teachers College, 1930. A possibly related phenomenon of developmental lag is revealed in Carroll Eugene Weber, "A Study of Sixth-Grade Children's Ability to Infer the Influence of the Natural Environment upon Man," *Dissertation Abstracts,* 25 (January 1965), 4012.

[15] Jerome S. Bruner, *The Process of Education.* Cambridge, Mass.: Harvard University Press, 1961. P. 47.

[16] Bruner. P. 53.

There is no essential contradiction. A primary-grade teacher can assume, as would Bruner, that the geographical theme of man's use of the land can be taught at any age. In applying the principle of readiness in accordance with Piaget, the primary teacher emphasizes those applications which the child can observe and test at firsthand. The central problem of readiness is a question of fitting instruction—whatever its content may be—to the mental horizons and thought pattern of children at each successive stage of growth, whatever the pace of that growth.

The point needs to be stressed that some elements of the "unknown" lie close to home. We should avoid being misled, by children's glib talk about foreign places, to the conclusion that they know all they need to know about that which is close at hand.

Readiness of Children
for Depth Studies

The reader may wonder whether or not the young child's intellectual power is sufficiently developed to enable him to study social studies content with profit—except, perhaps, in a purely descriptive way. Some writers, unlike Bruner, doubt that the child has sufficient critical understanding.[17] The issue cannot be definitively settled because of a lack of rigorous evaluation of children's responses to social studies instruction. On the basis of teachers' anecdotal reports, however, and those of careful classroom observers, it can be assumed that children of elementary school age quite spontaneously engage in social studies learning and show a capacity for understanding social concepts.[18]

By way of example, Rusnak reports that children possess the capacity for depth study, and that they are fully challenged by content dealing with

[17] Erich Fromm, *The Sane Society*. New York: Holt, Rinehart and Winston, 1955. P. 346; Richard Livingston, *On Education*. Cambridge, England: Cambridge University Press, 1954. P. 139; David Riesman, "Some Observations on Intellectual Freedom," *The American Scholar*, 23 (Winter, 1953–1954), 9–25.
[18] Barbara Biber, *et al.*, *Child Life in School: A Study of a Seven-Year-Old Group*. New York: Dutton, 1942; Alvina T. Burrows, *Teaching Children in the Middle Grades*. Boston: Heath, 1952. Chap. 7; Janice B. Goldberg, "Enrichment in Social Studies in an Enriched School," *Elementary School Journal*, 61 (May 1961), 418–423. Henry Harap, *Social Living in the Curriculum*. Nashville, Tenn.: George Peabody College, 1952. L. Thomas Hopkins (Ed.), *Lincoln School Curriculum Studies*: Titles include "Indian Life and the Dutch Colonial Settlement" (by Katherine L. Keelor and Mayme Sweet), and "Children and Architecture" (by Emily Ann Barnes and Bess M. Young). New York: Teachers College, 1931–1932. Lucy Sprague Mitchell, *et al.*, *The People of the U.S.A.: Their Place in the School Curriculum*. New York: Progressive Education Association, 1942; Mary M. Reed and Lula E. Wright, *The Beginnings of the Social Sciences*. New York: Scribner, 1932. For a systematic study of children's gains from social studies instruction, see Melvin Arnoff, "Adding Depth to Elementary School Social Studies," *Social Education*, 28 (October 1964), 335–336.

home and community.[19] She experimented informally for three years with teaching children in the first grade about "home" and "community." Her report gives an apt illustration of teaching in depth. Her pupils learned the profound aspects of "home" and "community" through analysis of historical sequence, cause-and-effect relationships, environmental adaptation, and contrasts between simple and complex societies. They learned how to collect information, how to organize it, and how to report it. It well may be that the proper issue regarding readiness is not "here and now" versus "remote," but rather superficial study versus study which brings out underlying principles, relationships, and processes.

PRINCIPLES OF LEARNING SOCIAL STUDIES

Whatever a child may be learning—concepts, values, behavior, or skills—the teacher can help make that learning substantial and satisfying by seeing that certain principles operate. This section will discuss six of the basic principles which are essential to successful learning in social studies.

First Principle: The Child Requires a Suitable Background

The child is unable to learn a generalization if he lacks its underlying component concepts. Take the generalization: "Our expanding population needs more places of recreation such as are provided by our national forests." How much does the child know about a forest? Does he understand its vastness, its density, its relative coolness in summer? Does he know its flora and its wild life? Does he know the difference between national forests and other types of forests? Does he know what is implied by the term "recreation," or does he associate it entirely with the play activity of a school recess period? It is obvious that a child who has visited a national forest, responded emotionally to its majesty, gone swimming in its lakes, used its camping facilities, and, perhaps, seen a deer, will instantly recognize and understand the generalization.

On the other hand, a child, whose only comparable experience is a walk past a patch of woods containing a dump, forms a very inaccurate and incomplete picture of the generalization. Before the latter child can learn the generalization, he will need at least a good verbal description through reading or listening, preferably supplemented by pictures, a film, or colored slides showing the appearance and recreational possibilities of a national forest. This suggests that if children lack the background for learning something, the teacher can often supply it by direct, on-the-spot instruction.

[19] Mary Rusnak, "Introducing Social Studies in the First Grade," *Social Education*, **25** (October 1961), 291–292.

Sometimes, however, children are not ready for such instruction. The teacher's best efforts may be of little avail in attempting to teach a primary-grade class the meaning of generalizations like the following:

A flat map cannot be wholly accurate in all respects.

Canada has a shorter growing season than Mexico because of the inclination of the earth's axis.

The *Mayflower* reached Plymouth toward the end of the first quarter of the seventeenth century.

Similarly, an intermediate-grade class would probably find it difficult to learn with real understanding such generalizations as these:

On a map which represents one mile by one inch, every unit of map distance represents 63,360 units of ground distance.

Wars are often followed by monetary inflation.

A long period of time elapses following important technological changes before people change their social institutions and beliefs to conform to the new situations.

Some of the background for generalizations such as these can be supplied immediately by the teacher, with the result that they can be understood, at least partly, by many children. For other children, however, learning the generalizations must await greater maturity and experience.

Skills, as well as generalizations, require a background for their learning. A child cannot take adequate notes from his reading, for example, until he knows how to spot the main ideas in a paragraph and how to express them by cue words. Nor can he interpret a physical map until he has learned directly, or through pictures, the landscape features which are represented on the map by color or other symbols.

The importance of this principle places a heavy responsibility upon the teacher. There is no master list or formula to tell him the degree of readiness of a particular child for learning a given concept. That information comes only through careful observation and study of each pupil, and through introducing new concepts and skills slowly, in order to give each child a chance to master them.

*Second Principle: Motivation toward Learning Goals
Increases the Effectiveness of Learning*

A sense of direction is essential for effective learning. The teacher should help a class identify and clarify desirable goals. He can do this by asking the class: "What questions about this subject we are going to study would you like to find answers to?" If the answers are shallow, he should supplement them by discussing the central questions as he sees them. Subsequent to the identification of some questions, he might ask further: "In what ways will this study be useful to us?" The goals should be reexamined, clarified, and expanded as the study continues.

Some of the private goals of children may have nothing to do with the subject matter. A child may apply himself for any one of several reasons of his own: to please the teacher, to do better on a test than his classmates, to impress his family with his knowledge, or to get a favorable report card. While these goals denote an extrinsic kind of motivation which is natural enough, the teacher, by emphasizing intellectual goals and by exhibiting his own intellectual curiosity, can help his pupils keep in mind the goals which reside in the social studies content.

Motivation is basic to effective learning. A well-motivated learner throws himself into the work at hand, giving it his sustained attention and obtaining satisfaction from it. Well-motivated learning tends to yield better retention than learning which is undertaken halfheartedly or unwillingly.[20]

MEDIUM OF LEARNING	SUBJECT OF LEARNING
Teacher presentation and class discussion	Growing of wheat and converting it to flour
Reading of textbook	Where wheat is grown and how it is harvested
Viewing film	Wheat, from farm to bake shop
Construction of mural	The work of the wheat farmer
Recitation	Growing of wheat
Taking test	Growing of wheat
Discussion of test	Correction of misconceptions
Arranging bulletin board display	Steps in the baking of bread
Teacher presentation and class discussion	Ways in which wheat flour is used
Erecting classroom exhibit	Samples of wheat, flour, wheat products
Making chart	Nutritional ingredients of wheat flour
Research	Man's early methods in use of wheat flour
Recitation	Review of all above subjects
Taking test	Covering all above subjects
Discussion of test	Correction of misconceptions and final summary

[20] John M. Stephens, *The Psychology of Classroom Learning.* New York: Holt, Rinehart and Winston, 1965. Pp. 210–211.

Among conditions contributing to favorable motivation, the following are important:

1. Having the child work toward goals which he recognizes as worthwhile. This is the point of the Second Principle.
2. Enabling the child to grasp the structure of the topic he is studying. In the words of Dewey: "No experience is educative that does not tend both to knowledge of more facts and entertaining of more ideas and to a better, a more orderly arrangement of them."[21]
3. Providing opportunities through which the child enriches the meaning of what he learns. An example of enriching meaning, which follows, presents a teacher's plan in teaching about the role of wheat in our economic life.
4. Providing opportunity for depth of understanding. It is advisable to dwell in detail on a few significant areas in preference to spreading out superficially over many. As previously noted, a certain amount of variety is needed for a balanced program. Yet, including too many topics necessitates skimming the surface, and scatters effort. Whitehead wrote:

> Do not teach too many subjects. . . . What you teach, teach thoroughly. . . . Let the main ideas which are introduced into a child's education be few and important, and let them be thrown into every combination possible.[22]

Nothing defeats this simple truth so effectively as requiring that a class cover massive subject matter (such as the geography of Europe) in a few short weeks and expecting thorough coverage of each of its political or cultural divisions. Such a comprehensive study can be self-defeating. Writes Dale:

> Some of these orientation courses have been like the Powder River in Montana, a mile wide and a foot deep. They do not really orient and are quickly forgotten. Certain so-called broad courses have been unsuccessful because they have attempted to cover the ground rather than to uncover it.[23]

The alternative is to select segments of the topic for intensive treatment—a procedure once called "type-study" and more recently "post-holing."[24]

---

[21] John Dewey, *Experience and Education.* New York: Macmillan, 1938. P. 102.
[22] Alfred North Whitehead, *The Aims of Education and Other Essays.* New York: Macmillan, 1929. P. 2.
[23] Edgar Dale, "Generalized Education," *The News Letter,* Ohio State University, Vol. 16, No. 7, (April 1951).
[24] Donald L. McMurry, "Type Study Units in the Social Studies," *Historical Outlook,* **24** (December 1933), 431–441.

5. Seeing that each pupil has an opportunity to participate in learning exercises. After asking a question orally, the teacher should allow time for each pupil to think through his own responses before calling on anyone to reply. Workbooks and programmed materials are intended to provide opportunities for individual participation, and some are well planned and challenging. But such devices may not meet the child's basic need in learning how to make a satisfactory response. Pupils often have difficulty because they do not know how to think about the question. They lack logical thought processes and need to be helped to develop them. Teachers, workbooks, and programmed learning devices have tended to concentrate on the *products* of acquiring knowledge, not the *process*. That is, the concern has been about the correctness of the pupil's answer. It has been a common practice that, if one pupil cannot answer correctly a question about whether or not a particular governmental act was an example of imperialism, the teacher asks another pupil. It is a better practice to ask, "How can you decide? What are the characteristics of imperialism? And what things are true of the action of this government?" When the pupil has named both of these, he can be helped to make a one-to-one comparison between both sets of characteristics. Pupils need to know that there are certain mental operations in which one engages to answer questions of logic, and how to perform these operations.

6. Seeing that many of the exercises require the pupils to apply a learned generalization to fresh problems. For example, if the children have learned how fruit prices are related to demand and supply conditions, they might be asked to explain how demand and supply figures in the regulation of a commodity such as steel, the price of which is not fixed by open competition, and to postage stamps, which are produced and sold by the Federal government.

Third Principle: Learning Is Promoted
by Reinforcement

Learning social studies involves a host of minor tasks. Some of those employed are: giving an oral report before classmates, locating cities on a map, answering questions in a workbook or on a test, and responding orally to a teacher's question during a discussion period. Any child may have a number of such tasks to perform each day. One important factor in determining the quality and permanence of the insights acquired by the child as he undertakes a given task appears to be the promptness and strength with which his performance is *reinforced*. (When a pupil gives a correct answer or otherwise performs satisfactorily, and the teacher reacts with a smile of approval or rewards him in some other way, the child's response is said to be reinforced.) Praise is a time-honored reinforcer for success. Feedback to the pupil in the form of recognition of the correctness (or appropriateness)—or the incorrectness—of one's responses has been proposed by psychologists as another reinforcing agent.

Many potentially important learning activities are seldom reinforced in any systematic way by the teacher. Present knowledge about the effects of programming on learning is impressive enough to justify the teacher's rigorous attention to the pupil's need to know the degree to which his daily responses are satisfactory, and then providing opportunities for him to correct unsatisfactory responses, with subsequent suitable reinforcement.

Fourth Principle: Insight Is Aided through Discovery

The child learns much through reading, hearing, and being informed in other ways, but to acquire insight of a high caliber, he requires opportunity to learn through discovering relationships. Bruner has popularized the discovery principle, advocated earlier by many, including Spencer, Dewey, and Mitchell.[25]

Opportunities for discovery are present in both deductive and inductive learning. These two methods of learning may be summarized as follows:

Deductive method: From generalization to facts.
Inductive method: From facts to generalization.

The child learns by both methods. He needs experience with the thinking peculiar to each type.

In applying the deductive method to learning through discovery, the teacher presents a principle or a generalization for the class's consideration. One generalization might be this:

Settlements located at mouths of navigable rivers with access to deposits of coal and iron have tended to become important industrial centers.

The teacher assists the class in finding examples of this generalization, and the pupils, from the information at their disposal, draw inferences which explain the generalization (the inferences are "discovered").

The inductive method is appropriate whenever a generalization is needed to solve a problem. We might convert the generalization in our example of

[25] Bruner, *The Process of Education*; John Dewey, *How We Think*. Boston: Heath, 1910; Lucy Sprague Mitchell, *Young Geographers*. New York: Day, 1934. Pp. 33–35, 52–54 (Reprinted: New York: Basic Books, 1963); Herbert Spencer, *Education: Intellectual, Moral and Physical*. New York: Mershon, n. d. Pp. 126–127.

the deductive method into a problem to illustrate the settting for inductive learning:

What makes a city an important industrial center?

In this case, the children's search for data will be focused not only upon location and resources, but also on the city's history, its industrial pioneers, and other factors in its growth. Following their search, the pupils will not be trying to test or explain a generalization as in the deductive method, but will be formulating their own generalizations.

The discovery approach slows up learning. A child would never be able to acquire all he needs to know about his environment if that were the sole method at his disposal. He would have to start all his learning from scratch, almost as though others had not made discoveries before him. On the other hand, the discovery method does develop his powers of creative thought and becomes an indispensable tool to him later on in drawing conclusions from scattered information.[26] Further applications of this principle are given in Chapter 4.

As mentioned earlier in this chapter, the child may seem content to deal with fragments of social studies content. He often finds generalizations in textbooks tedious. Yet, he is quite capable of generalizing, as he does about school, his teachers, and his siblings. One purpose of the school is to teach him how to generalize in a disciplined manner, with discovery of principles as the object.

Despite the values of "pupil discovery," its limitations should be faced candidly. Learning through discovery involves more or less random groping. There is much more to learning than that. For example, there is learning by imitation and by verbal instruction.[27] "Telling" the learner the principle is certainly quicker than having him "discover" it, and it is often more effective and appropriate. Furthermore, as Ausubel points out, ". . . actual examination of the research literature allegedly supportive of learning by discovery reveals that valid evidence of this nature is virtually non-existent."[28] Although it is up to teachers to see that their pupils are kept on their toes by being expected to engage in the hard thinking demanded by discovery, it would be a grave error to think that this should constitute the whole of instruction.

[26] The value of discovery procedures in solving map problems was brought out by Wilma Martens Possien, "A Comparison of the Effects of Three Teaching Methodologies on the Development of the Problem-Solving Skills of Sixth Grade Children," *Dissertation Abstracts*, 25 (January 1965), 4003.

[27] D. E. Berlyne, "Curiosity and Education," in *Learning and the Educational Process*, John D. Krumboltz (Ed.). Skokie, Ill.: Rand McNally, 1965. Chap. 3. Robert M. Gagné, *The Conditions of Learning*. New York: Holt, Rinehart and Winston, 1965. P. 53.

[28] David P. Ausubel, *Psychology of Meaningful Verbal Learning*. New York: Grune & Stratton, 1963. P. 165.

*Fifth Principle: The Child Needs Opportunity
to Practice and Review
What He Has Learned*

Study is necessary in order to help the child retain his learning. This is the goal of practice and review. Two methods of practice and review are of particular help: (1) *recitation* and (2) *application*.

1. Recitation consists of repeating the learned material. It is indispensable to good retention, but for best results must be well motivated. Arbitrary material, such as dates, proper names, the position of national boundaries, and known routes of explorers, constitutes traditional data for recitation. Ideas, likewise, should be recited in the child's own words, in order that the teacher be able to determine whether the material is really understood. Recitation may follow the reading of a passage, a chapter, or a book; the viewing of a film; the completion of a unit of study; or it may take place at other times. Having one child recite before the class on occasion may be useful in demonstrating the process, after which the children may recite quietly to themselves, each at his own desk, or to one another in groups of two or three. When assigning such practice, the teacher should stress the value of overlearning—continuing to practice *after* mastery is reached.

2. *Application* is equally important in fixing social studies concepts. Media which can be used include preparation of reports; creation of informal dramatics; execution of murals; keeping of scrapbooks or notebooks; and construction of maps, time lines, and charts. As children select and arrange data in such activities, the teacher is enabled to note what each child has learned, how he interprets concepts, and what misconceptions or errors may be present. The errors which are caught in these ways supply content for further teaching aimed at clearing up the mistakes and misunderstandings.

SEX DIFFERENCES
IN SOCIAL STUDIES LEARNING

Surveys of social studies achievement generally show boys exhibiting superiority to girls.[29] Boys also tend to like social studies better than do

[29] Val E. Arnsdorf, "An Investigation of the Teaching of Chronology in the Sixth Grade," *Journal of Experimental Education*, 29 (March 1961), 307–313; William H. Burton, *Children's Civic Information, 1924–1935.* Los Angeles: University of Southern California Press, 1936; L. C. Day, "Boys and Girls and Current Events," *Elementary School Journal*, 36 (January 1936), 354–366. Arthur W. Foshay, et al., *Educational Achievements of Thirteen-Year-Olds in Twelve Countries.* Hamburg,

girls.[30] The differences between the sexes in both achievement and interest actually are small, and they are not always statistically significant. Nevertheless, just as girls in our culture tend to exceed boys in language development and school marks, so boys rather consistently obtain higher average scores on standardized tests of social studies and science.

The differences most evident to teachers of Grades 5–7 are most likely to occur in a division of interest in particular topics. Thus, during a study of, say, the furnishings and arrangement of the colonial home, the girls, as might be expected, may be agog, sitting on the edges of their chairs, and the boys bored and slumped in their chairs, or restless. The next day, in a discussion of a campaign of the Revolutionary War, the situation is likely to be reversed. The teacher's job here is to see that every topic is dealt with in such a way that there will be plenty of material to challenge both boys and girls.

But even such differences may exaggerate the situation. The responses of the sexes are by no means always divergent in this age group. For example, Baker found that the questions asked by boys were not markedly different from those asked by girls. She found that questions concerning animal life, industries, and commercial products were the most frequently raised by boys and also by girls.

ATTITUDES OF CHILDREN TOWARD SOCIAL STUDIES

A child's interest in what he studies helps to carry him through the laborious steps he must take in order to master the essential concepts and skills. If he finds satisfaction in the learning process, his interest in the subject of his learning tends to remain. It is a matter of concern, therefore, that surveys of subject preference reveal that the social studies are relatively unpopular among children.

Chase and two of his students at Boston University studied subject preferences of fifth-grade children.[31] They found, as did an earlier investi-

---

Germany: UNESCO Institute for Education, 1962. Pp. 52–53; Fred I. Greenstein, *Children and Politics*, New Haven, Conn.: Yale University Press, 1965. Chap. 6; Charles Guzzetta, "Children's Knowledge of Historically Important Americans," Ed.D. dissertation, Temple University, *Dissertation Abstracts*, **25** (September 1964), 1653–1654; Wolfgang Hilligen, *Plan und Wirklichkeit im socialkundlichen Unterricht*. Frankfurt am Main Germany: Jährig, 1955. P. 91; Hyman Meltzer, *Children's Social Concepts*, New York: Teachers College, 1925; Ralph C. Preston, *Children's Reactions to a Contemporary War Situation*, Child Development Monographs, No. 28, New York: Teachers College, 1942; Cathryn A. Probst, "A General Information Test for Kindergarten Children," *Child Development*, **2** (June 1931), 81–95.

[30] W. Linwood Chase and Gilbert M. Wilson, "Preference Studies in Elementary School Social Studies," *Journal of Education*, **140** (April 1958), 1–28 (entire issue); Robert L. Curry, "Subject Preferences of 1,111 Fifth Graders," *Michigan Education Journal*, **40** (April 1963), 567.

[31] Reported by Chase and Wilson. Pp. 1–5.

gator,[32] that social studies ranked below reading, arithmetic, and other subjects. Among girls, even spelling proved more popular. Only 9 percent of the first choices were social studies. (The most popular subject, reading, received 23 percent of first choices.)

Jersild and Tasch found that almost twice as many children mentioned social studies unfavorably as mentioned them favorably—a situation almost completely reversed in the case of reading and arithmetic. Their data reveal also that social studies suffered in comparison with other subjects children indicated they would like to learn more about.[33]

Mosher asked children in Grades 4–12 to mark their subjects as "preferred" and as "liked" or "disliked." Social studies were not among the "liked" subjects at any level, and were among the "disliked" subjects at the elementary and junior high school levels.[34]

More recent surveys show a continued relatively unfavorable view of social studies. Curry, in two separate studies, found that fifth-grade pupils ranked social studies last among nine subjects.[35] Rice turned aside from the usual device of having pupils rank subjects, and instead, sought data from teachers who ranked academic interests on the basis of their observations of pupils, their obtaining of pupils' expressions of interest, and their study of the activities in which pupils wholeheartedly engaged. His findings showed that, of nine "interest areas," teachers ranked social studies fifth for accelerated pupils, sixth for average pupils, ninth for pupils whose grades lagged below average, and eighth for educable mentally retarded pupils.[36]

All this dislike of such an important subject is discouraging. Fortunately, it is a situation teachers can do something about, as we shall see.

First of all, why this unpopularity of a subject of so much variety and of interest to so many adults? For one thing, many parents and teachers believe in the old theory that the three R's and spelling are the most important school subjects, and so, place a higher premium on them. By their greater concern and praise for the child's achievement in those subjects,

[32] Ethel E. Holmes, "School Subjects Preferred by Children," *Appraising the Elementary-School Program*; Sixteenth Yearbook of the National Elementary Principal. Washington, D.C.: National Educational Association, 1937. Pp. 336–344.

[33] Arthur T. Jersild and Ruth J. Tasch, *Children's Interests and What They Suggest for Education*. New York: Teachers College, 1949. P. 77. Survey covered approximately 2,000 children in Middle West, South, and the metropolitan area of New York City.

[34] Howard H. Mosher, "Subject Preferences of Girls and Boys," *School Review*, **60** (January 1952), 34–38. Survey covered approximately 2,000 children from three school systems classified, respectively, as urban, rural, and mountain.

[35] Robert L. Curry, "Subject Preferences of 1,111 Fifth Graders" and "Subject Preferences of Fifth-Grade Children," *Peabody Journal of Education*, **41** (July 1963), 23–27.

[36] Joseph P. Rice, Jr., "A Comparative Study of Academic Interest Patterns among Selected Groups of Exceptional and Normal Intermediate Children," *California Journal of Educational Research*, **14** (May 1963), 131–137.

they transmit their feelings and values to him, and thus, influence his preferences. Furthermore, many children like those other subjects and find them easier because of the emphasis which schools tend to place on their clear-cut, precise nature. Children may also find security in having an immediate check upon their success, such as they often receive on an answer in arithmetic or a spelled word, which is unequivocally either right or wrong.

Social studies, by way of contrast, may appear:

1. More involved,
2. Less practical,
3. Less concrete and definite,
4. More complex, with their indefinite and ambiguous concepts and their subtleties of cause and effect, how's, why's, maybe's, but's, and if's,
5. More abstract in their concepts, such as "responsibility," "progress," and "climate."
6. To require the effort of original thinking and much "digging."

Today's emphasis on the practical, on job preparation, and on speed may make children impatient with such an involved subject.

Another factor is the deficiencies to be found in social studies textbooks. Those for the primary grades tend to be content-thin, and those for the intermediate grades often contain too many topics, are hard to read, and are dehumanized, according to reports from key supervisors.[37]

Herman brought out another probable factor: the teacher's verbal behavior.[38] The pupils of teachers whose remarks in the classroom were predominantly encouraging of pupil efforts and accepting of their ideas were more interested in social studies than pupils whose teachers were inclined to lecture, command, and criticize.

A final possible contributor to dislike of social studies deserves mention. Challenging problems are often omitted on the grounds that children are not mature enough to deal with them. Children who study the local community, for example, may not be given an opportunity to look at the question of why Negroes live in ghettoes, or why there are no Negroes in town. As a result, the study may take on a flat, unreal aspect.

All these factors contribute to children's lack of interest in social studies; but probably the most potent factor, and the one teachers can do the most about, is inferior teaching. Despite the dramatic, human-interest content, some teachers manage to make social studies a dreary, colorless subject by

[37] This was one of the findings in unpublished questionnaire studies conducted by the author covering supervisors and principals throughout the country.

[38] Wayne L. Herman, Jr., "The Relationship between Teachers' Verbal Behavior and Children's Interests in the Social Studies," *Peabody Journal of Education*, **43** (November 1965), 157–160.

overemphasis on memorization and recitation. The effect of such drab social studies teaching upon pupil attitudes was brought out by students of Chase in an evaluation of 20 classrooms, ten of which had a majority of children who said they preferred social studies to other subjects; in the other ten, no child accorded first choice to social studies, and few accorded it second choice.[39] All 20 teachers reported that the social studies area was the one they preferred to teach over all others. Great differences were found in the teaching in the two sets of classrooms. The following practices were common in classrooms where social studies were popular, and uncommon in classrooms where social studies were unpopular:

1. Employment of the unit method,
2. Careful planning of objectives by the teacher,
3. Use of resource visitors,
4. Use of a wide range of activities (trips, committee work, dramatics, and so on),
5. Specific development of pupils' study and research skills.

In other words, when teachers succeed in making social studies attractive and meaningful to children, the children are enthusiastic. They learn, and the significant aims of social studies are more likely to be achieved.

Finally, mention must be made of the teacher as a person. A teacher who is warm, just, and sincere toward his pupils, finds them more receptive to his teaching and likely to enjoy those subjects about which he himself is enthusiastic.

FOR REVIEW AND REFLECTION

1. What factors other than that cited by Jersild might account for the decline in intellectual curiosity observed in many children as they advance in age?
2. What facts underlie the argument that children should study about remote times and places at an earlier age than has been customary? What facts are used to support an opposing view?
3. Name a social studies concept in connection with a study of colonial history and give examples of how it could be enriched for presentation to a class.
4. Explain the term "reinforcement" as it applies to learning.
5. Explain and evaluate deductive and inductive learning.

ASSIGNMENTS

1. Study a reading-readiness test or intelligence test and the manual for its administration. What, if any, of its contents might be regarded as clues to the readiness of kindergarten children for social studies?

[39] Reported by Chase and Wilson. Pp. 26–27.

2. Visit a classroom during a social studies period. What leads do you find concerning pupil interests in social studies, social concepts, and gaps in knowledge and understanding?
3. Observe a social studies class with a view to finding examples of the principles of learning as discussed in this chapter.
4. Read Inhelder and Piaget *Early Growth of Logic in the Child*, especially Chapter 3. What are the implications for social studies in their discussion of all–some relations?

SUPPLEMENTARY READING

Baker, Emily V., *Children's Questions and Their Implications for Planning the Curriculum*. New York: Teachers College, 1945. A collection of more than 9,000 spontaneous questions of children, almost half of which relate to social studies. The vast range of their content is impressive.

Brownell, William A., and Gordon Hendrickson, "How Children Learn Information, Concepts, and Generalizations" in *Learning and Instruction*, Nelson B. Henry (Ed.); Forty-ninth Yearbook of the National Society for the Study of Education, Pt. I. Chicago: University of Chicago Press, 1950. Chap. 4. A helpful, clearly written summary of children's learning.

Burrows, Alvina T., *Teaching Children in the Middle Grades*. Boston: Heath, 1952. Chap. 3, "Psychological Considerations in Middle Childhood," brings out aspects of children's characteristics, such as the absorption in detail, and indicates their implications for teaching.

Chase, W. Linwood, and Gilbert M. Wilson. "Preference Studies in Elementary School Social Studies," *Journal of Education,* **140** (April 1958), 1–28 (entire issue). Reviews a series of studies on children's social studies interests undertaken by students at Boston University.

Dale, Edgar, "Learning by Discovery," *The News Letter* (Bureau of Educational Research and Service, Ohio State University), **30** (November 1964), 1–4. A brief treatment of some of the knotty problems arising when we try to apply the "discovery principle" to classroom teaching.

————, "Principles of Learning," *The News Letter* (Bureau of Educational Research and Service, Ohio State University), **29** (January 1964), 1–4. A Presentation of seven "common sense" principles which, writes Dale, "have helped me as a teacher and a learner."

Dinkmeyer, Don, and Rudolf Dreikurs, *Encouraging Children to Learn: The Encouragement Process*. Englewood Cliffs, N.J.: Prentice-Hall, 1963. Chapter 7 deals with "Encouragement Techniques Adapted to Developmental Levels." The authors (a psychologist and a psychiatrist) cite the role of encouragement in the development of children in classroom settings in the primary grades, intermediate grades, and junior high school.

Easton, David, and Robert D. Hess, "The Child's Political World," *Midwest Journal of Political Science,* **6** (August 1962), 229–246. Report of study showing rapid expansion of certain political concepts during elementary school years.

Gagné, Robert M., *The Conditions of Learning*. New York: Holt, Rinehart and Winston, 1965. Has a particularly fine treatment of the formation of generalizations and problem-solving.

Hawkes, Glenn R., and Demaris Pease, *Behavior and Development from 5 to 12*. New York: Harper & Row, 1962. Chap. 11. "The Developmental Process and Principles of Growth" is a succinct discussion of the child as a unique individual and of the continuous, orderly process of his growth.

Huck, Charlotte, "Children Learn from Their Culture," *Educational Leadership*, 13 (December 1955), 171–175. Based on an interview study of 115 suburban first-grade children on 75 social concepts. Contends that children's contact with their culture has expanded in recent years.

Inhelder, Bärbel, and Jean Piaget, *Early Growth of Logic in the Child: Classification and Seriation*. New York: Harper & Row, 1964. Presents evidence on children's acquisitions and limitations in dealing with logical relationships.

————, *The Growth of Logical Thinking from Childhood to Adolescence*. New York: Basic Books, 1958. Based on experiments with children's reactions to physical phenomena: a persuasive presentation of the proposition that the preadolescent's mental operations are simple and essentially attached to empirical reality, not going beyond logical groupings or into the propositional logic of adolescents.

Jersild, Arthur T., *Child Psychology* (5th ed.). Englewood Cliffs, N.J.: Prentice-Hall, 1960. Chapters 14–16 present a balanced account of the child's intellectual development. Chapter 16 deals with children's reasoning and concept formation, including analysis of children's response to the world, their capacity for generalizing, their capacity for inductive reasoning, and their concepts. Chapter 19 deals with children's interests.

Loomis, Mary Jane, *The Preadolescent: Three Major Concerns*. New York: Appleton, 1959. This volume, oriented toward classroom application, is organized around the following aspects of development: aspiring to greater independence, striving for sexual identification, and looking ahead to junior high school and adolescent living.

Murphy, Gardner, *Freeing Intelligence through Teaching*. New York: Harper & Row, 1961. Reflections by a leading psychologist on the post-Sputnik preoccupation of educators with intellectual values and processes to the neglect of creativity, brotherhood, and other values. Relationships between contributions of James, Dewey, Piaget, Thorndike, Freud, and others are developed.

Ojemann, Ralph H., "Social Studies in Light of Knowledge about Children," in *Social Studies in the Elementary School*, Nelson B. Henry (Ed.); Fifty-sixth Yearbook of the National Society for the Study of Education, Pt. II. Chicago: University of Chicago Press, 1957. Chap. 4. Shows the relationship between the development of social concepts and social behavior.

Stephens, John M., *The Psychology of Classroom Learning*. New York: Holt, Rinehart and Winston, 1965. An introduction to child development and the principles of learning.

Taba, Hilda, "Learning by Discovery: Psychological and Educational Rationale," *Elementary School Journal*, 63 (March 1963), 308–316. An analysis of the implications of the "discovery" principle, with a section on teaching strategies upon which learning by discovery is dependent.

Tuddenham, Read D., "Jean Piaget and the World of the Child," *American Psychologist,* **21** (March 1966), 207–217. A summary and interpretation of Piaget's work.

Wallen, Norman E., and Robert M. W. Travers, "Analysis and Investigation of Teaching Methods," in *Handbook of Research on Teaching,* N. L. Gage (Ed.). Skokie, Ill.: Rand McNally, 1963. Chap. 10. Presents six principles of learning (pp. 494–500) ". . . to illustrate the limitations of most teaching methods and perhaps also the difficulties involved in designing a method consistent with many principles."

PART TWO

SOCIAL STUDIES UNITS

4

The Unit Method

*Instruction ladled out in
a hurry is not education.*
LORD CHARLES BOWEN

The unit method is both a way of organizing learning experiences and a way of teaching. Briefly, it consists in providing a wide range of learning experiences for the pupil concerning a topic or problem, and planning active pupil involvement in each phase of the teaching process.

The unit method is one of the substantial contributions of the educational experimentation of an earlier generation. Its success can be attributed to several factors:

1. It is flexible, allowing the teacher to develop fully his own unique teaching style.
2. It conforms to the psychology of childhood, permitting the teacher to work with the child, rather than engage in a kind of tug of war with him.
3. The unit method yields superior learning (an advantage discussed on pages 104–105).

The teacher, of course, needs to steep himself in the unit topic. That calls for wide reading. The reading should not be regarded as a burden. One of the satisfactions of teaching comes from the deepening of one's scholarship in this way. The teacher needs to plumb deeper than his pupils can be expected to. He should steep himself in the content, satisfying his own curiosity and obtaining as firm and scholarly a grasp of the subject as time permits. A teacher with a rich store of knowledge is able to know whether or not his pupils are obtaining a well-rounded picture, and he is able to supply information to which they do not normally have direct access.

ARRANGEMENT OF CONTENT

Scope of the Unit

A unit may be organized around any significant content. It is desirable that, in most instances, the teacher approach the unit primarily from the point of view of the content and the method of a particular social science (economics, anthropology, and so forth) as already explained on page 48.

Unit topics are sometimes worded as problems ("Finding Ways to Conserve Our Limited Natural Resources") or as questions ("How Did England Become a Nation?"). Such unit titles are misleading when, as is usually the case, they denote a focus which is narrower than the planned scope of the unit. A straightforward statement of a topic is to be preferred. Problems and questions can be raised as the unit progresses.

The suitability of the scope of a unit topic can be judged by the ability of a given group of children to encompass it as a whole during an orientation period—that is, before engaging in its systematic study. Under the unit method, the child is able to discern the "forest" before he analyzes the separate "trees." He gets a general, overall picture of the community, of farming, or of a nation, whatever the topic may be, before he is confronted with masses of detail.

The teacher should guard against including loosely related material in a unit, keeping in mind the child's limited background and his confusion when presented with too much disconnected content. Remember that the child's experience will not end with this one unit. Furthermore, too comprehensive a study which appears to present all that is worth knowing about a subject, may give the child a false sense of thoroughness and discourage further thinking in the area. If, on the other hand, the teacher concludes the unit with the frank statement that study of the topic has been merely begun, that the information is far from complete, and that many questions remain to be answered, he presents a truthful picture and leaves the door open for future inquiry.

Unity of the Unit

The central principle of a unit is that the diverse aspects of its content are tied together. For example, colonial life, when organized as a unit, is pursued intensively in many relationships. The class investigates colonial commerce, schools, recreation, ideas about government and education, housing, agriculture, crafts, and transportation as they interact with one another, as they are pervaded by common motives and values, and as parts of community life. Thus, the content grows into a web of connecting threads. It is this which forms the closely knit internal structure of the unit—in a word, its *unity*.

The premise underlying the idea of the unit is that the child who learns only a few distinct, fairly well-rounded concepts, but learns them intensively in their interrelationships, has learned to better purpose than one who memorizes a host of independent concepts that fail to cross-fertilize each other.

Duration of the Unit

The length of time a class should study a unit depends upon the school's curriculum plan for the year. If the plan for a given grade is divided into six units, deemed of equal importance, and contains an equal amount of content, and if there are 42 weeks in the school year, then it is a matter of simple arithmetic to determine that each unit can be allotted approximately six weeks. Such neat equality, of course, is seldom merited. Many experienced teachers believe that six weeks is the optimum period for a typical unit. Some, however, prefer fewer units, with more time devoted to each one.

Obviously, the relative importance and volume of content of each unit should determine the amount of time to be devoted to it. Other factors to be considered are (1) the amount of weekly time provided for social studies, (2) the availability of supplementary books and other learning material, (3) the extent of the teacher's experience with the unit, and (4) the degree of maturity and the extent of intellectual background of the class. Because of these factors, it seldom occurs that every unit can or should be accorded the same amount of time.

Units on topics as vast as Africa or transportation can extend profitably for as long as three months, because they contain so much potentially significant material, and because so much has been written for both teachers and children on these subjects. Such an exceptionally prolonged study of one topic can rarely be justified, however, unless the teacher has taught the unit before and has, thereby, had a chance to build up a reservoir of teaching materials. Even under such circumstances, the teacher must keep in mind the total curriculum design for the entire year. Restraint is called for! Furthermore, it is always better for a unit to end with the pupils still eager about the topic and anxious to learn more, than for it to run to the point of satiety.

TASKS IN PLANNING A UNIT

The Teacher Tentatively Organizes
the Content of the Unit

Using notes he has made while studying, the teacher reviews all aspects of his subject and decides which ones should be emphasized. He should construct an outline, no matter how strictly he plans to stick to the sequence of topics which appear in the textbook he proposes to use. The teacher who develops scholarship will almost invariably discover ideas and information which are not treated in the text and which he will wish to include. Or he may have ideas about amplifying portions of the textbook.

In drawing up such an outline, the teacher need not worry about wording his thoughts in children's language. His notes are for his use alone. A preliminary outline in planning a unit on transportation might start out like this:

I. The development of modern transportation changed community life
   "Commuting" unknown before railroads and buses
   The megalopolis grew along the Eastern seaboard, Great Lakes and West Coast
   Food, clothing, building materials, and the like, had no longer to be confined to local products
   The middle class moved to the suburbs and cities subsequently underwent decay
   "Mass travel" introduced; traveling ceased to be a luxury of the few; vacation habits changed; more visitors, mail, newspapers, and so forth, from outside local community
   Modern transportation an example of industry requiring more capital than one man possesses and calling for organization of corporations
II. Transportation lines affected by terrain, condition of atmosphere, and other geographic factors
   Natural land obstacles overcome by bridging, tunneling, grading, filling, which sometimes shortened routes

Some teachers prefer to organize a unit in terms of topics rather than of generalizations like the example above. In a study of the Westward Movement, such a teacher might have three major topics:

I. The Successive Frontiers
II. Daily Life on the Frontier
III. Famous Frontiersmen
IV. Contribution of the Frontier to American Democracy

He would then arrange subtopics under each of these headings. This procedure is acceptable, provided the teacher thinks through the generalizations and attitudes he wishes his pupils to gain as a result of studying these topics.

The Teacher Roughs out a Scheme
for a Daily Lesson Plan

A lesson plan is a helpful device for preparing the presentation and activities for a given day. It can be blocked out on a day-to-day basis, or a week or more in advance. Following is a sample lesson plan for first grade:

> *Generalizations to develop:*
> There are many ways to earn an income.
> Most workers today are specialized.
> Certain types of jobs are filled mainly by men; others mainly by women; others by both men and women.
> A housewife does not earn a money income as a homemaker, but she contributes to the standard of living of a family in various ways.
> *On chalkboard:*
> Have children dictate names of occupations described in textbook; list on chalkboard.
> Have children dictate names of additional occupations not from textbook, but from personal knowledge; list on chalkboard.
> *Questions for discussion:*
> Which of these jobs usually require a uniform? Why?
> Which of these jobs are usually jobs for men only?
> Which are usually jobs for women only?
> Which are given to either men or women?
> What abilities are needed for the various jobs?
> What kind of training?
> Does a mother earn an income from her work as a homemaker? How does she add to the family's standard of living?

Another lesson plan consisted only of questions the teacher wished to raise for guiding a lesson. The class had already learned that The Netherlands is a small nation with heavy population pressure on the land, and with about one third of its land below sea level; a nation faced with the disappearance of the Dutch East Indies as a Dutch colony, with insufficient coal, petroleum, and timber, and with a cool, damp climate.

> What can the Dutch do to raise their standard of living?
> What industries might be encouraged?
> If the Dutch succeed in rapidly industrializing their land, what will be the benefits?

One lesson plan mapped by a teacher in connection with a community study began with a statement of the lesson's purpose: To develop an understanding of fire insurance. It listed the activities which the teacher wished to set in motion in the order in which she believed they should occur:

1. Arthur presents his picture-chart on how fire insurance works.
2. Questions and discussion are invited on the picture-chart.
3. The teacher encourages children to help construct a list of risks other than fire (weather, shipment of goods, travel) and to consider how insurance can enable the buyer of insurance to avoid these risks.
4. The teacher introduces concepts and terms of anticipated difficulty (law of large numbers, mutual insurance, and so on).
5. Volunteers dramatize contrasting home situations. In one home— initial visit of insurance salesman, start of blaze and its extinguishment, investigation, estimation of loss, settlement by insurance company. In the contrasting situation, the owner declines to buy insurance, and the financial consequences are depicted. Pupils encouraged to use newly acquired concepts and terms in the dramatization.
6. The teacher raises questions: Does fire insurance prevent fires or loss from fires? What are the risks of the insurance company? etc.
7. Individual children are called upon to summarize the purpose of fire insurance and how it works.

There are many forms of lesson plan. They all contain a statement of the objectives which the teacher seeks to achieve through the lesson, a list of pupil activities and the order in which they are to occur, the nature and order of teacher presentations, questions for the teacher to ask and examples to give, and necessary materials or equipment. The exact form and content is preferably left to the individual teacher who should be allowed to fit the plan to his own style of planning and teaching. He should look upon it as a useful, flexible guide rather than as a straitjacket.

TEACHING THE UNIT

Because the unit method is flexible, teaching procedure varies widely from teacher to teacher. Although the suggestions offered here are representative, the reader is cautioned against slavish acceptance of them. The teacher should feel free to modify these suggestions if his judgment so indicates, and to add his own creative touch.

Assessing the Pupils' Background

At the outset, it pays to discover the children's present knowledge of the subject matter of the unit. It would be a waste of time to teach what most members of the class have already mastered. The teacher may, accordingly, prepare and administer a pretest, covering the essential content of the unit, or, with children in the beginning school grades, conduct one or more oral discussions with the class, probing for the pupils' background information.

Some children offer glib answers or comments which seem to indicate wider knowledge or understanding than they actually possess. When the teacher suspects shallowness in an answer, further questioning is in order. For instance, a child might contribute this statement: "We already know about the United Nations. Its headquarters are in New York and a lot of countries belong." The teacher should question him further to learn whether the child's knowledge goes deeper. Does he know *any* of the major purposes of the United Nations? Is he familiar with some of its successes and failures? Does he know which countries do not belong and why? Additional probing will help determine what concepts the teacher can take for granted and what ones he will need to stress during the course of teaching the unit.

Introducing Pupils to the Unit

Before systematic study begins, the teacher can profitably spend several days acquainting the children with the topic. During this period of initial exposure, he presents the all-important overview of the topic and encourages them to relate the new topic to their present knowledge. This he accomplishes through discussion and written assignments. He raises relevant questions and presents glimpses of part of the content of the unit in order to arouse interest and curiosity.

His introduction to the topic need not be elaborate. For example, in a unit entitled "Clothes for the Community," a third-grade teacher might plan to do the following:

1. Place on the bulletin board or wall, for discussion, a set of pictures dealing with some phase of textiles and clothing, here and in other lands.
2. Read aloud to the class a portion of Lazarus' *Let's Go to a Clothing Factory.*
3. Show the film, *Choosing Clothes for Health.*
4. Ask the pupils to tell of the different fabrics with which they are familiar.
5. Display felt, knitted, and woven articles, and have the children learn the differences in structure of knitted and woven fabrics.

Arousing Pupil Curiosity

The interest of many pupils will be aroused through the teacher's introduction of the unit if it embraces such procedures as have just been described. Every teacher has discovered, however, that initial interest may be of a passive sort and not necessarily transformed into active curiosity.

One effective way of arousing curiosity is to jar the conceptual complacency that is such a common human condition and which is such a formidable barrier to learning. The jarring of this complacency involves introducing an idea that is contrary to what the pupil has been thinking, thereby inducing disequilibrium in his thinking. It is natural for a child to try to answer a question or solve a problem in terms of his present beliefs. When his anticipated answer or solution is sharply challenged and is revealed to be faulty, he receives a jolt. If the contradiction is one with which he can cope (and obviously, a frustrating type of contradiction should not be considered), he becomes curious and motivated to explore further.

The teacher should not find it hard to discover ways of introducing motivating types of contradiction. This is because much of children's knowledge in social sciences is distorted. If the class is about to study the tropical deserts, for example, the teacher might begin by attempting to modify the narrow ideas about deserts which his pupils had previously expressed, that a desert is nothing but endless stretches of sand with, perhaps, camels and Bedouins scattered about. The teacher, for contrast, may then produce desert pictures showing various types of desert shrubs with their thick leaves and stems, of a heavy rainfall, and of an oasis; and may read a description from T. E. Lawrence or some other desert explorer which describes the great range of desert temperatures. Or, at the outset of a study of American Indians, the teacher may find that the children have the stereotyped notion perpetuated by so many television "westerns" of the Indian as a wicked, ruthless, unprincipled person. The teacher might then read selected portions of Harrington's *Dickon among the Indians*, Wilson's *The White Indian Boy*, or other authentic accounts of Indian culture to present more valid and typical Indian characteristics.

Formulating Learning Goals

The teacher should show the class a plan for the study of the unit derived from his own tentative outline. The main headings of the outline may be written on the chalkboard, by distributing duplicated sheets, or by referring the class to the table of contents in their textbooks. By knowing the framework, the children will be able to perceive the scope of the unit and the interrelationships of its parts. Such knowledge is a large part of the goal-setting. The outline should be referred to frequently as study of the unit progresses, so that the children may keep the topic's structure in mind.

It must be pointed out, however, that to be handed an outline, already cut and dried, can have a stultifying effect on young learners. They should be encouraged to regard it as a piece of unfinished business, and perhaps, be invited to suggest additional topics or subtopics which are of special interest to them as individuals. (Some teachers report that immature classes in the lower primary grades are not ready for this activity.) These suggested topics are recorded by the teacher, or by a child who serves as secretary, on the chalkboard where they can be seen by all, for comparison and possible revision. Class and teacher discuss each topic for its merits as a subtopic, and obtain concensus regarding its inclusion.

Often, one or more new subtopics are thus added to the outline. One class, in studying transportation, wished to add consideration of certain mechanical matters, such as the difference between a Diesel and other types of engines. So, a new topic, "The Engine," was inserted in the outline. This enhanced the learning goals for many of the pupils in the class. In another class, which was beginning to study the contributions of various national groups to community life, one child said, after examining the outline: "But there is nothing here about the French. My great grandfather arrived here from France seventy years ago, and he helped design several big bridges." The teacher had omitted the contributions of the French because of the scarcity of known French descendents in the community and because those who were present had, apparently, largely lost the identity of their forebears' origin. But, as it turned out, there was excellent reason for adding the French to the list, and the teacher did so.

Another way to obtain thoughtful pupil involvement and positive goal-orientation is to find out what questions about the topic the pupils would like answered, and what activities they would like to pursue in connection with the topic. Questions and suggestions, offered by a class in their study of a unit, "Life in Norway," follow:

1. Questions
    (a) Is there proof that Eric the Red discovered America before Columbus?
    (b) Are there any Vikings left today?
    (c) About how many whales does a Norwegian whaler get on one trip?
2. Suggested activities
    (a) Exchange letters with children in a Norwegian school.
    (b) Read a story about a Norwegian boy which Claude has at home.
    (c) Invite Mrs. Andersen, who lived in Norway, to come to our classroom to tell us about daily life there.

Some class-initiated questions and suggestions may appear to be trivial or based on misconceptions. They should, nevertheless, be recorded along with the others. All are indicators of the various levels of maturity of the class. Take the second question, concerning Vikings: it stems from ignorance, and should be recorded. Before the unit is over, the teacher will make sure that the pupils understand that "Vikings" refers to the Norsemen of the Middle Ages, known for their skill as shipbuilders and sailors and for their exploits as traders and raiders.

On the third question, the teacher may regard the number of whales a whaler can load as of small importance. However, this question is useful in at least four ways:

1. It is a reminder of children's preoccupation with, and need for, concreteness and detail.
2. It is a logical lead into an examination of the methods used by Norway's modern whaling fleet.
3. It suggests to the teacher where the unit might be broadened to include matters close to the interests of one or more members of the class.
4. It is a lead into a study of the ecology of the sea, of the need for regulating the whaling industry, and of how nations compete for limited resources such as whales.

A child's questions and suggestions often reveal something about himself —his interests, background, and personality. It is in the teacher's interest as well as the child's to try to identify what each question reveals and to capitalize on it for educational ends.

No part of the unit method is more misrepresented and misunderstood than this step in which children help to formulate questions. "They study whatever they want!" is a frequent accusation. But they do not! In the situation described, the topic is selected for them by the teacher. They are then carefully oriented to it, so that they become informed about it and can ask appropriate questions. If their questions were listed *before* such orientation, many would be irrelevant and trivial. When faltering occurs in this step, it is usually due to the teacher's expecting the class to ask questions "out of the blue" or without proper orientation. It is important that the teacher act as guide when the questions are asked, helping the children to make them clear and significant.

This approach, combining a study of the structure of the unit with a formulation of questions and activities, enables the teacher to know the limitations of the class's background, the gaps in its knowledge, and the level of comprehension on which it can be expected to operate. But the special significance of this approach is that it causes the pupils to become goal-oriented.

Collecting Data

Data are collected by children through various means.

READING TEXTBOOKS AND SUPPLEMENTARY MATERIAL   This process is so important that an entire chapter—"Improving Reading in Social Studies" —is devoted to it. Reading should be part of the social studies program almost daily, beginning with the first grade.

LISTENING TO AND INTERVIEWING AUTHORITIES   Teachers should not overlook the rich contributions to social studies that may be made by specialists from the community. They may be parents or other local residents. Often, they are able to impart the enthusiasm that comes from expertness. While some of them may not know much about children and may use terms and concepts which are over the heads of children, their statements may be clarified by the teacher. The stimulation these outsiders can supply is invaluable, not only for their zeal, but also because their novelty as outsiders—not school teachers—arouses special attentiveness.

One teacher invited a policeman to her classroom to give instructions and answer questions on safe bicycling in traffic in connection with a unit "Safety in Our Community." Another took her class, which was studying the history of its community, to see an old resident and his collection of pictures of the neighborhood as it appeared fifty years ago. He reminisced for them about changes that had taken place since then. Another class, in its study of ancient Egypt, visited a museum and interviewed the curator on methods of archeologists in unearthing the past. Adult members of the community who have collected photographs or slides in their travels or who are engaged in a specialized occupation, often are glad to show their pictures or share their knowledge and experience with school groups.

OBSERVING AND EXPERIMENTING   A teacher, in conducting a unit on "Shelter," took advantage of a nearby building program in order to teach the children at firsthand about house construction procedures, materials, tools, and division of labor. Another class, studying textiles in connection with "Food, Clothing, and Shelter," experimented with making and using natural dyes. Still another class, in studying "Air Transportation," conducted experiments with air in order to understand how airplanes fly. Firsthand experiences of this kind make a lasting impression on children and therefore have especial potency. The teacher should try to arrange for perhaps one such experience a week, making sure that the observations and experiments are suited to the children's age and comprehension.

LISTENING TO TEACHER PRESENTATIONS   The teacher frequently presents fresh data to the class, drawing upon appropriate material to which the class lacks access, such as that written for adults. He may tell about Benjamin Franklin's contributions to American independence or explain the difference between a cantilever and a suspension bridge. Sometimes, the presentation is a reading. There is value in readings, from such books as Hamlin Garland's *Boy's Life on the Prairie,* during a unit on farming or the North Central states—to give children a feeling for farm life of a century ago—or *The Odyssey,* as a sample of Greek literature in a study of ancient Greece. Or, the teacher may present statistics on the comparative speed and safety of various forms of transportation in a unit on transportation. At other times, he may introduce concepts by means of maps or globes (see Chapter 10), or pictures, films, or recordings (see Chapter 12). Variety in the form of the presentation strengthens learning and helps maintain interest.

Presenting, Discussing, and Recording Data

Children should have opportunity, from time to time, to report to their classmates. Until an effective pattern of presentation is established, each child who is preparing a presentation should go over his plans with the teacher, who can help him in various ways where necessary—in pronouncing certain words, encouraging him to look for pictures, or guiding him concerning a time limit. Because of the limited time the teacher can devote to giving this assistance, it is seldom wise to plan to have more than one child make a report on any one day.

Some teachers feel that the child will learn more if put on his own and allowed to sink or swim. However, a major purpose of social studies presentations is to build up the knowledge and understanding of class members and to stimulate their thinking. Unplanned and undirected presentations will not, of course, accomplish this. The teacher should bear in mind, however, that it takes more time to help a child prepare a presentation than for the teacher to undertake it himself, and he should plan his time accordingly. In the discussion that follows the presentation, every child should have the chance to speak freely to the subject without special preparation.

Discussions are frequently planned by the teacher for the purpose of presenting data which will stimulate and guide the thinking of either the entire class or a group within the class. As the children participate, they may raise new ideas or introduce new information. The teacher spots and corrects misconceptions. Rather than let the discussion peter out—when enough data have been covered and before interest flags—he should help his pupils draw conclusions or make a summary.

There are various ways in which the teacher initiates a discussion. Typical introductory remarks for a discussion about wheat follow:

What are the pros and cons of government subsidies for wheat farmers?

Why do you suppose winter wheat is named winter wheat?

Yesterday I overheard someone say that whole wheat bread comes from brown wheat and that white bread comes from white wheat. Who knows what is wrong with that idea?

Discussions are also helpful in evaluating methods of work. The teacher starts these off in some way, such as this:

What are good ways for a research committee to begin its work?

How can we best explain our study of Australia at a school assembly?

How can we plan our visit to the museum so that we shall be quieter than we were on our last visit?

Other discussions deal with the comparison, location, authenticity, or appropriateness of materials:

These two geography books give different figures on the length of the Mississippi River. How can that be?

Our textbook does not tell much about the boyhood of Lincoln. How can we find a book which gives more information about his early life?

Below this picture of the *S. S. Normandie*, it says: "The fastest ocean-going ship." How can we tell if this book is up-to-date, or whether we should look further to find out if today there is a faster ship?

The discussion period can be one of the most stimulating and fruitful parts of the school day. It is treated further, later on in this chapter.

As the class accumulates information, the teacher provides means for recording it, such as notebooks, scrapbooks, murals, maps, dramatic play, time lines. Use of these media is explained in the following four chapters, and treated in further detail in Chapter 11, "Teaching about Maps and Globes," and Chapter 12, "Planning Creative Experiences." Suffice it to say that when a child records his learning, he not only engages in self-expression but, more significantly, unknowingly reviews and recites it, and thus, fixes it for future recall and use. William James aptly expressed the need for recording activities: There can be no impression without expression.

Summarizing and Reviewing the Unit

Summary and review may be carried out in a variety of ways.

ORAL SUMMARIES   The teacher summarizes the unit and also asks individual children to tell the group what they know about particular phases of the topic. For example, in a unit, "Colonial United States," one child is asked to give reasons why the early settlers left their European homes.

WRITTEN SUMMARIES   Each child can be assigned the responsibility of summarizing the unit in his notebook. Here is an opportunity for teaching the desirability of using headings for the central divisions when reporting on a large topic.

CULMINATING ACTIVITIES   Toward the close of the unit, teacher and pupils together select one of the recording activities (see page 95), such as preparing a notebook, writing a report, or creating a play or a mural to serve as a culminating activity, which becomes a major means for bringing together the important concepts and generalizations of the unit.

TESTS   The teacher prepares a test covering the unit. (Test construction is dealt with in Chapter 13.) After the test is taken and corrected, he returns the test papers to the class for reexamination and discussion. He encourages the children to raise questions, and corrects misconceptions.

GROUP EVALUATION   A class discussion is conducted in order to evaluate the success of the unit. The children are questioned about the value and interest they have found in the study, what content and activities they have found valuable, what additional content and activities they wish might have been included, and methods of work they found satisfying or which they feel might have been improved upon. This evaluation should be helpful to the teacher in planning the next unit.

OTHER ASPECTS OF UNIT TEACHING

Class Discussions

The foregoing step-by-step description of unit teaching emphasizes teacher-pupil discussions in the development of a unit. Such discussion sessions are basic in planning, in evaluating, and in exploring ideas. Planning obviously is necessary in many procedures—to obtain pupils' reactions to the unit's outline, to prepare for a trip, or to divide assignments. Evaluation is involved whenever the pertinence of a learning experience or of instructional material is reviewed. The exploring of ideas is involved when conflicting data are studied, when an analogy is proposed, when fresh information is furnished, and the like. The teacher should prepare with care for each discussion session, deciding ahead of time what topics, materials, or problems to introduce, and how to introduce them. Successful discussion depends on careful planning and hard work.

If the teacher sometimes wonders if holding discussions is worth the effort, he should remind himself that, quite apart from the immediate purpose, a discussion is an important means to developing the democratic attitude which is desirable in a democratic nation—an attitude which induces one to operate constructively and generously with others in working out solutions to group problems. Several research investigations have shown that democratic learning situations produce children who are more cooperatively minded, better workers, more courteous, and more responsible than children subject to more authoritarian control.[1] Democratic methods of education may be regarded as scientifically defensible, as well as philosophically desirable.

One of the leader's tasks is to keep the discussion moving steadily toward a solution of the problem or a conclusion. Teachers are often tempted to short-circuit the process by "selling" their own solution or plan to the class. It would defeat the purpose of group planning for them to impose a ready-made solution upon the class or to capitalize on their own prestige and authority by subtly pressing for its acceptance. On the other hand, they, as leaders of the group, should participate in the planning, see that all available data and points of view are conscientiously considered, and help the class think through the probable consequences of alternative plans and decisions. This is done by mentioning points overlooked and asking leading questions.

One of the difficulties encountered in class discussion is the likelihood that a few children will monopolize it. One study of children's participation in discussions reports that the most loquacious child may make as many contributions as the 16 least talkative children, and that the most loquacious quarter of the class may supply more than half of the total contributions. Furthermore, this study found that the most talkative children were by no means necessarily the best informed. Obviously, the teacher must take steps to establish as large a measure of equality of participation as possible. This may be accomplished through several avenues: through discussing frankly with the class the need for full representation during planning sessions, in spite of the tendency on the part of a few to say too much while the others say too little; through aiding the loquacious to

[1] Ronald Lippitt, "An Experimental Study of the Effect of Democratic and Authoritarian Group Atmospheres," *University of Iowa Studies in Child Welfare*, 16 (1940), 43–195; Kurt Lewin, *et al.*, "Patterns of Aggressive Behavior in Experimentally Created 'Social Climates,'" *Journal of Social Psychology*, 10 (May 1939), 271–299; Robert L. Thorndike, *et al.*, "Observation of Excursions in Activity and Control Schools," *Journal of Experimental Education*, 10 (December 1941), 146–149.

accept a heavier responsibility for listening; through declining to recognize a child's request for the floor when he is monopolizing too much of the talk; through encouraging shy children by specifically calling upon them when their interest or knowledge is thought to bear upon the matter at hand; through building their confidence by bringing them together occasionally in smaller discussion groups; and through dealing with extreme cases at both ends of the scale by trying to get at the causes of their overassertiveness or their shyness.

The tendency for a few children to monopolize discussions appears much more marked when a pupil serves as chairman than when the teacher so serves. In one class, it took more than twice as many of the quietest pupils to equal the verbosity of the most talkative child when the chairmanship shifted from teacher to child![2] Teachers are well advised to think twice before delegating the critical role of discussion leader to a child. It will work only where the pupil chairman is sensitive to the need for wide participation and can exert the skill, authority, and skill necessary to secure it. Such a child is, of course, rare, especially in the elementary grades.

A discussion period should be set aside daily if possible. If the pupils have movable chairs, they may form a circle or adopt some other seating arrangement that will encourage and facilitate free discussion, but this is optional. The period's length cannot be prescribed. It should last no longer than is necessary to carry out its purpose, but it should not be hurried. In the primary grades, it would rarely last as long as 20 minutes, and might be as brief as five. In the intermediate grades, good discussions can successfully run for 20 to 30 minutes.

Committee Work

It is often desirable to have children work in small groups while carrying out some of the tasks required in the various steps of the unit. Such committee work gives children valuable experience in working independent of the larger class group and, when well managed, contributes significantly to social maturation. Occasionally, committees may be formed on a purely voluntary basis, but preferably, the teacher guides their formation to avoid having social studies become a vehicle for perpetuating and entrenching social cliques. Children who are shy, retiring, and fearful often should be placed on committees where their special knowledge or interest can be used and where they may develop assurance and a measure of leadership. Fixed patterns of committee membership should be avoided. Thus, it would be a mistake to appoint only dexterous children to committees for performing handwork; for, less skilled children also need such experience, perhaps

---

[2] Arthur T. Jersild, *Child Psychology* (3d ed.). Englewood Cliffs, N.J.: Prentice-Hall, 1947. P. 218.

more so, in order that they may try themselves out and develop better motor coordination.

A committee's assignment should be clear-cut and definite, involving only tasks which are more effectively performed by a committee than by either a single child or by the entire class. Such tasks include these:

> Obtaining suitable books from the public library to keep on hand in the classroom during the study of the unit
>
> Interviewing an old resident of the community for information about community history
>
> Constructing a large bar graph to show the world's diminishing oil resources
>
> Constructing a large map locating sources of products used in the manufacture of automobiles
>
> Constructing a model of a reaction turbine
>
> Previewing a film with the teacher
>
> Drawing a mural to summarize a unit
>
> Reading and reporting on a phase of the unit which the class as a whole will not study

The size of a committee is important. Rarely is it efficient to have large committees (more than, say, five members), unless the task requires that many children as actual participants. A committee of three is not too small. Having committees which are larger than the job requires is wasteful of time, productive of poor work habits and attitudes, and likely to create discipline problems, horseplay, and noise. Anything that detracts from the dignity of the social studies period will also detract from the learning that should take place.

The practice of dividing the content of a unit and parceling out different phases to various committees is not, as a general rule, sound. The teacher is not able to supervise adequately the work of several such committees working simultaneously each with its own subject. Poor work habits are often developed under such circumstances, and the reports are usually lacking in authenticity and accuracy. Children need considerable help in selecting good source material, in taking notes, in making decisions concerning the content and organization of their reports, and the like. Few teachers are able to keep abreast of the work of several committees at once, each of which is developing an important area of content for the class. The quality of learning is improved if all the members of a class investigate important phases of a unit together under the teacher's direction.

To be sure, there are exceptions, as when there are few books available or when a few children are especially desirous of pursuing a specialized phase of the subject. Committee work, however, should never wind up with the class having to listen to a round of dull or inaccurate reports from the committees. Committee work can add much to the interest and value of a unit when used in moderation and for carefully selected purposes, such as those listed above, which cannot be well achieved by the class as a whole.

The Technique of Discovery

As mentioned in the preceding chapter, the idea that the child can generate information on his own was brought to the fore by Bruner. He termed this "the technique of discovery."[3] The technique may take either the deductive or the inductive form.

In the deductive form, the class is presented with a principle or generalization and is called upon to draw inferences from it. Bruner gives an example from the practice of a fourth-grade teacher who begins with the generalization that civilizations have most often begun in fertile river valleys.[4] The pupils are asked to figure out why this is so, and why civilizations are not so likely to begin in mountainous countries. Examples of other problems to which solutions could be deductively solved are:

> The invention of farm machinery over the last 100 years has increased farming efficiency. How has the increased efficiency affected the proportion of farmers in the population and of workhorses, size of farms, etc.?
>
> Are vegetable prices lower when vegetables are scarce or higher when they are scarce? (In this case, two conflicting propositions are offered for analysis.)
>
> Political parties are necessary for democratic government. In what ways?

In the inductive form, the class becomes acquainted with a set of facts and is then challenged to infer (discover) principles or generalizations which the facts seem to signify. Thus, a class studies the history of the formation of various kinds of national boundaries—mountains, rivers, and artificial boundaries. After amassing a body of information, the class draws conclusions about the respective stability and utility of the various types of boundaries. The generalizations thus formed are "discovered." The question explored is: "What kinds of demarcation make the best national boundaries?"

Examples of other questions lending themselves to inductive thinking are:

> Why did the population of many large cities (Chicago, Boston, Detroit, San Francisco, and so on) drop between 1950 and 1960, a period when the total national population rose rapidly?

[3] Jerome S. Bruner, *Process of Education.* Cambridge, Mass.: Harvard University Press, 1961. P. 51.
[4] Bruner. Pp. 50–51.

How does a storekeeper decide what to charge for his merchandise?
Why did the Plains Indians choose skin for their shelters, the
Woodland Indians wood, and so on?

Needless to say, in either method the pupils may make a wrong discovery.
This risk can be minimized by the teacher's seeing to it that the necessary
facts are supplied (through books, trips, invited authorities, or the like)
and duly considered. After the class draws its tentative conclusions, the
textbook or other source should be consulted by the class for verification.

As pointed out, learning through discovery is slow and should not be
regarded as the only method. Obviously, a child would never have time to
learn as much about the diverse elements of society as he should if he used
the discovery method only. Furthermore, as also pointed out, some of the
claims made for it have not been substantiated by research. It does, however, supply a versatile tool, not only for use in the school years, but also
for the many situations in life which also demand the drawing of inference
or the formulation of sound generalization.

Providing for Individual Differences

The intellectual stimulation and encouragement afforded by individual
pupil participation in various phases of the unit, as outlined and illustrated
earlier in this chapter, give *every* child daily opportunity to grow in mental
stature and social understanding. The principles of learning (see Chapter 3)
apply to individuals only. Hence, it is desirable for teachers to be constantly
on the lookout for chances to apply them to individual children. Experienced, sensitive teachers do this intuitively.

Provision for *total* individualization of instruction requires either tutoring or providing materials of a self-instructional sort. Examples of the latter
are programmed textbooks and teaching machines. These present the
elements to be learned in series of closely integrated steps, constituting a
well thought out sequence. The learner thus proceeds, by easy stages, from
step to step. At each step, the pupil responds to a question or a problem in
textbook or machine and checks the correctness of his answer. Because of
the gradualness of the program, error is reduced to a minimum, and reinforcement is frequent and assured. The extent to which social studies
content lends itself to programming will be discussed in Chapter 12.

In any case, short of tutoring or providing self-instructional devices,
individualization of instruction must be a compromise. Differences in
reading ability constitute a special problem. (1) They can be handled in
part by providing pupils whose reading skills do not permit much success
with the textbook, with reading material parallel to the textbook's content,
but written more simply. Unfortunately, such material for most topics is
meager or, when available, often thin in content. (2) Poorer readers in the

class can be taught how to make the most of a difficult textbook, as described in Chapter 9. (3) Team learning can be tried, also as described in Chapter 9. (4) Outside reading assignments in biography, historical novels, and other literature related to the social studies unit take care of differences in outlook, cognitive style, and interests in addition to differences in reading ability. This, too, is treated in Chapter 9. (5) The assignment of what Durrell calls "pupil specialities" is a tried procedure well known to many teachers. A side topic is assigned for exploration by a pupil. He is challenged to become the class "expert" on the subject. The teacher and librarian give him what help they can in exploring it in depth, and later, he reports on it to his class. In the course of a school year, every child in the class should have one such assignment.

Informal Units in the Primary Grades

Children display an eager and vigorous curiosity in the primary grades which spreads out simultaneously in many directions. To catch and harness as much of this spirit of inquiry as possible often requires several informal units that run more or less side by side. The reading limitations of children during this period restrict the volume of reference work they can undertake, lending further need for the introduction of many units. The unit plan as described earlier in this chapter normally works well; however, many primary teachers have found a need for a more informal approach. A single unit pursued alone in the primary grades often fails to offer the rich, many-sided programs demanded by the growth needs of children in kindergarten, first grade, and second grade.

One teacher planned the following units for a first grade class, which well illustrates the nature of informal primary grade units: (1) machines, (2) licensing, (3) the school plant. Each of these units represented a major concept which the teacher planned to illustrate and expand as the year progressed. She had no foreknowledge of the pace or rhythm at which the units would proceed, nor which ones would receive the greatest emphasis. She did have, however, a list of materials and activities to draw upon and questions to raise during discussions.

These social studies units were developed over the entire school year, leisurely and intermittently. Questions raised by the children, and others formulated by the teacher, were fully discussed and served as points of departure. None of the units had the neat beginning or the clear-cut ending characteristic of the formal unit, nor were they pursued so intensively. An examination of the content of the units may further clarify this point.

UNIT ON MACHINES   The teacher aimed to bring the children to a realization of the significance of the machine as a labor-saving mechanism.

Special attention was called to the pencil sharpener, lawn mower, paper cutter, typewriter in the school office, electric saw and joiner in the school shop, steam shovel operating near by, and machine-driven looms in a small local textile mill. In each case, the teacher arranged for direct experience or trips in order to provide initial orientation. She then provided materials so that the class could perform each process through handwork. For example, the children sharpened pencils with sandpaper, as well as with the mechanical sharpener, and discussed the differences in quality of the product and speed of the operation. They performed simple hand-weaving after visiting a textile mill. The teacher constantly was alert to experiences that the children were having, or might have, that would enlarge the concept of the meaning of technological advance which the unit was designed to build.

Many pertinent books were kept on hand. Most of them contained selections and stories which the teacher read to the class, but some of them were read, toward the end of the year, by a few of the children themselves.

UNIT ON LICENSING   The teacher's objective was to bring the children to some appreciation of the extent and purpose of certain curtailments which citizens through organized government find necessary to impose upon themselves. This unit began during the hunting season for pheasants, which had point for the children because some of their fathers hunted these birds. Discussions were conducted concerning the need for, and merit of, licensing hunters. A child whose father was a barber told about the license a barber must obtain. This started a rapid expansion of the theme, which continued throughout the year. Specimens of licenses were brought in, and soon, a table was set aside to exhibit them. Licenses for automobiles, dogs, bird-banding, and retail selling were among those collected, and their need was often warmly debated. Questions such as why cats, which kill so many wild birds, should not be licensed, occasioned further discussion. The class was proud of its growing collection, and any member could take a visitor to the "license" table and explain the purpose, cost, if any, and significance of each specimen.

THE SCHOOL PLANT   Every few weeks, the teacher planned a trip to enlarge the children's knowledge of their school building, increase their familiarity and security concerning it, and build an appreciation of certain differences between maintaining a large public building and a house. Many features of the plant were explained, explored, mapped, and discussed, including the basement, furnace, overhead pipes, fuse box, storage rooms, assembly room, library, and attic. The data for this unit were obtained from firsthand observation and from explanations by the teacher, janitor, principal, nurse, and other members of the school staff.

Unit Resource Collections

A unit resource collection (often misleading called a "resource unit") is a body of suggestions and materials for use by the teacher in developing a unit. The teacher starts such a collection when he is preparing to teach a unit, and he can add to it each year. This collection may consist of newspaper clippings, books, bibliographies, lists of illustrative community resources, pictures of landscapes and economic activities, scale models of vehicles or buildings, lists of classroom activities—whatever might aid in enriching the unit.

In time, the accumulation may become very large. But that is, after all, the aim—to create a rich reservoir of ideas and materials. Sometimes a central repository for resource collections is kept in the school office or library, to which all teachers may contribute and from which all may borrow. Because a successful unit depends upon an abundance of ideas and materials, the building of unit resource collections is strongly recommended.

THE EFFECTIVENESS OF UNIT TEACHING

Types of teaching which possess at least some of the characteristics of the unit have been carefully studied, and appear to possess superiority over oldfashioned, routine recitation procedures. At the elementary school level, they appear superior in terms of acquisition of good work habits,[5] achievement in geography and history,[6] ability to apply new generalizations in social studies,[7] creativity,[8] use of reference materials,[9] and scope of out-of-school intellectual pursuits.[10]

The difficulty in drawing precise conclusions from the research is that the unit is not a clear-cut teaching device. When unit teaching is compared with its opposite, namely, a method consisting mainly of memorization and recitation of textbook material, it becomes evident that the two methods

[5] Frederick Pistor, "Evaluating New School Practises by the Observational Method," in *Appraising the Elementary School Program*; Sixteenth Yearbook of the Department of Elementary School Principals. Washington, D.C.: National Education Association, 1937. Pp. 377–389.

[6] Pistor; Charles Guzzetta, "Children's Knowledge of Historically Important Americans," Ed.D. dissertation, Temple University, *Dissertation Abstracts*, 25 (September 1964), 1653–1654.

[7] Saul B. Sells, *et al.*, "Evaluative Studies of the Activity Program in the New York City Public Schools: A Preliminary Report," *Journal of Experimental Education*, 9 (June 1941), 310–322.

[8] Arthur T. Jersild, *et al.*, "An Evaluation of Aspects of the Activity Program in the New York City Public Elementary Schools," *Journal of Experimental Education*, 8 (December 1939), 166–207; J. Wayne Wrightstone, *Appraisal of Newer Elementary School Practices*. New York: Teachers College, 1938.

[9] Wrightstone.

[10] Wrightstone.

cannot be clearly differentiated from each other. The miscellaneous host of activities which characterize the unit contrasts fuzzily with the similarly diffuse memorizing-recitational activities. The methods overlap. For example, each may employ devices such as films, textbook reading, and discussions. There is need for research in which selected variables are studied.

Nevertheless, unit teaching recommends itself on several grounds. First, the favorable evidence cited is, at least in part, valid and, to a considerable extent, supports the acceptance which unit teaching has received. Second, reports of unit teaching in action supply strong empirical evidence of its success in the hands of talented teachers (see the references cited in Chapter 3, Footnote 18). Third, the unit method ideally executes those aspects of educational policy which emphasize the goals of critical thinking (checking and comparing sources, marshaling evidence, analyzing arguments in a newspaper editorial, and so on) and class discussion (for purposes of planning work and exchanging points of view). Fourth, unit teaching is in accord with psychological principles which tend to view favorably active pupil participation[11] and provision of realistic experiences[12] in the learning process as means of increasing pupil understanding.

FOR REVIEW AND REFLECTION

1. What are the essential features of a unit?
2. In what respects is a unit dependent upon the teacher's judgment and style of teaching?
3. What is the purpose of pupil participation in planning a unit, in view of the fact that the teacher has already drafted a tentative plan?
4. Supply an example of a culminating activity. What is its value?
5. What differences exists among pupils in the primary grades and pupils in the intermediate grades that call for corresponding differences in application of the unit method?

ASSIGNMENTS

1. Describe how you would conduct the orientation phase of a unit on communication for a second grade.
2. Observe a social studies discussion period in an elementary school. Make as complete a transcription as you can of what is said. Evaluate the discussion from the standpoint of its probable purpose.
3. Make a list of suitable reading materials on transportation which you can locate in a school or public library. Indicate how adequately this library

---

[11] "Procedures which foster active student response are generally, though not uniformly, favored by experimental evidence over procedures which do not." (A. A. Lumsdaine, "Instruments and Media of Instruction," in N. L. Gage (Ed.), *Handbook of Research on Teaching*. Skokie, Ill.: Rand McNally, 1963. Chap. 12, p. 610.)

[12] ". . . experience with the concrete situation is the base for understanding." (Lee J. Cronbach, *Educational Psychology*. New York: Harcourt, 1963. P. 456.)

could fill the needs of a class studying transportation. Where could you locate additional reading material on the subject?

4. Draft the design of an experiment to test some aspect of unit teaching.

SUPPLEMENTARY READING

Burns, Paul C., "A Re-examination of Aspects of Unit Teaching in the Elementary School," *Peabody Journal of Education*, **40** (July 1962), 31–39. Analyzes certain excesses and misinterpretations of unit teaching.

Chambers, J. Richard, "The Social Studies," in *Providing for Individual Differences*. Norman E. Cutts and Nicholas Moseley (Eds.) Englewood Cliffs, N.J.: Prentice-Hall, 1960. Chap. 8. Suggestions for grouping, study guides, reference works, and pupil specialties.

Chase, W. Linwood, "Individual Differences in Classroom Learning," in *Social Studies in the Elementary School*, Nelson B. Henry (Ed.); Fifty-fifth Yearbook of the National Society for the Study of Education, Pt. II. Chicago: University of Chicago Press, 1957. Chap. 7. Includes description of group learning with study guides and pupil specialties.

Clements, H. Millard, William R. Fielder, and B. Robert Tabachnick, *Social Study: Inquiry in Elementary Classrooms*. Indianapolis: Bobbs-Merrill, 1966. Describes and illustrates the role of inquiry and discovery in social studies learning.

Clymer, Theodore, and Nolan C. Kearney, "Curricular and Instructional Provisions for Individual Differences," in *Individualizing Instruction*. Sixty-first Yearbook of the National Society for the Study of Education, Pt. I, Chicago: University of Chicago Press. 1962. Chap. 14. Includes section on "Working with Instructional Groups," which deals with fundamental requirements for successfully reaching individuals in a classroom setting.

Dale, Edgar, "Principles of Learning," *The News Letter*, **29** (January 1964), 1–4. Presents seven generalizations about learning which Dale states have helped him as both teacher and learner.

Dewey, John, *How We Think*. Boston: Heath, 1933. Five suggestions for conducting a recitation are given on pages 266–267. "The art of questioning is . . . the art of guiding learning."

Fenton, Edwin, *Teaching the New Social Studies in Secondary Schools: An Inductive Approach*. New York: Holt, Rinehart and Winston, 1966. Packed with illustrations of teaching and materials used in teaching by the "discovery" method.

Goldberg, Janice B., "Enrichment in Social Studies in an Enriched School," *Elementary School Journal*, **61** (May 1961), 418–423.

Hanna, Lavone A., *et al.*, *Unit Teaching in the Elementary School* (2d ed.). New York: Holt, Rinehart and Winston, 1963. Describes in detail unit teaching procedures.

Hanvey, Robert, "In Pursuit of Reason," *School Review*, **69** (Summer 1961), 127–135. Views discussion as "the life stuff of the social studies."

Hill, Wilhelmina, *Unit Planning and Teaching in Elementary Social Studies*. Washington, D.C.: U.S. Government Printing Office, 1963. Pamphlet. Contains suggestions for unit teaching, including detailed description of "resource units."

Hock, Louise E., *Using Committees in the Classroom*. New York: Holt, Rinehart and Winston, 1958. Pamphlet. Discusses use of committees for studying, reporting, and evaluating.

Loomis, Mary Jane, "Confusions Concerning Unit Teaching," *Childhood Education*, **32** (December 1955), 171–174. Clarifies misunderstandings about pupil participation in initiating, planning, and evaluating a unit.

Massialas, Byron G., and Jack Zevin, "Teaching Social Studies through Discovery," *Social Education*, **28** (November 1964), 384–387, 400. Report of application of the discovery technique in a high school course in world history. Students appeared well motivated and quite capable of formulating and testing hypotheses. Points up need for parallel investigation at elementary school level.

Muessig, Raymond H., "Bridging the Gap between Textbook Teaching and Unit Teaching, *Social Studies*, **54** (February 1963), 43–47. Presents "a temporary measure to aid teachers in getting a feel for unit teaching."

Preston, Ralph C., "Working with Primary Children in the Social Studies," *The Packet*, **18** (Winter 1963–1964), 3–15. Outlines some general procedures.

Sanders, Norris M., *Classroom Questions: What Kind?* New York: Harper & Row, 1966. Describes questions that will "insure a varied intellectual atmosphere," utilizing Bloom's *Taxonomy of Educational Objectives*.

Taba, Hilda, "Learning by Discovery: Psychological and Educational Rationale," *Elementary School Journal*, **63** (March 1963), 308–316. Briefly presents a history of the discovery concept of teaching; develops the point of view that it is "the chief mode for intellectual productivity and autonomy"; and sketches requisite teaching strategies.

Zelko, Harold P., *Successful Conference and Discussion Techniques*. New York: McGraw-Hill, 1957. Although written with adult discussions in mind, presents generally applicable analysis of the discussion process, the role of the leader, and the dynamics of participation.

5

TEACHING GEOGRAPHICAL CONCEPTS: REGIONS AND CULTURES

The earth is given as a common stock for man to labor and live on.

THOMAS JEFFERSON

Through units which emphasize geographical concepts, the child learns of the interrelationships between a people, their culture,[1] and their environment, and about important differences and similarities between places. The units are organized around regions or areas of the earth's surface, each of which is homogeneous with respect to specified features. The features may be environmental or cultural, or both. It is from their homogeneity that the region derives its character or individuality.

Geographic units deal with the processes which have resulted in the region's present appearance and human activity. Some of these processes are purely physical (such as drainage and erosion); some are biological (such as grown-over New England farms and the work of the destructive wheat rust); and some are cultural (such as innovations in manufacturing and governmental controls). Man is shaped by these processes, but he, in turn, exploits or modifies them as his drive, imagination, energy, and technical skill permit.

Geographic units should do more than describe. They should lead to generalizations about regions and processes such as: "No region is self-sufficient in terms of modern living needs" and to explanations such as relating a population shift to the discovery of a mineral resource (for example, the discovery of iron mines in the area of Atlantic City, Wyoming, which has given that former ghost town a rebirth). Geographic units should consider the movements of peoples from one region to another, and

---

[1] The culture of a group is the sum total of its values, customs, laws, religious beliefs, technology, language, social institutions, and creative products. The term, "way of life," is sometimes used popularly to denote culture.

the exchange of goods and ideas. They explore the kinds of transportation and communication which make such migration and exchange possible.

ENVIRONMENT AND CULTURE

In teaching geographical concepts, we are not justified in taking the once-popular but one-sided position that man's culture is determined by his environment; we are compelled by geographic fact to bring out that man and his environment mutually shape and affect each other. Geographers today stress the fact that the physical environment has no human significance *per se*; that its significance is determined by the culture of the inhabitants. A given environment means one thing to one cultural group, and it is used accordingly; it may mean something quite different to another cultural group. Broek gives an apt illustration of this by citing the manner in which southern California was used by three different groups:

> The Indians found California a good land for gathering, hunting, and fishing; the Spaniards introduced their Mediterranean forms of land use; the Americans made it a commercial fruit and vegetable garden and found it a pleasant place in which to retire.[2]

Although the culture of primitive man is sharply conditioned and restricted by his environment, man in his more advanced stages clearly dominates many aspects of his environment. He is not always wise in his manipulation of it, as when he abuses or wastes water resources, but he certainly succeeds in changing and utilizing his habitat in ways which he *believes* will serve his needs. He has the equipment to mine minerals, dig canals, drill tunnels, span rivers and bays, destroy insect pests, and meet the challenge of his environment in other ways.

AREAL VARIATION

Geography contains descriptive concepts of "areal variation"— concepts centered on differences and similarities between places. Thus, a geographic study of a city would reveal differences between the sections of a city and might lead to the identification of a commercial core, an industrial area, a residential area. In a world-wide comparison of farms, the conclusion reached would be that most farmers in the world live in villages, but that exceptions are to be found in the United States, Canada, New Zealand, in certain remote mountainous regions of Europe, and elsewhere. In a study of the United States, data would be examined and

---

[2] John O. M. Broek, "Progress in Human Geography," in *New Viewpoints in Geography*; Twenty-ninth Yearbook. Washington, D.C.: National Council for the Social Studies, 1959. Chap. 4, p. 35.

generalizations would be sought to give each region distinctiveness. For example, southeastern United States is an area of humid, subtropical climate with relatively poor soil, largely dependent on an agricultural economy, but making rapid growth in the manufacture of steel, aluminum, farm machinery, airplanes, and other products; and New Englanders' efficient use of

---

Some Basic Generalizations of Geography[3]

A. Formulation of Regions
 1. People and environments differ from place to place.
 2. A region may be based on political, physical, economic, or other features, or on a combination of features.
B. Environment and Man
 1. Man's achievements and way of life within a region are influenced by a combination of factors: climate, soil, vegetation, water, and other environmental factors; and by his energy, intelligence, tradition, and wisdom in determining personal and public policy.
 2. Man determines the significance of the physical features of his environment; he has learned to use and control parts of it through his intelligence, energy, and ability to apply natural laws.
 3. The development of transportation and communication in many places has freed man from complete dependence upon products afforded by his immediate environment and has led to the interdependence of the regions of the earth.
 4. Man constantly seeks better ways to use the earth and its products to satisfy his needs for food, clothing, and shelter.
 5. Man uses natural resources in accordance with his needs, desires, and level of technology.
C. Spatial Relationships
 1. The shape, movements, and inclinations of the earth cause day and night, the seasons, and climatic differentiation.
 2. The earth is divided into climatic regions created by the distribution of heat and moisture in various combinations.
D. Tools of Geography
 1. A map is a diagram representing part or all of the earth and showing the location and relationship of selected places and features.
 2. A globe is a scale model of the earth; the scale remains constant over the entire globe.

---

[3] These generalizations are, in part, a streamlined version of some of those appearing in *Report of the State Central Committee on Social Studies to the California State Curriculum Commission.* Sacramento: California State Department of Education, 1961; Bernard Berelson, *et al., The Social Studies and the Social Sciences,* New York: Harcourt, 1962; and Henry J. Warman, "Major Concepts in Geography," in Wilhelmina Hill (Ed.), *Curriculum Guide for Geographic Education.* Chicago, Ill. 60602: National Council for Geographic Education, 1964. Chap. 2.

their limited resources in the past enabled the region to structure a human-capital resource base which supports its population today. The study of areal variation is geography's principle objective and is a unique contribution of geography to the social studies.

MAPS AND GLOBES

Geographical concepts should be taught with abundant use of maps and the globe. These tools give precision to the location of a place under study and clarify directional, and distance relationships. Maps are invaluable aids in demonstrating terms (such as "peninsula" and "continent"), in explaining drainage systems, landforms, and other physical arrangements, in showing the distribution of natural resources, crops, population, and other aspects of geography, and in numerous other ways. Children should be introduced to geographical concepts so that they are "genuinely uncomfortable about studying an area they cannot visualize" on a map and so that they will, as a matter of course, visualize "the stage upon which the human drama" takes place.[4] A separate chapter is devoted to maps and globes.

TEACHING GEOGRAPHY AS METHOD

Geographic information is based on geographers' observation of numerous features. These include: (1) kinds and amounts of things in a specific place, (2) differences and likenesses between regions, and (3) man's relationship with his environment. Part of the school's responsibility is to develop reflective thought through learning how difficult it is to obtain reliable information and to form sound conclusions. Experiences should be provided for the child to collect information at firsthand and to draw generalizations from the data. He can also learn about how the geographer works and thinks in map exercises. Through the use of transparent overlays, or through side-by-side comparison, maps can be used to note "areal associations" between geographical features—for example, between population density and centers of industrial activity. Or, they can be used to note evidence of "spatial interaction" such as the utilization made by the Chicago-Gary steel complex of the iron ore from the Lake Superior iron ore district. "Areal association" and "areal interaction" are good geographical concepts which can be introduced to aid children in analyzing a region. While these methods should be in the teacher's mind during every unit which emphasizes geography, particularly favorable opportunities are present in studying the geography of the local community, as explained in ensuing pages.

[4] Edward Coleson, "The Elementary Social Studies: Sense and Nonsense in Integration," *Journal of Geography*, **57** (April 1958), 196–202.

DIVIDING THE WORLD INTO REGIONS

Physical Regions versus Culture Regions

What system should be used to divide the earth into regions (or areas) suitable for study? This question has been admirably analyzed by Pearson.[5] He discusses two schemes of presentation: (1) organizing the world into physical regions (dry lands, rainy tropical lands, polar lands, and so on), and (2) organizing it into culture regions (Europe, the Orient, the Soviet realm).

While both schemes have their adherents among geographers, Pearson notes a trend toward regions based on cultural characteristics (regions which consist of groups of nations which have common cultural traits). He notes that it is the most common organization of introductory geography courses in college. This seems a desirable approach in elementary school, too, in that it encourages the study of selected cultures with a degree of intensity. In contrast, the physical-regions approach encourages jumping around from one culture to another. The pupils, in learning the different adaptations made in, say, the dry regions of the world, study such diverse peoples as the shepherds of Patagonia, the nomads of the Gobi desert, the Arabian Bedouins, the aborigines of the Australian desert, and the Navajo Indians in Arizona. Such a plan is not conducive to understanding a few culturally related nations in depth, and tends to give undue prominence to the influence of the physical environment.

Divisions Based on Culture Regions

Various ways of dividing the world into culture regions have been devised by geographers. "No one system of dividing the earth into homogeneous areas is inherently better than any other," writes Pearson. "No one is right and the others wrong."[6] One scheme that has attracted much interest is that of James, who outlines seven major "culture areas," "each of which possesses distinctive characteristics related to these world-wide processes of change," namely, the Industrial Revolution and the Democratic Revolution: (1) European, (2) American, (3) North-African-Southwest Asia, (4) Oriental, (5) Soviet, (6) African, and (7) Pacific.[7]

Another scheme is found in a college geography by Wheeler and others.

---

[5] Ross N. Pearson, "Progress in Regional Geography," in *New Viewpoints in Geography*; Twenty-ninth Yearbook. Washington, D.C.: National Council for the Social Studies, 1959. Chap. 6.

[6] Pearson. P. 77.

[7] Preston E. James, "The Use of Culture Areas as a Frame of Organization for the Social Studies," in *New Viewpoints in Geography*; Twenty-ninth Yearbook. Washington, D.C.: National Council for the Social Studies, 1959. Chap. 10.

It outlines the following eight areas: (1) Europe, (2) Soviet Union, (3) Middle East, (4) Orient, (5) Pacific World, (6) Africa, (7) Latin America, and (8) Anglo-America. Wheeler and his associates emphasize that their scheme ". . . is only one among various alternative methods of subdividing the world for purposes of study."[8] An inspection of college textbooks on world geography will reveal numerous variations of the James and the Wheeler organizational schemes.

Making a Representative Selection

When the child has completed elementary school, he should have studied his own culture area in detail, and representative nations of the remaining culture areas.[9] Some teachers are reluctant merely to sample a culture region. They prefer to cover an entire region, usually nation by nation. Nevertheless, selection is essential. The accelerating expansion of knowledge threatens to bulge the curriculum to a point where the child becomes stuffed rather than enlightened. We have no alternative to selecting and discarding.

To be sure, there remains the hazard of *too* fragmented a presentation of a culture. It is a hazard which can be reduced by the following plan:

1. Employ the old "type-study unit" idea,[10] more recently called "post-holing." It is still probably as satisfactory a compromise as any yet achieved between the opposed and equally undesirable practices of (a) frantically trying to "cover" all nations of a culture region, and (b) lopsidedly dwelling on one nation for an entire semester or year. The type-study unit provides for the intensive, detailed study of one segment of a culture region, as Brazil is sometimes chosen for Grade 3 or 4 to sample the Latin-American culture region. Similarities and differences with respect to other Latin American cultures should be noted. Or, in the upper elementary grades (5 to 6, or 5 to 8), the type-study unit is more likely to provide for a unit embracing a more thorough study of a culture region (say, all of Latin America). In that case, one subculture region (say, the three Inca countries with predominantly Indian populations) may be studied by post-holing in Peru, and then merely surveying, and making brief comparisons with, Ecuador and Bolivia.

2. Before, and again after, each unit, have the pupils examine the culture area as displayed on a map and on a globe. Have them trace

---

[8] Jesse H. Wheeler, Jr., *et al.*, *Regional Geography of the World.* New York: Holt, Rinehart and Winston, 1961. P. 4.

[9] Culture regions need not be subdivided exclusively into national units, although this is the usual teaching practice.

[10] Donald L. McMurry, "Type Study Units in the Social Studies," *Historical Outlook*, **24** (December 1933), 431–441.

with their fingers the boundaries of the total culture region and to identify the various subregions of the area. Supply pictures which will illustrate major similarities and differences between the subregions of the unit and the other subregions of the culture area.

Plan for This Chapter

The remainder of this chapter will give suggestions for teaching about the following culture regions:

1. The local community
2. Anglo-America
3. Latin America
4. Europe
5. Africa
6. The Middle East
7. The Soviet realm
8. The Orient
9. The Pacific

It will be assumed that the teacher will wish to post-hole. The chapter contains suggestions of selections that could be made appropriately, but in so doing, there is no intent to close the door to other possible selections. After all, which particular subregions or subcultures are most representative is a matter about which curriculum workers might argue endlessly and futilely.

THE LOCAL COMMUNITY

Through community units, the school beginner is appropriately introduced to some of the techniques of social science investigation—collecting data through observation, interviewing, and reading; then weighing information, drawing conclusions, and formulating generalizations. Because community units lend themselves particularly well to data-collecting, it is not surprising to find them recommended by curriculum specialists, not only for the primary grades, where they are most commonly found, but for upper grades as well.

Some of the examples of classroom activity which follow describe the study of isolated features or processes. While they are valid illustrations of teaching procedure, they should not be interpreted as describing all the necessary activities of a unit. Only when features (such as a school) or processes (such as renting a home) are compared from place to place is geography *per se* being taught.

The Home

Through carefully planned units containing discussions and excursions, the primary-grade child may discover a wider range of types of houses and functions of the home than he had previous knowledge of. The study enlarges his concept of homelife with respect to such factors as size of family, contributions of various members of the household, standards relating to behavior, hours of rising and retiring, habits of television viewing, types of housing and furnishings, kinds and timing of meals, and home chores.

In schools in disadvantaged areas where the majority of children may be from Aid-to-Dependent-Children families and where the father may be compelled by welfare requirements to live outside the home, the special problems of the fatherless home need to be discussed, and how children can assist mothers with housekeeping chores. In some schools, parents' meetings have become parent-child meetings with both mothers and children attending and planning together how to bring some order into a chaotic environment. Mothers have been alerted to the fact that children will be bringing home samples of the schoolwork—papers or art products—and that the recognition given to such samples by parents can help to build in the child a drive to do well in school.

The fact that the child deals with an institution with which he has surface familiarity is an aid to his understanding, and "the home" thus provides him with ideal content on which to cut his teeth as a data collector and a generalization-formulator in the social sciences.

Suggestions for Teaching

1. Early in the unit, draw a large map of the community, showing all the houses, based on a local map from a real estate office or chamber of commerce, or use a three-by-three-foot blowup of a vertical areal photograph of the neighborhood available from local government agencies, planning commissions, state highway departments, or the Map Information Office of the U.S. Department of the Interior. Have each child locate his home. (Obviously, this cannot be done in classes attended by children from other neighborhoods.) The teacher might draw such a map, approximately 4-by-5 feet, showing the shape of each building on each block (see Figure 5.1). This map may be used in studying the school neighborhood as well as the home.

2. You might want to try out some of the possibilities of a unit dealing with the home which were brought out in a study conducted by a first-grade teacher whose class observed the construction of new houses in the neighborhood. After reporting, discussing, and recording what they had seen,

each child drew and painted plans of what he considered a model house. They read about homemaking in available preprimers, and story books. They considered the issue of renting versus buying a house, and the father of one of the children, a banker, explained mortgages in simple terms. The teacher rated these children's understanding as high.

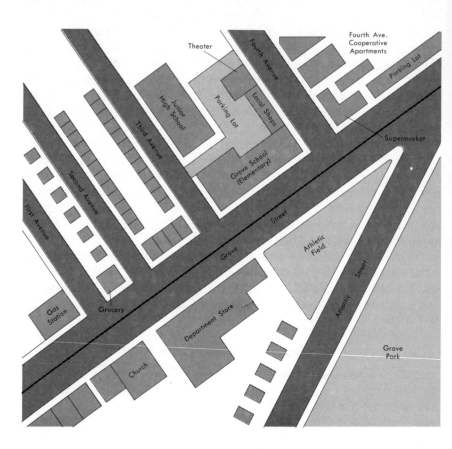

Figure 5.1. A portion of a map prepared for a first-grade class.

Obviously such an approach would have little relevance for the disadvantaged child. Here the teacher can be of help in getting pupils to conduct surveys of housing problems—for example, garbage collection, protection from rats and insect pests—and in finding out what steps, if any, are being taken and need to be taken to improve such unsanitary housing conditions. Where some agency has taken steps to clean up a portion of the slums, it might be possible to organize an excursion to visit the project and see what has been done.

3. If you teach older children, they, too, can study the home. They can gain insight into the great change in homelife brought about by the industrial revolution. Portions of autobiographies dealing with early American farm life and pioneer days furnish data that help children to see vividly the "old-time home" depicted by Dorothy Canfield Fisher as follows:

> . . . the old time home was not only kitchen, sleeping-rooms, and living quarters for a father, mother, and their children, as it is now; but also school, grocery, textile mill, butcher shop, shelter for the aged and insane, hospital—unit of life for a clan rather than a family. . . . we find in the American account books of pre-industrial general stores practically no purchases of food or clothing. Nor were there hospitals, except for soldiers. Nor insane asylums. All the sick of the clan were nursed under its own roof. . . . Most of the education of the boys took place there, and all of that of the girls.[11]

The purpose here is not to make the child sigh for a return of the past, but rather to have him understand the change in conditions brought about by the industrial revolution, such as more mothers going out to work, the resultant growth of the child-care center, the change in family chores, the reduced size of the average family, and new patterns of recreation.

Some Teaching Materials: The Home

Books for Children
Beim, Jerrold, *Who's Who in Your Family?* New York: F. Watts, 1954.
Miles, Betty, *A House for Everyone.* New York: Knopf, 1958.
Preston, Ralph C., *et al., A New Hometown.* Boston: Heath, 1964.
Zim, Herbert, *Things around the House.* New York: Morrow, 1954.

Films
Moving Day—Timmy's New Neighbors. Chicago: Coronet Instructional Films, 1960.
Our Family Works Together. Chicago: Coronet Instructional Films, 1958.
What Do Fathers Do? Los Angeles, Calif.: Churchill-Wexler Film Productions, 1958.

Filmstrip
All Kinds of Houses. Wilmette, Ill.: Encyclopedia Britannica Films, 1960.

Pamphlet
Steps to Home Safety. Hartford, Conn.: Aetna Casualty and Surety Co., 1962.

---

[11] Dorothy Canfield Fisher, *Our Young Folks.* New York: Harcourt, 1943. P. 168.

4. Consider any study of the home as a "type-study unit," with the impli-cation that it should be concluded with a study of homes in other parts of the world and in other times. Preston and Clymer have provided a lead for this in a book for third-grade children.[12]

5. With the attention of America focused on the disadvantaged, raise such questions as: Can all people live in the kind of houses they would like to? Bring out the wide variety of homes—firetraps, rat-ridden, poorly constructed, and so forth. Avoid dwelling on the middle-class home. Your pupils should learn that, with respect to homes, there is considerable unfinished business.

The School

The study of the school is customarily undertaken during the child's first year at school. In many instances, it deals with stale ideas and under-estimates the child's capacity for substantial learning.

Suggestions for Teaching

1. Take up such questions as "Who pays the teacher?" and "Who buys the textbooks?" Help the children understand how money is obtained from

---

Some Teaching Materials: The School

Books for Children
Bailey, Carolyn, *The Little Red Schoolhouse*. New York: Viking, 1957.
Beim, Jerrold, *Country School*. New York: Morrow, 1955.
Preston, Ralph C., *et al.*, *In School and Out*. Boston: Heath, 1964.

Filmstrip
Our Homes and Our School. New York: American Book, 1961. Set of six.

Other Teaching Materials
Casper, the Friendly Ghost. Lima, Ohio: Superior Coach Corp., 1962. Free (school bus safety).
My Own Safety Story. Traffic Safety Guide—Primary Grades. American Automobile Association, local chapter, 1962. Free.

For the Teacher
Alford, John J., and George L. McDermott, "Climates of the School Yard," *Journal of Geography*, **64** (April 1965), 177–181.

---

[12] Ralph C. Preston and Eleanor Clymer, *Communities at Work*. Boston: Heath, 1964. Pp. 176–178.

local and state taxes to support public schools and other public institutions. The concept of "tax" is essentially simple, and children achieve a satisfying sense of mastery when they learn about it.

2. Conduct a class tour of the school building and grounds. The children should be able to identify the centers and equipment which play a part in the school's operation—other classrooms, principal's office, nurse's headquarters, heating system, water pipes, storage space, and so forth.

3. Use a blueprint of the school, if one is available, as the basis for constructing a large floor plan for help in directional orientation and the relationships of portions of the plant. Refer to the cardinal directions, and "right," and "left," applying these terms to the floor plan and the actual plant and grounds.

4. Conduct a survey of fire hazards. One teacher has her class make a study of fire hazards in the school and consider what the school has done to minimize the hazards through fireproofing, storage, placement of fire extinguishers and fire alarm boxes, and the like. She explains fire insurance (how the pooling of many premiums makes fire insurance a workable concept) and the major provisions of the school's fire insurance policy.

Neighborhood, Town, City

The local region can be taught profitably at any grade level to introduce and illustrate geographic principles.

Suggestions for Teaching

1. Emphasize a survey of the locality on foot where information can be collected at firsthand. In this way, the pupil learns in an elementary way how geographic data are collected by a geographer engaged in scientific work—by observing landforms, man-made structures, and work patterns; taking notes; sketching; mapping; noting distances and directions. Anderzhon and Newhouse give examples of things to observe which contribute to geographical generalizations.[13] These include:

(a) The sun: noting its position and its resultant shadow as it varies with the time of day and the seasons,

(b) Temperature and precipitation: Keeping a record as these phenomena vary seasonally,

(c) Cultural and physical features: finding directions, differen-

[13] Mamie L. Anderzhon and Hazel R. Newhouse, "Teaching Geography Out-of-Doors," in *New Viewpoints in Geography*; Twenty-ninth Yearbook. Washington, D.C.: National Council for the Social Studies, 1959. Chap. 11.

tiating physical and natural features, and seeking to discover their relationships,

(d) Distance, area, and extent: developing realistic concepts of a mile, an acre, etc., and how they are scaled on a map,

(e) Places and directions: orientation by the cardinal directions and by conventional map arrangements and symbols,

(f) Selected features: noting the patterns of such community functions as the postal service, a dairy delivery route, sources of supply, and markets,

(g) Selected features: traversing a busy stretch or area and recording on an outline map the important buildings, transportation routes, sources of supply, and the like.

2. If you are an intermediate-grade teacher, the following illustrations may prove suggestive.

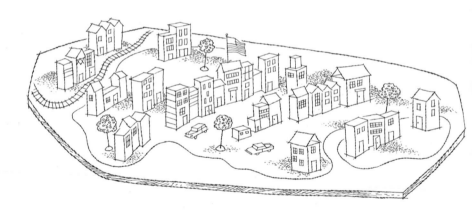

Figure 5.2. Model of the community.

FOURTH GRADE   One fourth grade extended its study of the community to include its history, government, important persons, and miscellaneous pertinent facts. A major project was the construction of a 6-by-8-foot floor "map" (see Figure 5.2). Its base was beaver board covered with sawdust, which was arranged to show the hills. White sand in elongated strips represented the roads; blue paper under glass, the rivers and streams; toothpicks, the railroad line; and sponges dipped in green paint affixed to twigs stuck in clay, the trees. Buildings were carved out of 2-inch balsa wood. Each child carved his own house and one important building. The experience was an enjoyable one, which taught the children the layout of their community, and its orientation to the points of the compass.[14] Such a map could also be used to teach areal variation within the city, such as the commercial core, industrial area, residential area, and the like.

FIFTH GRADE   A fifth-grade class surveyed its city (Philadelphia) in quite a different manner.[15] Each pupil selected a point of interest which he wished to study intensively, and was excused for one school day for an on-the-spot study, provided one of his parents consented to accompany him. He then pooled his data and wrote a report. Among the topics chosen were:

> The Zoo
> The Newspapers
> Women's Medical College
> The Delaware River
> Elfreth's Alley
> Philco Corporation Plant
> Carpenters' Hall

3. Compare the local area with contrasting areas and with similar areas. The comparison most important for the primary grades is between rural, urban, and suburban areas. Younger children will do much of this through the medium of construction and play. Children of all ages can take imaginary trips from their own community to another, and back again. Discussion, too, is a good medium for making community comparisons. For example, when discussion focuses upon the hour that marks the beginning of the farmer's day, immediate reference can be made to the hour on which office and factory workers report for duty. To provide graphic representation of the comparison, charts and notebooks with parallel columns may be constructed. Informal debates may be held on the relative advantages of being raised in one as opposed to the other community. It is to be hoped that it will be developed through discussion that, although communities differ widely, one type is not necessarily "better" than another; that is, a city is not superior to a rural town or a suburb. Children should learn that differences between habits, occupations, appearances, and customs among communities are natural and reasonable, given the communities' respective origins, traditions, and environments, and that in today's specialized industrial age, communities are dependent upon each other as never before.

---

[14] This unit was taught by Barbara Winslade Dugdale.
[15] This unit was taught by Esther Reagan.

One first-grade teacher in a suburban area organized a unit for comparing the local suburban area with urban and rural areas—a country store, a city store, a farm, and a large railroad freight terminal. The class had already surveyed a number of the community's workers in its suburbs and had some understanding of the suburb's "parasitic" status—being neither at the source of economic raw materials nor at the point where the raw materials are converted to manufactured articles. A general store in the country was visited, and the next week, a wholesale grocery in a nearby city. The next trip was to a dairy and truck farm, followed by one to a large railroad freight terminal in the city, where the loading and unloading of freight cars was observed. Discussions following the trips pointed up the contrast between the city and the rural life, with its closeness to the source of food, and the rapid tempo, complicated mechanical operations,

---

Some Teaching Materials: The Community

Books for Children
Evans, Eva, *Why We Live Where We Live.* Boston: Little, Brown, 1953.
Hammond, Diana, *Let's Go to a Hospital.* New York: Putnam, 1959.
Hastings, Evelyn, *The Department Store.* Chicago: Melmont, 1956.
Miner, Irene, *The True Book of Our Post Office and Its Helpers.* Chicago: Childrens Press, 1955.
Peattie, Roderick, and Lisa Peattie, *The City.* New York: Schuman, 1952.
Preston, Ralph C., and Eleanor Clymer, *Communities at Work.* Boston: Heath, 1964.
Schneider, Herman, *Let's Look Under the City.* Chicago: Scott, 1954.
Urell, Catherine, *et al., Big City Workers. Big City Water Supply.* Chicago: Follett, 1953.

Cut-out Kit
Gas Serves Your Community, Ed-7. New York: American Gas Association and local gas company, 1962.

Film
Helpers in Our Community. Chicago: Coronet Instructional Films, 1958.

Filmstrips
Farm and City. New York: Young America Films (McGraw-Hill), 1956. A series of 4 films.
Learning about Community Services. New York: American Book, 1961.

For the Teacher
McIntosh, C. Barron, "Geography in the Grocery Store," *Journal of Geography,* **64** (March 1965), 123–126.

and mass distribution characterizing the city. A textbook was used, as were a number of pictures and supplementary books, that brought out clearly the contrast and interdependence of city and farm, and the role of the suburb.

An intermediate-grade class in a city rich in historical lore and important among the early colonies concluded its community study by comparing their community with Williamsburg, Va., also of early origin and with traditions growing out of a long and colorful history. A class committee wrote directly to Williamsburg for information. The present status of each of the two communities was considered in terms of population, economic importance, points of interest, and ways in which old historical sites have been preserved and restored. Then a study of the origin and early days of each of the communities was made. Questions were considered, such as why one had become a major industrial city and the other had not.

4. Establish contact with a teacher in another community, and plan for the exchange of letters between your respective classes. This need not be limited to American communities. One enterprising fourth-grade teacher of Margate City, N.J., arranged for such a correspondence between members of her class and children in a school in Margate, England, for which the American city was named. The letters introduced the pupils in both cities to similarities and differences in ways of life in communities on opposite sides of an ocean.

ANGLO-AMERICA

Children should become steeped in the geography of their own country. Because children of the United States and children of Canada are neighbors who share important cultural traditions, they should know about each other's countries as well as about their own.

State or Province

The state or province, often taught in one of the intermediate grades, is a convenient and logical political unit for study. It is a unit which, on a small scale, illustrates characteristics and problems of the country at large. Thus, it has its own history, geography, combination of cities and rural areas, leaders, laws, and institutions; it has flag, motto, seal, and other symbols; it engenders pride and loyalty among its citizens. The child's study of his state should lead him to appreciate its historical significance and its geographical character. Its geographical significance is in its relationship to the rest of the nation and world. Some of the aspects that can be studied profitably are these:

TOPIC	QUESTIONS TO EXPLORE
Boundaries	Which are natural?
	Which are man-made?
Name	How did the name originate?
Physical features	What are the natural regions and where are they?
	What prominent physical features are present?
	Is the state known for its natural beauty?
	Is its beauty being considered in the building of highways, airports, etc.?
	What are the chief resources and where are they?
	What are its recreational areas?
	Are they enough to accommodate the population?
Early settlers and settlements	What Indians occupied the region?
	Who were the first white settlers?
	Where did they come from and what were their traditions?
	How has their way of life influenced ours today?
Relationship to nation	When was it admitted to the nation?
	What contribution has it made to the life of the nation?
Relationship to our own community?	What does our community contribute to the state?
Today	What is the population and how is it distributed?
	How do its people make a living?
	What are some of its customs? problems? plans?
	How is it governed? Where is the seat of government?
	Which of its problems can be solved only in cooperation with other states?

An abundance of published material and pictures concerning the past and present of states and provinces is obtainable from various departments of state provincial governments, state and provincial historical societies, and chambers of commerce.[16]

[16] Examples of state periodicals are *Arizona Highways*; *New Hampshire Profiles*; *Vermont Life*; and *Virginia Cavalcade*.

Nation

Teaching about the country as a whole, also, is usually undertaken in one of the intermediate grades. The study should provide the child with a bird's-eye view of his entire homeland.

Suggestions for Teaching

1. Start off with a view of the country as a whole. An imaginary trip across the country is a good introduction. Identify the national boundaries. Using maps and photographs, give an over-all picture of the topography of the country—locating its mountains, deserts, plains, swamps, rivers, large lakes, and so on. Discuss facts of general significance. The following are true of both the United States and Canada.

(a) The chief ranges run north and south. They are historically significant barriers to east-west travel. The long, high mountain ranges of the West force the prevailing winds into high altitudes, causing them to give up their moisture as rain and thus to irrigate the region west of the mountains, but leaving great dry stretches in those states or provinces just east of the mountains.

(b) The country lies between the two largest and most important oceans in the world and contains several large rivers and lakes. Aside from their value to trade and transportation, these bodies of water have a moderating effect upon climate and supply moisture to the winds which sweep over them.

(c) The country contains extensive plains with relatively fertile soil, a warm, long growing season, and adequate rainfall, which lend themselves to the growing of large quantities of wheat and many different kinds of crops, supplying not only the country's own needs, but those of other countries as well.

(d) Alone in the world, the United States and Canada together have almost all the important resources which make nations wealthy and strong. We are lucky to live in such a well endowed land.

Children may help the teacher construct a large plastic relief map to learn details of the country's physical geography. Many teachers have found it helpful to have jigsaw puzzle maps of the country on hand in which each state or province is a separate piece. They are popular with children and help draw their attention to details of the country's political components.

2. Subdivide the country into a few significant geographical regions. A number of systems have been proposed. Each has its merits—also its arbitrary elements. The following breakdown is a common one.

UNITED STATES	CANADA
New England	The Maritime provinces
Middle Atlantic states	Ontario and Quebec
The South	The Prairie provinces
North Central states	Southern British Columbia
Rocky Mountain states	Sparsely settled and empty lands
Pacific states	

These regional divisions are not to be confused with units. A unit should constitute a more comprehensive grouping. Thus, one textbook combines the regions of the United States in consecutive pairs—New England and the Middle Atlantic states constituting one unit, and so on.[17]

3. Emphasize unique aspects of each region. For example, New England, although deficient in natural resources, is occupied by people who have, in the past, made the most of its timber, water power, maritime trade, and fish. The past efficient use of these resources gave New England the wherewithall to structure a human-capital resource base which, along with favorable location, supports its population. The Prairie provinces produce abundant wheat on their broad plains, but because of low rainfall grow limited amounts of other crops.

4. After a brief survey of the region, select typical places for intensive study. For example, after a survey of the South, detailed attention could be given to the city of Winston-Salem, N. C., an important textile and tobacco center; the Tennessee Valley, with its concentration of cotton farms; and the Oklahoma oil fields.

5. Take a close look at how the people live. The need for this is one of the reasons for spending some time studying selected spots in a region. Give plenty of attention to building a vivid picture of the landscape and of the customs with respect to such aspects of life as food, clothing, shelter, education, recreation, dialect, and observance of holidays. Relevant pictures and films should be displayed in the classroom during this part of the study. Even though gross regional cultural differences are dwindling in consequence of television, national advertising, the standardization of products, governmental controls, and other regimenting influences, distinctive traits persist, and they should be brought out.

6. Take a look at the traditional character of the people. What are some of their values? Who were their heroes? Regional literature will bring out many of the answers. Some of the writings of Edward Eggleston, John Muir, and Hamlin Garland, for example, convey a feeling for the people who settled in the Middle West, and portions can be read profitably to children

[17] Ralph C. Preston and John Tottle, *Geography—United States and Canada.* Boston: Heath, 1966.

during study of that region. Children can themselves read such well-liked juvenile material, on the same region, as *Caddie Woodlawn* by Brink, *Corn-Belt Billy* by Hunt, and *Daniel Boone* by McGuire. Here, too, it is well to recall that regional differences are shrinking and to avoid the teaching of stereotypes.

7. Examine some of the area's central problems and discover how they are working to solve them. For example:

(a) How New England is meeting the removal of its textile mills to the South through diversifying its industry,

(b) How southern California is seeking to replenish its dwindling underground water supply by concentrating surface water at strategic points by means of damming rivers, digging canals to spread the water where it is most likely to infiltrate the soil, and seeking to convert ocean water to fresh water,

(c) How the national and provincial governments in Canada are subsidizing transportation and communication operations in order to reduce the sectionalism resulting from geographic barriers, scattered settlements, and diverse language.

8. Spend time generously in developing key geographic concepts. Some examples follow:

(a) The regions into which the country is divided should be discussed. Are there other regions into which it could be divided? By considering relative similarity with respect to *landforms, climate, resources, work, traditions,* and *location,* members of your class should be encouraged to demarcate on outline maps other defensible divisions than the one you are following. After developing regional concepts, some work might be done with areal association and spatial interaction which are not difficult ideas.

(b) The Continental Divide should be learned as a line connecting high points of land such as hills, ridges, and mountains from which streams flow to opposite sides of the continent.

(c) The Great Plains is a term which should create an image of the attractive strip of land extending east of the Rockies, for the most part level or slightly rolling grasslands with extensive wheat farming and cattle grazing—once the territory of the cowboy and later, in the winter wheat section, the location of the "dust bowl."

(d) The Great Glacier, moving because of the weight of its ice (accumulated from snow), shaped the land in Canada and northern United States by rounding off hills and broadening valleys. Upon melting, the glacier left some areas devoid of soil, stripping them down to bare bedrock. Other areas were left with deep fertile soils; still other areas, with sand or boulders; some areas, with a mixture of these deposits. All areas were left with lakes, ponds, marshes, and newly directed wandering streams.

(e) The United States contains 50 states; it is made up of *continental* United States plus Hawaii; *conterminous* United States consists of the 48 states, which, before 1959, constituted the entire country.

9. Throughout the study, emphasize the attractions of the homeland. Through the use of folk stories and folk songs, tales of adventure, descriptions of the wildlife, scenery, recreation and sports facilities, interesting cities, and other aspects and qualities of the homeland which are emotionally satisfying, you help to build patriotism. Avoid a cold, academic survey!

Some Teaching Materials: Anglo-America

Books for Children
Banta, Richard, *Life in America: The South*. Grand Rapids, Mich.: Fideler, 1960. (One of a series; other regions covered in other books.)
Lent, Henry, *Men at Work in the Great Lakes States*. New York: Putnam, 1958. (One of a series; other regions covered in other books.)
Miers, Earl S., *Our Fifty States*. New York: Grosset & Dunlap, 1961.
Preston, Ralph C., and Eleanor Clymer, *Communities at Work*. Boston: Heath, 1964.
Preston, Ralph C., and John Tottle, *Geography—United States and Canada*. Boston: Heath, 1966.
Ross, Frances, *The Land and People of Canada*. Philadelphia: Lippincott, 1960.

Films
Cotton Belt: Yesterday and Today. Bloomington, Ind.: Indiana University, Audio-visual Center, 1961.
Geography of the U.S.: An Introduction. Chicago: Coronet Instructional Films, 1958.

Filmstrips
A Look at Canada. Valhalla, N.Y.: Stanbow Productions, 1959.
United States—Its History and Geography. New York: McGraw-Hill, 1954. Color. Buy. (Set of 14, 7 areas, 2 for each.)

Other Teaching Materials
Canadian Travel Kit (Special Teachers' Package). Ottawa: Canadian Government Travel Bureau, 1962. 5 booklets.
Teachers' Kit on Canada. New York: Canadian Consulate General, 1962. One to a teacher.

The foregoing point to only a random selection from the many concepts which study of our native land could develop.

LATIN AMERICA

The Good Neighbor Policy (of the United States toward Latin America), in order to be more than a slogan and in order to become actually a part of our national policy, needs the support of education. All Latin-American cultures are still unknown, misunderstood, or antagonistically regarded. Our Latin-American friends are sometimes annoyed with our ignorance of their cultures, our tendency to lump them together, our incorrect pronunciation of Latin-American names and terms, our past carelessness in describing their cultures in our books, and our neglect of their cultures in the curriculum of our schools.

The difficulty in drawing generalizations that are true for all of Latin America is made evident by Augelli's analysis of two persistent ideas, namely, that Latin-American cultures are uniform and homogeneous, and that the unprepossessing physical environment of Latin America is an obstacle to the settlement and development of its empty lands.[18] Augelli regards the alleged homogeneity as at best dubious, pointing out that the types of environment and resources "run virtually the entire gamut of possibility"; that economic conditions range from subsistence farming to agricultural and commercial affluence; that the allegedly unifying Spanish language is neither the language of the tens of millions of Portuguese-speaking Brazilians nor of millions in the Indian sections of Latin America who "either do not speak Spanish or use it only as a second language"; and that, while most Latin Americans are Roman Catholics, the Catholicism of the masses is nominal and skin deep. Insofar as the difficult environment is concerned, Augelli finds no evidence that it is unconquerable. He makes a convincing argument for dividing the continent into cultural complexes rather than strictly-adhered-to national lines. Teaching children to think in terms of the cultural complexes, he believes, will lead to sounder generalizations than are currently being taught about Latin America.[19]

Suggestions for Teaching

1. In any of the lower grades, probably including Grade 4, present a single country. Have the children study in depth whatever country is chosen

[18] John P. Augelli, "The Controversial Image of Latin America: A Geographer's View," *Journal of Geography*, **62** (March 1963), 103–116.

[19] Augelli. Pp. 104–108. As far as the uniformity of the physical environment is concerned, however, children who have previously studied Anglo-America will realize that there is a greater degree of uniformity in Latin America than in Anglo-America. It should also be added that, although the Latin American environment is not unconquerable, it is certainly a difficult one for man to manage.

(Mexico and Brazil are favorites with many teachers). Deal realistically with how the people live—their work and play, their religious life, their government, their heroes, their national holidays, their physical environment, and how they have utilized their environment. Avoid creating such stereotypes as were cited above. Following the study of one nation, make brief comparisons with two or three other Latin-American countries.

2. In one of the intermediate grades, approach Latin America more thoroughly. With the aid of a wall map and a small map for each pupil, take a look at the all-important highlands of Latin America—in Middle America, the mountain ranges and the Plateau of Mexico; in South America, the Andes, the Guiana Highlands, and the Brazilian Highlands. Identify the dramatic volcano of Mexico, Popocatepetl. Note how the range extending from Mexico to South America undulates—is not really a mountain at all in the area of the Panama Canal. The Andes are the longest mountain range in the world, contain the highest mountains in the Western Hemisphere, and are an obstacle to easy east-west land transportation. The major river systems, the coast lines, the vegetation, and other natural resources would be taken up next. Emphasize the wide diversity of all these natural phenomena throughout Latin America.

3. Follow Augelli's cultural complexes when introducing Latin America in the intermediate grades.[20] As slightly revised in a textbook for the intermediate grades,[21] in consultation with Augelli, the zones are (1) Tropical Plantation Zone; (2) Indian Subsistence Zone; (3) Mestizo Zone; (4) European Commercial Zone; (5) Zone of Little Change.

4. Deal sufficiently with the history of a region so that current problems and progress will be comprehensible. For example, the situation in Brazil of vast open spaces devoid of settlement juxtaposed with crowded cities, the lack of adequate food for many, and the need to import food can be understood only superficially without delving into Brazil's past. Begin with the early Portuguese settlements, the practice of reliance upon single products (successively, sugar, gold, rubber, and coffee) for varying periods of time, and the eventual disastrous results of this practice; then deal with the more recent diversification of industry and agriculture and the introduction of scientific land management.

5. Make use of the exceptional opportunity offered by a study of Latin America to dramatize the fact that climate is produced by a combination of factors, not by a single factor. For example, the South American countries on the Pacific Ocean (except for the southern part of Chile) are within the tropics; yet the air temperatures from northern Chile northward prac-

[20] Augelli. Pp. 110–112.

[21] Ralph C. Preston and John Tottle, in *Latin American Lands.* Boston: Heath, 1966. Chap. 6. These culture zones are described in the first chapter of the unit on the geography of Latin America. The subsequent chapters are organized in terms of groups of related countries.

tically to the equator are about ten degrees cooler than "typical" tropical temperatures. Why? Have your pupils check the altitude along the western South American coast, and compare it with information they have from other sources about high-altitude temperatures. Also, have them read about the cold Peru Currents off the coast of Chile and Peru, caused by its pole-ward origins and by the rising of cold water from the ocean's depths, which, in turn, cools the air along the coast.

6. Bring out how the formidable topography and vegetation of much of Latin America makes transportation difficult. The building of highways and railroads is costly. Can your pupils see how this fact may have prevented a more widely distributed population and greater exploration of Latin-America's mineral possibilities? In this connection, it is worth getting information about the airways, which now promise to offset, in part, the difficulties of establishing long-distance ground transportation. In addition to the need for better transportation to develop the unsettled areas, a pioneering psychology is necessary. This was the hope of the Brazilian government in building the new city, Brasilia, for its capital. Located 500 miles from the coast, it would, the government believed, dramatize un-developed Brazil, and would lead people to look to the west and to "think" west.

7. Your pupils should understand the problems of Latin America stem-ming from lopsided land ownership, high birth rate, and poverty; and why there is a need for foreign aid. On the other hand, avoid having your pupils regard Latin America as a bundle of problems; remind them of its solid achievements. The metropolitan area of São Paulo has over 36,000 manu-facturing establishments. Millions of tons of steel a year are produced. Successful shipbuilding and auto industries are in operation. Rio de Janeiro is one of the world's handsomest cities (but also contains some of the world's worst slums—*favelas*). Illustrate how the nations of Latin America are striving to build economic systems which will bring about a higher standard of living.

8. Help your pupils draw useful generalizations about national bound-aries. What difficulties face Bolivia by its being landlocked? To be so near the sea without a seacoast—could this produce friction with her neighbors? The series of boundary disputes can also be profitably explored, with emphasis upon the good example often set in settling them by peaceful means. (For example, the Colombia-Peru dispute of 1932, which was settled by the League of Nations; the Ecuador-Peru dispute of 1941, settled at the Rio de Janeiro Conference of Foreign Ministers; and the Chile-Argentina dispute, arbitrated by Edward VII of England in 1900. The point at issue in the latter dispute over the discrepancy between the main crest of the Andes and the water divide is worth discussing with your class. Have some of the pupils, with clay models, demonstrate how a point of water divide may not be on the line connecting the highest peaks.)

Some Teaching Materials: Latin America

Books for Children

Faraday, Margaret, *The Young Traveler in South America*. New York: Dutton, 1957.

Goetz, Delia, *Neighbors to the South*. New York: Harcourt, 1956.

Peck, Anne, *Young Mexico*. New York: Dodd, Mead, 1956.

Preston, Ralph C., *et al.*, *Four Lands, Four Peoples*. Boston: Heath, 1966. Unit V, "Brazil, Nation in the New World." Grades 3–5.

Preston, Ralph C., and John Tottle, *In Latin American Lands*. Boston: Heath, 1966.

Quinn, Vernon, *Picture Map Geography of Mexico, Central America and the West Indies*. Philadelphia: Lippincott, 1943.

Teaching Tips

Kenworthy, Leonard S., *Studying South America in Elementary and Secondary Schools*. New York: Teachers College, 1965.

Kit of Materials on Mexico. Washington, D.C.: Mexican Embassy, 1962. Folders, leaflets, maps, fact sheets.

EUROPE

Europe comprises little more area than the United States. Yet, its more than 19 languages, accompanied by other distinctive cultural idiosyncracies, have contributed to political fragmentation, nationalism, and cleavages. These factors have played a major role in West European politics and international relationships, sometimes with world-wide repercussions.

Europe's economy is varied, ranging from its industrial centers such as those of England, France, Belgium, The Netherlands, and Germany, where a relatively high standard of living is maintained, to the rural areas of the south, where the standard of living is low.

Europe's geographic importance arises from its generally favorable climate for work, the diversity and richness of its resources, and a long period of "ageing." Europe took the lead in science and technology and in ushering in the machine age, with the resultant benefits (and problems!) of modern civilization.

Suggestions for Teaching

1. In one of the lower grades, have the unit concentrate upon one country which maintains a democratic society, which has achieved success in both manufacturing and agriculture, which conspicuously illustrates man-environment interrelationships, and which has sufficient structural simplicity to enable the child to grasp its totality. Switzerland comes close to meeting these criteria and is a common choice. In addition to Switzerland, The

Netherlands would be almost as good to work with. Switzerland has more internal areal variation than The Netherlands, however, and provides, therefore, a better lesson in geography.

No country more forcefully indicates the compatibility of unity and diversity. Here is a land where the citizens lack a common language— French, German, Italian, and Romansh all being spoken; where they lack a common religion, being divided between Protestants and Catholics; where they lack common interests and occupations, some being shepherds, others industrial executives; some farmers, others scientists. These people—almost five million of them—with all their differences, are squeezed together between mountains in a tiny area which is half the size of Maine, and one quarter of which is unproductive. We should direct children's attention to discovering how the Swiss have managed their society so that it runs smoothly. How is it that diversity, a troublemaker in most countries, has not prevented the achievement of Swiss unity?

American children, accustomed to having a "head man" in governmental as well as in private organizations, are sometimes mystified by the structure of the Swiss republic. At the head of each agency is a group of men rather than one man. There is a President, but he is merely temporary chairman of the Federal Council, which consists of seven members. He is not prominent in the public eye, occupies no executive mansion, and after one year is succeeded by another council member. A government operated on a cooperative basis, freed from the domination of offices that grant power and prestige, may be an important factor in the unified character of modern Switzerland.

The unit should be realistic, so that children will not be left with the idea that Switzerland is or has been a Utopia. Its present unified state did not always exist. Its history of warfare until 1515, the bitter internal struggles continuing into the nineteenth century, and its conquest by France should be reviewed. This content should help establish for children the gradualness and difficulty of progress. The present harmony of the Swiss federated state will be better appreciated when viewed against the background of struggle. Children should also understand that a stable federated state does not ensure democracy for all. Women still are not permitted to vote in Switzerland. The country also has stringent regulations governing the lives of workers from other countries. While a government can help a country to run smoothly, smooth-running is not to be confused with functioning for the welfare of everyone.

2. For older children, teach Europe as a single unit. Organize it into subregions and "post-hole" each subregion. One possible division is as follows: (a) Western Europe (United Kingdom, Ireland, most of France, Germany, Benelux countries, Switzerland, Austria); (b) Mediterranean Europe (Portugal, Spain, Italy, Greece; (c) Fenno-Scandia (Sweden, Norway, Denmark, Finland, Iceland).

3. When dealing with a subregion, emphasize the factors which unite it. The Fenno-Scandic countries, for example, occupy a section of the earth which is located in latitudes well north of the bulk of the world's inhabitants; the subregion is influenced by the warm North Atlantic drift as it warms the winter air moving onshore and thus has a moderating effect upon the climate of the western coasts; with notable exceptions, its land is rugged and its soils mediocre; there is homogeneity of religious belief; the nations have had singular success with democratic government and international relations; they maintain a balance between free enterprise and "welfare state" practices, avoiding extremes.

4. Be sure to avoid overemphasizing the unity of the subregions; each country has distinctive individuality. It is desirable to have your pupils read widely on individual countries—stories of travel, descriptive accounts, native children's literature—to bring out individual characteristics.

5. Here is an opportunity to see how well pupils can apply and clinch principles of climate which they have probably learned previously. Can they explain, for example, the year-long open harbors of the Norwegian Atlantic coast in terms of the North Atlantic drift; and the moderating effect upon European climate of the ocean and seas which indent the circumference of Europe in many places?

6. Present information about the European Economic Community (the Common Market). Discuss its advantages (a free flow of goods between member nations such as exists between the states of the United States), ways in which it would be to the advantage of European nations to become

---

Some Teaching Materials: Western Europe

Books for Children
Berner, E. R., *Germany*. New York: Holiday, 1951.
Clement, Marguerite, *In France*. New York: Viking, 1956.
DeJong, Dola, *Picture Story of Holland*. New York: McKay, 1946.
Lauber, Patricia, *Getting to Know Switzerland*. New York: Coward-McCann, 1960.
Portraits of the Nations Series. Philadelphia: Lippincott. Titles include "The Land and People of Austria," and ". . . of Belgium," ". . . of Finland," ". . . of France," ". . . of Germany," ". . . of Greece," ". . . of Iceland," ". . . of Switzerland."
Preston, Ralph C., *et al.*, *Four Lands, Four Peoples*. Unit III, "Switzerland, Land of Mountains." Boston: Heath, 1966.
Toor, Frances, *Made in Italy*. New York: Knopf, 1957.

For the Teacher
Prittie, Terence, *et al.*, *Germany*. New York: Time, 1961.

a union of states, conditions which make it more difficult than it was for the 13 American colonies in 1776 to form a union (differences in language, political aspirations, age-old habits of independence, deep-seated mutual suspicions, entrenched customs, and nationalistic prejudices).

AFRICA

This section follows the common practice of today of focusing the study of Africa upon that portion of the continent south of the Arab-speaking countries of North Africa. The latter are included among the countries of the Middle East.

For many years, African cultural development was retarded, first by its lack of contact with the outside world, then by its dependent, colonial status. Although Africa is still referred to as the "Dark Continent" and as "underdeveloped," it has rapidly attained political consciousness and a strong desire for independence. Since the Second World War, it has largely emerged from a collection of colonial possessions to a dynamic group of nearly forty independent countries, promising, at this writing, to grow in numbers still further. The new countries are not only struggling for stable governments and economic progress for themselves, but they are contributing support to freedom movements in the remaining colonial territories as well. Talk of freedom is stirring the entire African continent.

The problems of the new African states start with poverty and illiteracy. They are being helped to solve both problems by outside governments on both sides of the Iron Curtain. The United States, for example, has sent large amounts of food for famine relief, funds to support native African programs for roads, railroads, and power, advisory services to African farmers, and technicians of all sorts to aid in developing a machine industry. Recognizing the importance of education, the United States has given aid to African educational systems, and Africans have been brought to the United States for technical training.

The continent is so large physically and so varied in terms of resources, language, persisting influences of the several colonial powers of the past, and other factors, that it is difficult for children to grasp its unity, on the one hand, and its complexity on the other. One thing is certain: the school curriculum can no longer neglect Africa.

Suggestions for Teaching

1. In the early grades, try a single unit on one of the older independent African countries. Liberia, relatively small and with an important historical link to the United States, is an interesting possibility. Liberia is roughly divided into three geographical divisions: a coastal area, a plateau of grassland and forest, and low mountains. It has a republican form of govern-

ment. The original settlers, who had been slaves in the United States, were, beginning in 1820, sent by a private group of Americans to the African land which the group had purchased. The bulk of Liberians, however, are not descended from these coastal settlers, but are members of tribes inhabiting the interior of Liberia. The official language is English. As yet, printed matter on Liberia for American teachers and their pupils is scarce. Teachers may write for suggested study material to the Department of Information and Cultural Affairs, Monrovia, Republic of Liberia.

2. For older children, divide Africa into a few sections, or perhaps only two—the emerging nations (such as Nigeria and Ghana) and the older nations (such as Liberia and the Union of South Africa). There are, of course, other bases of organization (Mediterranean Africa, tropical Africa, and South Africa). Mediterranean Africa—the upper tier of countries on the continent of Africa—may be included in the unit when considering the physical aspects of Africa. Culturally, however, they belong to the Arab world, and as such, would be studied as part of the Middle East as well.

3. Raise the question of why non-Africans were so slow in exploring the continent and why trade was so late in developing. Have your pupils study the coast line and compare it with the coast lines of Europe, Asia, and the Americas, noting Africa's relative regularity, almost completely lacking in good natural harbors. A physical map will reveal the generally narrow coastal plane and the extensive Sahara Desert which cuts off the Mediterranean countries of Europe from Africa's interior. Photographs and written accounts of some of the great rivers will show the falls and rapids which render the rivers unnavigable.[22] Review the period before the building of the Suez Canal when ships would take the long detour to India around the bulky continent of Africa, noting how the early explorers neglected, for the most part, the inhospitable-looking continent (see Figure 10.3).

4. Emphasize that here is one continent whose climate corresponds rather neatly to the latitude zone (especially in comparison to South Africa). Except in east equatorial Africa, there are no highlands of sufficient altitude to offset significantly the effect of distance from the equator. Africa is rimmed north and south with areas enjoying the typical Mediterranean climate. Then come strips of desert, caused by the two corresponding belts of trade winds. Between these is the large tropical rain forest.

5. Include in the unit information about the varied races and religions on the continent. In addition to the Negroes, there are Arabs and other Semites, the Bushmen and Hottentots (mixtures of Mongolian, Negritoes, and Mediterranean), and even Nordic types in the Atlas mountains.[23]

---

[22] Ralph C. Preston, Caroline Emerson, et al., Four Lands, Four Peoples. Pp. 63–70. This feature is brought out vividly in the designated pages, where an account is given of Stanley's adventurous exploration of the Lualaba-Congo River sytem.

[23] G. Etzel Pearcy, et al., World Political Geography. New York: Crowell, 1948. P. 395.

Some Teaching Materials: Africa

Books for Children

Horrabin, J. F., *An Atlas of Africa* (Rev. Ed.). New York: Praeger, 1961.
50 excellent maps. (Text not designed for children.)

Kaye, Geraldine, *Great Day in Ghana*. New York: Abelard-Schuman,
1962.

Perkins, Carol and Marlin, *I Saw You from Afar*. New York: Atheneum,
1965.

Quinn, Vernon, *Picture Map Geography of Africa*. Philadelphia: Lippincott, 1952.

Sutherland, Efua, *Playtime in Africa*. New York: Atheneum, 1962. (Ghana.)

Wattenberg, Ben, and Ralph Lee Smith, *The New Nations of Africa*. New
York: Hart, 1963.

Film

This Is Nigeria. New York: Contemporary Films, 1959.

Periodical

Africa Report. African-American Institute, 345 East 46th Street, New
York. Monthly.

6. The stunning landscape and the appealing human beings (and their
attitudes and feelings) are subjects which should be developed through
films, pictures in *National Geographic Magazine*, and selections from the
writings of Albert Schweitzer, Alan Paton, and others. It is all too easy for
a geographic study to be so detached as to appear unreal. When your pupils
study Rhodesia, for example, supply the detail which will enable, at least
the more sensitive ones, to picture it as a beautiful and spacious country,
with clear, dry air resembling that of our own Rocky Mountains.

THE MIDDLE EAST

The Middle East, as defined here, includes northern Africa and
southern Asia, from Turkey to West Pakistan. The peoples of this region
are predominantly Moslems. The area of the Middle East is predominantly
desert, forcing most of the people to live on oases. But to say that over-
simplifies matters. The region is highly diversified culturally (for example,
the language and literature of the North African countries are Arabic; those
of the Turks are Turkish; those of the Pakistani are Urdu, an Indic tongue).
Most of the Middle East is Moslem, but Israel is Jewish. Although the
Middle East is well known for its forbidding deserts, it also contains important agricultural areas, most of which border on the Mediterranean Sea with
some exceptions such as the historically significant "fertile crescent" in Iraq
and larges oases such as that created by the Nile.

Suggestions for Teaching

1. Introduce Egypt in one of the earlier grades as a representative country, emphasizing village life, the important role of the Nile in its history and agriculture, Cairo as a trade center, Egypt's cotton crop and its growing cotton manufacture, its petroleum production, its iron mining and infant steel manufacturing industry, and ancient Egypt's creative achievements such as the use of copper, its system of writing, papyrus paper, and the calendar.

2. In the upper grades, teach the Middle East as a unit. In passing, it should be noted that many teachers like to include North Africa in a unit on Africa when considering the physical integrity of the continent of Africa, as well as to deal with it when taking up the Middle East.

3. Prevent formation of the common stereotype of the Middle East as merely desert by showing pictures of forests, farms, oil wells, and cities. Obtain or construct a map which shows symbolically the distribution of forest, arable land, oil resources, steppe, and desert.

4. Emphasize the central importance of irrigation in the vast desert areas for raising the region's standard of living. Your pupils should learn what has been done so far—what is being planned in the building of dams on the Indus, Karun, Nile, and other rivers for irrigation, land reclamation, and electric power. Irrigation is particularly important because three-fourths of the population are farmers, most of them subsistence farmers. Egypt is a good illustration of a country in need of irrigation. Have your pupils document this need (its population is crowded and rapidly mounting along the banks of the Nile, and the acreage of productive land remains restricted). The High Dam in Egypt offers an illustration of the sacrifice of one value for the sake of giving priority to another. For, the rising water at the dam will cover, probably forever, many of the ancient and irreplaceable tombs and temples of interest and beauty along the Nile. Your pupils should know how organizations throughout the world have helped to dismantle, move, and reassemble some of these treasures, at great expense and effort, in order to preserve them in a safe place.

5. Your pupils should look into the extent of the rich petroleum deposits in the Middle East, the effect their presence has had in stimulating foreign investment and efforts of foreign governments to improve economic and political ties with governments of the region, and the ultimate effect this wealth will have on the region's prosperity. Petroleum is just about the only mineral deposit of consequence in the area. It has the unfortunate effect of inhibiting the growth of other industry in the Middle East. Furthermore, the petroleum industry is vulnerable to the discovery of new deposits nearer to the world's major markets.

6. Do not let your pupils conclude that the desert is simply wasteland. Aside from acquainting them with its mineral deposits, have them investi-

gate details of desert ecology and read samples of the writings of those who have found interest and beauty in desert life.[24]

7. Your pupils will discover that much of the Middle East is a politically troubled, unsettled area. To help them understand the turmoil and unpredictability, underscore (a) the prevalence of poverty among the masses and the concentration of land in the hands of a few—facts which are related to the limited resource base of the area and the structure of society; and (b) the important and historically well known crossroads character of the central area of the Middle East, how it is a sort of span between Europe, Asia, and Africa, and how armies and traders have found it a convenient one to cross in their intercontinental movements. The building of the Suez Canal a hundred years ago increased its strategic importance, and the discovery of its vast petroleum resources resulted in competition among outside nations for influence and control. The consequence of these conditions and pressures, over many years, has been a unique social and political climate.

Some Teaching Materials: Middle East

Books for Children
Copeland, Frances, *Land Between: The Middle East.* New York: Abelard-Schuman, 1958.
Gunther, John, *et al., Meet North Africa.* New York: Harper & Row, 1957.
Holding, James, *The King's Contest.* New York: Abelard-Schuman, 1964.
Joy, Charles, *Island in the Desert: The Challenge of the Nile.* New York: Coward-McCann, 1959.
Portraits of the Nations series. Philadelphia: Lippincott. Titles include "The Land and People of Egypt," and ". . . of Turkey," ". . . of Israel."
Preston, Ralph C., *et al., Four Lands, Four Peoples.* Boston: Heath, 1966. Unit II, "Egypt, Land of One River."
Steintorf, Louise, *Children of North Africa.* Philadelphia: Lippincott, 1943.

Filmstrip
I Live in Egypt. New York: Museum Extension Service, 1954.
Living in Egypt and Sudan. Chicago: Society for Visual Education, 1956.

Teaching Ideas
Egypt, the Youngest Republic . . . 6000 Years Old. Washington, D.C.: United Arab Republic Embassy. Pamphlet.
Kenworthy, Leonard S., *Studying the Middle East.* New York: Teachers College Press, 1965.
Kit of Travel Material. Washington, D.C.: United Arab Republic Embassy.

---

[24] A vivid description of the Sahara is given in Philippe Diole, *The Most Beautiful Desert of All.* London: Cape, 1959.

THE SOVIET REALM

A communist culture is being vigorously promoted by the Union of Soviet Socialist Republics among its own people, including those in appropriated countries, such as Estonia, and among the citizens of its satellites, such as Hungary. This culture goes well beyond political considerations, finding expression in literature, architecture, education, agriculture, and other aspects of life. The Soviet leaders are establishing a way of life which contrasts in many ways with that of the Western world. Representative government, one of the West's great innovations, together with associated terms like "democracy," "republic," and "elections," has been applied in the Soviet realm in a way that does not grant to the individual citizen the rights and opportunities which Westerners take for granted. Although the Chinese-sponsored communist world has much in common with the Soviet realm, a distinction must be made between the two Communist blocs. They differ not simply in matters of strategy, but, at least equally, in fundamental traditions and geographical relationships.

The Soviet realm is largely Slavic in language and culture. The population of its five predominantly Slavic countries is approximately four times that of its non-Slavic countries. The largest of the Slavic countries is the U.S.S.R., comprising 15 Republics, 12 of which represent non-Slavic languages and cultures, yet the total population of the latter constitutes a distinct minority.

Suggestions for Teaching

1. In any of the lower grades, have the unit concentrate upon one of the nations which is relatively homogeneous in its composition, such as Poland. This country is a good selection, in part because of the freedom-loving nature of the Poles, which has led to such singular events as the famous uprising of impoverished factory workers in Poznan in 1955, the Poles' effective protest against the workers' trial, their success in getting Russian troops withdrawn, and the like. The architecture and arts of Poland, including handcrafts and painting, are probably more representative of Polish culture than its present political regime, but both should be presented—the beauty of the former as well as the harshness of the latter.

2. Help your pupils evaluate the physical resource base of the U.S.S.R. For example: (a) The Soviet Union is three times larger than the United States, but most of it is either too cold, too dry, too rough, or too poorly drained to be used effectively by man. (b) The Soviet Union has a wealth of mineral resources but those that complement one another are separated by great distances or are far from the factories that use them. (c) In the southwestern part of the U.S.S.R. there are excellent soils, but the growing season is either too short or rainfall is too small to get maximum production.

(d) The Soviet Union is a very important agricultural nation, but it has serious agricultural problems because of its climates and agricultural systems.

3. In the upper grades, the entire realm should be studied, with post-holing in the U.S.S.R. This is not a simple task because of the many nations which form the country and because of the diversity of climates and resources extending from the Arctic Circle to the subtropics.

4. The political doctrine of the communists should be openly examined and critically appraised. See Chapter 8, where teaching about communism is discussed. Advances in social welfare and education should be readily acknowledged, but it should be made clear that these advances are the fruits of sensible public policy, not political philosophy.

5. The polyglot nature of the Soviet Union should be surveyed and the hypothesis offered that one source of internal support in the early period of the U.S.S.R. lay in its toleration, even encouragement, of the traditional languages and customs of the Armenians, Georgians, and other national groups in the U.S.S.R. The demarcation of the land into mountains, steppes, and deserts tends to make considerable separatism a natural condition. On the other hand, the government subsequently attempted to Slavicize the nation, and many Slavs have moved into non-Slavic republics, particularly in the cities. In Kazakh, for example, over half the population is now Slavic.[25]

6. Dig sufficiently into the history of the Soviet Union to develop an understanding of how it was able to revolutionize Russian society, establish communism, and continue as a strong power. Acquaint your pupils with the feudal Czarist regime, which was out of step with Russia's needs and

---

Some Teaching Materials: The Soviet Realm

Books for Children
Gronowicz, Antoni, *Piasts of Poland*. New York: Scribner, 1945.
Portraits of the Nations series. Philadelphia: Lippincott. Titles include "The Land of the Polish People" and ". . . of the Russian People."
Shapovalov, Michael, and W. B. Walsh, *Let's Read about Russia*. Grand Rapids, Mich.: Fideler, 1950.
Slesser, Malcolm, *Red Peak*. New York: Putnam, 1964.
Vandivert, Rita, *Young Russia: Children of the U.S.S.R. at Work and at Play*. New York: Dodd, Mead, 1960.

Film
Soviet Union: The Land and the People. Chicago: Coronet Instructional Films, 1956.

---

[25] Paul E. Lydolph, *Geography of the U.S.S.R*. New York: Wiley, 1964.

with the twentieth century; how, after the Revolution, the peasants resisted communization of their farms, forcing a compromise; and how, subsequently, there has been some reversion to private ownership in industry in a search for increased productivity.

THE ORIENT

We Westerners too readily shrug off our failure to comprehend Oriental ways by quoting the dubious and hackneyed lines: "Oh, East is East, and West is West, and never the twain shall meet." It must be acknowledged that the pattern of political units and cultures in even a single one of its countries, such as India, is so complex as to challenge the skills of a social studies teacher to the utmost. Furthermore, many aspects of Oriental culture are unique and strange to Westerners. Nevertheless, the basic aspirations and drives of Orientals are not unlike those of Westerners, and understanding is a realizable goal.

Suggestions for Teaching

1. In one of the lower grades, select for study a country with a background of political independence, such as Thailand; or a larger, dynamic, industrial country such as Japan; or a country with a variegated culture and economy such as India. Each has its own appeal and value for study by young children.

2. In the upper grades, conduct an intensive study of China, India, and Japan—although if one of these has been studied in depth in a lower grade, it would not need intensive treatment again in these grades. For purposes of comparison, conduct briefer studies of the remaining Oriental countries.

3. Emphasize the factors that are common to the nations of the Orient: they contain much poverty and hunger; most of the inhabitants of the Orient are subsistence farmers and are concentrated on river plains; the region contains very old civilizations, in which creativity has flourished in many branches, from philosophy and religion to art and technology; economically, and in the diets of the people, cereals dominate, and rice is the most important and dominant; the nations share a colonial background; the indigenous Oriental religions emphasize contemplation.

4. As your pupils investigate the region, call their attention to the fact that no single physical feature dominates (as in the case of the Middle East, dominated by the desert). Yet one physical factor, the monsoon, exerts a pervasive influence. In summer, the monsoon is in the form of warm, humid air moving from the ocean northerly and northeastwardly over India, Indo-China, and China, permitting abundant rainfall. In winter, the monsoon circulation is outward from deep in Asia toward the ocean, resulting in clear, dry weather over the land. Your pupils should understand

the convectional nature of the monsoons: In summer the land warms up more rapidly than the ocean, and the atmospheric pressure is, hence, lower. The pressure differential between the moist ocean and the heart of Asia results in the summer monsoon. In winter, the heating and pressure conditions are reversed.

Another fact about the physical environment is that the Orient has a higher percentage of rough land than does the West. The plains are usually small and of alluvial origin. There are no large plains of structural origin such as the North European plain.

5. Devote time to exploring Oriental contributions to the civilized world —silk, tea, porcelain, paper, printing, lacquer, kites, and a score of other items.[26]

6. Show pictures of the Orient's temples, pagodas, palaces, and gardens; prints of their paintings and Japanese color prints; and read a few of their folk tales. These will help transmit the elegance and uniqueness of Oriental artistic expression.

7. Because these lands cannot be understood without some knowledge of their civilizations' long history, have some of your pupils read about and report on their readings to the rest of the class.[27]

8. Chinese communism should be studied candidly and not concealed under the romantic aspects of traditional China.[28] It is a fact of life that the communist nations hold values at variance with those of the Western democracies. Discuss with your pupils how civilization takes a step backward when religious and political freedom are denied, together with the right of individuals to think and speak freely and to work creatively, without fear of being deprived of livelihood or freedom. A study of Chinese history and philosophy will reveal that the Chinese people are not inherently evil, that they have produced noble works and deeds, and that these are grounds for believing in their ultimate return to a freer society.

THE PACIFIC

The Pacific region includes Australia, New Zealand, and the South Sea Islands. Australia and New Zealand are tied culturally to European

[26] See Derk Bodde, *China's Gifts to the West*. Washington, D.C.: American Council on Education, 1942; Cornelia Spencer, *Made in China*. New York: Knopf, 1952.

[27] See Elizabeth Seeger, *Pageant of Chinese History* (4th ed.). New York: McKay, 1962; Cornelia Spencer, *Ancient China*. New York: Day, 1964; Howard E. Wilson, *et al.*, *Out of the Past*. New York: American Book, 1950. Chap. 13, "Chinese Civilization."

[28] The teacher will need to read, select, and present material to the class. Pertinent information will be found in Robert Loh, *Escape from Red China*. London: Michael Joseph, 1963; Tibor Mende, *China and Her Shadow*, New York: Coward-McCann, 1960; and Audrey R. Topping, "Through Darkest Red China," *New York Times Magazine* (August 28, 1966), 26–27, 89–90, 92. Consult the *Readers' Guide to Periodical Literature* for strictly current reports.

civilization, but due to differences in climate, topography, and isolated location, they have developed social and economic patterns peculiar unto themselves.

It is recommended that study of these sturdy outposts of the British Commonwealth, and the South Sea Islands, be studied in one of the intermediate grades.

Suggestions for Teaching

1. Organize the region in five parts: Australia, New Zealand, Melanesia, Micronesia, and Polynesia. Concentrate on Australia, and make a brief survey of the other Pacific islands at the conclusion of the unit.

2. Your pupils can observe the relative isolation of Australia by holding a globe in their hands, turning it until they look directly at Australia, and noticing the immense expanse of ocean surrounding it and separating it from other continents. This isolation is one reason that it was not discovered until 1606, not actually seen by white man until 1642, still not settled when Captain Cook made his voyage in 1769, and its center not reached until 1860. Although it should be made clear that Australia's barrenness and scarcity of good harbors have played their part in delaying settlement, it must still be noted that southeastern Australia offers a pleasant climate and that some adequate harbors do exist. A time line plotting the important discoveries and settlements will make graphic how casually Australia was regarded and how unalluring it must have appeared. Selected accounts of discovery will add to the significance of this part of the unit.[29]

Emphasize the effect of isolation on the civilization of the aborigines. Reference reading concerning the weapons (such as the famous boomerang) and utensils and techniques of the aborigine will reveal the remains of a Stone Age culture. Yet, despite the fact that the Australoids have retreated for the most part to the isolated, unfertile northwest, even they have not escaped the influence of outside civilization. An outstanding authority on Australia writes that he "has travelled very widely in Australia and has never seen absolutely primitive aborigines."[30] Mankind's dreams of isolation and seclusion do indeed seem doomed. However, the effect of isolation upon plant and animal life is striking. Reading material and pictures should be secured to show the abundance of primitive forms of wildlife and to point up other effects of isolation.[31]

Study of contemporary Australia will effectively dispel any lingering beliefs that its geographical isolation, its comparatively smooth, inhospitable

[29] See Thomas K. Butcher, *Great Explorations: Asia and Australasia.* Toronto: Saunders, 1955; and T. M. Perry, *Australia's First Frontier.* New York: Cambridge University Press, 1963.

[30] Griffith Taylor, Australia. New York: Dutton, 1943. P. 426.

[31] See film, *Aussie Oddities*, on loan from Australian News and Information Bureau, 636 Fifth Avenue, New York, N.Y.

coast line, and its aridity still keep it insulated from the outside world. Publications of the Australian News and Information Bureau, New York, N. Y., offer evidence that innovations of the West have entered in the form of modern cities with their traffic, subways, and tall buildings; sports familiar to Americans such as tennis; and up-to-date schools, hospitals, and other community institutions.

3. Obtain or make a map of Australia, showing the distribution of population. This will reveal the mass of Australians to be concentrated along the eastern, southeastern, and southwestern shores. It will show that people avoid settling in those areas known as "empty Australia," which constitutes three-fourths of the continent and contains much adequate pastoral land, but which is, nevertheless, largely tropical, arid, or desert in character. A vivid description of this hot, barren country can be found in the thrilling accounts of Sturt and other explorers of Australia's interior.[32] Consider also what the potential development of "empty Australia" may be when advances are made in the desalting of sea water.

4. On an outline map of the world, have your pupils shade Australia's barren interior; then, have them shade other tropical deserts such as the Sahara, Kalahari, and Atacama. They should note the comparative similarity in the position of these deserts with respect to the equator. All these areas are dry for the same reason; namely, they are dominated by semipermanent subtropical high pressure cells—centers of descending dry air. If your pupils have studied a unit on weather, climate, or meteorology, this phenomenon can be tied into their understanding of the world's circulation system. Discuss with your pupils, while their maps are before them, a secondary factor in Australia's aridity, the absence of any large indentation of sea, such as the Gulf of Mexico in the United States.

5. Make a brief study of the history of Australian settlements. Among other values, it will clear up the persistent misconception that the old families of Australia are descendants of hardened convicts. It is necessary to know how severe some of the laws of eighteenth-century England were to realize that relatively slight offenses could make one a convict. With America no longer an outlet for convicts after the Revolutionary War, Australia became a logical point to ship these outcasts.

FOR REVIEW AND REFLECTION

1. Define the terms "culture," "state," "country," "nation," and "society."
2. How can a unit on one's country be taught so that children will develop feelings of appreciation and loyalty, as well as factual knowledge?
3. Select five diverse regions of the world and show how the environment of each has influenced the way of life of its inhabitants.

[32] Butcher, *Great Explorations*; and C. Manning Clark, *Short History of Australia*. New York: New American Library, 1963.

4. What concepts can be effectively taught through a unit on an isolated region?
5. What experiences, aside from formal study, will contribute to a child's sympathetic understanding of another culture?

ASSIGNMENTS

1. Ask a group of children (or a single child) for facts about a region recently studied. Note any misleading stereotypes which may have been formed, and consider how they might be corrected.
2. Select a little-known and remote society, and search a library or bookstore for children's books dealing with it. Write a critical review of what you consider to be the best of these books.
3. Have the class construct a simple interview test for primary grades, dealing with foreign regions and cultures. Have each member of the class administer it to one primary-grade child. Pool your results, and draw conclusions regarding the information possessed by primary children. Discuss the educational implications.

SUPPLEMENTARY READING

Geographic School Bulletin. C/o National Geographic Society, Washington, D.C. 20036. Monthly.

Hanna, Paul R. *et al., Geography in the Teaching of Social Studies.* Boston: Houghton Mifflin, 1966. Presents an "expanding environment" program.

Hartshorne, Richard, "Why Study Geography?" *Journal of Geography,* **65** (March 1966), 100–103. Succinctly and lucidly describes the field of geography and its goals.

Journal of Geography. Official organ of the National Council for Geographic Education, 111 W. Washington Street, Chicago, Ill. 60602. Monthly.

Kenworthy, Leonard S., *Introducing Children to the World.* New York: Harper & Row, 1956. Contains teaching suggestions for developing world-mindedness in children.

Kenworthy, Leonard S., *Studying South America; Studying the World; Studying Africa; Studying the Middle East.* New York: Teachers College, 1965. Gives sources of maps, pamphlets, films, books.

Kolevzon, Edward R., and Rubin Maloff, *Vitalizing Geography in the Classroom.* Englewood Cliffs, N.J.: Prentice-Hall, 1964. Written with high school in mind, but contains many ideas equally pertinent to the elementary school.

Lobeck, Armin K., *Things Maps Don't Tell Us.* New York: Crowell-Collier and Macmillan, 1958. Treats the "whys" of shape, location, and the like with illustrative drawings on every page.

Mitchell, Lucy Sprague, *Young Geographers.* New York: Basic Books, 1963. Proposes ways of teaching geography to promote relationship thinking and discovery.

Pearcy, G. Etzel, *et al., World Political Geography* (Rev. ed.). New York: Crowell, 1957. Gives solid information to the adult on the historical, cultural, and geographical backgrounds and potential political roles of all regions of the earth.

Strahler, Arthur N., *Physical Geography* (Rev. ed.). New York: Wiley, 1960. Describes with refreshing thoroughness the principles of physical geography—the earth as a whole, weather, climate, soil, landforms.

Thralls, Zoe A., *The Teaching of Geography*. New York: Appleton, 1958. Presents systematically the elements of geography teaching.

Tooze, Ruth, and Beatrice Perham Krone, *Literature and Music as Resources for Social Studies*. Englewood Cliffs, N.J.: Prentice-Hall, 1955. Refers teacher to folk and other material organized by country and culture.

UNESCO, *Source Book for Geography Teaching*. London: Longmans, 1965. Geographers from four nations offer suggestions for content, techniques, and materials.

Wheeler, Jesse H., Jr., *et al.*, *Regional Geography of the World* (Rev. ed.). New York: Holt, Rinehart and Winston, 1961. A college textbook useful to the teacher for checking facts and for reference.

6

TEACHING HISTORICAL CONCEPTS: UNITS EMPHASIZING THE PAST

Life must be lived forwards, but can only be understood backwards.
SÖREN KIERKEGAARD

The study of history contributes to the child's development in many ways. It gives him perspective—a framework for looking at, and judging, current affairs. It contributes to his maturity by adding another dimension to the impressions he is gradually accumulating about society. When the child learns to think in terms of the past, he possesses a powerful tool for the establishment of sound judgment in assessing the present.

Gustavson makes an excellent analysis of the nature of historical-mindedness.[1] Although he writes with the college freshman in mind, Gustavson describes seven qualities which the teacher of children can appropriately aim to cultivate in the child, if in only primitive form. Briefly, they are (1) sufficient curiosity to be dissatisfied with purely surface phenomena and to wish to get at the underlying causal phenomena; (2) instinctive search for historical parallels or relationships when viewing a contemporary problem; (3) instinctive search for the dynamic forces (class differences, loyalty, and the like) behind events; (4) recognition of the superficiality of one's grasp of a situation unless it is traced back to its beginnings; (5) acceptance of the inevitability of change; (6) ability to brush aside wishful thinking and examine the facts; and (7) recognition of the uniqueness of an event, and restraint from attempting positive prediction of the future.

If a teacher starts off a unit on history with the foregoing attributes as goals, his pupils may be less inclined than adults normally are to develop the dangerous misconceptions which Gustavson explores, such as exaggeration of the effect on history of particular personalities (the Great Man

[1] Carl G. Gustavson, *A Preface to History*. New York: McGraw-Hill, 1955. Chap. 1.

theory), looking for a *single* cause of an event, and making black-white judgments of peoples and issues.[2] It cannot be overemphasized that, in all units embracing history, the teacher should read the foregoing seven characteristics frequently and should make sure that his teaching is really giving the pupils an opportunity to develop them. Once a week, the teacher might have his class think about the connection between the period studied and the contemporary period (in line with item 2). Although we know that

---

Some Basic Generalizations of History[3]

A. Chronology
   1. Space and time form a framework within which all events can be placed.
   2. The times of past occurrences can be identified with varying degrees of precision in terms of dates.
   3. The period of recorded history and of man's struggle for freedom and human dignity has been relatively brief as compared with the total span of man's existence.
   4. Events occur in a sequence, past ones influencing present ones.
B. Bases of History
   1. Changes in society are continually taking place, but not all change is progress.
   2. Human drives and the impulse to discharge basic social functions have remained much the same throughout recorded history.
   3. Man has been motivated in all ages by morals and ideals on the one hand and by material wants and needs on the other.
   4. Many events and periods in history are associated with specific persons, ideas, or institutions.
   5. A limitation upon man in any period of history is the level of technology in his culture.
C. Uses of History
   1. Man can derive principles, ideals, and implications for present citizenship from study of the past.
D. Historical Judgments
   1. The passing of time, and advances in historical scholarship, produce new perspectives and understandings of the past.
   2. History is historians' interpretations of what happened.
   3. The sources of history are varied; they require critical examination and sifting.

---

[2] Gustavson. Pp. v–vi.

[3] These generalizations are, in part, a streamlined version of some of those appearing in *Report of the State Central Committee on Social Studies to the California State Curriculum Commission.* Sacramento: California State Department of Education; 1961 Bernard Berelson, *et al., The Social Studies and the Social Sciences.* New York: Harcourt, 1962; and Henry J. Warman, "Major Concepts in Geography," in Wilhelmina Hill (Ed.), *Curriculum Guide for Geographic Education.* Chicago, Ill.: National Council for Geographic Education, 1964. Chap. 2.

history does not repeat itself (or at least cannot be counted upon so doing) and that it is a poor predictor of the future, origins of a modern situation can be found often in the past, or a useful comparison can be made.

CHILDREN'S TIME CONCEPTS

It stands to reason that the study of history will not have much value for children until they gain some insight into the relationship between past and present. Studies have shown that such insight develops rather late in childhood, and imply that poor chronological sense is at least in part due to slow maturation.[4] The inference has sometimes been drawn that the study of history should, therefore, be postponed until sixth or seventh grade. On the other hand, it is possible that children could grasp time relationships earlier than they do if schools emphasized them from the very beginning— indeed, from kindergarten. Primary teachers who do so report gratifying results.

The abstraction of a yesterday not experienced is an elusive one, even for many an adult. It is known that children who are plunged into the study of history before having become "time conscious" tend to think of an episode of the past as cut off from the present, assuming fairy-tale qualities. They become absorbed in the color and uniqueness of the period—the dress, language, architecture, and quaint ways of living; but they do not see how the lives of these men, women, and children have influenced their own lives, or how certain present-day problems are the old problems in a different setting.

Words alone will not fully convey to children the impact of the past upon the present. This abstraction, the past, must be given flesh, and its relationship to us must be expressed in graphic terms.

Teaching Time Concepts

In the area of time relationships, the elementary school has responsibility for helping children in a fourfold manner: (1) to form an understanding of terms that designate temporal units; (2) to think of an event as part

---

[4] Paul Fraisse, *The Psychology of Time*. New York: Harper & Row, 1963; K. C. Friedman, "The Growth of Time Concepts," *Social Education*, **8** (January, 1944), 29–31; E. C. Oakden and M. Sturt, "Development of the Knowledge of Time in Children," *British Journal of Psychology*, **12** (April 1922), 309–336; F. Pistor, "How Time Concepts Are Acquired by Children," *Educational Method*, **20** (November 1940), 107–112.

That training can promote development of time concepts at least at the sixth-grade level is shown by Val E. Arnsdorf, "An Investigation of the Teaching of Chronology in the Sixth Grade," *Journal of Experimental Education*, **29** (March 1961), 307–313; O. L. Davis, Jr., "Children Can Learn Complex Concepts," *Educational Leadership*, **17** (December 1959), 170–175; and Edith L. Dodds, "A Study of the Sequential Development of Time Sense and Chronology in the Elementary School." Ed.D. dissertation, University of Kansas. *Dissertation Abstracts*, **24** (June 1964), 5075.

of a chronological series of events; (3) to think of the separation of an event from the present in measured units; and (4) to form an understanding of the differences in duration of various historical periods. *The teaching of these concepts should be tied into every unit in which historical content is prominent.*

FORMING AN UNDERSTANDING OF TERMS THAT DESIGNATE TEMPORAL UNITS   Primary-grade teachers can take advantage of daily opportunities to help children build mental images of time units. Children may take turns each morning writing the day's schedule and the day or the date on the chalkboard and marking the weather each day on the calendar. Teachers may consciously use and emphasize conventional symbols and abbreviations, both orally and on the board, that denote hours, days, and other units: A.M., P.M., min., hr., wk., mo., yrs., Mon., d.s.t., Feb., and the like.

In the intermediate grades "generation," "decade," "century," and other temporal terms are encountered. A class can furnish data to illustrate "generation" as follows: Each member supplies the date of his own birth and that of his father and grandfather. All these dates are then arranged along a line, as shown in Figure 6.1, with the average date of birth for each generation prominently marked. Finding the differences between these average dates will reveal that a generation is about thirty-three years and that there are about three generations in a century.

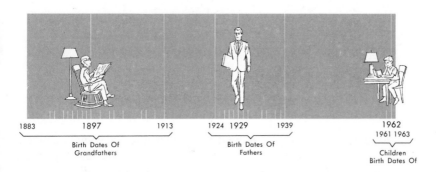

1883	1897	1913	1924 1929	1939	1962
					1961 1963
	Birth Dates Of		Birth Dates Of		
	Grandfathers		Fathers		Children
					Birth Dates Of

Figure 6.1. Time line: the concept of "generation."

THINKING OF AN EVENT AS PART OF A CHRONOLOGICAL SERIES OF EVENTS   Since history is a continuum from ancient times to the present, the correct concept of chronology is an important one. It can be introduced early in the school life of a child. Countless opportunities present themselves in the typical classroom, even in kindergarten. For example, when a caterpillar is brought to school and later enters the chrysalis stage, and eventually, emerges a butterfly, a strip of pictures may be prepared by the teacher to show this sequence of development, giving to each stage a proportional share of the strip. This is one kind of time line. Children usually are stimulated by graphic and systematic reviews of this sort concerning experiences which they are inclined otherwise to recall only in loose fragments. Teachers have found a host of experiences which, when similarly summarized, help the child to grasp the flow of events. Typical time lines for use in the early school years include the following:[5]

1. A series of pictures of children at various stages to show their progression at intervals from birth to their present age (see Figure 6.2),
2. A series of pictures to show the child's daily routine, each picture depicting an event such as eating breakfast or arriving at school,
3. A line drawn along a lengthy stretch of chalkboard, divided to show the weeks and months of the school year and providing the opportunity to enter words or sketches to record significant school events as they occur,
4. Rearrangement of a calendar by clipping it to make the dates of a month run in a continuous horizontal line.

Just Born   One   Two   Three   Four   Five   Six

Figure 6.2. Time line: development of a child, birth to age six.

Later on, time relationships more directly related to the content of social studies will need clarification. Thus, a chronology of certain significant developments in the history of man may be presented as in Figure 6.3.

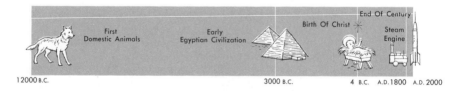

First Domestic Animals   Early Egyptian Civilization   Birth Of Christ   End Of Century   Steam Engine

12000 B.C.   3000 B.C.   4 B.C.   A.D. 1800   A.D. 2000

Figure 6.3. Time line: points in the development of civilization.

[5] Directions for constructing time lines appear in Chapter 12.

Apt verbal descriptions of a relationship often help to make it more apparent that time is all of one piece. The author, when a boy, heard a speaker make the statement that he once met a man who had seen George Washington. As a consequence, for the first time, the father of his country seemed within reach! This seemed incredible and yet brought the formerly remote and unreal great man infinitely nearer, timewise. Rufus Jones implied a similar feeling of closeness to the early days of the country in writing of one of his grandmothers, who ". . . was born just as the Revolutionary War was ending, so that her life and mine together spanned the entire history of the United States."[6] In addition to the verbal approach, however, graphic techniques should be employed. For example, in connection with a study of inventors and inventions, the overlapping of historical figures and generations and their closeness to each other and to contemporary times may be shown in chart form as in Figure 6.4.

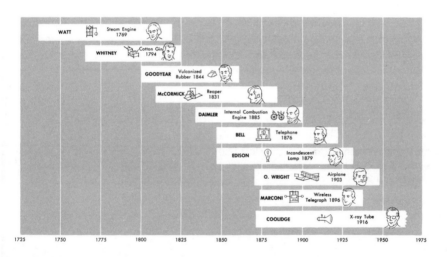

Figure 6.4. Time chart: overlapping life spans of some important inventors.

THINKING OF THE SEPARATION OF AN EVENT FROM THE PRESENT IN MEASURED UNITS   This capacity, too, can grow early in school life. Before a child tells time, clocks with hands appropriately arranged may be drawn in the background of each section of a time line to summarize the order of events in a school day. Cardboard clocks can be used in various ways. For example, just before the class is dismissed for lunch, one second-grade teacher sets the hands of two cardboard clocks at 12 and one respectively,

6 Rufus Jones, *Finding the Trail of Life*. New York: Macmillan, 1927. P. 26.

saying, "We leave for lunch at 12," pointing to the hands of the first clock; "and we come back to the classroom at one," pointing to the hands of the second clock.

Other examples of measured time which the child can learn in elementary school include these: (1) The calendar shows there are 30 days between the beginning and ending of September. (2) Today is Arbor Day—365 days since last Arbor Day. (3) Your little brother was born in 1967— almost 2,000 years since the birth of Christ. If the teacher encourages his pupils to think of the separation of events in measured units, they soon become familiar and convenient devices.

FORMING AN UNDERSTANDING OF THE DIFFERENCES IN DURATION OF VARIOUS HISTORICAL PERIODS When children reach the intermediate grades, they are capable of appreciating some of the vastness of time and the differences in length between various historical periods. Such appreciation, however, is inclined to be inaccurate and vague unless, again, graphic foundations for thinking are provided. Grasp of the concept that recorded history covers a relatively brief period (about 6,000 years) of the estimated total tenure of man upon earth (about one million years) requires tangible representation upon a time line. Contrast of shorter periods, too, requires time lines, such as comparison of the youthfulness of the government of the United States with the maturity of the government of England in point of time. Where very prolonged periods are to be compared with very brief periods, temporary outdoor time lines are often advisable. Points in time may be indicated by driving stakes into the ground or making chalk marks on the pavement. Space can be measured off in steps. For example, a contrast of the period of prehistory with that of history may be illustrated by allowing 167 steps to represent prehistory and one step to represent history (the ratio of 1,000,000 years to 6,000 years).

TEACHING HISTORY AS METHOD

The attributes of historical-mindedness discussed in the opening paragraphs of this chapter are more likely to develop if the subject matter includes the *method* of the historian as well as the *information* which his methods have yielded. The habit of looking reflectively and critically beneath the surface of events can be cultivated through occasional discussions of how historians work—their search for documents and their evaluation of them. Pupils can be given opportunities to collect historical data about their own communities, learning to judge the authenticity of old letters, diaries, newspaper clippings, and other documents. Who are the authors? Is there evidence that they were reliable eyewitnesses? Do they betray a tendency to exaggerate or overdramatize their observations and experiences? Is there evidence that they have prejudices or interests that might lead them to distort the facts?

It is desirable, also, to have children become aware of how historical evidence is turned up by archeological excavation, and how the age of ancient remains (an ancient beam, a piece of cloth, charcoal from an unearthed campfire) can be measured by instruments which measure the radioactive carbon contained in the objects.

Primary Sources

One way to develop in the child an understanding of an important aspect of historical method and also a feeling of intimacy with the past is by providing contact with primary sources—autobiographies, diaries, letters, photographs, newspapers, family stories, oral testimony of eyewitnesses, films, church or court records, tangible remains (tools, clothing, buildings, and so on). Many written reports of eyewitnesses have been copied, compiled, and published as "source books."

Some source books of value to the elementary school teacher in teaching American history are listed below. When teaching units which emphasize the past, teachers may select from these books relevant and interesting portions of eyewitness accounts which effectively convey the flavor of the period under study, and read them to the children. They should be presented to the class as building blocks of history, for such accounts are indeed the foundation of all potentially trustworthy history and the material against which to test the truth of other accounts.

O'Neill, Edward, *A History of American Biography, 1800–1935.* New York: Barnes & Noble, 1961.

Eisenschiml, Otto, and Ralph Newman, *Eyewitness: The Civil War as We Lived It.* New York: Grossett & Dunlap, 1960.

Commager, H. S., and A. Nevins, *The Heritage of America.* Boston: Little, Brown, 1949.

Abbott, E. C., and Helena H. Smith, *We Pointed Them North: Recollections of a Cowpuncher.* Norman, Okla.: University of Oklahoma Press, 1955.

Stefansson, Vilhajalmur, *Great Adventures and Explorations.* New York: Dial, 1947.

Driggs, Howard R., *The Pony Express Goes Through: An American Saga Told by Its Heroes.* Philadelphia: Lippincott, 1936.

Commager, Henry S., *The Blue and the Gray: The Story of the Civil War as Told by Participants.* Indianapolis: Bobbs-Merrill, 1954.

————, *Documents of American History* (7th ed.). New York: Appleton, 1963, 2 vols.

Angle, Paul M. *The American Reader*. Greenwich, Conn.: 1964. 5 vols.
Neider, Charles, *The Great West*. New York: Bonanza, 1958.
Downs, Morton, *Medieval Pageant*. Princeton, N. J.: Van Nostrand, 1964.

A feeling for the lure and excitement in looking for primary sources is
conveyed by Deuel's work listed at the end of the chapter. Portions of it
may be beneficially retold to children.

The significance of primary sources, of course, to the historian, is their
indispensability to history, and their usefulness in filling in missing information or in confirming a hitherto unverified report. The teacher frequently
should encourage children to examine relevant primary sources and to
compare them with a secondary source, such as the textbook or a reference
book. Such a comparison would point up the scientific value of the validated
primary source and the utility of the secondary source.

DEVELOPING INTEREST IN STUDY OF THE PAST

The purposes of studying the past will be achieved only if children's
interest is aroused. History is one of the most disliked of school subjects.
One of the main reasons for this aversion is the emphasis some teachers
place upon memorization of facts, making this an end in itself. Facts are
obviously indispensable in any study. Their memorization should come
about largely as a by-product of gathering and using them. Those few, really
essential, facts that still do not "stick" then can be made automatic through
drill.

The clues to making history attractive are (1) making the objectives
clear and meaningful; (2) providing a variety of learning activities (reading, discussion, trips, drill, dramatics, and so on); (3) emphasizing matters
of personal interest to children, such as accounts of colorful personalities,
home life, schools, details of work, games, folklore, and other details that
create a feeling for the times; (4) emphasizing biography; (5) bringing
history "home" by making connections with the present; and (6) restricting
the scope of a unit to one period in history to avoid overloading so that
through concentration, children may have ample opportunity to discover
how people lived.

Study of the past has a potent role to play in developing sturdy citizenship. The historian Strayer points out that if the pupil's ". . . courses were
well taught he would have acquired a taste for history and a continuing
interest in the problems of society."[7] If a continuing interest is achieved,
he goes on to say, ". . . omissions of certain information in school courses

[7] Joseph R. Strayer, "History," in Bernard Berelson, *et al.*, *The Social Studies and
the Social Sciences*. New York: Harcourt, 1962. Pp. 20–41.

do no harm, for the gap will be filled in later life. If it is not achieved, the most carefully planned selection of facts will be futile."[8]

ASPECTS OF HISTORY TO EMPHASIZE

Many years ago, the Committee on American History in Schools and Colleges expressed the view that the major emphasis of the elementary school in the teaching of American history should be upon cultural history, that is, upon how the people lived.[9] There has been widespread opinion among teachers that this should be the emphasis in other branches of history as well. There can be little doubt that one factor in the lack of interest among children not mentioned in the preceding section is the heavy emphasis in elementary school upon political as opposed to cultural history.

That the emphasis is, indeed, upon political aspects is brought out by an investigation by Guzzetta.[10] He submitted a frequency count of historic persons named in fifth-grade social studies textbooks to a panel of fifteen historians. The historians criticized the absence from the list of representative Americans from the broad spectrum of cultural fields, and its overweighting with political personalities. The list failed to reflect the trends of recent historiography, thus rendering the textbooks deficient in introducing fifth-graders to the cultural and intellectul threads of American history. This is a situation which textbook writers and teachers should seek to correct.

SELECTION OF HISTORICAL PERIODS

The history of man can be only sampled in the elementary school. One approach to sampling would be to select successive periods, beginning with primitive man, and to introduce them chronologically, one by one, throughout the school years. The rationale of such a scheme is that the child will see civilization unfold in proper sequence. The notion is intriguing but unproved, and inconsistent with what is known of the average child's chronological sense. A more plausible scheme would probably observe the principle of relevance during the first few grades, scheduling in the first years such history which attends the holidays and other special days which play a large part in the child's culture, and the history of the Indians' use of the natural features and products of our environment—largely an anthropological study. Thereafter, the child could be taught history chronologi-

[8] Strayer. P. 41.

[9] American Historical Association, *et al.*, *American History in Schools and Colleges.* Committee on American History in Schools and Colleges. New York: Crowell-Collier and Macmillan, 1944.

[10] Charles Guzzetta, "Children's Knowledge of Historically Important Americans," Ed. D. dissertation, Temple University, *Dissertation Abstracts,* **25** (September 1964), 1653–1654.

cally, with greater opportunity for profiting from scanning the orderly development of man and society. This chapter will give suggestions for teaching the following aspects of history:

United States history
Origins of special days
The American Indian
Local and state history
The early explorers
The early American period
The Westward Movement
Ancient civilization
The Middle Ages
Current history

Not all the history a child learns, of course, is acquired from units which are labeled "history." It was made clear in Chapter 5 that a study of a culture region includes material on the historical background. As James points out, "geography cannot be strictly contemporary. All geographic study must be approached historically if it is to be complete."[11]

UNITED STATES HISTORY

Strayer reminds us:

> The schools can never teach everything. . . . Some choice has to be made. . . . One basic rule is clear enough: the student should have more information about his own country and his own age than about remote areas and times.[12]

The primary-grade child is ready to develop concepts about his nation's history, such as the cultural origins of American society, the process of settlement, the Puritan tradition, religious persecution, and religious freedom. One means of supplying them is in connection with the commemoration of national holidays. Many schools plan a unit on the early American Indian in Grade 3 and a unit on state history in Grade 4. When he reaches Grade 5, therefore, and typically begins his first systematic study of the United States, the child should have a foundation of elementary concepts and a familiarity with a few personalities and events.

United States history is taught systematically at three points in most school systems—once in the elementary school (usually in Grade 5), once

---

[11] Preston E. James, "American Geography at Mid-Century," in Preston E. James (Ed.), *New Viewpoints in Geography*; Twenty-ninth Yearbook. Washington, D.C.: National Council for the Social Studies, 1959. Chap. 2, p. 18.

[12] Strayer. Pp. 26–27.

in the junior high school (usually in Grade 7 or 8), and once in the senior high school (usually in Grade 11). Because the offerings at these three levels are often uncoordinated, the pupil at each of the three levels may be presented with practically the same content, presented in approximately the same fashion. This monotonous duplication induces boredom among pupils. It has resulted in a salubrious curriculum examination on the part of teachers, other social studies educators, and curriculum specialists.

The solution does not lie in simply reducing the number of years in which United States history is offered. As Cartwright points out, three years are not excessive when we consider the subject's importance and complexity.[13] Cartwright calls attention to the suggestion of the Committee on American History in Schools and Colleges, formulated in 1944, to the effect, in Cartwright's words:

> . . . that differentiation be achieved through changing emphasis in central theme and in chronology, although all three cycles would give some attention to the whole period of American history. Thus in the middle-grade cycle the emphasis would be on how the people lived, and two-thirds of the time would be allotted to the period before the establishment of the government under Washington. The junior high school cycle would emphasize the growth of a free nation, with two-thirds of the time allotted to the century from 1776 to 1876. The senior high school cycle would emphasize a democratic nation in a world setting, with at least half the time devoted to the period since 1865.[14]

Cartwright continues: "The middle grades might well follow its (the Committee's) recommendations." He believes a more valid division between the two upper cycles, because of the rapid accumulation of events since 1944, would be much later than 1865.[15] Cartwright's analysis of the problem merits the attention of all curriculum workers. His article is the most penetrating, thoughtful, and authoritative evaluation of the problem that has been published in 25 years. If his suggestions on the subject (which are not confined to the organizational problem discussed here) were adopted, the quality of the learning of United States history and pupil interest in the subject would be enormously enhanced.

Origins of Special Days

Commemoration of special days should have a prominent place in the primary grades as a vehicle for deepening loyalties and building appreciation of our cultural heritage. The units should be short, probably not started

[13] William H. Cartwright, "Selection, Organization, Presentation, and Placement of Subject Matter in American History," *Social Education*, **29** (November 1965), 435–463.

[14] Cartwright. P. 36.

[15] Cartwright. Pp. 436–437.

before a week or ten days prior to the date of the celebration and not extending beyond that date. Although important days deserve some recognition in every grade, their use as content for units is considered here as belonging chiefly to the primary grades. Such units should embody the important events, personalities, concepts, and ideals which the day symbolizes.

Suggestions for Teaching

1. Bring out the original meaning of the celebration of a special day. Thanksgiving Day, for example, should be looked upon, not only as the Pilgrims' first harvest celebration, but also, and especially, as the American form of ancient harvest ceremonies. So many of our population today are removed from the actual harvest processes that its significance tends to become obscure. A Thanksgiving unit should, above all else, bring children close to the original religious character of harvest festivals, the importance of the soil, and the hard labor as well as the drama in harvest production.

2. Locate authentic fiction of interest to children about special days. By reading aloud to the class a good story about an approaching commemoration, you can provide a valuable and enjoyable experience. The class may read simple stories and plays and act them out. Realistic material should be used and the usual trite situations avoided. (See the books listed at end of this section.)

3. Give special attention to commonly observed holidays in commemoration of national heroes such as George Washington. A unit centered on a man or woman should include the following:

(a) Authentic accounts of the life either told or read to the class, to bring out his essential character. For example, in a study of Washington, material should be sought which reveals Washington's sense of duty, selflessness, and integrity.

(b) Information about the period. Many of the facts concerning dress, transportation, customs, events, and the like can be conveyed through pictures. Written accounts which vividly transmit the spirit of the times should be located.

(c) Critical examination of legends which have arisen about the person, such as that about George Washington's chopping down of his father's cherry tree. Illustrate how legends grow about most important people; how it is not always easy and sometimes not possible, to separate fact from legend; and how we accept as folklore, not as history, tall tales which have been passed on to us about the historical figure.

4. Do not be too indulgent toward legend when teaching historical concepts. Make a sharp distinction between legend and history. In the opinion

---

Some Teaching Materials: Special Days

Books for Children
Bartlett, Robert M., *Thanksgiving Day*. New York: Crowell, 1965.
Burnett, Bernice, *First Book of Holidays*. New York: F. Watts, 1955.
Dalgliesh, Alice, *The Thanksgiving Story*. New York: Scribner, 1954.
Fisher, Aileen, *Arbor Day*. New York: Crowell, 1965.
Hastings, Evelyn, *All Kinds of Days*. Chicago: Melmont, 1955.
Les Tina, Dorothy, *Flag Day*. New York: Crowell, 1965.
McGovern, Ann, *Why It's a Holiday*. New York: Random House, 1960.
Parlin, John, *Patriots' Days*. Scarsdale, N.Y.: Garrard, 1964.
Showers, Paul, *Columbus Day*. New York: Crowell, 1965.

Film
Special Days in February. Chicago: Coronet Instructional Films, 1953.

Filmstrip
Our Holidays and What They Mean. New York: Filmstrip House. A set of eight strips.

For the Teacher
Holidays . . . 1962. New York: Manufacturers Hanover Trust Co., International Division. Booklet of information on holidays.

---

of A. B. Guthrie, Jr., Pulitzer Prize-winning writer of historical novels, "The little story of George Washington and the cherry tree has muddied history. And they (such stories) seem to me to be almost acts of disrespect, like disfigurements of headstones."[16]

The American Indian

The study of the American Indian affords an opportunity for children to examine environmental features and conditions in this country at an early period and to discover how the aboriginal American adapted to them. By contrasting features and conditions then and now, children learn how man, through the knowledge and techniques of European civilization and in the same environment as that of the Indian, tamed the wilderness.

Suggestions for Teaching

1. In organizing the unit, select several Indian groups representing contrasting environments (often the Woodland, Plains, Pueblo, and Northwest groups) and teach about them consecutively. The Preston-Clymer book

[16] "Fiction with a Hold on History," *New York Times Book Review* (December 3, 1950). P. 1.

listed in the accompanying box follows this approach. Another method of organization is to teach intensively about the tribe which formerly occupied your local area, and later, make brief comparisons with tribes of other groups. This requires that substantial information about the local tribe be at the teacher's disposal.

2. Emphasize that the way of life of a primitive people is shaped largely by its environment, whereas a civilized people modifies the environment in many and sometimes spectacular ways.

3. Include material which shows Indian usages which were taken over by the settlers, some of which are still with us today. Early settlers recognized and adopted Indian place names, with the result that half of our states and many of our largest rivers have Indian names. The Pilgrims' Thanksgiving was inspired by the Indians' ceremony of thanks to the Great Spirit for his gifts of crops and game. Many plants which supply present-day items of food and drugs had been discovered and used similarly by Indians. These include tomatoes, pumpkins, lima beans, maple syrup, strawberries, cocaine, and sassafras. The settlers, moving into an unfamiliar environment (new and strange to them), wisely learned from the natives how to get along in it. They adopted Indian ways of hunting, raising and preparing food, preparing skins, clearing wooded land by ringing trees, making baskets from grass, twigs, and bark, making snowshoes, canoes, moccasins, and of adapting in other ways, too, to their new environment.

4. Avoid the common error in the teaching of Indian units of combining the culture of several Indian groups as though they had been practiced by one tribe. Such units have created the false stereotype of *the* American Indian in the minds of many. The need is to create the concept of a diversity of Indian groups, each conditioned by the type of country it occupied and adapting to it in its own unique way.

5. Plan for the reproduction by your pupils of some of the Indian handcrafts. It will teach them something about the Indian's use of the environment and his adaptation. Thus, if the child were to make a Navajo drum he would cover a pottery jar with skin, whereas if he were to make a Delaware drum, he would construct it from folded dry skin, or by stretching a skin on a hoop. A few projects should be planned to show the steps involved in Indian industrial processes. The Lenapes, for example, ground their grain in logs which they had hollowed out by transferring hot coals from a wood fire to the middle of the log, blowing the coals until they burned out, scraping out the charcoal with a shell or stone scraper, and repeating the process until a sufficient depth was reached.[17] Art teachers and industrial arts specialists in some school districts have assisted classroom teachers in carrying out such enterprises. Some have taken a few pupils into a studio or laboratory, or to a campground, carrying out the processes jointly

[17] M. R. Harrington, *The Indians of New Jersey: Dickon among the Lenapes.* New Brunswick, N.J.: Rutgers University Press, 1963. P. 154.

to a point at which the children understood it and could report to the class. Another group of children, using a regular mortar and pestle to grind up a little acorn or corn flour, will discover the great patience that was required in preindustrial society. Other suggestions will be found in some of the books in the accompanying box listing teaching materials.

6. Lead your pupils to think about the effects of isolation upon a society. Place emphasis upon the Indians' lack of opportunity for centuries to exchange inventions and ideas, except with other Indian tribes, with the result that iron was unknown or, at least, unused when the first white men come

---

Some Teaching Materials: The American Indian

Books for Children

American Heritage, *Indians and the Old West. The Story of the First Americans.* New York: Golden Press, 1958.

Bleeker, Sonia, *The Delaware Indians, Eastern Fishermen and Farmers.* New York: Morrow, 1953.

Dorian, Edith, *Hokahey! American Indians Then and Now.* New York: McGraw-Hill, 1957.

Fletcher, Sydney, *Big Book of Indians.* New York: Grosset & Dunlap, 1950.

Harrington, M. R., *The Indians of New Jersey: Dickon among the Indians.* New Brunswick, N.J.: Rutgers University Press, 1963.

Preston, Ralph C., and Eleanor Clymer, *Communities at Work,* Unit 4, "Indian Communities of Long Ago." Boston: Heath, 1964.

Salomon, Julian Harris, *The Book of Indian Crafts and Indian Lore.* New York: Harper, 1928.

Underhill, Ruth, *Indians of the Pacific Northwest.* Washington: Bureau of Indian Affairs, U.S. Department of the Interior, 1944. Intermediate Grades. (See also, by same author and from same publisher, *The Indians of Southern California, Workaday Life of the Pueblos, Here Come the Navahos,* and other titles.)

Wilson, E. N., and Howard R. Driggs, *The White Indian Boy.* Yonkers, N.Y.: World Book, 1919.

Film

Indian Family of Long Ago. Wilmette, Ill.: Encyclopedia Britannica Films, 1957.

Way of the Navaho. New York: McGraw-Hill, 1956.

Maps

Three Maps of Indian Country. Lawrence, Kansas: Haskell Institute, Public Service, 1962.

Pictures

Blackfeet Indian Portraits. 24 colored portraits. St. Paul, Minn.: St. Paul Book and Stationery Co., 1961.

along, the plow had not been developed, and the wheel as a labor-saving device had not been invented.

7. From time to time, have your pupils make comparisons between impressions of the Indian which they are getting in school, with impressions gained from television and movie "westerns." The study should offset the erroneous concept of the Indian created by the popular representations of mass entertainment media, in which his hostility to the white man and warlike, evil acts are so often given distorted emphasis. The unit should teach about Indian warfare, but it should also show the Indian as a constructive, industrious member of a community who took family and community responsibilities seriously. To this end, teachers and pupils should have access to such books as are listed in the accompanying box of teaching materials.

8. Have your pupils do some reading and engage in discussion about the Indian's being driven back by the white settlers and placed on the reservations where they now are. The following periodicals contain news items about contemporary Indians and will be found useful sources of information concerning their current status.

Indian Progress (Friends on Indian Affairs, Hinsdale, Illinois, 60521)

Indian Truth (Indian Rights Association, 1505 Race Street, Philadelphia, Pa., 19102)

Indian News (Indian Affairs Branch, Department of Citizenship and Immigration, Ottawa)

Local and State History

The chief value of a unit on local history is the opportunity provided for pupils to learn at first hand what is involved in compiling and interpreting historical data. (It must be recognized, of course, that some communities lend themselves better to a study of local history than others.) If the unit is well taught, the pupil will learn the differences between evidence and unsupported hearsay, and he will have experience in judging the authenticity of a document, the validity of an oral report from an eyewitness, the weighing of alternative explanations of an event, and the like. He should end up with greater respect for evidence and a greater liking for recorded history; also, a less naïve attitude toward hearsay and unsupported evidence in print.

Suggestions for Teaching

1. Set your class the task of writing a guide to local history. Its creation should be the main project of the unit. If your class is too immature or if you have too little time for the completion of such a guide book, aim to have your class compile an organized, indexed scrapbook.

The nature of a guidebook may be clarified by the following introduction to one:

> Last year, when we were in fifth grade, we used these maps [of the local township] when we discussed our local history and decided that next year, when we were in sixth grade, we would prepare a historical guide book.
>
> In January of this year we were taken by bus to the historical places in which we were most interested. Several periods were devoted to discussing the trips and deciding upon the subjects which should be included in the book. It was so much easier to decide which places to select because of our visits when we actually saw where the place was located and what its appearance really is now.
>
> Each pupil was allowed to select the topic which most appealed. Some wished to write articles; others wished to make drawings. Those desiring to draw had already made sketches while on the trip or taken photographs which were used as models from which to draw.
>
> Several of the group learned to use the mimeoscope. This is a machine for transferring original drawings and printing onto stencil which is then run through the mimeograph, a machine which many of the boys learned to operate.
>
> We have had fun and learned much while preparing "Our Township's Past". . . .[18]

Another class, in a different community, prepared a similar guide and described the process as follows:

> First we looked in all the history books we could find, to see what they said about our Town. We found some things in these reference books. . . . But actually, we are only a small Town, in a large County, in a large State in the United States. It is understandable, therefore, why we could not find a great deal in books about just how the people of North Salem lived when they first settled our Town, and all the other things we wished to know.
>
> So we started asking questions of our older neighbors whose ancestors came here in the early days. And we became quite excited about the stories they told us. . . .
>
> . . . collecting and writing down the stories printed here has been one of the many interesting things any of us has ever done. . . .[19]

2. Organize the study by topics such as founders and early settlers, architecture, government, business, churches. Have each pupil sign up for work on a committee concerning one of the topics. See what your pupils

---

[18] The author is grateful to William J. Laramy for a copy of the mimeographed report.

[19] Francis Eichner and Helen Ferris Tibbets (Eds.), *When Our Town Was Young.* Purdy Station, N.Y.: Board of Education, Central School District No. 1, 1945. Pp. xii, xviii.

can turn up in the way of heirlooms, old newspapers, letters, photographs, in the discovery of old tombstones with significant inscriptions, and in other ways. While a given pupil is working primarily on one topic, he should be encouraged to report material he comes upon that would help other study groups.

3. Contact older citizens in the community who may be willing to contribute oral accounts of changes they recall. Invite them to the classroom, or arrange for a few pupils to interview them at their homes. Many adults are pleased to have such chances to share their recollections.

4. Reserve a corner of the classroom for a miniature museum in which your pupils can exhibit articles from earlier days—tools, household equipment, and other items.

5. Utilize the historical research that has already been undertaken by others, evidences of which may be in a museum, in books, or memorialized on a roadside historical marker.[20]

6. You will find the foregoing activities applicable to units on the history of the state as well as to units on the local community. State units are also enriched by the materials of state historical societies, visits from invited officials of such societies, Chamber of Commerce brochures, and historical material on the state, written for children.[21]

Early Explorers

The study of the early explorers necessarily encompasses more than the history of the United States. Much of the story took place in Europe and in portions of the Americas outside of the United States. The need to embrace such material becomes evident upon considering the following points:

MOTIVATION OF THE EXPLORATIONS   There were reasons why a new trade route to the East was sought—the routes employed in the 15th century were long and difficult, necessitating loading and unloading as a trip proceeded from sea to land and from land to sea, traveling over poor roads,

---

[20] A class trip to a nearby roadside historical marker can be an opportunity for stimulating the imagination. For example, a sign near Southampton, Pa., marks the place where John Fitch tested his model steamboat in 1785. "What would Street Road have looked like then?" the teacher could ask. "What 'traffic' noises would we have heard? What comments might John Fitch's neighbors have made about the model boat?"

[21] An example of the latter is the periodical, *The Junior Historian*, official publication of the Pennsylvania Federation of Junior Historians, State Museum Building, Harrisburg, Pa. It is written by and for junior and senior high school pupils, but many of its articles are suitable for use with elementary school pupils. Fourteen other states have junior historical organizations, most of which have similar publications. The organizations are usually associated with a state's department of education. The states, in addition to Pennsylvania, which have these organizations, are California, Colorado, Illinois, Indiana, Kentucky, Minnesota, Mississippi, Nebraska, New Jersey, New York, North Carolina, Ohio, Texas, and Wisconsin.

paying tolls, and the like. For Portugal, a leader in the promotion of exploration, religious motives were important. In addition to seeking commercial goals, the Portuguese desired to flank the Moors in Africa and to convert the American Indians to Christianity.

TIMING OF THE EXPLORATIONS   There were reasons why the new explorations were not made in earlier centuries—the quadrant and the square-rigged caravel had not been developed, knowledge of geography was limited, and what geography *was* known did not become widespread because the printing press with movable type had yet to be invented in Europe.

REGIONS EXPLORED   Some of the most significant discoveries, including those of Columbus and Magellan, did not include land now part of one of the 50 states. It would be highly artificial to confine a study of the explorers to those who set foot on the mainland of the United States.

Suggestions for Teaching

1. Post-hole, rather than cover, the explorers. Some teachers take up Spanish explorations and give most attention to Columbus (sometimes almost equal attention to Magellan); English explorations, giving John Cabot major emphasis; Dutch explorations, with chief attention given to Hudson; and French explorations, with primary emphasis upon La Salle.

2. When grouping explorations by nation, it is wise to spend time having children establish the discrepancy in the case of some of the explorers (such as Columbus, Magellan, and Hudson) between their nationalities and the flags under which they sailed.

3. Discuss the evidence on the often emotionally charged question of who discovered America. In 1963, the Norwegian explorer, Helge Ingstad, discovered the remains of a Norse settlement in Newfoundland dating several hundred years before Columbus and, in 1965, American scholars found a map drawn in 1440 showing North America and containing a note of Leif Ericson's visit. This is a topic from which children may get an early lesson in looking to evidence and disregarding feelings when searching for facts.

4. Encourage your pupils to think through (a) the labeling of the period of explorations as one in which the iron age (symbolic of the European stage of technology) sailed to the stone age (symbolic of the American Indians' stage of technology);[22] (b) the motivation for the explorations.

5. Ask your pupils "why" questions frequently: Why some Europeans thought that Columbus would not reach Asia by sailing west; why the

[22] Ralph C. Preston and John Tottle, *In These United States*. Boston: Heath, 1965. Chap. 3.

Some Teaching Materials: Early Explorers

Books for Children
Berger, Joseph, and Lawrence Wroth, *Discoverers of the New World.*
New York: American Heritage, 1960.
Dalgliesh, Alice, *America Begins; the Story of the Finding of the New World.* New York: Scribner, 1958.
Rich, Louise, *The First Book of New World Explorers.* New York: F. Watts, 1960.
Syme, Ronald, *Vasco da Gama. Sailor Toward the Sunrise.* New York: Morrow, 1959.

Filmstrip
Age of Exploration. New York: Museum Extension Service, 1954.

Resource Unit
The Discovery and Exploration of the Americas. Louisville, Ky.: The School Board, 1959.

---

explorers sailed *westward* to reach the *east*; why the natives of the new land were called Indians; etc. Discourage guessing and handwaving following "why" questions. Tell your pupils you want them to think not only of possible answers, but also of *reasons* for their answers. Then wait before calling upon a child to give his answer. Sometimes, it is better to assign a "why" question to a committee for research and give-and-take discussion and then for reporting to the rest of the class.

6. Read to the class from the explorers' own accounts of their journeys (see the list of primary sources). Through these accounts, the children will get a clearer picture of the explorers' personalities, their decisions in small as well as major matters, daily life on shipboard, problems in preparing for a long ocean voyage in that prerefrigeration age, attitudes toward the Indians, and so on.

The Early American Period

The seventeenth and eighteenth centuries, cited by an historian as one of the richest and most picturesque eras of our history, has been a common and favorite subject of study in the elementary school. By understanding the simple processes of life of early America, the child begins to appreciate the hard struggle of the settlers with a tough environment, a struggle which set the foundation for our relatively easy life today. He will come to respect the character, traditions, and the profound devotion to liberty of some of the early colonial people which so largely fixed the pattern of later American life.

Attention should be given to the three groups of colonies: New England, Middle, and Southern. However, the teacher is advised to select one for particular emphasis, and to treat the other two more briefly at the conclusion of the unit, bringing out similarities and differences.

Suggestions for Teaching

1. Give as much time as possible to the daily life of the colonists. Several books furnish details about their homes, schools, work, and play.[23] This material lends itself well to informal dramatization and creative writing, through which children will consolidate their learning and identify themselves with the period.

2. Bring out the strong continuing bonds of the colonists with European culture, and the European influences upon the colonies as revealed in their representative government and their religious character.

3. Provide industrial arts experiences in which the children can reconstruct colonial processes of making such objects as buttons, candles, soap, and lanterns.[24]

4. Have your pupils explore the geographical features and resources of the colonies and draw inferences. The relatively poor soil of New England, for example, required that the pioneer farmer be painstaking, industrious, and frugal; and the shallow waters of the New England coast, attracting abundant fish which fed on the marine life associated with the undersea vegetation, account for the early dependence of the coastal colonies upon fish.

5. Include content about early American naturalists such as Alexander Wilson, the ornithologist, and John Bartram, the botanist; and about inventive engineers such as John Fitch, Benjamin Franklin, and Thomas Jefferson. Have your pupils compare the training and professional status of these men with those of contemporary scientists and engineers.

6. Introduce the significant political achievements of the colonists, such as their formation of a union and the creation of the Constitution; and some of the important political personalities, such as Benjamin Franklin and

[23] Alice M. Earle, *Home Life in Colonial Days* and *Child Life in Colonial Days*. New York: Macmillan, 1898 and 1899; William C. Langdon, *Everyday Things in American Life, 1607–1876*. New York: Scribner, 1937, 1941. 2 vol.; Mary H. McElroy, *Work and Play in Colonial Days*. New York: Macmillan, 1917; Edna McGuire and Thomas B. Portwood, *Our Free Nation*. New York: Crowell-Collier and Macmillan, 1954. Pp. 101–112. Edmond S. Morgan, *Virginians at Home: Family Life in the Eighteenth Century*. New York: Holt, Rinehart and Winston, 1959. Information on colonial schools is contained in Clifton Johnson, *Old Time Schools and School Books*. Magnolia, Mass. The old horn books are described in Beulah Folmsbee, *Little History of the Horn-book*, Boston: Horn Book.

[24] Robert J. Babcock and Carl Gerbracht, *Industrial Arts for Grades K–6*. Milwaukee, Wis.: Bruce, 1959; Dawn E. Schneider, *Correlated Art*. Scranton, Pa.: International Textbook, 1951.

George Washington. However, the political (and also the military) aspects should be in the nature of "a few bold brush strokes on the canvas."

7. A study of the American Revolution offers a chance to teach some of the elements of historical-mindedness outlined earlier in this chapter: search for the role of diverse forces behind the Revolution, and examination of its multiple causes.

8. It is advisable to include topics dealing with the intellectual history of the period, such as ideas about religious freedom, freedom of speech, and education, as reflected in the newspapers, books, laws, and schools of the times.

Some Teaching Materials: Early American Period

Books for Children

Aulaire, Ingri and Edgar d'., *Benjamin Franklin*. New York: Doubleday, 1950.

Daugherty, Charles M., *Benjamin Franklin, Scientist-Diplomat*. New York: Crowell-Collier and Macmillan Library Service, 1964.

Emerson, Caroline, *Pioneer Children of America*. Boston: D. C. Heath, 1959.

Fenner, Phyllis R. (Compiler), *Price of Liberty*. New York: Morrow, 1960.

Fisher, Margaret, *Colonial Children*. Grand Rapids, Mich.: Fideler, 1960.

Hanff, Helene, and L. L. Smith, *Early Settlers In America*. New York: Grossett & Dunlap, 1965.

Heilbroner, Joan, *Meet George Washington*. New York: Random House, 1965.

Johnson, Gerald, *America Is Born; A History for Peter*. New York: Morrow, 1959.

Langdon, William C., *Everyday Things in American Life 1607–1776*. New York: Scribner, 1937.

Rich, Louise, *The First Book of the Early Settlers*. New York: F. Watts, 1959.

Tunis, Edwin, *Colonial Living*. Cleveland: World Publishing, 1957.

Ziner, Feenie, and George Willison, *The Pilgrims and Plymouth Colony*. New York: American Heritage, 1961.

Films

Colonial Living. Chicago: International Film Bureau, 1957.

English and Dutch Colonization in the New World. Chicago: Coronet Instructional Films, 1956.

Plymouth Colony: The First Year. Chicago: Coronet Instructional Films, 1961.

Filmstrip

Jamestown: The Settlement and Its People. Wilmette, Ill.: Encyclopedia Britannica Films, 1959.

The Westward Movement

Few subjects of American history have proved as persistently popular as the settlement of the West. Its popularity over the years is evidenced by the widely read and enjoyed Leatherstocking tales of James Fenimore Cooper, Francis Parkman's *The Oregon Trail*, Bret Harte's stories, Mark Twain's *Roughing It*, Owen Wister's *The Virginian*, the autobiographical writings of Hamlin Garland, and the novels of Willa Cather and A. B. Guthrie, Jr.—not to mention the seemingly endless (if often misleading) outpouring of movie and television "westerns." Units on the Westward Movement can serve to correct the distorted impressions and jumbled ideas which children receive from unauthentic sources.

Suggestions for Teaching

1. Organize the unit so that your pupils will have an orderly view of the Westward Movement. Here is an example:

(a) The pioneer and his way of life,

(b) The major road and waterways used by the first waves of pioneers,

(c) The Louisiana Purchase,

(d) The Lewis and Clark Expedition,

(e) The westward trips between 1812 and the Civil War—the condition of roads, vehicles used, river craft used, and problems in breaking the prairie,

(f) The pathfinding of Lieutenant Frémont and Kit Carson and the movement of wagon trains on the Oregon Trail,

(g) The Gold rush of 1848,

(h) Communications between West and East studied chronologically—the ocean trips around Cape Horn or by way of the Isthmus of Panama, the stage coaches and freight wagons, the Pony Express, the telegraph, the railroad, and finally (for the Westward Movement has not halted), the automobile and the airplane.

To maintain a narrative thread, you may want to weave political and military events into the above: General Wayne's successful campaign against the Indians in northern Ohio, as a part of (b); the War of 1812, preceding (e); the war with Mexico, the annexation of Texas, and the acquisition of California and the Southwest, preceding (f).[25]

2. Build a clear concept of the frontier, as follows: (a) It was a buffer

---

[25] An organization approximating this appears in Ralph C. Preston and John Tottle, *In These United States*. Boston: D. C. Heath, 1965. Chap. 6.

area between the builtup sections to the east and the wilderness to the west. (b) It was an area in which the pioneers cleared land for their homes and fields. (c) It was a moving area; as the families moved from the east and settled, the frontier advanced westward. (d) It was more than an advancing buffer zone; the process of settlement which took place within it produced an atmosphere in which the democratic spirit and individualism of the pioneers could flourish—qualities which remain parts of the national character. It also produced an atmosphere of "frontier justice" where man took the law into his own hands, a fact which may account for a kind of "gunsmoke" morality often observed in the national character.

3. Make ample use of physical maps. Point out the successive physical obstacles to westward migration—the fall line, the Appalachians, the Ohio, Mississippi, and Missouri rivers, the semiarid plains, and the Rockies—and the dangers and hardships: Indians, uncertain supplies of game and water, lack of access to accustomed markets, and absence of skilled artisans.

4. Have the class make a detailed study of the Wilderness Road, the Oregon Trail, the Erie Canal, or some other artery of the settlers to the West and mark them on the map. The child should know about them and their status today. A chart organized along the lines of the following plan might be made.

ARTERY	FIRST USED BY PIONEERS	EXAMPLE OF ADAPTATION TO LAND	PRESENT STATUS
Wilderness Road	1775	Use of Cumberland Gap (Tennessee)	Natchez Trace Parkway
Oregon Trail	1811	Use of South Pass (Wyoming) in Rockies	U.S. Route 30 in Oregon follows part of trail
Erie Canal	1825	Use of Mohawk Valley (New York)	Part of New York State Barge Canal

5. Make the most of the strong appeal of the adventurous frontier life to children by providing them with books on well-known frontiersmen— Daniel Boone, Kit Carson, Davy Crockett, Wild Bill Hickok, Buffalo Bill, and others. Use of biography makes concepts such as "pioneer" and "Mountain Men" more vivid—for example, the lives of Daniel Boone and Kit Carson, respectively, help make those two terms concrete.

6. Keep the class on the lookout for news items which are related to the old West. As this is written, the author has at hand three clippings with

the following headlines: "Wilderness Path Now a Speedway"; "The Pony Express: Colorful Business Flop"; "Buffalo May Find New Home to Roam." Such material adds relevance and interest to the study.

7. Have some of the better readers in your class read and report on eyewitness accounts. Consult the list of source books. Neider's book, for example, contains excerpts from Frémont's autobiography, giving an account of his hazardous crossing of the Sierra Nevada in midwinter, an account of Mountain Man James Bridger by an officer for whom he had served as guide, and Robert Louis Stevenson's fascinating description of his transcontinental railroad journey in the Fall of 1879.

Some Teaching Materials: Westward Movement

Books for Children
"American Adventure" Series. Titles include *Alec Majors, Kit Carson, Wild Bill Hickok, Davy Crockett, Fur Trappers of the Old West.* New York: Harper & Row, 1941–1953.
Donovan, Frank R., and J. Bell Whitfield, *The Many Worlds of Benjamin Franklin.* New York: Harper & Row, 1964.
Harmer, Mary, *True Book of Pioneers.* Chicago: Childrens Press, 1957.
Jones, Evan, and Dale Morgan, *Trappers and Mountain Men.* New York: American Heritage, 1961.
Josephy, Alvin M., Jr., *History of the Great West.* Marion, Ohio: American Heritage, 1965.
"Landmark Books." Titles include *Daniel Boone, Lewis and Clark Expedition, Louisiana Purchase, Santa Fe Trail, To California by Covered Wagon, Erie Canal, First Overland Mail.* New York: Random House, 1950–1954.
McNeer, May, *The California Gold Rush.* New York: Random House, 1950.
Ross, Nancy, *Heroines of the Early West.* New York: Random House, 1960.
Tunis, Edwin, *Frontier Living.* Cleveland: World Publishing, 1961.

Film
Frontier Boy of the Early Midwest. Wilmette, Ill.: Encyclopedia Britannica Films, 1961.

Filmstrips
Pathfinders Westward. Chicago: Society for Visual Education, 1961. A set of six strips, with disc recordings at 33⅓ rpm.
We Travel the Mormon Trail. We Travel the Oregon Trail. Philadelphia: Your Lesson-Plan Filmstrips, 1960.

Teaching Tips
Pioneer Life and *Westward Movement.* Unit Teaching Plan. Field Enterprises, Educational Division, Merchandise Mart Plaza, Chicago.

ANCIENT CIVILIZATIONS

This chapter begins with the statement that the study of history contributes to the child's development by giving him perspective—a balanced way of looking at the modern world. Perspective cannot be attained with any degree of completeness unless the historical framework includes the fascinating story of ancient civilizations. The manner in which we live today is possible because the ancients prepared the way. Their influence reaches through the centuries. One means we have of increasing our understanding and appreciation of the present is through increasing our knowledge of those ancient times.

Because of the decline of the study of ancient history in high school and college, the elementary school has an added responsibility for developing an appreciation among children for the rich contribution of ancient societies. Any one of the ancient civilizations—Egyptian, Hebrew, Greek, Roman, or other—may be studied with profit. After one is studied intensively, the others may be more quickly surveyed and compared.

Suggestions for Teaching

1. Develop the concept of change, starting with changes the children have witnessed or experienced. Lead the discussion to greater changes they know about which occurred long ago. Then introduce the great changes in living which occurred when man in ancient times abandoned his nomadic existence and settled down to grow crops.

2. Read to the class portions of the table of contents and selected passages from Kramer's *From the Tablets of Sumer*[26] to convey the inventiveness of the ancients in the Fertile Crescent. Each of the 25 chapters deals with a "first" in the development of civilization—the first schools, the first bicameral congress, and the like. Have children read about other early civilizations such as those in the Indus River valley, Babylonia, and Egypt.[27]

3. It is probable that the child would gain more of an appreciation of the background of our culture from the study of ancient Greece than from the study of any other ancient civilization. Greek achievement ". . . shows the high-water mark reached in every region of thought and beauty the Greeks entered. . . . (They) were the first Westerners; the spirit of the West, the modern spirit, is Greek discovery. . . ."[28]

[26] Samuel Noah Kramer, *From the Tablets of Sumer*. Indian Hills, Col.: Falcon's Wing Press, 1956.

[27] Ralph C. Preston, *et al.*, *Four Lands, Four Peoples*. Boston: Heath, 1966. "Early Civilization in India"; "Earliest Times in Egypt." Pp. 123–133, 224–226. H. W. F. Scaggs, *Everyday Life in Babylonia and Syria*. New York: Putnam, 1965; E. M. White, *Everyday Life in Ancient Egypt*. New York: Putnam, 1964.

[28] Edith Hamilton, *The Greek Way to Western Civilization*. New York: New American Library, 1942. Pp. 8–9.

Some Teaching Materials: Ancient Civilizations

Books for Children
Cottrell, Leonard, *Land of the Pharoahs.* Cleveland: World Publishing, 1960.
Cowell, F. R., *Everyday Life in Ancient Rome.* New York: Putnam, 1961.
Falls, C. B., *The First 3000 Years: Ancient Civilizations of the Tigris, Euphrates, and Nile River Valleys, and the Mediterranean Sea.* New York: Viking, 1960.
————, *Stories from Herodotus.* New York: Dutton, 1965.
Meadowcroft, Enid, *Gift of the River.* New York: Crowell, 1937.
Mellersh, H. E. L., *Finding out about Ancient Egypt.* New York: Lothrop, 1962.
Quennell, Marjorie, and C. H. B., *Everyday Things in Ancient Greece.* New York: Putnam, 1954.
Robinson, Charles, *The First Book of Ancient Greece; The First Book of Ancient Egypt.* New York: F. Watts, 1960; 1961.
Unstead, R. J., *Looking at Ancient History.* New York: Crowell-Collier and Macmillan, 1960.

4. When dealing with Greece, you may wish to focus on Athens, where an early form of democratic government was established and where artistic and intellectual genius reached a distinguished level of achievement. Such a unit would include, of course, details of the daily life of the Athenians.[29]

5. If you concentrate upon Greece, devote part of the unit to a study of Greek art, legends, and heroes. The *Iliad* and *Odyssey* have been edited for children and are well suited for reading aloud.

6. The independence of the various city-states of Greece can be explained through work with physical maps. Greece has aptly been called "a wild scramble of mountain ranges." These mountains form the country into a network of plains and valleys, making communication among the isolated communities difficult, even today.

7. The great artistic expressions of the ancients—such as the Egyptian pyramids and temples, Greek sculpture and architecture, and the magnificent public buildings of the Romans—are deserving of emphasis.

THE MIDDLE AGES

The Middle Ages bridges ancient and modern times. A well-conducted unit will heighten a child's understanding of the revolutionary developments that have taken place as feudal institutions were gradually

[29] D. R. Barker, *Story of Ancient Athens.* New York: St. Martin's, 1960; Olivia Coolidge, *Men of Athens.* Boston: Houghton Mifflin, 1962; Leonard Weisgard, *The Athenians in the Classical Period.* New York: Putnam, 1963.

replaced by representative government and a broader base of economic opportunity.

Suggestions for Teaching

1. Give your pupils intimate glimpses of life in a monastery—workshop activities, teaching, scriptorial work, and so on[30]—and of life on a manor[31] —castle life, life of the serfs, and training of knights.[32]

2. Present the Middle Ages as one in which many modern institutions and ideas took shape. Children sometimes come from its study with the notion that the period was a uniform one, free of change. Stress the development of a merchant class, the origin of ideas of Protestantism, and the growth of secular interests as expressed in literature and trade.

3. Capitalize on the strong appeal which the romance and chivalry of

---

Some Teaching Materials: The Middle Ages

Books for Children
Buehr, Walter, *Knights and Castles and Feudal Life*. New York: Putnam, 1957.
Price, Christine, *Made in the Middle Ages*. New York: Dutton, 1961.
Pyle, Howard, *Men of Iron*. New York: Avon, 1965.
————, *Otto of the Silver Hand*. New York: Random House, 1960.
Tucker, Ernest, *The Story of Knights and Armour*. New York: Lothrop, 1961.

Films
Medieval Guilds. Wilmette, Ill.: Encyclopedia Britannica Films, 1956.
Medieval Knights. Wilmette, Ill.: Encyclopedia Britannica Films, 1956.
Medieval Manor. Wilmette, Ill.: Encyclopedia Britannica Films, 1956.

Filmstrips
Life in the Middle Ages. St. Charles, Ill.: DuKane Corp., 1955. A series of six strips.
When Knights Were Bold. New York: McGraw-Hill, Text-Film Dept., 1957.

Teaching Tips
"Life in the Middle Ages," *The Packet* (Heath), **12** (Spring 1957), 31–37.
A Medieval Tournament. Teachers Lesson Unit Series, No. 62. New York: Teachers College.

---

[30] Read to class, or have children read, Evaleen Stein, *Gabriel and the Hour Book*. Boston: Page, 1906.

[31] Detailed references for the teacher are G. G. Coulton, *Medieval Village, Manor and Monastery*. New York: Harper & Row, 1960; and William S. Davis, *Life on a Medieval Barony*. New York: Harper & Row, 1928.

[32] For excellent children's reading, see the books by Howard Pyle in the accompanying box of teaching materials.

knighthood has for children by encouraging informal dramatization of a few episodes.

4. Survey with your class the factors in the decline of feudalism—the Crusades, which led to a drop in fighting among the nobles and, consequently, to increased trade; to the development of towns; to the formation of workers' guilds and their achievement of political power; and to the development of the pike and longbow, which could decimate cavalry.

CURRENT HISTORY

The current history class gives pupils a chance to practice those qualities of caution and judgment which are among the goals of all history teaching. Rarely pursued as a regular unit, the study of current history should comprise 15 or 20 minutes a week. Use of one of the publications of current events for children provides all pupils with a restricted number of news items, making it possible for each to equip himself to contribute as an informed person to a current events discussion. The more informal and enjoyable the discussion, the more it will resemble a gathering of adults at which news is exchanged and discussed, and the greater will be the interest and the learning.

Suggestions for Teaching

1. Aim to develop through these discussions the ability to maintain open-mindedness even when controversial matters are discussed. Children should be encouraged to see how new facts often make it necessary to modify old ideas. For example, a child who, on hearsay, gives unqualified blame to the pilot for an air crash for which the cause is actually uncertain, should be directed to the news passage where the probable causes are discussed.

2. Aim also to develop a willingness to listen courteously and attentively to another's point of view. Children should be encouraged to raise questions about sources of news whenever conflicting reports occur, and to weigh the relative authenticity of each. The explanatory statement from a director of public safety concerning the need of new restrictions on parking of automobiles may be compared with an angry editorial in the local press on the same subject.

3. In summarizing, beware of finishing and polishing a problem too neatly or making any solution appear too pat. It is usually better to end a discussion with a question for children to think about than with a final categorical word.

4. Be prepared for some children to display naiveté in regard to the relative significance of events. One fourth-grade pupil of superior intelligence was asked to bring to school three items of national news. Her articles had the respective headlines: "Man Killed in Tool Factory," "Two Children

---

Some Teaching Materials: Current History

Newspapers for Children
Current Events. Wesleyan University, Middletown, Conn. 06458. Grades
7 and 8.
My Weekly Reader. Wesleyan University, Middletown, Conn. 06458. Editions for each grade, K–6.
The Young Citizen. Civic Education Service, 1733 K Street, N.W., Washington, D.C. 20006. Grades 5 and 6.

Periodicals for Children Containing News
American Junior Red Cross Journal. American National Red Cross, Wash-
ington, D.C. 20006.
Children's Digest. 52 Vanderbilt Avenue, New York, N.Y. 10017.
Children's Playmate Magazine, 6529 Union Avenue, Cleveland, Ohio
44104.
Highlights for Children. 2300 West Fifth Avenue, Columbus, Ohio 43212.
Jack and Jill. Independence Square, Philadelphia, Pa. 19105.
Junior Natural History Magazine. American Museum of Natural History,
New York, N.Y. 10024.

Teaching Tips
Civic Education Service, *Teaching Current Affairs.* Pamphlet. Washington,
D.C. 20006: The Service, 1963.
Smith, Lloyd L., "Current Events for the Elementary School," *Social Edu-
cation,* **25** (1961), 75–78, 81.

Saved at Fire by Mother," "Women Shoppers Injure Vet's Ankle." When
her teacher said they were not items of national news, she protested, "It all
happened within the nation!" It is important for you to know the level at
which your pupils think about the news; you can then quietly start broadening their understanding from that point. A useful technique is to present
pairs of headlines of widely differing importance, and ask the class which
of each pair is of greater importance in the lives of most people.

FOR REVIEW AND REFLECTION

1. What are some ways in which teachers can make the study of the past
   attractive and challenging?
2. What aspects of the past can appropriately be studied in the primary grades?
3. How should folklore and legends about George Washington, Davy Crockett,
   and other historical figures be handled by the teacher?
4. What are some of the values that accrue to the child from a study of an
   ancient civilization?
5. What are the essential characteristics of a time line? How does a time line
   help the child understand time relationships?

ASSIGNMENTS

1. Take any one of Gustavson's attributes of historical-mindedness, and indicate in detail how it can be developed in a specified grade and through a specified unit.
2. Plan a short unit to prepare primary children for the celebration of a special day. Keep it in its historical context and avoid trivial art activities and other busy-work.
3. Evaluate any modern social studies textbook prepared for elementary school in terms of the contribution it makes to the child's understanding of the past.
4. Select any aspect of the past which you believe has value for children, and construct a time line.

SUPPLEMENTARY READING

American Heritage: The Magazine of History. New York: American Heritage. Bimonthly.

Brown, Ralph Adams, "Biography in the Social Studies," in Michaelis, John U. (Ed.), *Social Studies in Elementary Schools*; Thirty-second Yearbook. Washington, D.C.: 1962. Pp. 243–255. Reviews values of biography in teaching history, gives leads to biographies, and suggests methods of use.

Carson, George Barr, Jr., "New Viewpoints in History," in Roy A. Price (Ed.), *New Viewpoints in the Social Sciences*; Twenty-eighth Yearbook. Washington, D.C.: National Council for the Social Studies, 1958. Chap. 2. Gives examples of changing historical perspectives and discusses the contribution of history to modern education.

Cartwright, William H., and Richard L. Watson, Jr. (Eds.), *Interpreting and Teaching American History*; Thirty-first Yearbook. Washington, D.C.: National Council for the Social Studies, 1961. Brings together recent scholarly interpretations of American history and suggests ways of teaching history through using geographic materials, local resources, and similar materials.

Chace, Harriet, "Using Maps in Teaching History," *Journal of Geography*, **59** (November 1960), 380–385. Contains good examples of combining map work with use of primary sources.

Deuel, Leo, *Testaments of Time: The Search for Lost Manuscripts and Records*. New York: Knopf, 1965. Gives a glimpse into the interesting work of a historian.

Fraisse, Paul, *The Psychology of Time*. New York: Harper & Row, 1963. Reviews research and reports original investigations which emphasize maturational aspects of development of time concepts in children.

Gottschalk, Louis, *Understanding History: A Primer of Historical Method*. New York: Knopf, 1950. Deals, among other things, with principles for the critical examination of records and the reconstruction of the past from the data revealed by the records.

Gustavson, Carl G., *A Preface to History*. New York: McGraw-Hill, 1955. Tells what is involved in historical-mindedness, and problems in identifying causes of revolutions and other events, disentangling the respective roles of "great men" and determinism, and the like.

Johnson, Henry, *Teaching of History in Elementary and Secondary Schools* (Rev. ed.). New York: Crowell-Collier and Macmillan, 1940. Contains wise observations and suggestions. A classic, deserving continued use.

Lord, Clifford L., *Teaching History with Community Resources*. New York: Teachers College, 1964. Presents a remarkable range of resources and activities which teachers would do well to examine when planning units on local history or when wishing to draw upon local resources to illustrate the history of other periods.

Palmer, John R., "The Place of History in the Curriculum," *School Review,* **71** (Summer 1963), 208–221. A highly critical essay on history teaching and the history curriculum as promoters of understanding of the past.

Rogers, Vincent R., "History for the Elementary School Child," *Phi Delta Kappan,* **44** (December 1962), 132–135. Discusses the structure of history.

Shaftel, Fannie R., "Industrial Arts in the Social Studies Program," in Michaelis, John U. (Ed.), *Social Studies in Elementary Schools*; Thirty-second Yearbook. Washington, D.C.: National Council for the Social Studies, 1962. Pp. 212–218. An important statement on the educational benefits of industrial arts and construction activities.

Strayer, Joseph R., "History," in Bernard Berelson, *et al., The Social Studies and the Social Sciences.* New York: Harcourt, 1962. Contains penetrating remarks about the teaching of history.

United States Department of Housing and Urban Development, *Preserving Historic America.* Washington, D.C.: Superintendent of Documents, 1966. Describes projects in many states involving historic preservation of buildings and areas representing various periods. Well illustrated.

Wesley, Edgar Bruce, "Let's Abolish History Courses," *Phi Delta Kappan,* **49** (September 1967), 3–8. Proposes that history be viewed as a source in the learning of social studies and not offered as a series of courses which are alleged to "close rather than open doors to the past."

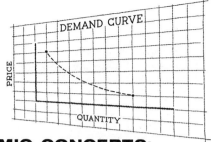

7

TEACHING ECONOMIC CONCEPTS:
UNITS EMPHASIZING GOODS
AND SERVICES

*Citizens cannot check the performance of
legislatures unless they have some idea
of how the economic machine works.*
STUART CHASE

Economics is an area from which teachers shy away. As Senesh points out, teachers often explain cooperation among the people of a community to their pupils "purely in terms of the moral obligation of helping each other, and not in terms of the necessity for division of labor to assure greater efficiency and a higher standard of living." He points out, further, that teachers, in directing attention to "things" (in itself commendable), may neglect ideas. Of a trip to the bank, he states, "Children are so preoccupied in inspecting the safe or the armed guard in the bank, for instance, that the idea of banking gets lost in the shuffle."[1]

Instruction should go beyond such externals and lead to consideration of *why* the institution was established in the first place, and what purposes it serves. Write two authorities:

> The fifth-grader, learning the complexities of the American banking system, should also understand why banks exist as well as how they operate as financial institutions. The student should be led to understand the importance of money in an economy and the role of banks in fostering economic activity.[2]

[1] Lawrence Senesh, "The Emerging Pattern of Economic Education in Public Schools," *Iowa Business Digest*, **28** (March 1957), 25–28.

[2] Lorraine H. Scheer and Vincent Patrick, "Guidelines for Incorporating Economics in the Intermediate Grades," *Social Education*, **20** (April 1966), 256–258.

The Ups and Downs of Mr. Boot

LAWRENCE SENESH
Professor of Economic Education
Purdue University

ONCE upon a time there was a town where everyone went around barefooted because there was no shoemaker.

One day a shoemaker named Mr. Boot came into town. He had heard that many people in the town would like to have shoes. He built a shop.

Other shoemakers found out about the good fortune of Mr. Boot. Another shoemaker arrived in the town . . . and another . . .

. . . and another . . .

They all thought that they could produce just as good a pair of shoes as Mr. Boot for $6.00.

Now all the shoemakers were unhappy because the price of shoes dropped to $4.00. What could the shoemakers do?

Should they continue to produce as before—but sell the shoes at a very low price and eke out only a meager living for themselves?

Should some of them move to other towns where they could sell their shoes at a higher price?

Figure 7.1. A lesson in economics for children. Courtesy of Dr. Lawrence Senesh and *The Instructor.* "[This figure] can be used to introduce the role of *price* in our economic system. The chart shows that if the demand for something goes up, then the price is likely to increase, and human and other resources will be attracted to the industry. But if the demand for it decreases, the price drops, and human and other resources usually go elsewhere.

The teacher may quote other examples where this law of supply and demand is in operation. For instance, when electric refrigerators were invented, the price of iceboxes fell and the people and materials and tools employed in the icebox factories found more profitable use in other places.

Some farmers also face a dilemma similar to Mr. Boot. When wheat farmers produce too much wheat, prices for wheat drop. If they cannot earn enough on their wheat, they can leave their farms. But it is not easy for farmers to leave their country homes

He bought leather, glue, thread, and nails; and with the tools he brought with him, he was ready for business.

He sold every pair of shoes he made for $6. With this money, he paid for his materials, the shop he built, the wear and tear on his tools, the wage he would have earned if he had worked for another shoemaker.

The shoemaker was very happy because everyone wanted to buy his shoes, and he made a good profit for being willing to take a chance.

As more people had more shoes, and more shoes were produced, the shoemakers had difficulty selling them for $6.00. The price of a pair of shoes started to get lower. . . .

. . . and lower. . . .

. . . and lower. The shoemakers made less and less profit, and some started to show losses.

Or should some of them try to find another occupation in this town?

Should they all agree not to produce too many shoes, and so keep the price up?

Should all or some of them advertise their shoes so the people would want to buy more than one pair?

What Would You Do ?

to go and work in the city. Nor is it always easy for them to learn a new trade.

It is equally hard to persuade the American people to eat more bread so farmers can sell more wheat. Many farmers choose to stay on their farms and make out the best they can.

Some people believe that the best way to solve the problem of overproduction is to have the government tell the farmer how many acres of wheat he can grow each year. What do your pupils think about this?

Although *The Ups and Downs of Mr. Boot* happened long ago, price still largely regulates production and consumption in our economy. The picture story helps children discover that: raw materials, labor, and tools (capital) are needed to produce goods; resources tend to move from less profitable to more profitable businesses and occupations; advertising helps to increase sales because it increases the customers' knowledge of possible choices; prices are determined by the relationship between the quantity of goods produced and the quantity demanded."

DESCRIPTIVE VERSUS ANALYTICAL APPROACHES

The National Task Force on Economic Education expressed dissatisfaction with the tendency of social studies teachers to teach economics descriptively rather than analytically.[3] A descriptive study of the economic activity of farming, for example, might include the social utility of farming, farm tools and machinery, the relation of crop yield to soil and weather, types of crops, markets for farm products, and the geographical distribution of various kinds of farms.

An analytical study, on the other hand, while including the foregoing, would lay emphasis upon such other matters as how the price of a product is affected by the interplay of demand and supply—what happens, for example, if drought reduces the supply of a product, causing it to become scarce. The Task Force suggests that analysis of the farm problem would also treat "governmental policies for dealing with low farm incomes and farm surpluses" and include an examination of alternative courses of action in search of that which promises best to achieve higher living standards and maximum economic freedom of the individual.[4]

It must be remembered that the Task Force report was written with the high school student in mind. Some of its suggested content may strike the elementary school teacher as too advanced for his pupils. There is a place in the elementary school for purely descriptive detail in teaching economic concepts. Many young children have firsthand knowledge of only a fragment of the world's economic relationships. They require an introduction to the function of economic institutions (banking, advertising, public utilities) before they can analyze problems in which these institutions are involved. Children and even adolescents frequently reveal a naiveté concerning economic matters.[5] The depth of the analysis undertaken in a classroom is dependent upon the intellectual maturity and sophistication of the pupils. Teachers of slow learners or of pupils of meager background may find it necessary to confine a unit on economics primarily to describing an economic activity—its role and organization.[6]

[3] National Task Force on Economic Education, *Economic Education in the Schools.* New York: Committee for Economic Development, 1961.

[4] National Task Force. P. 67.

[5] Robert V. Duffey, "Children's Knowledge of Income Levels," *Peabody Journal of Education,* **43** (July, 1965), 28–32; Edward G. Sewell, "Effects of Classwork in Economics on Attitudes and Understanding of a Select Group of Secondary School Pupils," *Journal of Educational Research,* **57** (November, 1963), 131–136; Dale D. Simmons, "The Development of Concepts about Occupational Status," Ph.D. thesis, University of Oregon, 1961, *Dissertation Abstracts,* **22** (December 1961), 2066–2067; M. C. Templin, "General Information Test for Kindergarten Children: A Comparison with the Probst Study after 26 Years," *Child Development,* **29** (March 1958), 87–96.

[6] Economic analysis is essentially a problem-solving activity and, as might be expected, problem-solving is positively correlated with intelligence. See David P.

Nevertheless, the Task Force's call for economic analysis to accompany economic description cannot be ignored. It has worked in many classrooms. Skeptical teachers should consult Senesh's pioneering in teaching economics to elementary school children[7] and should study the illustration of it in Figure 7.1. Most children are capable of learning the "why's" of the economic system and are interested in doing so. Earlier in this book, the author told of one teacher's successful teaching of first-grade children about the pros and cons of renting versus buying a house, and the concept of mortgage. This was not an exceptional case, as may be seen from reports on the teaching of economic concepts in the primary grades of Elkhart, Ind., and elsewhere.[8]

Some Basic Generalizations of Economics[9]

A. Production
   1. Resources are scarce, and human wants are unlimited.
   2. The total income of a society is determined by its total output of goods and services.
   3. The standard of living of a society is increased by increases in productivity.
   4. Economic welfare (measured by the total product of goods and services) is determined by the extent and nature of (a) natural resources, (b) working population, (c) capital goods, and (d) opportunity for economic initiative.
   5. With increased technological knowledge comes increased division

[continued]

Ausubel, *Psychology of Meaningful Verbal Learning,* New York: Grune & Stratton, 1963. P. 155; John M. Stephens, *Psychology of Classroom Learning.* New York: Holt, Rinehart and Winston, 1965. P. 185–186; Robert M. W. Travers, *Essentials of Learning* (2d ed.). New York: Crowell-Collier and Macmillan, 1967. P. 350. See also studies of critical thinking such as Edward M. Glaser, *An Experiment in the Development of Critical Thinking.* Contributions to Education No. 843. New York: Teachers College, 1941.

[7] Lawrence Senesh, *Our Working World.* Chicago: Science Research Associates, 1966.

[8] See two articles by Anne R. McAllister, Coordinator of Elementary Education in Elkhart during the early years of the experiment there in economic education: "Economic Education: A New Horizon," *Instructor,* **73** (January 1964), 7, 15; "Teaching Profit to Second Graders," *Grade Teacher,* **82** (March 1965), 68–70. See also Jane M. Gross, "Economics in the First Grade," *The Instructor,* **74** (September 1964), 63, 76; Helen F. Robinson, "Clarifying Ideas in the Kindergarten," *Instructor,* **73** (May 1964), 32–95; Rachel S. Sutton, "Behavior in the Attainment of Economic Concepts: II," *Journal of Psychology,* **58** (October 1964), 407–412.

[9] These generalizations are, in part, a streamlined version of those appearing in *Report of the State Central Committee on Social Studies to the California State Curriculum Commission,* Sacramento: California State Department of Education, 1961; Bernard Berelson, *et al., The Social Studies and the Social Sciences,* New York: Harcourt, 1962; *Economic Education in the Schools,* New York: Committee for Economic Development, 1961; and Lawrence Senesh, "The Organic Curriculum: A New Experiment in Economic Education," *The Councilor,* **21** (March 1960), 43–56.

of labor, increased mechanization of industry, increased exchange of goods, increased efficiency, and a potentially larger total quantity of goods and services.

6. The division of labor has destroyed man's self-sufficiency and has resulted in interdependence which, in turn, has led man to discover ways of facilitating the exchange of goods (substituting money and banking systems for barter, improving transportation, among others).

7. Many economic resources may be threatened by man's reckless use of them or by his upsetting the balance of nature. Man can offset the danger through conservation practices and through the development of new products.

B. Consumption

1. Consumer decisions concerning spending and saving determine what and how much is produced.

2. Income received from wages, dividends, and rents determines the size of an individual's claim to goods and services.

3. The most basic economic wants are food, clothing, and shelter.

C. Role of Government

1. Government influences economic life through its fiscal policies, through regulations affecting economic life (e.g., tariff regulations), through foreign policy (e.g., loans, support of U.N., participation in the World Bank), through domestic loans (e.g., F.H.A., N.D.E.A. student loans), through regulating prices, through public ownership, and so on.

2. Taxes are the main means of diverting income from private hands to government.

3. The government charges for many services.

ECONOMIC CONCEPTS IN ALL SOCIAL STUDIES UNITS

Man's economic activities are vast and complex. How can we chart a course between feeding the child meaningless bits and pieces of economics on the one hand, and on the other, overwhelming and confusing him in trying to present the intricate network of factors underlying our economy?

The problem can be solved, in part, by teaching some economic concepts through every social studies unit, regardless of the unit's emphasis. For example, in geographical studies of the community, food markets are commonly studied, and the class may trace a certain food product from the planting of a crop to its arrival on the market shelf. In planning the unit, the teacher can teach his pupils something about how the price of a product is affected by supply and demand, analyzing such factors as are mentioned in the preceding section in connection with the cost of bringing a product to market.

Similarly, in a study of Brazil, the risk involved in a nation's placing all of her eggs in one basket as Brazil did through her former overreliance, one at a time, successively, on sugar, gold, rubber, and coffee, and conversely, the advantages of diversified industry may be profitably analyzed. Or, in a study of city government, the way in which government influences economic life may be developed by examining how it affects prices through a sales tax and restricts commercial activity through zoning. Every social studies unit, regardless of its emphasis, can be enriched at one point or another by detailed consideration of economic concepts.

But this is not enough. There is an important place for units which *focus* upon economic activities. The remainder of the chapter will be devoted to discussion of such units.

SOME BASIC ECONOMIC PROCESSES

Before proceeding to suggestions for teaching economics-centered units, it seems necessary to consider some of the basic economic processes which should, in one form or another, become part of the content of any unit designed to promote economic understanding.

Determination of Prices

In our free enterprise economy, demand and supply with respect to goods and services play an important part in the determination of prices. Consumers shop around for the best buy, and producers charge what they think consumers will be willing to pay.

If a large number of people are prepared to buy apples at a given price, and if they try to buy more apples than are available, the price of apples goes up. On the other hand, if there are more apples for sale than people are prepared to buy at the asking price, apple dealers will reduce the price. In general, the price of apples will be one at which the quantity that buyers are prepared to buy approximates the quantity that are available.

But prices are not always so neatly determined. Not all buyers shop around. Some will always patronize certain stores and brands, regardless of price. Furthermore, some producers have a monopoly (such as a patented drug) and may charge more than if there were other products to compete with it.

For the most part, however, an increase in demand tends to raise prices (and a decrease in demand to lower them), and an increase in supply tends to lower prices (and a decrease in supply to raise them). These relationships can be grasped by children when applied to concrete situations. The consequences of a change in demand and supply can be illuminated through having a few children act out the situation. For example, Farmer Jones has an orange grove. Each orange tree may be represented by a pencil or a stick. Let us suppose he has 100 orange trees. Half are destroyed by frost. Your pupils can then figure out what is likely to happen to the price of oranges, now that the supply is reduced, assuming that all his customers continue to be eager to buy his crop.

A seller cannot normally stay long in business if the price he asks for his product does not cover the cost of its production. Pupils in one class expressed the belief that the cost of a farm product is the farmer's cost of raising the crop, and that this amount should be the market price. The class was directed by its alert teacher to analyze the cost of bringing a product to the market—beginning with the expenses of farming, of course, but looking, as well, at the costs of trucking, storing, retailing, and the like, including interest on capital and rent for land.

Banking

Some adults as well as many children have a restricted view of the services of banks. They think of a bank as a place to deposit their savings for safekeeping and for withdrawal when they wish. Some children also know about checking accounts. As part of any unit on economics, this service should be reviewed, or taught if the pupils are ignorant of it, with stress upon how the commonest form of payment today, for both businesses and individuals, is through checks, without the actual physical transfer of money.

Banks perform a more important job than keeping money and processing checks. They play an indispensable part in the manufacture and distribution of goods. This role, though unfamiliar to children, is one which they can readily understand. A businessman (or it could be a partnership or a corporation) may not have enough money on hand to buy what his business requires—a new truck, a larger warehouse, new machinery, additional merchandise, or the like—so he goes to a bank and applies for a loan. The bank investigates the businessman's reputation and the soundness of his business before making a decision concerning his request. If the loan is granted, the bank charges him interest as payment for the use of its capital.

The credit aspect of the bank's work can be clarified through role-playing. One group of children might represent a group of entrepreneurs who want to begin a new business—who, perhaps, are planning to open a hardware store. The teacher may have to guide the first group which enacts the steps in securing a bank loan. They could conduct a conference around a table to determine their needs. Perhaps, they will decide that they might use a building which was formerly occupied by a clothing store and which, to be converted for a different purpose, will require the hiring of a carpenter. How much rent must they pay for the building? How much money will they need to lay in a stock of tools and other hardware? One of them visits a child who represents a bank official. What information will he need to give the official in order to persuade him that the store will succeed? The banker will wish to know whether it is the only hardware store for miles around and in a thickly settled community, or whether it will have to compete with already established hardware stores in the same neighborhood. What experience in the hardware business have the owners had? What are their assets? Eventually, the banker may grant or deny the loan, explaining to the class the grounds for his action.

Risk-Taking

Profit is a commonly misunderstood concept, yet one which it is entirely possible for children to grasp. Briefly, it is the reward for the risk-taker—the entrepreneur who planned and established the business. If he is setting up a hardware store, it would be up to him to rent, buy, or build a store, employ a manager and other employees, purchase hardware stock, and borrow money for the purpose of getting started. Then he must regularly pay rent (or taxes on his property), salaries, interest on money borrowed, and such miscellaneous expenses as are involved in lighting, heating, air-conditioning, and repairs. If anything is left over after, say, three months, or after a year, it is his profit. There is no guarantee there will be any. He may only cover expenses, or he may even incur a loss. He may have a profit only in certain years. Thus, a successful entrepreneur must have sound business judgment and the courage to risk his reputation and capital. He is not going to undertake the planning, risks, and responsibilities unless he has a chance of making a profit.

The concept of risk-taking is a comparatively simple one for children to understand. In a classroom in Elkhart, Ind., in which risk-taking and profits were being studied, the author saw a pupil-constructed poster which suggested one approach to clarifying the role of the entrepreneur. The poster bore this caption: "I want to start a new business. What do I need?" Depicted below were land, energy, raw materials, capital, labor, and a market. Role-playing, as illustrated in the case of banking, can also be helpful to a class thinking through the meaning of risk-taking.

Paying Taxes

Children should learn early in school that no goods or services are free—even when they appear to be so. Children may be misled because they observe that the letter carrier does not charge for delivering a letter nor a fireman for putting out a blaze; and the public school teacher does not send a bill to parents for his services. Every unit on economics should bring out that these and numerous other public services are provided by some unit of government, that the government is created and operated by all of us, who are "we, the people," and that the people pay the government, largely through taxes, to provide the services. Since the citizens of most modern countries, including our own, pay large portions of their income to the various units of government in the form of taxes, the process cannot be glossed over if we are to give children a realistic view of our economic system.

More concerning the teaching of taxation appears in the next chapter.

Labor-Management Bargaining

Most workers today are employees. They are told how many hours they are to work each day, how much they will be paid, what tasks to perform, and how to perform them; and there are normally rules about lunch periods, coffee breaks, sometimes even what clothing to wear, and other matters. It is not surprising that employees should frequently find themselves in conflict with their employers over working conditions and that they should form organizations to protect their interests. Teachers should plan to have their pupils acquire an understanding of collective bargaining —that process whereby appointed representatives of a union confront the employers with grievances and requests on behalf of all the union's members. When collective bargaining fails to bring about agreement between labor and management, a strike may result. The factory or store is forced to close (although sometimes management personnel and "scabs" keep the business at least partially operating). During the period of a strike, the workers are not paid their wages, the business loses its income, and the goods and services of the business are no longer at the disposal of the consumers. Some economists believe that this is a small cost in the long run; that, if the dissatisfactions were allowed to continue, there would be a greater cost in the form of lowered worker morale and a consequent drop in productivity.

Touchy though the subject of labor-management disputes may be, it is inconceivable that teachers, in introducing children to the economic world, should ignore this conspicuous aspect of it. Part of the training offered by the study of economics lies in the opportunity for the learner to step aside from private partisan feelings and examine the factors contributing to labor-management disagreement, understand the process of collective bargaining, and recognize its relatively orderly and civilized character.

Children should learn that employees are not totally reliant on collective bargaining for the protection of their welfare. Federal and state laws have been passed to minimize industrial accidents and disease, to compensate workers who meet with industrial accidents or contact industrial diseases, to pay annuities for retired employees, and to provide unemployment insurance.

Advertising

In this age of television, advertising is an inescapable element in the child's environment. To most children—and perhaps to most adults—the "commercials" of television and radio, the billboards, and the numerous advertisements of newspapers and magazines signify little more than a jockeying for a favored position in the shopper's deliberations. To be sure, businessmen who advertise are seeking to widen the market for their goods and services. But the social utility of advertising is all too likely to escape attention. Children should be encouraged to trace the steps whereby advertising affects the production process.

Advertising enables manufacturers to sell larger quantities of goods and stimulates mass production. Mass production, in turn, lowers the cost of production per unit of product and, thereby, prices. To the extent that advertising accomplishes this, it helps to raise the standard of living.

Advertising aids the consumer further by drawing his attention to features of a product or process that he might otherwise not have been conscious of, such as safety features of an automobile tire, length of life of a fountain pen, or extra space in a refrigerator. The consumer may not accept the word of the advertiser that his product is the best, but he may become aware for the first time of the features mentioned and be led to shop among competitive items with greater discrimination and judgment. Thus does advertising contribute to improved economic decision-making.

It is evident, however, that advertisements frequently encourage "keeping up with the Joneses," snobbery, extravagance, and other questionable values. Moreover, some advertisements are lurid, and others are placed outdoors where they may mar some feature of natural beauty. So, while children need to learn of the positive economic role of advertising, particular advertisements relevant to the unit in progress should be critically analyzed.

Receiving External Benefits
and Incurring External Costs

An external benefit is one not paid for, such as a benefit received from a park or golf course adjoining one's home which provides play space, shade, and a wide expanse of grass and plantings which the home owner did not create and does not pay for. A newsboy selling his wares at a shopping center receives the external benefit provided by the stores' attraction of crowds of shoppers. A local airport benefits a manufacturer by making the firm more readily accessible to its customers and its suppliers.

An external cost, on the other hand, is a loss suffered at the hands of others quite apart from any action of the person or persons harmed. For example, a fisherman must pay the cost of a depleted catch caused by the chemical wastes that a nearby factory discharges into the river in which he fishes. A home owner who lives by an airport suffers from the noise and vibration caused by jet airplanes. Those with respiratory ailments risk serious health loss from city smog created by the burning of coal or petroleum products by industries and homes.

Most units dealing with economics provide occasion to examine external benefits and costs. Pupils will quickly learn that not all gains and losses involve money received or expended.

ORGANIZATION OF CONTENT
FOR THE STUDY OF ECONOMICS

Courses in economics at the high school and college levels are organized by topics such as Money and Banking, International Trade, and the Business Cycle. There is no reason why the elementary school curriculum should attempt to parallel those courses. It would appear more suitable for the young child to learn economics by seeing how basic economic processes operate in areas with which he has had prior experience. Those areas which will be chosen for illustration in this chapter, and which will be discussed as teaching units, are:

Community Work and Workers
Farming
Industry
Transportation
Invention
Conservation and Use of Resources

COMMUNITY WORK AND WORKERS

During the primary grades, children will profit from surveying work patterns in the community. Among the purposes of such survey are the following learnings:

1. The variety and types of jobs that must be performed to keep the wheels of a community turning,
2. The kinds of "intermediate goods" (buildings, machinery, raw materials, and the like used by the producer to make other goods which will satisfy consumer wants) which are prominent in local industry,
3. The role of banks in supplying some of the capital needed to obtain "intermediate goods,"

4. The division of workers between blue-collar and white-collar occupations; and between jobs which are distributed more or less regularly throughout the year and those which are seasonal,

5. The division of workers between those who own their own shops and tools and those who work for others; between those wearing uniforms and those not wearing uniforms; and between those in private employment and those in government employment.

Children have more information about such matters than is sometimes assumed. When they pool it, the total amount of material is considerable. Its accuracy needs to be verified by the teacher in many instances. After appropriate excursions to stores, repair shops, and the like, opportunity should be given the children for discussing and "playing out" the experiences, through informal dramatic play. Realistic stories for young children about workers and work will help them generalize their limited firsthand impressions of community workers.

Suggestions for Teaching

1. Plan to give your class a comprehensive view of the work of the community, including the following categories:
   (a) Work that provides the basic physical necessities of living—food, water, clothing, shelter,
   (b) Work that contributes to cultural and religious life through home-making, education, and religion,
   (c) Work that contributes to bodily and mental health through medicine, sanitation, and recreation,
   (d) Work that contributes to protection and conservation of life, property, national security, and natural resources through police, fire, park, forest, and similar services,
   (e) Work that provides access to distant persons and places through devices of transportation and communication,
   (f) Work that involves the coordination of community life through administration of local government and the courts,
   (g) Work that involves financing production, providing a mechanism for making payments, and other banking functions.

2. Have your class discover the classes and variety of work by classifying community work and workers according to a scheme they work out themselves. Accept the children's own language, ignore naïve expressions and overlapping categories, but help them make a complete set of categories appropriate to the community.

3. Have your pupils think of examples within the community of external benefits and costs. This analysis might begin by having each pupil think of those enjoyed or incurred by himself or his family.

4. Lead your class to identify workers who furnish goods and those who furnish services, and to understand that services (medical advice, teaching, acting) which are nonmaterial, are economic "goods" as much as are commodities (lumber, gasoline, food, and so on). In other words, services and commodities both satisfy human wants.

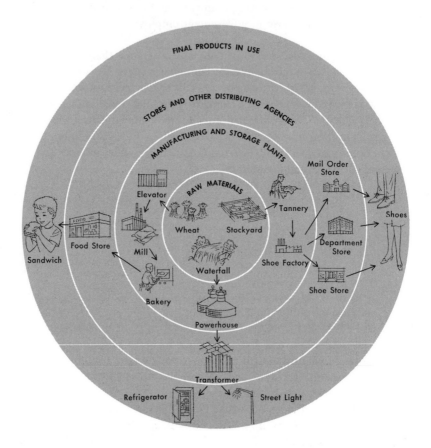

Figure 7.2. Relationships between the community and the outside world.

5. Concentrate on three or four types of work for intensive study. Develop those basic economic concepts which are appropriate to the work in question and in accordance with the maturity and ability of your class.

6. Discuss with your class the family as a consumer. What determines which of the many products available in the community to buy, what to postpone buying, and what not to buy? Are a family's wants greater than its income (or purchasing power)? To what extent is a family led to buy

---

Some Teaching Materials:
Community Work and Workers

Books for Children
Hammond, Diana, *Let's Go to a Hospital.* New York: Putnam, 1959.
Hastings, Evelyn, *The Department Store.* Chicago: Melmont, 1956.
Miner, Irene, *The True Book of Our Post Office and Its Helpers.* Chicago: Childrens Press, 1955.
Preston, Ralph C., *et al., Greenfield, U.S.A.* Boston: Heath, 1964.

Cutout Kit
Gas Serves Your Community. New York: American Gas Association.

---

something because of persuasive advertising or salesmen? Why does a family try to save part of its income?

7. Introduce experiences whereby your pupils will sense the relationship between the economic life of the community and that of the outside world. Figure 7.2 shows characteristic relationships to be sought. The four sections of the figure correspond to four successive states in the production of economic wealth. Starting at the hub and proceeding to the periphery, they are: (a) sources of raw materials, (b) manufacturing plants, (c) stores and other distributing agencies, and (d) consumers. The stories of three products—electricity, bread, and shoes—have been simplified and plotted on the accompanying chart. Some children will know these products only at the consumer end. Children in the wheat belt will know the bread story in at least two of its phases, and children in other specialized regions may know other phases of other processes. Their understanding of the complete chain of most economic processes is probably fragmentary. Studying the economic community should involve studying much that is not in the community, in order that the child may understand exactly where and how his community fits into the four-phase economic scheme. Tracing these relationships saves community study from provincialism.

FARMING

Farming is, of course, one of the most basic of all economic processes, since it produces most of our food. Few units can illustrate as effectively the absolute dependence of man on the soil and the elements. Even with modern farm machinery, scientific plant and animal breeding, and new knowledge of soil management, the farmer still, as always, has no certain protection against drought, frost, violent storms, and pests. Like his primitive forerunner, he is still subject to the blessings and curses of his environment. But in other respects, the American farmer has little in common with his primitive forerunner. Modern farm tools and machines have drastically reduced the man-hours needed in performing such operations as plowing, harrowing, and harvesting; and new knowledge of how to increase soil fertility enables today's farmer to exceed his ancestors' yield per acre.

Suggestions for Teaching

1. Ascertain, through discussion, how much your pupils know about farms. Because of our shrinking rural population, fewer and fewer children know anything about the most elementary farm practices. It is helpful for a farming unit in the primary grades to include some gardening experiences on the school grounds, if this is practicable, and the construction of a model farm.[10] Read to your class stories and descriptive accounts of farm life.

2. Introduce pictures which portray man tilling the soil and keeping herds in various periods of history, representing various levels of technological development, and in various regions of the earth today. Have the children make rough comparisons in terms of acre yield per man-hour and decide in which situation the food is probably being raised for a market (as opposed to subsistence farming).

3. Bring out the regional specialization in farm products fostered by climatic differences and made economically advantageous by modern transportation and modern methods of food storage and preservation. Your pupils should be able to identify on a map some of the regions which are major producers of certain crops, such as Florida and California for citrus fruits; Texas, Louisiana and Arkansas for rice, and the heart of the North Central States region for corn. Ask your pupils to reason out the advantages to society in having a degree of regional specialization over having regional self-sufficiency.

4. Develop the concept of the typical farmer as a risk-taker—a capitalist. Since almost three-fourths of American farms are operated by their owners, stress the fact that most farmers are entitled to salaries as managers of their farms and as farm workers, as well as to profits.

5. Provide your class with some information of major trends in farming, and see if, working from that information, they can discover reasons for today's (a) bigger farms, (b) fewer farmers, and (c) greater farm productivity. They will need, first, to know that today one man can do more work than one man could do in years gone by, thanks to the tractor, combine, and other farm machines; that he has better seed, fertilizer, irrigation, and insect control, thanks to the work of scientists; and that the phenomenal

---

[10] Franklin L. Hillenberg, "A Model Farm: A Third Grade Project," *Journal of Geography*, **62** (November 1963), 375–376.

Some Teaching Materials: Farming

Books for Children
Coatsworth, Elizabeth, *The Secret*. New York: Crowell-Collier and Macmillan, 1964.
Goodspeed, J. M., *Let's Go to a Dairy*. New York: Putnam, 1957.
Ipcar, Dahlov, *Ten Big Farms*. New York: Knopf, 1958.
Riedman, Sarah, *Food for People*. New York: Abelard-Schuman, 1961.

Films
Where Does Our Food Come From? Chicago: Coronet Instructional Films, 1960.
Where Does Our Meat Come From? Chicago: Coronet Instructional Films, 1960.

Filmstrips
Farmer and City Man Need Each Other. Philadelphia: Your Lesson Plan Filmstrips, 1958.

---

growth of American industry has provided occupational opportunities in cities which has caused many farmers to leave the farm.[11]

6. Be sure to supply examples of the various ideas which are discussed. Thus, when talking about how farm machines stimulated productivity, give explicit illustrations, such as the tomato-picking machine which, when introduced in Sacramento Valley, Calif., required only 13 workers to do the job previously requiring 60 workers. Supply pictures and details whenever possible.

INDUSTRY

To the curious child, much of the activity of industrial society is mysterious. The interdependence of its participants is not evident on the surface, and the functions of many of its institutions (such as insurance companies and law firms) are guessed at only hazily. The elementary school teacher can make a substantial beginning in building the child's understanding of the industrial complex.

The topic, "Food, Clothing, and Shelter," is often taught as a unit (or as three successive units) in one of the primary grades and provides a means of introducing the child to industrial society.[12] In the intermediate grades,

[11] For a brief account of these and other aspects of farming, see the United States Department of Agriculture pamphlet, *Farming in the United States* (Agriculture Information Bulletin No. 246). Washington, D.C.: Superintendent of Documents, 1961.

[12] For the treatment of "Food, Clothing, and Shelter" as three successive units, see Ralph C. Preston and Eleanor Clymer, *Communities at Work*. Boston: Heath, 1964.

a unit on the topic, "Industry," offers an overall view of economic processes as they apply to two or three pivotal industries chosen among the following: meat, textile, lumbering, rubber, leather, or steel. The unit covers the stages of the production, distribution, and consumption of the industry's products and considers such economic matters as the form of business organization characteristic of the industry, how labor is divided, how it is organized, the degree of competitiveness of the industry, insuring the product during shipment, problems of retailing, and the human wants which are satisfied by the product.

Suggestions for Teaching

1. Your pupils will discover, as they study almost any major industry, that its products are diversified. For example, in studying the cotton industry, they will see that cotton fibers are used in making cloth, that cottonseed provides a nutritious oil used as the base of many food products, that the fuzz (linters) on the seed are used in making cellulose products, and that still other by-products are yielded. These may be listed on a chart, with samples of the cotton product beside each item. In connection with this activity, bring out the role of large-scale production in securing by-products. It would not pay to grow cotton just to obtain some of its by-products, and if cotton were not processed on a large scale, no one would trouble with the linter, for example, or the hull. A large business, however, is able to reduce costs through mass production, to hire expert managers, and to maintain a research laboratory staffed with competent scientists. It is thus in a position to discover various ways of using its raw materials and of profitably marketing the by-products.

2. Your pupils can learn of the greater economy of labor in mass production through first-hand experience. Senesh tells of how two teams of first-grade pupils produced gingerbread boys.[13] One team formed an assembly line, each child performing a separate function. One rolled the dough, another cut the forms, and so on. Each child on the second team, on the other hand, did all the jobs himself. Comparisons were then made in terms of waste of materials, duplication of equipment, and speed. The assembly-line team was ahead on all counts.

3. Plan a trip to a manufacturing plant to illustrate the efficiency of modern assembly-line production; or, if a trip is not feasible, show a film which describes an industrial process.

4. Provide experiences which will give children an understanding of the underlying process of an industrial machine. For example, if they are studying the cotton industry, have them take a piece of cotton batting and pull out some fibers and then, with wet fingers, twist the fibers together into

[13] Lawrence Senesh, "The Economic World of the Child," *The Instructor*, 72 (March 1963), 77–79.

yarn. Have them repeat the process, attaching each piece of yarn to the preceding piece by twisting the two ends together until they have spun a piece of yarn several inches long. The underlying processes of other industries may be illustrated through consulting Harold G. Gilbert's *Children Study American Industry* (see "Supplementary Reading" at the end of this chapter) and publications of School Products Co., 330 East 23 Street, New York, N.Y.

5. Have the children compare some samples of natural and synthetic products. Encourage them to find out some of the factors that led chemists

---

Some Teaching Materials: Industry

Books for Children

Adler, Irving, and Ruth Adler, *Houses: From Cave to Skyscraper.* New York: Day, 1965.

Bergere, Thea, *From Stones to Skyscrapers.* New York: Dodd, Mead, 1960.

Gringhuis, Dirk, *Big Mac.* New York: Crowell-Collier and Macmillan, 1959.

Hartman, Gertrude, *Machines and the Men Who Made the World of Industry.* New York: Macmillan, 1939.

Weisberger, Bernard A., and Allan Nevins, *Captains of Industry.* New York: Harper & Row, 1966.

Charts

See How Important Cotton Is to the U.S.A. New York: Cluett, Peabody and Co., 1962. (Project map shows where cotton is grown and illustrates manufacturing process.)

Wool Exhibit Chart. Portland, Ore.: Pendleton Woolen Mills, 1962 (shows seven stages of manufacture).

Films

An American Sawmill. Boise, Ida.: Film Originals, 1960.

Cavalcade of Fibers. Wilmington, Del.: E. I. duPont de Nemours and Co., Motion Picture Distribution, Advertising Department, 1959.

The Story of Leather. Bloomington, Ind.: NET Film Service, 1957.

Filmstrip

How We Get Our Homes. Chicago: Society for Visual Education, 1959.

Teaching Tips

The Growth of American Industry. New York: National Association of Manufacturers, 1962. (Booklet of information to be used with pupils.)

Making Iron and Steel—Picture Set. New York: U.S. Steel Corp., 1962. (Kit includes booklets for pupils and accompanying teacher's guide.)

Textile Teaching Kit. Charlotte, N.C.: American Cotton Manufacturers Institute, Inc., 1962. (Contains informative booklets on history and manufacture, with samples.)

to create synthetic rubber, textiles, building materials, tableware, and other products. They should not overlook the relative scarcity and expensiveness of natural raw materials.

6. Have your pupils read up on different sources of power required for driving the wheels of industry, such as water, steam, internal combustion, and atomic energy.

7. In studying an industry, do not neglect the consumer's end of the production chain. Thus, if the building industry is under consideration, you might ask your pupils to look carefully, with help from parents, at the way their own homes were constructed, and prepare a list of the building materials and trace the raw materials from which each was derived.

8. Have your pupils consider the economic role of advertising in the marketing of the product of a particular industry in terms of the concepts developed on page 191.

TRANSPORTATION

Developments in transportation are of supreme importance to modern specialized societies. The movement of goods and people binds geographic units together and has created the obvious interdependence of nations and of regions within nations. Few topics have been as commonly selected for social studies in all grades as transportation. Few are as popular with children—not surprising in view of the action and adventure connected with the movement of goods and people.

Suggestions for Teaching

1. Assist your class in making an inventory of transportation agencies. Discuss with the children the competitive advantages and disadvantages of each form of transportation. Here are some examples: The low cost of shipping goods by water gives an advantage to ships over airplanes, but the relative slowness of ships is a disadvantage when shipping perishables or goods urgently needed. Shipping crude oil and natural gas by pipeline is less expensive than shipping these resources by truck or railroad. The truck is a more flexible operating unit than the railroad train, which meets with delays in the assembling of cars for each trip; yet, the railroad controls a right-of-way and, hence, is spared the increasingly frequent traffic tie-ups encountered by trucks in metropolitan areas.

2. Deepen your pupils' grasp of the economics of transportation by devoting part of the unit to the history of transportation. Have them read up and consult pictures on transportation before the Industrial Revolution. They will discover how relatively slow and often cumbersome it was. As they trace the story of the introduction of steam-, electrical-, and gasoline-driven engines in transportation, they will learn the significance of the

Industrial Revolution. Have your pupils construct time charts of time lines to illustrate the sequence of major developments from human carriers and pack animals and the invention of the wheel and axle to the harnessing of the latter to mechanical power.

3. Bring out how modern transportation has helped to satisfy human wants through bridging the gap between producers and consumers; how it has been one of the most potent factors in expanding the market and in developing regional specialization; and how, by the means of rapid, dependable transportation, markets far and near can assimilate the products of specialized regional industry. This group of concepts will become part of a child's intellectual repertoire, in proportion to his intellectual maturity. Develop each concept slowly and with copious illustration. Younger children can make a start by tackling the problem of how a community without transportation—an isolated community—could subsist.

4. Have your pupils think through the knotty problem of the role of government in the development of transportation. Federal, state, and local governments have given land to the railroads for building their rights of way, state governments built the Erie and other canals, and the federal government has subsidized airlines and other agencies of transportation. Aid your pupils in seeing that such enterprises as beginning a railroad and building highways and airports require such large amounts of capital, and the prospect of return to the investor is so remote in time, that private enterprise cannot be expected to undertake the responsibility. Discuss with the class the public's gain in giving financial assistance to transportation.

5. Include in the unit a section on the relationship between transportation and communication. Bring out how transportation was the chief means of transmitting messages until the invention of the telegraph and the telephone. The messages and news had theretofore been carried by person-to-person visits or through some form of delivery system, such as messenger and postal services. Make available to your class books, pictures, and films which illustrate these forms of early communication and also other forms of communication which are not dependent on transportation (smoke signals, gun shots, or light signals). Emphasize the concept of communication's increasing independence of transportation and the further concept of how inventions, from the telegraph to television, have reduced the need for travel—that it is now possible to hold business conferences, to shop, to visit, and to witness theatrical, musical, and sports performances from one's office or home.

6. Develop the concept that in underdeveloped countries, lack of good transportation is a major factor in blocking economic growth. Most of the early loans to Africa from the World Bank were for transportation. Transportation is essential for what the underdeveloped nations seek most: to exploit their natural resources, increase agricultural productivity, and stimulate new industry.

Some Teaching Materials: Transportation

Books for Children
Bienvenu, Harold J., *Transportation: Lifeline of America.* Glenview, Ill.: Scott, Foresman, 1961.
Dalgliesh, Alice, *America Travels: The Story of Travel in America.* New York: Crowell-Collier and Macmillan, 1961.
Hebb, David, *Wheels on the Road: A History of the Automobile from the Steam Engine to the Car of Tomorrow.* New York: Crowell-Collier and Macmillan, 1965.
Hoberman, Mary Ann and Norman Hoberman, *How Do I Go?* Boston: Little, Brown, 1958.

Teaching Aids
Bulletin Board Kits—Automobile and Truck. Detroit: Automobile Manufacturers Association.
History of Land Transportation Chart. Washington, D.C.: American Trucking Association.
On the Track. Washington, D.C.: Association of American Railroads.

---

7. In discussing transportation difficulties in underdeveloped lands, your class should not lose sight of the fact that industrially advanced nations, too, have serious problems, although of a different nature. Among the problems are the moving of masses of commuters in metropolitan areas, checking air pollution by motor vehicles in cities, and controlling the often reckless acquisition of farmland, parkland, and residential acreage for building more and more superhighways.

8. Challenge your pupils to explain the statement: "For the first time in 5,000 years the wheel is being displaced as the symbol of transportation progress."[14] Have interested members of the class do some library research on vertical takeoff aircraft, pipeline transportation for gas, oil, and other products, and ground-effect (air cushion) vehicles which are supported by air and are potentially amphibious.

INVENTION

Units on invention deal with one of today's powerful forces—technological change. Through invention, man learns to perform old jobs more efficiently, and to perform tasks never before accomplished, such as the exploration of outer space. Through invention, some of the world's most

---

[14] Wilfred Owen, "Transport Technology and Economic Development," in United States Agency for International Development, *Transportation*; United Nations Conference on the Application of Science and Technology for the Benefit of the Less Developed Areas. Washington, D.C.: Superintendent of Documents, 1963. Vol. 5. P. 17.

backbreaking and dangerous labor has been eliminated, the length of the work day and work week have been reduced, and man's leisure has been increased. This has occurred without curtailing production—in fact, man-hour productivity has increased.

Suggestions for Teaching

1. Teach about a selected list of important inventions and their inventors. Emphasize that a single individual is not solely responsible for an invention, that each invention is the result of the work of several inventors who, basing their work on discoveries of men who went before them, work through the years, each adding his bit. When the final, critical step to economy, efficiency, and marketability is reached, no one man can truly be given sole credit for it. Bring out that the final step may be taken by more than one man at approximately the same time, perhaps working thousands of miles apart.

2. As your pupils read about the history of any process—providing illumination, weaving, or any other—they will become aware of the slow changes in development of the process for centuries, then a pyramiding from the time of the Industrial Revolution to the present. Focus their attention on this point. A time line can make it vivid.

3. Develop the concept that mechanized industry enables a comparatively small number of workers to turn out an enormous supply of goods. One worker in a textile factory today, for example, can manufacture as much yarn as it took tens of thousands of women in colonial days, working an equal length of time at their spinning wheels.

4. With the aid of dictionaries and reference books, your class should be directed to clarify the terms *automation* and *computer*. Automation employs devices which replace human regulation and management of machines. The worker, instead of being a machine tender, supervises the automated device. In many industries, relatively few men are required to perform such supervision, in that their automated systems are controlled by the electronic computer. Have the children consult books for detailed illustrations.

5. Have your pupils gather information about automation from current newspapers and magazines. The author has on his desk, at this writing, recent clippings describing automatic devices for unloading silos, feeding cattle, translating Russian into English, brewing tea, predicting weather, analyzing blood samples, supplanting the lighthouse keeper, sorting mail, guiding an automobile on the highway, and operating a typewriter by voice. Make a bulletin board display or a class scrapbook of the clippings your pupils bring in.

6. While the study of technological unemployment (displacement of workers by machines) is normally postponed until high school, some elementary school pupils will be quick to see that inventions tend to result

in technological unemployment, striking a serious blow to the displaced workers. If it becomes evident that the class has the maturity to explore the problem, delve into the history of industrial development which shows that labor-saving machines have reduced cost and increased the output of a product, thereby creating opportunities for new industries and new jobs. An example frequently given is of the displacement of horse dealers, blacksmiths, and the like by the invention of the automobile, which eventually led to new and increased demand for labor in auto factories, highway construction, and other fields. But the problem should not be dismissed so simply! There are those economists who fear that the revolution caused by automation may result in the abolition of whole categories of employment and with greater rapidity than society will be able to handle. Thomas J. Watson, Jr., President of IBM, has these sobering words:

> The fact that technological change may benefit all of us in the long run, or the fact that it may benefit us on the average, is small comfort to the man who is left wondering if he will be out on the street next year—or, perhaps, even five years from now. . . . If we permit it to penalize those who are least able to afford job change, if we permit it to bring on even temporary wide-spread hardship or unemployment, we shall deserve to be condemned for the mismanagement of what should be a great universal force for good.[15]

7. Examine with your class the external benefits received by the members of society from research activity such as that which yielded the polio vaccine or the transistor. Consider industrial research, how a firm's research results may be taken over by competing firms, and how even the protection

---

Some Teaching Materials: Invention

Books for Children
American Heritage (Michael Blow and R. P. Multhauf), *Men of Science and Invention.* New York: Golden Press, 1960.
Bonner, Mary G., *Wonders of Invention.* New York: Lantern, 1961.
Burlingame, Roger, *Scientists behind the Inventions.* New York: Harcourt, 1960.
Jolliffe, Ann, *From Pots to Plastics.* New York: Hawthorne, 1966.
Pratt, Fletcher, *All about Famous Inventors and Their Inventions.* New York: Random House, 1955.
Shippen, Katherine, *Mr. Bell Invents the Telephone.* New York: Random House, 1952.
Waller, L., *American Inventions.* New York: Holt, Rinehart and Winston, 1963.

---

[15] Thomas J. Watson, Jr., *The Power of Technological Change.* Pamphlet. Philadelphia: Wharton School, University of Pennsylvania, 1960.

of a patent is lost in time. Raise the questions: Is industry likely to do as much research as may be desirable for the welfare of man? Why is government justified to do research itself and to give money to universities and other institutions to do research?

CONSERVATION AND USE OF RESOURCES

A list of basic generalizations in economics appears on pages 185–186. The first reads: "Resources are scarce, and human wants are unlimited." A good way of documenting and underscoring this generalization is to make a survey of the world's natural resources and learn what is being done to conserve them, how wisely they are being used, and what remains to be done to protect them. While the invention of more efficient machines helps to narrow the gap between scarce resources and unlimited wants, the machines can do no more than process the raw material which they are fed. The raw materials of production are derived from nature's storehouse. It behooves society to use that storehouse with restraint and to assure its perpetuation. The present rapid acceleration of the world's population makes the problem an acute one. It is incumbent upon man to prevent needless washing away of topsoil, reckless cutting of timber, polluting of water and air, and waste in working of mines. Herein lies the urgency of effectively taught units on conservation and use of resources.

Suggestions for Teaching

1. Have your pupils trace the raw materials of a few common articles such as pencils, windowpanes, gasoline, and shoes. This activity will help direct their attention to our civilization's dependence upon natural resources.

2. Undertake with your class an inventory of natural resources. Samples of resources can be collected and placed in boxes, each bearing a label describing a different resource. Suggested labels and some of the objects that may be assigned to each are:

   (a) Can't be used up (for example, air, ocean, sand),
   (b) Can't be used up but can be spoiled (for example, rivers, scenery),
   (c) Can be used up, and can be used only once (for example, coal, oil, fertility),
   (d) Can be used up, but can be used more than once (for example, most metals),
   (e) Can be used up, and can be used only once (for example, coal, oil, gas).

This kind of activity will supply background. The children will see that not all resources are in danger of being snatched away, that the supply of certain ones is fully adequate, that others can be restored, and that still others require vigilant protection. Through such orientation the pupils will be in a position later to view in their larger setting the particular resources which may form the body of the unit.

3. Make an attractive display on a table or on an improvised magazine rack of samples of conservation magazines and pamphlets which will arouse interest and invite browsing.[16] Most conservation publications are written for adults, but children are often caught by the spirited, dramatic writing in some of them and by their many good illustrations. You may want to read to the class some portions of the writings of some of the pioneers in conservation.[17]

4. Set up an erosion demonstration model to illustrate the close relation between forest, soil, and water (see Appendix). The demonstration depicts vividly the role of vegetation in conserving water, preventing floods and duststorms, and holding precious topsoil in place. Follow up the demonstration by pointing out small-scale, close-at-hand evidences of rain-caused erosion. The hollowed-out faces of blocks of serpentine or other soft rock used in building are tokens of the work of rain upon an exposed soft material. Trips before and after a heavy rain may be taken by the class to observe a poorly seeded slope of lawn that, after a shower, loses soil to the sidewalk in the form of mud; or the detailed changes caused by rain on land in a garden, a neglected tennis court, or a sloping dirt road or driveway.

5. Explain through models and drawings the practices through which abused land is regaining its fertility and being conserved. "Contouring," "terracing," "crop rotation," and "cover cropping" are among the terms that should have meaning for every child, because it is through these farming practices that everyone, in city and in country, can look forward to a healthier, wealthier and more stable economy. Pictures of soil erosion on a large, socially disastrous scale, and of effective remedial measures should bring the story home graphically.

6. Emphasize the moral responsibility (particularly heavy in view of the rapid expansion of the human population) to preserve certain rare forms of wealth in their present state for the enjoyment of future generations. Examples are the recreational areas provided by the Grand Canyon, the

---

[16] *Audubon,* bimonthly publication of National Audubon Society, 1130 Fifth Avenue, New York, N.Y. 10028; *National Wildlife,* bimonthly for adults, and *Ranger Rick's Nature Magazine,* monthly for children, published by National Wildlife Federation, 1412 Sixteenth Street, N.W., Washington, D.C. 20036; *The Living Wilderness,* quarterly publication of Wilderness Society, 729 Fifteenth Street, N.W., Washington, D.C. 20005. A reference librarian can supply names of other conservation periodicals. Above organizations issue miscellaneous conservation publications from time to time. The National Wildlife Federation will supply "List of Conservation Education Publications."

[17] T. Gilbert Pearson, *Adventures in Bird Protection.* New York: Appleton, 1937; Gifford Pinchot, *Breaking New Ground.* New York: Harcourt, 1948. For biographies of Muir and Pinchot, consult accompanying box of "Some Suggested Teaching Materials."

redwoods, selected seashores, native prairies, marshes, and historical land-marks. Their preservation is a continuous battle, current campaigns of which are described in the news bulletins of the Nature Conservancy (see Footnote 21). Present these areas as types of *wealth*. (Wealth is defined by economists as anything possessing utility and physical substance, and is capable of being owned.

7. Include the topic of water conservation in the unit. The need for water conservation has become critical in consequence of the huge and steadily mounting water requirements of our expanding industry and our growing population. The problem is compounded by water pollution. For example:

(a) In industry. Industry, whose water wastes include enormous quan-tities of chemicals, oils, and greases, finds that it must treat the water it has helped pollute before the water can be used in some of its own manufacturing processes. The cost of the treatment, inci-dentally, causes the price of the industrial product to rise.

(b) In the home. Water must be treated for home use—drinking, cooking, and bathing.

(c) In agriculture. Water must be purified for irrigation lest crops be damaged, and for drinking water for cattle.

Assign some of your pupils to read about what steps are being taken to provide more clean water.[18]

8. A trip to a nearby resource can add a vivid touch of reality to dis-cussions of conservation. With respect to water, Mattison suggests:

> Any stream is an excellent teaching aid. Study it firsthand. Does it maintain a fairly constant flow of water the whole year? Why? Is it dry in summer? Again, why? What is its importance to the community? Is its water clean? Here, again, the teaching potential of water is limited only by the teacher's imagination.[19]

The following account of the firsthand experiences of an elementary school class in Texas and its study of oil resources makes it clear how a trip can enrich learning.

> C. M. Joiner drilled the first successful oil well in the county, and his granddaughter still lives near this original oil site. A committee from the

---

[18] Irma S. Black, *Busy Water*. New York: Holiday, 1958; Mart Casey and S. A. Lavine, *Water Since the World Began*. New York: Dodd, Mead, 1965; Bernard Frank, *Water*. Washington, D.C.: National Wildlife Federation, 1957; Iva Green, *Water: Our Most Valuable Natural Resource*. New York: Coward-McCann, 1958; United States Department of the Interior, *A Primer on Water* and *A Primer on Water Quality*. Washington, D.C.: Superintendent of Documents, 1960, 1965.

[19] Charles W. Mattison, "Teaching and Learning about Conservation," *Water: The Yearbook of Agriculture 1955*. Washington, D.C.: Superintendent of Documents. Pp. 681–684.

class wrote to her, inviting her to tell us what she could about this early adventure. She graciously accepted, and by anecdotes which no written material contained, personalized and made vivid what might have been to some of the children a purely historical fact.

We had another guest, the father of one of the boys, who was a crew foreman for a local drilling company. He did a thoughtful job of simplifying the processes involved in drilling a well. Following his visit, one group of children made a mural showing these steps, and another group made one depicting some of the uses of oil in the United States.

Two trips were made in conjunction with this study. We visited the drilling rig of the above-mentioned company, and the children saw the actual operation of the derrick. We saw firsthand operation of the enormous drilling machines, and how a "trip is made," i.e., pulling the pipe up to change a dull drilling bit. The crew also demonstrated the safety devices and the procedures used when a well "blows in" unexpectedly or the rig catches fire. It was the soil reports from this well which the children studied in deciding when it would be completed.

Our second trip showed dramatically how oil links us to the outside world. Another father, who was manager of Pioneer Airlines in Big Spring, became interested in our work; and he made arrangements for the class to take a 20-minute flight over the West Texas oil field. Words such as terrain, elevation, plateau, and so forth, took on new meanings. The plane was fueled after we were aboard, and the children thus had another concrete example of how one industry depends heavily upon another. The flight itself was a summarizing experience, giving a vivid over-all picture of Howard County's oil industry.[20]

To give such experiences economic teeth, the governmental favors granted the oil industry should be explored. A portion of the oil producer's income is tax exempt to make up to him for the depletion of his oil reserves, and oil imports are sharply limited. Children should become acquainted with the practice of governmental subsidy and the various forms it takes. Thus, water transportation receives a subsidy by the government's undertaking to widen and maintain river channels. Agriculture receives a subsidy from the government's support of the prices of certain agricultural products. Children should also become acquainted with the fact that government subsidy is not necessarily fairly or wisely distributed among the various industries—that pressure politics is part of the picture. Pressure is exerted on government officials and representatives by lobbies, some of which, such as the oil industry's lobby, are wealthy and powerful. However one might deplore particular subsidies, the teacher should emphasize that freedom to advance one's interests through propaganda and pressure groups is an essential of democratic government.

9. Give attention to attitudes toward conservation which your pupils are

[20] The author is grateful to Edythe Westmoreland Mullin for this account.

forming as the unit progresses. Aim to develop a rationally optimistic frame of mind among children concerning the future. Some conservation writers and speakers arouse a hopeless feeling about the problem. This can be counteracted by class projects, such as filling eroded gulleys with brush or stones, restoring the fertility of a worn patch of soil, establishing a small sanctuary with facilities for attracting birds, and planting, on an eroding hillside, trees supplied by the state government or interested local citizens. Through actual participation in such projects, the child will learn that even an unaided individual can do something. He also should learn about the constructive work of membership organizations through joining one that is geared to children.[21] The activity of private industry and of government agencies in conservation may be discovered by obtaining some of their publications.[22]

Discourage the notion that conservation requires hoarding. The solution to the problem of disappearing resources depends on preservation and increase of scarce items, and intelligent, efficient use of all resources. Teachers should point out that, probably, there are still undiscovered resources, that fuller use can very likely be made of our known resources, and that we are doing better than ever in renewing many of them.

Some Teaching Materials: Conservation and Use of Resources

Books for Children

Evers, Alf, *The Treasure of Watchdog Mountain*. New York: Crowell-Collier and Macmillan, 1953.

Hader, Berta, and Elmer Hader, *Two Is Company, Three's a Crowd*. New York: Harper & Row, 1965.

Lathrop, Dorothy P., *Let Them Live*. New York: Crowell-Collier and Macmillan, 1951.

Norman, Charles, *John Muir: Father of Our National Parks*. New York: Messner, 1957.

White, Dale, *Gifford Pinchot: The Man Who Saved the Forests*. New York: Messner, 1957.

---

[21] See the membership organizations given in Footnote 16. Write also to the Nature Conservancy, 1522 K Street, N.W., Washington, D.C. 20005. Information about the Audubon Junior Clubs may be obtained from the National Audubon Society, address in Footnote 16. See William L. Reavley, *Conservation Clubs for Juniors*, Washington, D.C.: National Wildlife Federation, 1957.

[22] For example: Dow Chemical Company, Agricultural and Industrial Bioproduct Sales, Midland, Mich.; American Petroleum Institute, 1271 Avenue of the Americas, N.Y.; American Forestry Association, 919 17th Street, N.W., Washington, D.C.; Forest Farmers Association Cooperative, 1100 Crescent Avenue, N.E., Atlanta, Ga.; United States Department of the Interior, Washington, D.C.

FOR REVIEW AND REFLECTION

1. Which economic (a) processes and (b) institutions do you consider most important and appropriate for systematic study in the elementary school? Why?
2. Describe an activity which could be carried out in connection with each of the proposed units in this chapter, in addition to those suggested.
3. Some industrial arts experiences are proposed in the chapter. How do they contribute to children's acquisition of economic concepts?
4. The Gross National Product is our measure of economic growth. How could the term and the concept be presented to children in a way that would make them meaningful and helpful?
5. To what extent, and how, should the subject of unfair business practices (false labeling, deceptive advertising, and other fraudulent business practices) be handled by the teacher?

ASSIGNMENTS

1. Draw up a lesson plan for teaching some aspect of money and banking. Indicate the grade or age of the children you have in mind.
2. Make a study of an industry dealing with a specified item of food, clothing, or shelter, and make a chart similar to the one in this chapter.
3. Carry out one of the industrial arts activities relevant to the study of a major industry. (Consult Gilbert's book listed in "Supplementary Reading.") Explain what new insight you acquired into the process through this experience, and the benefit of such an experience for children.

SUPPLEMENTARY READING

Annals of the American Academy of Political and Social Sciences, **345** (January 1963—entire issue). A comprehensive treatment of transportation contributed to by 17 specialists.

Crowther, James G., *Discoveries and Inventions of the Twentieth Century* (5th Ed.). New York: Dutton, 1966. A technical account of industrial development in transportation, chemical engineering, agriculture, and other selected fields.

Elgin, Keren, *et al., A Fifth Grade Studies the Results of a Forest Fire.* Pamphlet. San Francisco: Forest Service, California Region, U.S. Department of Agriculture, 1963.

Fair, Marvin L., and Ernest W. Williams, Jr., *Economics of Transportation* (Rev. ed.). New York: Harper & Row, 1959.

Fairchild, Fred Rogers, and T. J. Shelly, *Understanding Our Free Economy* (4th ed.). Princeton, N.J.: Van Nostrand, 1962. A textbook in economics for beginners, it should prove helpful to teachers who have not studied the subject formally.

Galbraith, John K., *The Affluent Society.* Boston: Houghton Mifflin, 1958. A provocative discussion of our economy's alleged overinvestment in goods and underinvestment in people.

Gilbert, Harold G., *Children Study American Industry*. Dubuque, Ia.: William C. Brown Co., 1966. Industrial arts for children, containing resource units on manufacturing, construction, and other industries.

Ginzberg, Eli (Ed.), *Technology and Social Change*. New York: Columbia University Press, 1964. A collection of papers on technology as it relates to such social problems as economic growth and government control.

Joint Council on Economic Education, "Check List: Materials for the Teacher." New York: The Council, 1963. A list of publications available on the teaching of economics, several titles of which are of special interest to the elementary school teacher.

National Academy of Sciences, *Conference on Transportation Research*. Washington, D.C.: National Academy of Sciences and National Research Council, 1960.

National Industrial Conference Board, *Road Maps of Industry*. New York: The Board. A periodical report of significant current statistics on the economic scene.

National Task Force on Economic Education, *Economic Education in the Schools*. New York: Committee for Economic Development, 1961. Report by an authoritative body on the need for economic education in the high school, essential economic understandings, and recommendations for the high school curriculum.

Nevins, Allan, *et al.*, *Energy and Man: A Symposium*. New York: Appleton, 1960. Deals with the history of energy development, the "petroleum revolution," energy and public affairs, and other topics.

New England Economic Education Council, *Toward Economic Competency: A Suggested Guide to Economic Education, Grades One through Six*. New York: Joint Council on Economic Education, 1960. Suggests objectives, topics, and activities.

Philipson, Morris (Ed.), *Automation: Implications for the Future*. New York: Vintage, 1962. A series of articles on possible consequences of automation for industry, labor, government, education, and leisure.

Senesh, Lawrence, *Our Working World*. Chicago: Science Research, 1966. A program for elementary school children including textbook, records, resource unit, and other teaching materials.

Social Education, 30 (April 1966), No. 4. Devoted to economic education, including one article on economics in the primary grades and another on economics in the intermediate grades.

Sutton, Rachel S., "Behavior in the Attainment of Economic Concepts: II," *Journal of Psychology*, 58 (October 1964), 407–412. Describes an experiment in which children in Grades 1, 3, and 5 were tested on economic concepts before and after six months of instruction in economics. The number of incorrect responses decreased significantly following the period of instruction.

United States Agency for International Development, *Transportation*. United Nations Conference on the Application of Science and Technology for the

Benefit of the Less Developed Areas. Washington, D.C.: Superintendent of Documents, 1963. Vol. 5.

United States Department of the Interior, *State Natural Resource Series*. Booklets. Washington, D.C.: Superintendent of Documents, 1963 and subsequent years. Lists resources and outlines conservation programs. A booklet will eventually be available for each of the 50 states.

Williams, Chester, "Teaching Economics to Elementary Pupils," *Chicago Schools Journal,* **45** (December 1963), 137–138. Presents a plan for introducing economic education into the curriculum for a selected group of pupils in Grades 5–8.

Woodbury, David O., *Atoms for Peace*. New York: Dodd, Mead, 1961. A popular description of the application of atomic energy to transportation, electrical power, and radiation.

8

TEACHING POLITICAL CONCEPTS: UNITS EMPHASIZING GOVERNMENT AND CITIZENSHIP

*Governments, like clocks, go
from the motion men give them.*
WILLIAM PENN

The study of government introduces the child to the system of authority and law within which society operates. It includes a study of the framework of government—its constitution, system of elections, executive agencies, legislative agencies, and the like—and the work performed by the various divisions and agencies. Although emphasis is properly placed upon our own local, state, and national governments, increasing attention is given in schools to international affairs—the relationship of our own government to others, comparisons of the governments of representative countries, and efforts at international political organization.

One prominent phase of the elementary study of government is citizenship training. According to Greenstein: "No topic of political science has a longer and more distinguished lineage than citizenship training."[1] He traces that lineage from Plato, who stressed the role of education in maintaining a stable political system, to contemporary legislative requirements for instruction about the Constitution. "Whether or not one believes that social studies in general and political science in particular have a primary responsibility toward citizenship education," writes Jarolimek, "those who are most directly responsible for the formulation of public school policies believe this to be the case."[2] Those formulators of school policy are justi-

---

[1] Fred I. Greenstein, *Children and Politics.* New Haven, Conn.: Yale University Press, 1965. P. 2.

[2] John Jarolimek, "Political Science in the Elementary and Junior High School Curriculum," in Donald H. Riddle and Robert S. Cleary (Eds.), *Political Science in the Social Studies*; Thirty-sixth Yearbook. Washington, D.C.: National Council for the Social Studies, 1966. Chap. 15, p. 238.

fied. Unless we teach about the responsibilities of citizenship, we can hardly expect our pupils, when they become adults, to vote intelligently, to be knowing about government and politics, to worry about the consequences of political decisions, and to have the urge to help bring about improvements in governmental policy.

HOW THE STUDY OF GOVERNMENT TEACHES CITIZENSHIP

The study of government has built-in elements which develop traits of good citizenship quite naturally and more successfully than the contrived and preachy devices which Mayer[3] and others have deplored. Government can be taught so as to impart a disciplined way of analyzing, classifying, and judging data; of comparing and evaluating sources of data; and of weighing conflicting data. The importance of the types of thinking underlying such activities when applied to public affairs is obvious. If free inquiry becomes a habit, it is perhaps the best defense against propaganda and subversion.

Knowledge of government contributes to citizenship in other ways. (1) It provides a basis for viewing current affairs with perspective—for appraising situations realistically, avoiding undue optimism or undue pessimism and avoiding the provincial outlook. (2) It provides an understanding of political traditions and thus promotes in the child a sense of continuity. He should be better able to live and work sympathetically, or at least tolerantly, with the generations which overlap his. (3) The child is brought to feel more at home in his world and to sense how his homeland is related to other lands. (4) The surface of political affairs may appear chaotic, but their systematic study reveals to the child some presence of order. For example, methods have been established for amending the Constitution, selecting juries, employing civil servants, and the like; and, "odd" (unfamiliar) political behavior often makes sense when examined in terms of human motives and customs.

A word of caution is in order. Cognitive learning may or may not have the affective results stated in (1) and (2). Provincialism is not necessarily the result, or solely the result, of inadequate information about other places or viewpoints. Nevertheless, the foregoing elements of citizenship can be taught indirectly and, perhaps, more effectively than through a frontal attack on citizenship itself. This is not to overlook the possibilities of a frontal attack.

Two political scientists, after studying children's interests, beliefs, opinions, and attitudes about political matters, concluded that:

[3] Martin Mayer, *The Schools.* New York: Harper & Row, 1961. Chap. 16.

. . . it is apparent that the elementary-school years rather than the high school years present the crucial time for training in citizenship attitudes and the wider range of behavior we have called political socialization. It seems likely that formal programs of citizenship training and education might be more effectively placed at the pre-high-school level than at later phases of formal education.[4]

Some Basic Generalizations of Government[5]

A. Nature and Purpose of Democratic Government
   1. The responsibilities of government are to provide (a) external security, (b) internal order, (c) justice, (d) services essential to general welfare which the people cannot provide so well for themselves, and (e) freedom.
   2. Political stability requires governmental flexibility to meet the changing conditions of a growing nation. The Constitution of the United States is an example of a governmental framework which provides such flexibility.
   3. Political parties and special interest groups perform necessary services in the governing process.
   4. Democracy implies a way of life as well as a form of government; the way of life is based on the dignity of the individual, equality of opportunity, and man's ability to govern himself.
   5. Man has the opportunity of developing his fullest potential in a climate of freedom.
   6. Civil liberty is the basis for human freedom.
B. Democratic Citizenship
   1. A citizen can do his part in making democracy work only if he is informed concerning the issues of the day.
   2. The citizen has civic responsibilities as well as rights.
C. International Government
   1. International political institutions and organizations have evolved over many years.
   2. International political institutions and organizations have special significance today because of the increasing interdependence of nations and considerations of national survival.

---

[4] Robert D. Hess and David Easton, "The Role of the Elementary School in Political Socialization," *School Review*, **70** (Autumn 1962), 257–265. The difficulty and complexity of shaping attitudes at more advanced age levels are brought out in Edgar Litt, "Civic Education, Community Norms, and Political Indoctrination," *American Sociological Review*, **28** (February 1963), 69–75; and Charles H. Stember, *Education and Attitude Change*. New York: Institute of Human Relations, 1961.

[5] These generalizations are, in part, a streamlined version of those appearing in *Report of the State Central Committee on Social Studies to the California State Curriculum Commission*. Sacramento: California State Department of Education, 1961; and Bernard Berelson, *et al.*, *The Social Studies and the Social Sciences*. New York: Harcourt, 1962.

Another factor which helps to mold citizenship is the influence of the teacher himself. Teachers sometimes despair when their citizenship training appears to be offset by destructive views prevalent in the child's neighborhood environment. Yet the teacher's potency need not be negated if he makes the most of opportunities for operant conditioning, using his rewarding power discriminately, if he is an attractive person in the eyes of his pupils, and if he is a warm, well-integrated person.[6]

The impact upon the child of living and learning in a civilized classroom setting can be considerable. After all, Monday through Friday, the number of hours an elementary school teacher spends in contact with a child approaches the number of hours a child is in similar contact with his mother per day, and exceeds the hours of such contact with his father. But the time factor is on the teacher's side only if the classroom climate is infused with a positive social and moral tone and if the teacher takes advantage of recent findings of social psychology.

CHILDREN'S UNDERSTANDING
OF THE POLITICAL WORLD

Recent studies by political scientists reveal that most primary-grade children are familiar with the concept of government. Children in the earlier grades associate government most commonly with personal figures of political authority, such as the President and the policeman.[7] Yet they do not necessarily know much about the work of these figures. For example, although most fourth-graders in one study rated the President's job as "the most important," less than one-third of them had a "reasonably accurate" idea of the President's duties.[8] Children are able to differentiate typical government personnel from nongovernment personnel—although at the second-grade level, a sizeable proportion of children in one study were unable to do so (32 percent misclassified the soldier and 43 percent misclassified the postman).[9] Younger children are inclined to look upon government as benevolent and to evaluate leaders favorably.[10] They do not share the widespread cynicism and distrust of adults toward politics.[11]

Older children, in Grades 6–8, show growth in a number of respects. They have more political information and more accurate information than

---

[6] Albert Bandura and Richard H. Walters, *Social Learning and Personality Development.* New York: Holt, Rinehart and Winston, 1963; and mimeographed report by L. M. Heil, M. Powell, and J. Feffer abstracted in N. L. Gage (Ed.), *Handbook of Research on Teaching.* Skokie, Ill.: Rand McNally, 1963. P. 424.

[7] David Easton and Jack Dennis, "The Child's Image of Government," *Annals of the American Academy of Political and Social Science,* **361** (September 1965), 40–57; Greenstein, see Footnote 1.

[8] Greenstein. Pp. 33, 58.

[9] Easton and Dennis.

[10] Easton and Dennis; Greenstein.

[11] Greenstein.

have younger children.[12] They are more inclined to associate government with elected legislative bodies and their lawmaking activities rather than with personal figures.[13] There is a shift from lofty idealization of leaders.[14] Party partisanship declines between Grade 4 and Grade 8 among upper socio-economic groups, and self-declared "independent" political status increases.[15]

Would more systematic teaching about government in the primary grades bring about earlier political knowledge and sophistication? There can be little doubt, on the basis of the aforementioned research, that "readiness" exists. That knowledge can be imparted was demonstrated by Arnoff. who found that after a five-week unit on government, even second-grade children were able to identify correctly definitions of terms such as "subpoena," "ballot," and "campaign."[16] How *rapidly* political sophistication can be brought about is another matter. Greenstein believes that ". . . young children probably are unable to engage in the abstract cognitive operations inherent in ideological thinking."[17] Another possibility is that the immaturity of younger children is due to adult attempts to shield the child from harsh political realities such as corruption and chicanery and to teach about political life in an unctuous and unrealistic manner.[18] As Greenstein puts it, ". . . adults . . . more or less unconsciously sugarcoat the political explanations they pass on to children."[19] At any rate, it is evident that primary-grade children possess a background and awareness of political personalities, institutions, and events which social studies programs have not developed as systematically or as energetically as appears justified.

SPECIAL TASKS IN TEACHING ABOUT GOVERNMENT

Teaching Patriotism

One aspect of citizenship training is to instill patriotism—pride in one's homeland, respect for its institutions, traditions, and aspirations, and desire to contribute to its progress and reputation. In this context, ceremonies like the flag salute and symbols such as the flag can be used as takeoff points for interpretations of what such symbols stand for. Children

[12] Greenstein.
[13] Easton and Dennis.
[14] Robert D. Hess and David Easton, "The Child's Image of the President," *Public Opinion Quarterly*, 4 (Winter 1960), 632–644; Greenstein.
[15] Greenstein. P. 73.
[16] Melvin Arnoff, "Adding Depth to Elementary School Social Studies," *Social Education*, 28 (October 1964), 335–336.
[17] Greenstein. P. 77.
[18] Ralph C. Preston, "Children's Reactions to Harsh Social Realities," *Social Education*, 23 (March 1959), 116–117, 120.
[19] Greenstein. P. 77.

in the primary grades discover that the flag possesses emotional significance. In the intermediate grades, they can consider the question: How do patriotic emotions differ from person to person? When they pool their experiences, they usually discover that for one person, the flag or the national anthem brings to mind a mental image of a loved feature of the landscape such as "amber waves of grain." For another person, it revives his tolerance of, and commitment to, the idea that unpopular ideas may be expressed. The flag or anthem for another person stirs his *intolerance* of unpopular ideas. Still another person (for instance, a rabid left-winger) will find his resentment of the federal government rekindled. The emotions aroused by patriotic symbols are thus varied. They drive one man to regret he has but one life to give for his country and another to protest his country's involvement in a conflict. Patriotism brings different individuals to support opposing causes; in the name of patriotism, conservationists battle anticonservationists and vice versa, and advocates of free enterprise for the power industry battle advocates of government ownership and vice versa. Yet, while the various forms of patriotism reflect the pluralism of society, patriotism also possesses a common denominator; if this were not the case, we would not be able to achieve the degree of unity and consensus which we enjoy.

Through consideration of these matters, patriotic symbolism offers a major entrée for elementary school social studies into civic education. The abstracting process, set in motion by patriotic symbols, is a major intellectual milestone that children can attain by introspective analysis and discussion. Patriotic ideas and symbols, if built into the intellectual content of the study of government, can lead to constructive reflection on what constitutes responsible civic behavior.

Stimulating Interest in Public Affairs

The low interest level of the average American in public affairs is a frequent subject of articles and editorials, in which schools are commonly held accountable. The lack of interest is not to be denied. One survey revealed that fewer than half of the adults of the United States were able to name the Congressman from their own district.[20] An earlier survey reported that only six percent ever wrote their Congressman.[21] In a tabulation of the voting turnout rates of 15 democratic nations, only India ranked lower than the United States.[22] In the closest presidential election of the century (1960), only 38 percent of a sample of adults stated they were

---

[20] George Gallup, American Institute of Public Opinion, Princeton, N.J., August 26, 1966.
[21] George Gallup, American Institute of Public Opinion, Princeton, N.J., April 6, 1957.
[22] Austin Ranney, *The Governing of Men* (Rev. ed.). New York: Holt, Rinehart and Winston, 1966. P. 287.

"very much" interested in the outcome, and only 63 percent of the age-eligible voters actually voted.[23]

It is unfair to shoulder teachers with all the blame for this situation. In the first place, not all political scientists are convinced that Americans' modest participation and interest in political affairs are necessarily pathological.[24] In the second place, there are cultural forces more powerful than classroom instruction which could account for the fact that public affairs apparently assumes a position of secondary importance in the lives of many Americans. On the other hand, interest could probably be raised if teachers were to focus less upon verbal and diagrammatic descriptions of government and more upon principles of government as it is seen to operate in current events and in people's everyday lives. Teachers will not have much impact upon their pupils' future political concern unless they can make the study of government more vital. The reader is referred to the suggestions for teaching "Current History"[25] and to the suggestions for handling controversial issues, (see pages 177–178) which follow.

Handling Political Controversy

In one survey of practices of elementary school teachers, 80 percent indicated they did not teach controversial issues.[26] It is doubtful if citizenship training can be accomplished while avoiding such issues. Wilson states that ". . . for a teacher of social studies to seek to avoid controversy is to surrender his function as a teacher."[27] He explains that some lessons can be learned only through examining such issues. How else, he asks, can the child learn that ". . . honest men may differ without rancor, without emotional outbursts . . . without doubting the integrity of those who hold different opinions"—and that much one may read and hear is quite subjective?[28]

[23] Ranney. P. 212.

[24] Gabriel A. Almond and Sidney Verba, *The Civic Culture: Political Attitudes and Democracy in Five Nations.* Boston: Little Brown, 1965; William G. Andrews, "Don't Blame the American Voter," in Bradbury Seasholes, *Voting, Interest Groups, and Parties.* Glenview, Ill.: Scott, Foresman, 1966. Pp. 19–21; Anthony Downs, *An Economic Theory of Democracy.* New York: Harper & Row, 1957.

[25] See also a summary of current events activities carried out at the elementary school level in Doyle Casteel, "Current Events and Political Science: Seeking a Functional Relationship," in Donald H. Riddle and Robert S. Cleary (Eds.), *Political Science in the Social Studies*; Thirty-sixth Yearbook. Washington, D.C.: National Council for the Social Studies, 1966. Chap. 20. Pp. 323–324.

[26] J. D. McAulay, "Controversial Issues in the Social Studies," *Education,* **86** (September 1965), 27–30.

[27] H. H. Wilson, "Values and Teaching in Controversial Areas," in Donald H. Riddle and Robert S. Cleary (Eds.), *Political Science in the Social Studies*; Thirty-sixth Yearbook. Washington, D.C.: National Council for the Social Studies, 1966. Chap. 19. P. 308.

[28] Wilson. P. 309.

The Harvard Social Studies Project demonstrated that junior high school pupils could learn to apply a method of analysis to controversial public issues which consisted, basically, of (1) settling factual issues, (2) handling problems of semantics, and (3) dealing with value conflicts.[29] In a study of Negroes and civil rights, for example, this might involve establishing or verifying facts about the Negro population in a given community, the rate of Negro unemployment, and so on; and agreeing upon the meaning of charged terms such as *black power* and *de facto segregation*. Dealing in this way with matters of fact and terminology separately keeps the value conflict "clean," and makes it possible to get at the heart of the clash over values—commonly so obscured by factual and semantic considerations that analytical procedures are blocked and no headway is made.

McAulay makes some suggestions which should also be given careful attention: The teacher's role should be one chiefly of suggesting the need for more information, to see that each child with something to say gets a courteous hearing, and to help the class summarize the pros and cons of an issue on the chalkboard.[30]

Teaching about Communism

The sharp challenge which communism addresses to the free democratic world makes it mandatory that it be studied and discussed whenever relevant—during the study of the Soviet culture realm (Chapter 5), during the study of our own system of government (whether at local, state, or national level), and during the discussion of current events (Chapter 6). The approach should be primarily a positive one, with emphasis on the nature of our freedoms as outlined in the Mayflower Pact, the Declaration of Independence, the Constitution, and other documents, and as embodied in our economic system of free enterprise (Chapter 7).

The fact that citizens participate vigorously in advancing the ideals embodied in those documents should be stressed as one of the significant characteristics of the free world which distinguishes it from the Communist world. Evidence of the participation should be freely referred to by citing instances of frank discussion occurring at public meetings, in the press, on television, and in the legislative halls. Many children are already aware of controversy: controversy growing out of efforts to protect the civil rights of all citizens; controversy over the limits of free enterprise (the extent to which business interests should be permitted to develop land and other resources without regulations governing land use, aesthetic values, hygienic

[29] James P. Shaver and Donald W. Oliver, "Teaching Students to Analyze Public Controversy: A Curriculum Project Report," *Social Education*, **28** (April 1964), 191–194, 248.
[30] J. D. McAulay.

standards, and the like); controversy over the persuasive inducement of young people to smoke cigarettes; controversy over the wisdom of permitting anyone with a few dollars to buy firearms in the face of an apparent relationship between the weapon controls of a state and the incidence of its violent crime. Free participation in such controversy should be cited as one of the hallmarks of a dynamic democratic society in which one need not abjectly accept public policy on a given issue as necessarily right; in which one is free to criticize a policy and promote alternative policies; and in which one is free to speak up for one's convictions.

Communist theory and practice should be examined. Children should become acquainted with the following facts:

1. There are dedicated communists throughout the world busily attempting to make converts. They are especially successful in their efforts among "have-nots" and some intellectuals who identify with "have-nots."

2. In the United States, they are relatively few in number. Although they infiltrate liberal groups, unions, the government, and other organizations, they do not presently threaten to undermine our system of government, even though they wish they could, and even though they have successfully affected certain leftist and black-power groups.

3. A series of anti-Communist laws were passed in the 1940s and 1950s as a result of a combination of factors, including evidence of the presence of active Russian and Chinese agents and widespread fear of internal subversion after the Second World War. These were intensified by events (the end of the nuclear bomb monopoly of the United States, the establishment of a Communist regime in China, Communist aggression in Korea, etc.) which required readjustments in foreign policy.

4. Communist tactics have created a knotty problem for free democracies which desire to guarantee individual political freedom and, at the same time, have the obligation to maintain national security.

5. Communists preach a cynical "ends justify means" philosophy used to exonerate their nations' denial of freedom, their "liquidation" of political opponents, their continuance of dictatorship, and their imperialist ventures. Such measures are alleged by communists to be taken for the purpose of advancing the welfare of the worker.

Teachers who wish to learn more about communism are referred to Scholastic Magazine Editors, *What You Should Know about Communism and Why* (New York: McGraw-Hill, 1962); John Gunther, *Meet Soviet Russia* (2 vols.) (New York: Harper & Row, 1962); Joint Committee of the National Education Association and the American Legion, *Teaching about Communism,* pamphlet (Indianapolis, Ind.: American Legion, 1962); and Rodger Swearingen, "Teaching about Communism in the American Schools," *Social Education,* 28 (February 1964), 68–70.

SELECTION OF UNITS

The following units on Government will be described below:

Local Government
State Government
National Government
Citizenship and Civil Rights
International Relationships

LOCAL GOVERNMENT

The local government as a topic for study (whether the government is thought of as county, township, town, city, or village) is much more important than its generally restricted size suggests. Local government is potentially a kind of laboratory for small-scale experimentation with new ideas. Furthermore, it can make allowances and adaptations, which state and national governments rarely can, for needs which grow out of indigenous religious, occupational, or other cultural patterns and problems.

Local government is the form of government in which most people have opportunity to become personally involved and which deals with matters which impinge visibly and directly upon them. A few of these, taken at random, are zoning ordinances to protect residential areas, provision of recreational facilities, law enforcement, and the levying of real estate taxes. When changes are made in any of these arrangements—revision of zoning, establishment of a new playground, reduction of the police force, or a change in tax assessments—many elements of the community become profoundly aroused.

Educators are justified in devoting a large portion of the curriculum to community study. We live in an age that overvalues size and organization. As Arthur E. Morgan, onetime chairman of the Tennessee Valley Authority, wrote: "The home and the community are not only the places of origin, but also the principal preserves, of the most intimate and sensitive values of our cultural inheritance, those elusive traits of good will, considerateness, courage, patience, and fellowship."[31]

A unit which emphasizes community government holds important educational possibilities. (1) It can cultivate in the child respect and loyalty for the community, based on realistic understanding of it. (2) It can reveal

[31] Arthur E. Morgan, *The Small Community.* New York: Harper & Bros. 1942.

the drama that lies close at home, checking the common tendency to regard commonplace, local problems as dull. (3) Finally, it can teach some of the techniques of investigation upon which social scientists ultimately base all their work—collecting data through observation, interviewing, and inspecting records; and drawing conclusions on the basis of these data.

Suggestions for Teaching

1. Make arrangements for your class to visit headquarters of your local government. One township manager volunteered to escort a third-grade class through the township offices himself. The tour included a visit to the tax offices, the engineer's office with its large map of the township, offices of those in charge of garbage and trash collections, and finally, the commissioners' room. There the children were seated and the manager told them how their township government operated, what a commissioner was, what the meetings were like, the meaning of taxes, and many other matters. The questions and discussions inspired by this trip continued for days.[32]

2. Have your class compile a scrapbook on the local community. The aforementioned third-grade class constructed one entitled "The Story of Elkins Park." It contained chapters bearing such titles as "The History of Elkins Park," "Our Community Government," and "The Future of Elkins Park." The book was complete with title page, table of contents, and an alphabetized index. It was copiously illustrated with drawings and photographs. It was pored over repeatedly by its young makers, eventually taking on a dog's-eared and much-loved appearance which betokened a well awakened interest in the community.

3. Organize part of the unit around some of the responsibilities of the local government, such as the providing of fire-fighting and police services. Your pupils can learn about fire protection in other times and places, common fire hazards, the costliness of fires, and the prevention of fires. Study of police protection, like that of fire protection, deals with its importance to society, the equipment, skills, and courage called for, and the training it requires. The limitations of police power should be clarified. Children see many television shows in which police violate constitutional rights and they often do not realize that a policeman does not have unlimited power. The need for training police to recognize the rights of minority groups in particular needs emphasis. The study should bring out the reasons for laws, how laws are made, the costliness of law enforcement, and ways apart from expense in which lawbreaking is harmful to society. Emphasize those laws which will have the most meaning for children, such as laws governing traffic, littering, zoning, the licensing of dogs, and the use of fireworks, to suggest a few.

[32] The author is grateful to Charlotte Werner Bernstein for this account.

One of the community's largest public undertakings is education. One fourth-grade teacher described part of her class's study of local education as follows:

> My class undertook to learn about the school organization in our District. A visit was made to the District Superintendent's Office. Here we examined the maps and charts of our District. We located other schools and districts on the maps and made a list of them. Upon returning to the classroom, the children discussed the number of schools they found and their classification. They decided to make a map of their District and put markers where each school is located, with a code number as to its type. After completing the map, a committee wrote a letter to the Board of Education for information on the other school districts in the city. They received from this office a sketch of the other five districts in the city, with the number of schools and their types listed for each district. From this the children learned the vastness and scope of our public educational system.[33]

4. Have the pupils consider how the community can be improved. This will introduce them to a wide range of possible governmental concerns, such as beautification. Arrange a survey of various ugly spots in the community —auto graveyards, dumps, the clutter of commercial signs, ranging from garish to dingy, that spoil the approaches to so many towns and cities. Discuss with the class how such conditions could be corrected.

5. Have your pupils think in terms of community planning. Children in several elementary schools of Philadelphia made an intensive study of their community's aesthetic needs. Before the study began, teachers found that many children thought of their neighborhoods as incapable of change or improvement. It was not difficult, however, to stimulate them to think in terms of what might be done to create greater beauty and more space. The pupils made detailed maps showing land use, each pupil taking a particular block. They placed their individual maps side by side. Then they listed both the neighborhood's assets and those spots that were ugly or harmful to healthful living. They drew up plans for the community of the future. Thus were citizens of the future led to think about the feasibility of improved surroundings. In view of the increased interest of all municipalities in planning for redevelopment, having pupils think in terms of redevelopment is a significant aspect of studies of local government. Many cities have models of their plans for urban renewal. A class excursion to study such a model might be an excellent experience for your class (see Figure 8.1).

Among the more vital aspects of community planning today are the preservation of urban open space and highway development—two needs which frequently clash. Of course, not all opponents of highways are promoters of open space. Most of the opponents are homeowners, tenants,

---

[33] The author is grateful to Olga C. Pennacchio for this record.

shopkeepers, and industries who face removal. As our population continues to expand, the need for long-term planning for both of these requirements will become increasingly apparent. Here is subject matter for citizenship of the most significant kind.[34]

Figure 8.1. A class studies urban renewal. Courtesy of Division of Visual Education, School District of Philadelphia.

Get information about "new towns" and cities which were planned completely before construction was begun in order to minimize traffic problems, preclude formation of slums and "urban sprawl," and build in safety, play space for children, and complete shopping and service facilities (Greendale, Wis.; Brasilia, Brazil; Levittown, Pa.; Columbia, Md.; and so on). Your pupils can consult encyclopedias under "city planning" and books on the subject.

6. Present your class with statistics on voting turnout obtained from an official of the local election board or the League of Women Voters. Have your class think of possible reasons for the usual poor voting turnout in

[34] See Urban Renewal Administration, *Preserving Urban Open Space*. Pamphlet. Washington, D.C.: Superintendent of Documents, 1963. For additional material on open space, write to Nature Conservancy, 1522 K Street, N.W., Washington, D.C. 20005—the only national conservation organization whose primary purpose is the preservation of natural areas having outstanding aesthetic or scientific importance. For an interesting account of how children in Grades 4 and 5 studied plans for an expressway, see E. Barry, "Economics Education in the East-West Expressway," *Childhood Education*, **42** (April 1966), 498–499.

Some Teaching Materials: Local Government

Books for Children
Brewster, Benjamin, *The First Book of Firemen*. New York: F. Watts, 1951.
Colby, Carroll, *Police; the Work, Equipment and Training of Our Finest*. New York: Coward-McCann, 1954.
Colonius, Lillian, *At the Library*. Chicago: Melmont, 1954.
Curren, Polly, *This Is a Town*. Chicago: Follett, 1957.
Dimond, Stanley E., and Elmer F. Pflieger, *Our American Government*, Unit 4 (Local Government). Philadelphia: Lippincott, 1963.
Elting, Mary, *We Are the Government*. New York: Doubleday, 1945.
Preston, Ralph C., et al., *Greenfield, U.S.A.* Boston: Heath, 1964. Pp. 44–78, 108–137.
Preston, Ralph C., and Eleanor Clymer, *Communities at Work*. Boston: Heath, 1964. Pp. 194–219.

Film
Day with Fireman Bill. Los Angeles, Calif.: Film Associates of California, 1958. Black and white or color.

Filmstrip
Learning about Your Local Government. Learning about the Growth of Towns. New York: American Book, 1961. Color.

---

local elections, in which often fewer than half of the eligible voters appear at the polls. Your class may be able to list probable reasons why there is greater interest in national elections, and to propose ways of increasing voter interest in local elections.

STATE GOVERNMENT

A unit on the native state is commonly taught in the fourth grade, sometimes an entire year being devoted to it. In the author's opinion, the state is more appropriately taught as a unit comprising four to six weeks. It must be remembered that the state is taught again in most schools in the junior or senior high school—sometimes, once in each. There can be little justification for a full year's study in the elementary school, to the exclusion of other social studies.

Two alternative plans are recommended for including the state in the elementary school curriculum. One plan consists of organizing a unit which is largely geographic in nature as suggested in Chapter 5, with a portion of it dealing with how the state is governed. The recommended alternative is to provide two units on the state—one emphasizing geography, to be followed by one emphasizing government and including narrative material on the origin and development of the state's political institutions.

Suggestions for Teaching

1. Make sure your class understands the hierarchical arrangement of governmental units—the organization of the United States into 50 states, the states into counties (called "parishes" in Louisiana), the counties of some states subdivided into townships (called "towns" in the New England states), and municipalities (ranging in size from tiny villages or boroughs to large cities) occurring as the smallest governing units. Of course, the *functioning* of the governmental structure is more important than the mere structure, but much of the confusion and ignorance among children concerning government comes about through their failure to learn initially about the governmental units and their interrelationships.

2. While it is necessary for your pupils to have the above relationships in mind while studying government, they will soon learn that these relationships are an oversimplification of the state of affairs. Supply concrete examples of how your state also designates school and park districts; of the powers granted by your state to municipalities to rule themselves; and of how the functions between counties and townships (or towns) are distributed.

3. On tracing historical developments, stress the sociological changes that have resulted in changes in the role of governmental units. For example: (a) The shift in population from our formerly largely rural population (85 percent of Americans lived in rural areas in 1790) to a largely urban population has reduced the power and significance of county government and has enhanced city government; (b) the shift from a largely rural to a largely urban population plus the United States Supreme Court ruling [1962] that state legislative districts must be based on the principle of equal electorates) is bringing about reapportionment of the state legislatures so that a legislative district will have representation based on population; (c) such diverse factors as the development of an economic system that cuts across state lines; increasing concern over foreign affairs and national security; and public sentiment favoring national standards with respect to social security, maintenance of fair trade practices, maintenance of regulation of air traffic and safety, and federal support of education, have led to an ever widening gap between the power and prestige of national government and state government.

4. Discuss with your class current state issues. (Local and state branches of the League of Women Voters keep abreast of them and issue literature giving details.) For example, certain states are being urged to make changes such as: (a) To extend home rule so that a municipality can adopt a

---

Some Teaching Materials: State Government

Books for Children
Preston, Ralph C., and John Tottle, *In These United States.* Boston: Heath, 1965. Pp. 249–250.
Ronan, Margaret, *Arrow Book of States.* New York: Scholastic, 1961.

Film
Inaugurating the Governor of Oklahoma. Norman, Okla.: Educational Materials Service, University of Oklahoma, 1955.

Source for the Teacher
Grant, David R., and H. C. Nixon, *State and Local Government.* Boston: Allyn & Bacon, 1963.

Materials for Particular States
Write to Department of Education in the state capital.

---

charter without waiting for a special act of the legislature; (b) to increase the frequency of legislative sessions (for example, the Pennsylvania legislature meets every second year—perhaps sufficient for the leisurely days of the nineteenth century); (c) to make it legally possible for a governor to succeed himself in office.

5. Develop an elementary concept of federalism in government—the scheme whereby political power is divided between the national and state governments. Your class should be able to list some of the reasons why a federation of states is advantageous (it increases security, facilitates trade between the states, and so on) and why, at the same time, a state wishes to retain its identity (it can act independently on many local matters, sectional pride preserves a healthy local initiative and interest in public affairs, etc.). At the same time, have your class identify and defend other alternatives such as abolition of states, regional agglomeration of states, and pure states rights. There is no need to make them think from the start that federalism is a logical concomitant of democracy.

6. Have your pupils think through what processes may be advantageously standardized on a national level (such as directing postal services) and what may more properly be left to the individual states (such as the determination of hunting laws, and operating state universities).

NATIONAL GOVERNMENT

It is customary for high school courses in government to describe in detail the three branches of the national government and the intricate, complex machinery by means of which governmental responsibilities are discharged. In the opinion of the author, such instruction should continue to be postponed until the high school years. The elementary school pupil can study the national government more profitably through a history unit on colonial United States, and through a short unit on government that places emphasis upon the citizen's individual responsibilities and upon governmental work carried out in his community.

Suggestions for Teaching

1. Provide a study of the fundamental rights and duties of citizenship. These have been presented in simple language for intermediate grade children by Preston and Tottle.[35]

2. Survey local institutions of the national government—the post office, perhaps a federal court, national park, passport office, office of the soil conservation service, or other agency. (Consult the local telephone book under "United States Government" for a list of U.S. agencies in your area.) Perhaps an official would come to your classroom to explain his work. Have the class make a large chart of federal agencies,[36] and mark those which have representation locally. A committee of children could be assigned the task of finding out the nature of their duties.

3. Create an understanding of a federal type of government. (Consult the fifth item in "Suggestions for Teaching" under the preceding section on "State Government.")

4. Prepare copies of an outline of the Constitution of the United States for your pupils. Read and discuss with them passages of the Constitution, taking time to explain legal and other unfamiliar terms. The author has found excerpts from the following passages to be particularly enlightening to children and capable of their understanding:

> Article 1, Section 7, method of passing laws
> Article 2, Section 3, duties of the President
> Article 6, part 2, supreme law of the land
> Amendment 1, freedom of religion, speech, and press

5. Familiarize the class with governmental aspects of Washington, D.C., as capital of the United States. Excellent photographs of the city are available in books, films, and filmstrips. Have the children become familiar with the Capitol, where laws are made; the White House, where the President may recommend laws to the Congress, sees to it they are carried out, manages foreign affairs, and commands the armed forces; and the Supreme Court Building, headquarters of the final court of appeal.

[35] Ralph C. Preston and John Tottle, *In These United States*. Boston: Heath, 1965. Chap. 9.

[36] See chart in the *United States Government Organization Manual*. Washington, D.C.: Superintendent of Documents. Revised annually.

Some Teaching Materials: National Government

Books for Children

Lawson, Don, *Young People in the White House.* New York: Abelard-Schuman, 1961.

League of Women Voters, *When You Come to Washington: How to Take a Look at the Federal Government.* Washington, D.C.: The League, 1964.

————, *You and Your National Government.* Washington, D.C.: The League, 1962.

Ross, George E., *Know Your Government.* Skokie, Ill.: Rand McNally, 1959.

Terrell, John U., *The United States Government Series.* Des Moines, Ia.: Meredith Press. Seven titles of various dates.

Torbert, Floyd J., *Postmen the World Over.* New York: Hastings, 1966.

Weaver, Warren, *Making Our Government Work.* New York: Coward-McCann, 1964.

Films

Our Country's Flag. Chicago: Coronet Instructional Films, 1960.

The American Flag. Wilmette, Ill.: Encyclopedia Britannica Films, 1959.

Filmstrips

Electing a President. New York: The New York Times, 1960.

Symbols of America. New York: Museum Extension Service, n.d.

Free Copies of Constitution

Hancock Life Insurance Co., 200 Berkeley Street, Boston, Mass. 02117. Limit of 50 copies.

CITIZENSHIP AND CIVIL RIGHTS

In these days of angry controversy over civil rights, the elementary school should utilize its opportunity to create rational discussion of the subject. An intermediate grade unit may be centered upon civil rights. Its content should embrace more than the Negro's civil rights in order that the topic may be viewed by the class in its proper broad perspective. While the teacher should avoid embarrassing pupils who belong to Negro or other groups striving to achieve civil rights, the civil rights problem simply cannot be understood without quoting or characterizing parties whose opinions are offensive to minority groups.

A portion of the study should focus upon the American people—who they are, who their forebears were, and what constitutes American citizenship. Such a study would reveal that most Americans speak English, but may differ in other respects—color of skin, religious belief, political allegiance, and in the nationality of their ancestors. It will become evident to the children that these variations help make the United States one of the most interesting countries in the world.

A second portion of the unit should deal with considerations of constitutional law. Citizens of all nations are formally assured by their constitutions of certain rights, such as freedom of speech and of press, and "due process of law." Constitutional guarantees are viewed by most citizens of free nations as safeguards against efforts of the majority to deny civil rights to members of minority groups. For example, the courts of the United States and Canada review cases of alleged oppression of minorities or individuals in the light of their constitutions. The cumulative decisions of these courts constitute a sort of index of the nations' regard for civil rights. The decisions of the United States Supreme Court often precipitate heated public controversy, such as the decision that membership in the Communist party was not, in itself, evidence of an individual's violation of anti-Communist legislation making it a crime to advocate the violent overthrow of the government; and when the Court ruled that separate schools for Negro children were unconstitutional.

Suggestions for Teaching

1. Explore with your class the means whereby a person attains citizenship through (a) birth and (b) naturalization.[37]

2. Discuss the proposition that all Americans are either immigrants or the *descendants* of immigrants—even the American Indian (whose forefathers came from Asia). Introduce the concept of the "melting pot."[38] See that your pupils understand that the melting pot is a factual characterization only up to a point—that in the extreme it would be the antithesis of diversity and would produce a far less colorful society than the one we are fortunate enough to have.

3. Have your pupils conduct a survey of the national backgrounds of the members of the class. This can be both enlightening and interesting. One sixth-grade teacher gave each member of her class the assignment to trace his ancestry back until he found the first relative who came from abroad. An interesting variety of backgrounds was revealed, since this class had such family names as Hougendobler, DiNatali, Bruno, McCulley, and Doyle. The teacher, Mrs. Patricia Farnan Pupo, writes:

Oh yes—we have a name like Pupo, too! My husband is of Italian-French ancestry while my own ancestory is Scotch and Welsh. Each child presented his information in the form of a tree showing branches bearing family names and their nationality from the central root. The project

[37] Ranney. Chap. 7; Preston and Tottle. Chap. 2.
[38] Preston and Tottle. P. 28.

awakened the children to the fact that peoples in their own ancestry come from foreign countries, and that in our classroom we have a melting pot of twelve different nations.

4. Have your class read and discuss the thirteenth, fourteenth, and fifteenth Amendments to the Constitution. These were adopted following the Civil War, and provided for the abolition of slavery and the extension of civil rights and suffrage to the Negro. Then review the long period of discrimination marked by noteworthy landmarks:[39] (a) The support of segregation by the Supreme Court in its "separate but equal" decision (1896); (b) the formation of the National Association for the Advancement of Colored People—the first of a number of organizations combining both Negro and white membership which have undertaken lobbying and legal and educational work to the end of securing equal rights and opportunities for Negroes (1909); (c) the refusal of the federal government to do business with firms that practiced employment discrimination against Negroes (1940); (d) the Supreme Court's rejection of its own earlier "separate but equal" concept and its ruling that separate schools for Negro pupils was unconstitutional (1954); (e) The enactment of the Civil Rights Act forbidding discrimination in public places (1964).

5. Have your pupils keep in touch with the civil rights issue as it is presented in periodicals for school children, newspapers, magazines, and broadcasts. Keeping abreast of current news will add life to the unit. But do not let news of the day overshadow the principles of civil rights growing out of the study of their history and legal basis.

6. See to it that your pupils do not form the narrow view of civil rights as having to do only with those of the Negro. The denial of rights to other minority groups should be considered (the Orientals, Jews, American Indians, and others).

7. Further broaden the concept of civil rights by bringing up some rights which relate to issues other than the protection of minority groups. A civil right is *any* freedom provided for by the Constitution. Civil rights range from protecting a citizen from being sentenced on the basis of evidence collected by tapping his telephone line to sparing a freethinker's child the necessity of hearing the Bible read in a public school. Of course, a person's claim to a "right" may be contested, and often the Supreme Court is called upon to render a decision as to whether or not some civic action interferes with a constitutionally guaranteed right of an individual. Political scientists make an important point about civil rights which can be understood by many children—legislators and courts make decisions about civil rights as they do about other controversial matters. The mood of the times, the convictions and judgments of the legislators and judges, and the strength

[39] Arnold M. Rose (Ed.), "The Negro Protest," *Annals of the American Academy of Political and Social Science*, **357** (January 1965).

Some Teaching Materials:
Citizenship and Civil Rights

Books for Children
Bard, Harry, et al., *Citizenship and Government in Modern America*
(Rev. ed.). New York: Holt, Rinehart and Winston, 1966. Chaps. 1, 2, 17.
Beard, Annie E. S., *Our Foreign-born Citizens* (Rev. ed.). New York:
Crowell, 1955.
Clayton, Ed, *Martin Luther King: The Peaceful Warrior*. Englewood Cliffs,
N.J.: Prentice-Hall, 1964.
Hine, Al, *This Land Is Mine*. Philadelphia: Lippincott, 1965.
Meltzer, Milton, *In Their Own Words: A History of the American Negro*
1865–1916. New York: Crowell, 1965.

Film
Good Citizens. Los Angeles: Educational Horizons, 1961.

Filmstrips
180,000,000 Americans. New York: The New York Times, 1961.
Growing in Citizenship Series. New York: McGraw-Hill Textfilms, n.d.

Teaching Tips
Payne, Rebecca S., "Focus on Primary Grades: Practicing Citizenship,"
Childhood Education, 42 (March 1966), 423.

---

and influence of the contesting groups all play a part. For this reason, we can expect that public actions on civil rights will shift from time to time, just as do actions on other governmental policies.

INTERNATIONAL RELATIONS

Elementary school teachers, anxious to make a contribution through their teaching to world peace, have hitherto relied on studies of various cultures of the world. These they have employed to break down provincial attitudes, to build tolerance and understanding, and to improve international relations. Can anything further be done in the classroom that might abate the grave threat to civilization of the nuclear arms race? Indeed, some teachers will wonder whether they should broach the subject of the nuclear threat to children of tender age.

The hard fact is that checking the arms race resides primarily in the realm of international politics. To a considerable extent, international politics operates independently of whatever "understanding" the citizens in hostile nations have of one another. So, apart from building under-standing (which *can* improve the international political climate and is not to be discounted), there is the task of achieving world peace through some kind of political agreement among nations, some kind of international law. As Oliver put it, it is on this issue that "the great debate of our time" will be centered. "Are we preparing our students for intelligent participation in this debate?"[40] Oliver had the high school student in mind, but the question is just as relevant for the elementary school pupil. The content must conform to the limited background and understanding of the younger child. He is not too young, however, to become prepared for grasping the necessity for the debate and, in broad outline, its content, even though we must postpone until he is in high school, a close analysis and evaluation of competing strategies.

Suggestions for Teaching

1. Acquaint your class with the major approaches to peace through various devices within the present "state system" (the system under which the world is divided into separate sovereign nations): (a) maintaining a balance of power between competing powers through "collective security" agreements and other means; (b) agreeing to disarmament; (c) submitting disputes to negotiation or arbitration; (d) submitting disputes to the International Court of Justice; and (e) working through the United Nations.[41] Give special attention to the United Nations—its structure and functions, its successes and problems. Make clear to your pupils that it is not a panacea for a warring world, but does represent a step toward international order and away from international anarchy.

2. Acquaint your class also with the concept of world government. One of its supporters (World Federalists) believes that the present international anarchy of our state system is the cause of war. This group finds the American federal system a useful model for relations between nations and a world government.[42]

3. Supply illustrations of peaceful settlement of disputes.[43] The study of international relations too often dwells upon the difficulties and creates a feeling of hopelessness and cynicism.

4. Encourage your pupils to correspond with children of foreign countries. Values of the culture and ways of thinking and doing are conveyed, as information about family and school life is exchanged. Names of "pen

[40] Donald W. Oliver, "Disarmament and World Law in the Social Studies Classroom," *Social Education*, **26** (November 1962), 363–366, 374.

[41] A scholarly description and appraisal of these approaches appears in Ranney. Chap. 23.

[42] Norman Cousins, *In Place of Folly*. New York: Harper & Row, 1961.

[43] Clark M. Eichelberger, *UN: The First Twenty Years*. New York: Harper & Row, 1965; James Avery Joyce, *World in the Making: The Story of International Cooperation*. New York: Abelard-Schuman, 1953; Arthur Larson, "Development of World Rule of Law," *Social Education*, **26** (November 1962), 390–396.

pals" may be obtained from International Friendship League, 40 Mt. Vernon Street, Boston, Mass. 02108; Student Letter Exchange, Wascea, Minn.; Letters Abroad, 45 E. 65 Street, New York, N. Y.; and People-to-People Letter Exchange, Box 1201, Kansas City, Mo. The problem of translating letters produces a difficulty, but not an insurmountable one. The experience of many schools has been that someone in the school or community can be found who is glad to help with translations. Sometimes teachers decide to learn the language of the "exchange" country and, in addition to translating, teach elements of it to the children.

5. Consider having your school form an affiliation with a foreign school. An affiliation is simply an informal partnership between two schools of two different countries. The partners keep in touch and in various ways build personal relations between pupils and teachers. In one school, affiliated with a school in France, every grade including kindergarten produced something to send to its affiliate—scrapbooks, Halloween masks, homemade stuffed animals, or school supplies. A school in Italy sent to its

---

Some Teaching Materials: International Relations

Books for Children
Bard, Harry, et al., *Citizenship and Government in Modern America.* New York: Holt, Rinehart and Winston, 1966. Chap. 18.
Cochrane, Joanna, *Let's Go to the United Nations Headquarters.* New York: Putnam, 1958.
Galt, Tom, *How the United Nations Works* (3d ed.). New York: Crowell, 1965.
Pierson, Sherleigh, *What Does a United Nations Soldier Do?* New York: Dodd, Mead, 1964.
Sterling Publishing Co., *Visual History of the United Nations, Year by Year* (Rev. ed.). New York: Sterling, 1966.

Filmstrips
We Are All Brothers. New York: Anti-Defamation League of B'nai B'rith.
Working Together for World Peace. Richmond, Va.: Visual Education Consultants.

Teaching Tips
Collings, Dorothy, "How to Put More Life into United Nations Studies," *Grade Teacher*, **83** (February 1966), 79, 124–127.
Martin, Clyde, "Introducing Children to Current World Problems," *Childhood Education*, **41** (March 1965), 349–352.
New York City Board of Education, *Toward Better International Understanding.* New York: The Board, 1960.
Robbins, Lois, "Training for Leadership: A World View," *Audio-visual Instruction*, **9** (December 1964), 668–671.

affiliate in the United States a booklet of crocheted lace, carvings, needle-work, and pictures of household appliances. From an affiliated school in France came mounted specimens of leaves, cutouts of girls' hair styles and clothes, and a notebook on holidays in France. Exchange of letters is a natural accompaniment to school affiliation where the language barrier can be overcome. Affiliations can be arranged directly or through the American Friends Service Committee, 160 N. Fifteenth Street, Philadelphia, Pa. 19102.

FOR REVIEW AND REFLECTION

1. What is involved in citizenship training? Do you agree with Hess and Easton that the elementary school years "present the crucial time" for it? Why or why not?
2. How can patriotism and world-mindedness be taught as complementary qualities?
3. What are the relative merits of the two plans for studying state government mentioned on page 226? What are other possible plans?
4. What are the major proposed approaches to world peace? How can each be simply yet accurately explained to children?
5. What experience aside from formal study will contribute to a child's under-standing of local government?

ASSIGNMENTS

1. Plan a lesson on the study of the organization of your local government.
2. Make a survey of the "open space" needs of an urban area with which you are familiar, and indicate how children could (a) cooperate in such a survey, and (b) learn the importance of planning for the preservation of open spaces. (See Footnote 34 for references to some source material.)
3. Make a plan for introducing children to the states' rights issue.
4. Construct a chart which would help children understand the concept of our federal government.
5. Plan an activity which you believe may contribute to children's sympathetic understanding of the needs of other nations.

SUPPLEMENTARY READING

Arnoff, Melvin, "Adding Depth to Elementary School Social Studies," *Social Education,* **28** (October 1964), 335–336. Summarizes a five-week study of government in Grades 2, 3, and 4, following which most children were able to identify correct definitions of terms such as "subpoena," "ballot," and "campaign."

Brown, Francis J., and Joseph Slabey Roucek (Eds.), *One America: The History, Contributions, and Present Problems of Our Racial and National Minorities.* Englewood Cliffs, N.J.: Prentice-Hall, 1945. A comprehensive source book.

Easton, David, and Jack Dennis, "The Child's Image of Government," *Annals of the American Academy of Political and Social Sciences*, **361** (September 1965), 40–57. Reports the results of an investigation of how children in grades two to eight orient themselves to the world of politics.

Estvan, Frank J., "Teaching Government in Elementary Schools," *Elementary School Journal*, **62** (March 1962), 291–297. Reports findings of a survey of the teaching of government in Wisconsin elementary schools.

Foreign Policy Association, *Intercom*. Issued six times a year, this periodical contains a section, "Memo to Teachers," with suggestions for dealing with world affairs in the classroom.

Greenstein, Fred I., *Children and Politics*. New Haven, Conn.: Yale University Press, 1965. Reports the results of an exploratory study of aspects of political knowledge and opinions such as sequences in learning, relationships between affect and knowledge, and class and sex differences.

Havens, Murray C., *The Challenges to Democracy: Consensus and Extremism in American Politics*. Austin, Tex.: University of Texas Press, 1965. Analyzes American politics and reports some serious threats of internal dissension to American unity and democracy.

Joyce, Bruce R., "Law in Elementary Social Studies," *Instructor*, **75** (February 1966), 32–33. Suggests legal concepts for the teacher to develop.

Kilpatrick, Franklin P., *et al.*, *The Image of the Federal Service*. Washington, D.C.: Brookings Institute, 1964. Reports results of a national survey on how the American citizen rates federal employment.

Litt, Edgar, "Civic Education, Community Norms, and Political Indoctrination," *American Sociological Review*, **28** (February 1963), 69–75. Presents results of an investigation of civics instruction in three contrasting communities, with conclusions drawn by comparing beliefs with those of control groups and in terms of social milieu.

McAulay, J. D., "Controversial Issues in the Social Studies," *Education*, **86** (September 1965), 27–30. Reports results of an interview survey of practices of elementary school teachers in relation to controversial issues, and gives suggestions as to how the issues may be handled.

McClintock, Charles G., and Henry A. Turner, "The Impact of College upon Political Knowledge, Participation, and Values," *Human Relations*, **15** (May 1962), 163–176. Reports little if any impact, and may leave the reader with a deepened realization of the importance of childhood education if civic goals are to be imparted.

Muessig, Raymond H., and Vincent R. Rogers, "Teaching Patriotism at Higher Conceptual Levels," *Social Education*, **28** (May 1964), 266–270. Tells how to give an intellectual base for teaching patriotism.

Niemeyer, John H., "Education for Citizenship," *in Social Studies in the Elementary School*; Fifty-sixth Yearbook of the National Society for the Study of Education, Pt. II. Chicago: University of Chicago Press, 1957. Chap. 9. Presents a program including personal involvement, student government, classroom citizenship, problem-solving, and the acquisition of information.

Preston, Ralph C. (Ed.), *Teaching World Understanding*. Englewood Cliffs, N.J.: Prentice-Hall, 1955. Gives suggestions for developing world-mindedness through service activities, current affairs teaching, school assemblies, school affiliations, and so on.

Rankin, Robert E., and Eugene A. Quarrick, "Personality and Attitude toward a Political Event," *Journal of Individual Psychology,* **20** (November 1964), 189–193. Indicates that personality (whether "compliant," "aggressive," or "detached") is related to how one reacts to a political event.

Ranney, Austin, *The Governing of Men* (Rev. ed.). New York: Holt, Rinehart and Winston, 1966. A college textbook on the governing processes in different contemporary societies.

Riddle, Donald H., and Robert S. Cleary (Eds.), *Political Science in the Social Studies*; Thirty-sixth Yearbook. Washington, D.C.: National Council for the Social Studies, 1966. Of particular relevance to the teaching of government and civics in the elementary school is the chapter by Jarolimek ("Political Science in the Elementary and Junior High School Curriculum").

Shaftel, Fannie R., and George Shaftel, *Role Playing for Social Values: Decision-Making in the Social Studies.* Englewood Cliffs, N.J.: Prentice-Hall, 1967. Suggests how civic values may be taught through dramatic play and role-playing.

PART THREE

SPECIAL TASKS
IN TEACHING
SOCIAL STUDIES

9

IMPROVING READING IN
SOCIAL STUDIES

*Read, mark, learn,
and inwardly digest.*
BOOK OF COMMON PRAYER

The child in kindergarten and first grade has a small reading vocabulary and must depend for much of his learning in social studies on nonreading activities. This situation rapidly changes. Even in first grade, instruction in social studies includes the use of books, and at each successive grade level, the child is expected to make wider use of social studies textbooks, reference books, biographies, and other supplementary reading materials.

THE RELATIONSHIP OF READING
AND SOCIAL STUDIES

The Development of Social Concepts through Reading

The child's improvement in reading skill tends to be accompanied by improvement in his grasp of social studies. As he becomes more adroit in reading, he reads more widely. He becomes less dependent upon adults and more dependent upon firsthand observation for new knowledge about the world. His textbooks and supplementary reading cover a wide range of information about previously unexplored activities and peoples. Reading has the power to carry him further and deeper, in a given time unit, than any other educational medium. Moreover, he can analyze more thoroughly what he reads than what he hears from teachers or in discussions, or sees in films or on television. A passage in a book can be reread as and when needed by the child; he can compare passages for corroboration or to check seeming inconsistencies; he can stop for reflection when he wishes; he can often choose a time for reading that will fit in with his mood or personal needs; he can carry books around with him and can take school-books home. The best of teachers, films, and guided trips have none of these advantages. Their ideas flow relentlessly and cannot be turned back at will like the pages of a book. Their pace may not be his. The book, in short, is the most adjustable, personally adaptable, and effective learning medium ever invented. It is not surprising, therefore, that growth in reading skill and learning in social studies (and most other kinds of school learning, for that matter) have been found to go together.

The Development of Reading Ability through Social Studies

One of the by-products of a successful social studies program is improved reading. As the child's knowledge of the world expands, his ability to carry out related reading is enhanced.[1] A social studies unit provides the child with incentive and opportunity for reading. He reads to get needed infor-mation for his committee, to write a report, to pass a test, or to satisfy personal curiosity. His feeling of responsibility to become informed, or his interest in a topic, frequently leads him to books which normally would be too difficult for him. Thus, social studies experiences propel many a child into reading situations which advance his vocabulary and reading skill by leaps and bounds. A fourth-grade teacher may be surprised to find a young-ster of mediocre reading ability, during a unit on Switzerland, reading the difficult Spyri book, *Heidi*, and another child using an adult encyclopedia to track down information about the timber line of the Alps. Because of stress by reading specialists on "reading level" and "readability," the fact may be overlooked that when a child is strongly motivated, he often will pursue a book regardless of its difficulty, and apparently with profit. He may gloss over some of the words and skip passages; yet, by the time he has completed the book in this fashion, he has acquired not only the gist of the book but the meaning of a number of the difficult terms. Seen repeatedly in familiar contexts, they have taken shape and become a part of his vocabulary. Consequently, the word difficulty of a book is sometimes a less important factor in determining the benefit a child derives from a book than his background for understanding the book's concepts, and his motivation.[2]

[1] Jeanne S. Chall, "The Influence of Previous Knowledge on Reading Ability," *Education Research Bulletin*, **26** (December 10, 1947), 225–230, 246; Sarah Smilansky, "Evaluation of Early Education in Kindergarten and Grades I and II of Elementary School," *UNESCO Educational Studies and Documents*, **42** Paris: UNESCO, 1961. Pp. 8–17; Theresa M. Wiedefeld, *An Experimental Study in De-veloping History Reading-Readiness with Fourth-Grade Children*. Baltimore, Md.: The Johns Hopkins Press, 1942.

[2] A. M. Williams, *Children's Choice in Science Books*. Child Development Mono-graphs, No. 27. New York: Teachers College, 1939.

DEVELOPING INTEREST IN STUDY-TYPE READING

Many children, who enjoy reading for pleasure, dislike the type of reading-for-mastery which is involved in learning social studies. The dislike is often due simply to lack of knowledge of how to perform study-type reading—ignorance of those skills which are called for in study-type reading which are not required in reading fiction. The subsequent section on "Developing Skills for Study-Type Reading" covers such cases. The present section deals with the more fundamental problem of children who exhibit little or no intellectual curiosity in the content of social studies. Teachers of such children are reminded of the proverb that a horse may be brought to water but cannot be made to drink. Probably every teacher has had the experience of bringing a class to the very edge of intellectual adventure, only to find that certain pupils—sometimes the majority—merely look at it and, at the first opportunity, turn away.

Those children most apt to develop intellectual curiosity are those who were stimulated at an early age by their parents to explore the world about them. The secret of turning children into students lies in the ability of parents and teachers to throw doors open to fresh ideas and broader perspectives, to sustain and build on the natural curiosity of the very young, and to arouse in children the desire for deeper inquiry. All this calls for inspired adults whose enthusiasm for learning and study is contagious.

Postponement of intellectual stimulation until the school years is risky. The early years of life in the formation of curious, productive students are of critical importance. It is during the preschool years that, in a real sense, an individual's later progress as a student is eased or blocked. Too often, parents tend to blame the schools for certain academic deficiencies in their children which more properly can often be laid at their own doorsteps. The suggestions which follow are made in the belief that it is never too late to develop new interests. Nevertheless, if the teacher must start from scratch, the difficulties for both teacher and child are augmented many fold, and the chances of complete success are not assured.

Primary Grades

Excursions in kindergarten and first grade contribute to intellectual interests. They should be planned with the children and undertaken in the spirit of adventure and wonder. The teacher during these early years should direct the child's attention to the teeming world and should help him to interpret it and to see its organization and order—people and their homes, people at work and at leisure, diverse buildings and their purposes, the characteristics which set off one store from another, and so on.

During the early years, if he is to develop intellectual curiosity, it is also necessary to introduce the child to the world of books. A browsing table with books should be in the classroom, and the titles changed frequently. Periods for exploring books should be scheduled even at the prereading age. Teachers should read to their pupils and take them to a library to browse among the children's collection, and should urge the parents of their pupils to do so, too.

Intermediate Grades

In the subsequent grades of the elementary school, the need continues for excursions, browsing, and reading to the class. An abundance of reference material should be kept on hand to enable children to go beyond their textbooks.

The nature of the reading assignments needs to be given care. Every experienced teacher knows that normal children enjoy work—even hard, tedious work. A reading-study assignment need not be sugarcoated.

During the period of the intermediate grades, it is common for the child to regress in the consistency of his performance. Sometimes he will start a job and fail to stick to it. His standards of workmanship often appear to be slipping. Why? And what can be done?

For one thing, the child is growing up and seeking greater independence. He wanders from his earlier, close identification with adults. Conflicts between child and teacher can be minimized if teachers will give this drive for independence an opportunity for expression in areas where it will be beneficial. Teachers can put children more on their own through assigning special tasks to individuals and small committees—the preparation of reports, the responsibility for supervising the social studies bulletin board, the composition of a letter of inquiry to a map publisher, and the like. Having such experiences makes it seem less important for a child to exhibit his independence by taking short cuts in schoolwork, and will, on the contrary, deepen his interest in the content of the social studies unit.

Teachers can also promote interest in assignments by making them precise and realizable. If a child is to do some reading in a reference book and report orally on it, the teacher can give him pointers on how to take notes from a book and organize them, and how to plan and practice delivering the report so that it will be clear and interesting. It would be a mistake to be deceived by the apparent maturity which some children display at this period. Their intellectual skills and their ability to do independent work are actually quite limited. They want to do a presentable job, and their interest can be maintained by giving them practical suggestions.

PROVIDING FOR INDIVIDUAL DIFFERENCES IN READING ABILITY

One of the most baffling problems of teaching social studies is what to do about individual differences in reading ability in a class. Eventually this problem may be solved, at least in part, through programmed materials (see Chapter 12). Meanwhile, other courses for mitigating the problem are open.

Some schools ease the problem by sectioning pupils in terms of reading achievement, thereby reducing the range of reading ability in each class. In such a school, a teacher of a class of accelerated readers need not worry about the textbook's vocabulary load, and he can even expect the class to do some extensive supplementary reading. If the section consists of lagging readers, on the other hand, the teacher seeks an easy textbook and slows up the pace of instruction—fewer concepts are introduced, and the teaching of them is more thorough.

Obviously such sectioning by reading ability does not obviate the need to consider individual differences in ability. There is likely to be a spread of several grades in any one "homogeneous" section, with overlap between pupils at the lower end of the high section and the higher end of the low section. For example, a score of 4.7 (fourth grade, seven months) on a reading test may place one pupil in the "high" section, while 4.6 (fourth grade, six months) may consign another to the "low" section; yet, the difference of one month is trivial in terms of classroom performance. Teachers cannot assume that individual differences are taken care of by assignment by reading ability to a section; they must continue to make some provision for the very real differences that exist.

Where teachers of accelerated classes fail to make provision for differences in reading ability, it is often the very bright pupil who is neglected. The fifth-grade teacher of a slow section may use fourth-grade books for slower readers, but rarely does the same teacher, when teaching an accelerated class, use seventh-grade (or more advanced) books for those who can read at that level. Yet such provision for the bright readers is not as difficult to arrange for as the needs of the slow readers. Upper-grade textbooks are more likely to cover topics studied in the middle grades than are the lower-grade textbooks.

A school may be too small to section pupils homogeneously, or its faculty may be opposed to the idea. In these schools, classes are undifferentiated with respect to reading ability. The teacher of a class in such a school may try to meet the problem by using parallel textbooks at various levels of difficulty. For example, he tries to find treatment of colonial life for some of his fifth-graders in third- or fourth-grade texts. Such parallel textbooks are increasingly available both in social studies and in science. Where such textbooks cannot be found, teachers often meet the problem with special assignments in trade or library books.

Some teachers of undifferentiated classes use "easy" books to the extent they are available and parallel, but also have the poorer readers use the reading materials assigned to the other pupils. The latter materials are used by the poorer readers in a limited way and often in conjunction with other pupils. One effective method for doing this is described later in the chapter in connection with the discussion of textbooks.

DEVELOPING SKILLS FOR STUDY-TYPE READING

Preparing the Class for Reading Assignments

Class reading assignments are specially productive when the teacher discusses with the class the purpose of the assignment, the kinds of questions it will supply answers to, and any special vocabulary or conceptual difficulties it contains. This implies, of course, that the teacher has read the assignment before giving it with a view to ascertaining the basic facts and ideas, any inferences or conclusions the pupils should draw, words which may need to be analyzed for meaning and pronunciation, and the like. Teachers' guides accompanying textbooks include suggestions to help teachers prepare pupils for a reading assignment. One teacher's preparation, reconstructed from notes, ran as follows:

> Today's reading is about a cattle ranch. It tells about another kind of work and another way of living.
> Some of the words you may not have seen before, but you have probably heard them spoken. I have written them on the board: *ranch, range, brand, cattle*. Can anyone tell me what they mean?
> The book does not tell exactly why calves are branded, but if you read carefully, I think you will discover why.
> The book tells how the rancher earns his income. I would like you to tell me about that when you have finished reading.

Teaching the Class How to Master
a Reading-Study Assignment

One of the average child's greatest needs is to learn how to master a reading assignment efficiently and confidently. It is a need often unfulfilled. A beginning can be made in the elementary school by teaching the following three skills.

How to preview an assignment   Previewing a reading assignment consists of examining the following items:

The title of the chapter or of the section
The subheadings
The first paragraph
The final paragraph
Pictures or other graphic aids, and their captions

After a preliminary examination of these features, the child should be able to tell roughly what topics or problems the assigned portion of the book will deal with.

Suppose the assignment comes in a unit on India and consists of reading the section entitled: "Farming the Rough Plateau."[3] The child reads the title. He also reads the subheadings: "Old Ways of Farming," "Better Ways of Farming," and "Government Help." He then reads the first paragraph, which tells that some of the farmer's problems are caused by the way he uses the soil. He reads the final paragraph, which tells of the need for fertilizer, better seeds, better tools, and stronger cattle. Finally, he studies the accompanying graph which compares the productivity of Indian farms with those of farms in three other countries.

When first teaching previewing, involve the entire class in the process. Children need practice in previewing aloud many assignments before they can be sure of its advantage and before it becomes a habit. If the foregoing illustration was part of a practice session, see how many children, after previewing, already have a reasonable idea of what the section is about; that its purpose is to tell about the primitive and wasteful farming methods, about better methods, and about how the government is helping the farmers to improve their practices. All this can be learned before systematic reading begins! (You and your class will discover, of course, that not all parts of the method are always equally applicable. For example, the first and final paragraphs are not always useful in introducing and summarizing a subject.)

Previewing puts pupils in an active frame of mind. As they start reading, they will look for details about tools and methods, about ways in which improvement might be made, and about what the government is doing to improve the situation. The all-too-common passive, purposeless reading of an assignment becomes active and purposeful.

How to read an assignment   How can we make sure our pupils will continue to be active and purposeful as they continue to read? One way is to teach them how to turn each heading and subheading into a question. Thus, "Old Ways of Farming" might become: "Just how did the farmer keep soil from washing off all those slopes?" or "What was the size of his crop?" This step, too, needs to be practiced repeatedly and orally until it becomes a habit.

How to recite   The key to mastery is self-recitation. Any reproduction of material may be called recitational: summarizing to oneself the contents of a passage just read; taking notes on a passage; memorizing a passage verbatim; reviewing a passage to oneself at odd moments during the day; going over the main headings of a passage and telling oneself the important

[3] Ralph C. Preston, *et al.*, *Four Lands, Four Peoples.* Boston: Heath, 1966. Pp. 250–253.

information contained under each heading, followed by checking with the passage.

Taking notes while reading is an exceptionally fruitful form of self-recitation and provides the child with something of an outline which he can use later in still a different form of self-recitation. However, taking notes is exceedingly difficult for elementary school pupils. Many pupils simply do not know what to record. Training should begin in the first grade. A teacher of this grade can have his pupils start in rudimentary fashion by cooperatively dictating to the teacher from something they have read or heard or otherwise experienced. The teacher writes on the chalkboard what is dictated and presents it next day to the class for reading. Such reading is a form of reciting. An example of one day's chart follows.

We watched workers make a sidewalk.
Concrete poured from a truck.
The men smoothed it with rakes and trowels.
They said it would not be hard till next day.

Thus, the pupils learn to recall an experience and to make a digest of it.

Later in the year, the teacher may call upon individual children to tell of something they have read. He writes on the chalkboard phrases of the main ideas of the report to indicate the sequence of ideas. Other children, with the help of the teacher, can then practice using these notes to retell the report. Thus, children learn to *study* a set of notes (written down by someone else) before trying their hands at *making* notes.

In the following years, children can take notes for oral or written reports by independently jotting down names, explanations, dates, and other needed information from their reference books. They should learn that anything copied which consists of more than key words or phrases must be enclosed by quotation marks, followed by the name of the author, the title, and date of the publication from which it was taken. Teachers should discourage children from the practice of copying whole sentences or passages, even when credit is given, as a substitute for taking notes in their own words. At any cost, they should never be permitted to form the notion that a passage copied from a reference book, without credit, is an acceptable report of their search for information. The author has seen such copies, in childish but well-formed handwriting, on classroom bulletin boards, with gold stars and commendatory words by the teacher across the top! Even if a pupil uses quotation marks and gives his sources, he should never get the idea that verbatim copying is all he needs to do when gathering information.

Skill in jotting down key words and phrases in one's own words develops slowly. The pupil can first try reading a passage and then writing a summary of it in his own words. He might begin with a passage in a book on water transportation, headed "Shipping on the Great Lakes." After reading the section, he closes the book, recites orally to himself, and then recites in writing some such note as this: "Before the building of the St. Lawrence Seaway, most of the ships on the Great Lakes carried iron ore which was mined in Minnesota. Today, however, ships carry goods from all over the world to the Great Lakes ports."

When material is difficult to recite, the teacher can show pupils how to make diagrams to help them in such instances. Figure 9.1 is an illustration of a teacher-made diagram.

Figure 9.1. Rough chalkboard sketch by teacher to clarify the relationship between wholesale and retail stores.

Enriching the Child's Vocabulary

There is no way to avoid the direct teaching of unfamiliar or unknown terms. The vocabulary of social studies is enormous. It includes technical terms (*rent, potlatch, erosion, raw material, fief, wholesale,* and so on) and other terms which have a general as well as a technical use (*democracy, power, colony, ranch, are some*). The social studies lexicon is burgeoning. New terms include *Apollo project, medicare, test-ban treaty, zip code,* and *supersonic transport.* As new nations emerge, the names of the regions they occupy and of their public leaders leap into the news, some of them into textbooks. The pronunciation problem alone is a demanding one. What is known about enriching vocabulary is modest in view of the need.

TEACHING ABOUT AFFIXES   An affix is a syllable attached to the beginning or ending of a word which gives the word a changed meaning (such as the attaching of *de* to *camp*, making *decamp*). Certain affixes can be profitably taught. The following are examples:[4]

[4] Lee C. Deighton, *Vocabulary Development in the Classroom.* New York: Teachers College, 1959.

PREFIXES	CHIEF MEANINGS
circum-	around, about, on all sides
equi-	equal
intra-	within
mis-	wrong, wrongly
non-	not
syn-	with, together

SUFFIXES	CHIEF MEANINGS
-able	able to
-ful	full of
-graph	something recorded
-less	lacking, not able to
-meter	instrument for measuring
-ology	a branch of knowledge

Affixes are not to be presented as lists for memorization. Rather, when a class is being prepared for a reading assignment and a new term (for example, *intratribal dispute*) comes up for preliminary analysis, the pupils can look up *intra-* in their dictionaries and venture their own interpretation of *intratribal dispute* as a dispute within a tribe. Every now and then, a list of affixes can be presented to the class and the children set the task of recalling familiar words in which the affixes appear, and discovering new words which contain the affixes. The list of affixes and the examples might be recorded by each child in his social studies notebook.

TEACHING BASE-WORDS   An English base-word is a "clearly recognizable and familiar English word. It is a common denominator for a whole group of related English words."[5] *Press* is a base-word which is found in *compress, impress, impression,* and *suppress.*[6] In each case it implies the application of pressure or the pushing down upon something. The pupils use their dictionaries to locate an adequate definition of the base-word, then apply it to the new word that has come up in their reading (perhaps *depression*). Other words containing the base-word can be recalled or discovered. Here, too, it is worthwhile for the child to keep a record in his notebook.

TEACHING THE MEANING OF FIGURATIVE LANGUAGE   Figurative language adds color and vitality to writing, but to some children it is a source of difficulty. For example, one textbook quotes from Guthrie's *The Big*

[5] Deighton. P. 38.
[6] Deighton.

Sky, in introducing the mountain states: "It was an enormous world. . . . Everything had been made to a giant's measure." If there are many literal-minded children in the class, the teacher may have to ask questions which will lead the pupils to the image of great heights and extensive views which indeed make the western mountains appear outsized. Figurative language can become less troublesome when children recognize it in their own expressions: I slept like a log; he acts chicken; my mother was crushed by the news; Tom passed the acid test; and so forth.

Aiding the Recognition of Main Ideas

To some children, every word seems as important as every other word, every idea as important as every other idea. In reading a biographical account of Benjamin Franklin, for example, they may attempt to remember everything, with the frequent result that they remember practically nothing; their minds become burdened with the weight of undigested detail. Franklin's inconsequential experimentation with vegetarianism may rank in importance for these children with his participation in the Constitutional Convention! This difficulty in differentiating important from unimportant ideas is a major block to successful reading comprehension.

Frequent practice sessions in spotting main ideas are needed in all grades which engage in independent reading. Select a passage from a juvenile newspaper which it is permissible to mark) for the underscoring of words and phrases embodying main ideas. Some children will start off by underscoring almost everything! They have to be taught which are the main ideas. Members of the class should be called upon to tell what they underscored and to explain why they chose certain words and phrases and rejected others. The teacher then comments on their choices and explains why they are right or wrong.

Teaching How to Locate Information

A four-year-old who received a trumpet for Christmas was confused when his sister referred to it as a horn. He went directly to a book with pictures of musical instruments which he had on his shelf of books, looked up the picture of the instrument most closely resembling his own, and found it was closer to being a trumpet than a horn. This illustrates how books can be used for reference: to furnish answers to live questions. A social studies unit affords many opportunities to look up answers to questions that arise.

Even first-grade children can learn how to use a table of contents and how books are arranged on a library shelf. A year later, they know enough about alphabetization to find the correct volume of an encyclopedia set when they are looking for information on a specified topic. By Grade 4, children can learn to use the index of a book and the library card catalogue.

In subsequent grades, all of these skills are applied and refined through practice.

Children become frustrated if directed to locate information not furnished in available books. It is important for the teacher to be sure before assigning reference tasks that a clear, direct answer is available in the classroom or the school library.

The teacher, who is unaided by a central school library and a librarian, is handicapped in teaching children how to locate information. What can be accomplished by schools with libraries staffed by professional librarians was shown in a study by Dale E. Becker at the University of Pennsylvania. Becker, writing his findings as this book goes to press, found that in selected schools the presence of central libraries and librarians was associated with significantly higher pupil scores in information-gathering skills as measured by the *Iowa Test of Basic Skills* than pupil scores in schools without libraries or librarians.

THE ROLE OF READING
IN THE SOCIAL STUDIES PROGRAM

Reading in the Orientation Phase of a Unit

The teacher plans the orientation phase of a unit so that the class will get a bird's-eye view of the new topic. He displays relevant pictures under which he places suitable and challenging captions. He encourages his pupils to write out descriptions to accompany pictures they bring in for posting. Exhibits and collections of objects pertaining to the unit, arranged on a table or window sill, should carry labels and descriptive cards. Periodicals and books with pictures or passages contributing to the unit should be displayed on a table at which the child can sit comfortably and read. Slips of paper may be inserted between pages to mark relevant material. Every few days new material should replace material already examined. The teacher may bring in relevant clippings and should encourage the children to do so, too. These may be read orally before the class. Finally, as part of the orientation, the teacher may wish to read to the class passages from books on the topic, to build class interest and to stimulate individual children to begin reading about the topic on their own.

Reading as an Aspect of Collecting Data

A textbook, aside from its role in presenting the unit as an organized body of content, provides the class with a common background of information and becomes the basic tool in the acquisition of data. The child must search in other printed material, however, for the answers to many questions that arise in the course of studying a unit, such as: Who is the editor of the local newspaper? Did Thomas Edison start inventing as a boy?

Where can information be found for constructing a time line of changes in water transportation?

The reading of "experience charts" is an important part of data-collecting in kindergarten and first grade. Several times a week, the class cooperatively "dictates" to the teacher an account of its social studies learnings. The teacher makes a chart of this account and presents it next day to the class for reading. It may be reviewed whenever desired thereafter.

To really know a subject, most children need to read widely about it. Reading about the subject also often increases their interest in it. A unit is considerably enriched by a supply of such materials as are listed in the boxes in Chapters 5 to 8. The most efficient way to track down supplementary reading on a given topic is through the *Children's Catalogue*—a standard library reference work. For more specialized references, see also:

Allen, Patricia H. (Compiler), *Best Books for Children*. Chicago: University of Chicago Press, 1966.

Crosby, Muriel (Ed.), *Reading Ladders for Human Relations* (4th ed.). Washington, D.C.: American Council on Education, 1963.

Eakin, Mary K. (Compiler), *Subject Index to Books for Intermediate Grades*. Chicago, Ill.: American Library Association, 1963.

Eakin, Mary K., and Eleanor Merritt (Compilers), *Subject Index to Books for Primary Grades*. Chicago, Ill.: American Library Association, 1961.

Huus, Helen, *Children's Books to Enrich the Social Studies* (Rev. ed.). Washington, D.C.: National Council for the Social Studies, 1966.

Metzner, Seymour, *American History in Juvenile Books*. New York: Wilson, 1966.

New York Public Library, *Books About Negro Life for Children* (Rev. ed.). New York: The Library, 1963.

Smith, Dora V., *Fifty Years of Children's Books, 1910–1960*. Champaign, Ill.: National Council of Teachers of English, 1963.

Critical Reading

As children collect data, they need to be prepared to read critically. They should be given special practice in comparing factual reports and expressions of opinion, and one-sided presentations and scholarly presentations of various points of view. The teacher can profitably devote time each week to having pupils read, or listen to the reading of, selections from books or newspapers which represent contrasting approaches. For example, one class, in its study of the local community, found that a burning issue was the wisdom of the state's condemnation, for the purpose of constructing a highway, of an unspoiled natural area bordering a creek valley. The local newspaper ran editorials on the issue and printed many letters from readers The teacher used these for training her pupils in critical reading.

An important outcome of learning in the social studies is the realization that sources may differ in presenting and interpreting facts. One textbook implies that all Eskimos live in igloos. A newspaper account of an interview with an Eskimo who was studying nursing in the United States, on the other hand, quoted her to the effect that she had never seen an igloo and never knew anyone who had seen one! In one book appears the statement that Mexicans are unable to run their affairs without a strong leader. Another book gives the Mexicans an idealized treatment. Press interviews reveal differing views concerning the placement of responsibility for a strike.

Introducing children to diverse accounts helps them to understand that in the search for truth, a single source may not be sufficient, that different observers do not always see the same things, that not all observers are equally openminded, and that different writers with the same facts may draw differing conclusions. Children should be helped to evaluate authenticity of sources and to distinguish between fact and opinion.[7]

Reading for Recreation

The reading of authentic story material (historical fiction, biography, adventure, explorations, and stories about life in other lands) has a solid place in social studies instruction. Examples of such material appear in the boxes in Chapters 5 to 8. Among the enjoyable phases of a unit are those moments when the teacher or a child reads to the class a rousing passage from a supplementary book he is reading in connection with the unit under study. Another satisfying and worthwhile experience is for a group of children to read aloud assigned parts in a play with content related to the unit.[8]

Reading to Organize and Summarize Knowledge

As data are collected through reference reading, taking trips, and seeing films, they may appear to the child jumbled and unorganized. This is where the textbook comes to the rescue. It helps pull ideas together and put them in order. The role of textbooks is our next consideration.

THE SOCIAL STUDIES TEXTBOOK

Textbooks are available for all the elementary school grades. Many are prepared with great care, painstaking attention being given to such

[7] The need for this is brought out by John E. Davis: "The Ability of Fourth, Fifth, and Sixth Grade Pupils to Distinguish between Fact and Opinion in an Experimentally Designed Reading Situation," *Dissertation Abstracts*, **25** (September 1964), 1781. How conflicting data was successfully dealt with by fifth- and sixth-grade pupils is described by Aletha Pitts Scarangello, "A Plan for Presenting Conflicting Data," *Elementary School Journal*, **65** (May 1965), 434–435.

[8] Plays, Inc., 8 Arlington Street, Boston, Mass. 02116, publishes *Plays: The Drama Magazine for Young People* and other plays suitable for classroom reading.

matters as vocabulary, organization, style of presentation, concept density, simplicity of ideas, and accuracy of text and illustrations. A good textbook can strengthen the teaching of any unit.

Status of Textbook Use

Surveys have produced some generalizations about the use of social studies textbooks:[9]

1. Systematic use of social studies textbooks is far more common in the intermediate than in the primary grades.
2. More schools favor "unified" textbooks than favor "separate subject" textbooks (which treat history and geography in separate books).
3. Many (but a minority of) schools purchase multiple textbooks for each classroom from each of several publishers in preference to buying copies of a basal textbook for each child.
4. Some schools do not purchase social studies textbooks at all, on such philosophical grounds as: "social studies should come from the experiences of the children," and "social studies learning should be inductive."

Using an Assortment of Textbooks in the Same Classroom

Some school systems encourage the teacher to use an assortment of textbooks—perhaps three or four different books will be represented in lots of eight or ten each. The supposed advantages of multiple textbook use is that it will prevent teachers from becoming slaves to a single textbook and that the textbooks will be used as reference books. There are several faulty elements in this reasoning.

Using three or four textbooks with their inevitable discrepancies in organization and scope can be confusing to teacher and pupils alike. Furthermore, a textbook is not a suitable reference book. It is claimed to be by advocates of multiple textbooks. Reference books which should be available to children are of two kinds: (1) those which expand, illustrate, and explain textbook content in greater detail than textbooks can possibly do; and (2) those which systematically catalogue information, such as almanacs. A second, third, or fourth textbook does not satisfy either of these requirements, nor could it do so and still remain a textbook. The author has met but few teachers who like the practice of multiple textbooks, and, in his opinion, it has no valid base.

[9] Ralph C. Preston and Byron O. Bush, unpublished surveys by 88 key principals and supervisors and 43 textbook salesmen, both groups representing regions in all parts of the United States, 1962.

The Relation of the Textbook to the Unit

The textbook is the teacher's tool. He should not let it be his master. Suppose the selected textbook contains more concepts on a topic, or more units, than the teacher feels his class can assimilate in the available time. Under such circumstances, he must be selective, using some portions of the textbook and omitting others. On the other hand, he may wish to add a unit not covered by the textbook, such as a unit on local or state government.

A frequently raised question is: "At which step in the unit should the textbook be read?" Some teachers like to have the class look over the book during the unit's stage of orientation, studying the table of contents, examining pictures and charts, and perhaps reading passages which introduce the subject matter of the unit. They postpone systematic study of the textbook until some time during the later stages. This seems like a sensible approach.

Judging the Difficulty of a Textbook

A textbook may be regarded as readable for a child if he can accurately read about 95 percent of running words of typical passages and give evidence of getting the gist of these passages after he has become fairly well acquainted with the new ideas and terminology of the subject. If a child reads fewer than 90 percent of running words, the book is probably too difficult for him. Using these percentage figures as rough guides, a teacher can estimate the appropriateness of a given textbook, so far as the readability is concerned, for the various members of his class. Rather than have every pupil make a test-reading, the teacher can judge a book's readability by calling upon one good reader, one average reader, and one poor reader to read scattered passages. This method is not only faster than the application of a readability formula, but in the author's belief, furnishes a more certain estimate of the book's difficulty. On the other hand, a formula can be of some use in judging a book before a decision is made as to whether to purchase it in quantity for the class. The Spache formula is widely used for judging the difficulty of primary-grade books, and the Dale-Chall formula for intermediate-grade books.[10] In these formulas, the difficulty level of a book is estimated by determining the average sentence length and the number of difficult words (words not contained in a list of "easy" words) from sample passages of the book. But readibility scores are often misleading and should be checked against test-reading, as suggested above.

[10] These and other formulas are described and evaluated in Jeanne S. Chall, *Readability: An Appraisal of Research and Application.* Columbus, Ohio: Bureau of Educational Research, Ohio State Unversity, 1958. Pp. 16–57; and George R. Klare, *The Measurement of Readability.* Ames, Iowa: Iowa State University Press, 1963. Chap. 4.

Introducing the Textbook to the Class

When a textbook is presented at the start of a school year, it should be systematically analyzed. First, the title page should be examined. The children should be asked to note the names of the authors and how recently the book was published. If it was published, say, in 1958, could the writeups of some topics (such as new developments in transportation and automation) be out of date, and could any information (such as the emergence of new nations) be lacking completely? The raising of such questions with a class does not disparage the textbook, but it does prepare the class for the need to supplement it. After all, the children should know that a social studies textbook cannot possibly be 100 percent up to date.

The class should also examine the table of contents to find out the number of units and of chapters and in what order they are arranged. Attention should be called to the sections of the book which can help in locating information. For example, the table of contents shows where treatment of the different topics can be found; if a pupil wants to locate the pages telling about a particular leader or place, he would use the index; a list of maps and a glossary may also be included in the book. Each of these aids should be discussed, and the teacher may want to provide informal drill in their use.

Correcting Inaccurate Images

No matter at what point in the unit the textbook is introduced, there is always the danger, because of its generalized, clipped, and compressed nature, that it will convey to children inaccurate images. Typical errors are these:

SENTENCES FROM TEXTBOOKS	INCORRECT IMAGES CONVEYED TO CHILDREN
Early stagecoaches between Boston and New York were very slow.	The trip probably took two days.
They succeeded in hacking a highway through the jungle.	Men with pneumatic drills were destroying a highway that had been laid through the jungle.
Few people live in northern Canada.	About 100 people live in northern Canada. Maybe 1,000 people live north of Montreal.

Thus, children are called upon to do a lot of "filling in" when reading textbooks. When their knowledge is limited, they "fill in" from imagination. Teachers need to be aware of this possibility and allot ample time for discussing textbook content both before and after the reading.

Using a Difficult Textbook
with Less Able Readers

A teacher may find that for as many as one third of his class the textbook is too difficult. If he likes its organization, treatment of topics, glossary, maps, and photographs, he may still wish to use it. But how can he use it with those pupils who can read only 50 to 90 percent of its running words?

He will probably find that even those children can learn to read its table of contents. Some of them may have to memorize certain of the words as sight words. But they can master the table of contents—a valuable achievement. It will acquaint them with the organization of the subject and with the relationship of the major topics to each other and to subtopics, and the relationship of subtopics to each other. Similarly, they can learn the captions of important pictures, charts, tables, and maps as necessary aids in interpreting this graphic material.

Another procedure for using a difficult textbook with poor readers was developed by Professor Donald D. Durrell of Boston University who calls it "team learning." It consists of dividing the class into "teams" of two or three pupils each. Each team includes one good reader who serves as "pupil-teacher." Each pupil is given a "study guide" (a teacher-prepared list of questions covering that day's "lesson"). Each pupil-teacher reads the first question aloud to his team. The pupils look for the answers in their textbooks and give them orally. When in doubt, members of a team discuss the question together. Then they consult an answer sheet. The other questions are read and answered similarly. This procedure allows pupils to work together, which, for some, is preferable to working alone. The scheme assures success and security for the child because it enables him to check the accuracy of his knowledge immediately. Every child responds to every question. This prepares him for whatever discussions and tests the teacher may have planned.

Despite the efficacy of "team learning," the reading of the less able reader should not be confined to difficult textbooks. As previously pointed out, he should have access to easy reading material which parallels some of the content of the textbook, whenever such material is procurable.[11]

---

[11] Consult Roy A. Kress, *A Place to Start*. Syracuse, N.Y.: The Reading Center, Syracuse University, 1963; and George D. Spache, *Good Reading for Poor Readers* (5th ed.). Champaign, Ill.: Garrard, 1966.

FOR REVIEW AND REFLECTION

1. Why can reading matter be more readily and critically analyzed than material that is listened to?
2. What steps should children learn to take before reading an assignment?
3. How can children be taught to separate central ideas from subordinate ideas?
4. What are the objections to initiating a unit with a textbook reading assignment?
5. If a good textbook is used, why does supplementary reading need to be supplied?

ASSIGNMENTS

1. Experiment with the practice exercise for recognizing main ideas. Have each member of your class bring in the same edition of a daily paper, and select a passage for all to read, underscoring words and phrases which describe the main ideas. Compare results. (An adult should be able to limit underscoring to 20 percent of the total number of words in a passage. A child should keep under 50 percent).
2. Select a unit topic and compile an annotated bibliography of books you have personally examined and which children could use. Indicate the grade or age you have in mind. Include books suitable for several levels of reading ability.
3. Write a critical review of a social studies textbook designed for use in the elementary school, judging the book in terms of the qualities which you think it should possess.

SUPPLEMENTARY READING

Aaron, I. E., "Developing Reading Competencies through Social Studies and Literature," in J. Allen Figurel (Ed.), *Reading as an Intellectual Activity*, Conference Proceedings, International Reading Association. New York: Scholastic, 1963. Vol. 8, pp. 107–110. Discusses teaching the special vocabulary, concept background, critical reading.

Allen, Patricia H. (Compiler), *Best Books for Children*. New York: Bowker, 1966. A useful annual compilation.

Arnsdorf, Val E., "Readability of Basal Social Studies Materials," *Reading Teacher,* 16 (January 1963), 243–246. Analyzes the readability levels and consistency of the books in four basal social studies textbook series.

Burrows, Alvina Treut, "Reading, Research, and Reporting in the Social Studies," *Social Studies in the Elementary School*; Fifty-sixth Yearbook of the National Society for the Study of Education. Pt. II. Chicago: University of Chicago Press, 1957. Chap. 8.

Crosby, Muriel (Ed.), *Reading Ladders for Human Relations* (4th ed.). Washington, D.C.: American Council on Education, 1963. Lists and discusses books which "offer readers an opportunity to identify emotionally with other human beings." Books for children are included.

Curry, James W., "Teaching Reading through the Social Studies," *National Elementary Principal,* 35 (September, 1955), 124–127.

Fay, Leo, *et al., Improving Reading in the Elementary Social Studies.* Washington, D.C.: National Council for the Social Studies, 1961. Supplies answers to nine questions about reading in the social studies which teachers frequently ask.

Hislop, George R., "A Study of Division Two Social Studies Reading Skills," *Alberta Journal of Educational Research,* 7 (March 1961), 28–38. Reports results of an experimental study in Grades 4, 5, and 6 in which training in problem-solving techniques appeared to contribute to improved social studies achievement.

Huus, Helen, *Children's Books to Enrich the Social Studies* (Rev. ed.). Washington, D.C.: National Council for the Social Studies, 1966. A careful selection of books organized in terms of divisions of the social studies curriculum.

Klare, George R., *The Measurement of Readability.* Ames, Ia.: Iowa State University Press, 1963. A scholarly report on readability.

Mingle, Benjamin R., "An Appraisal of Reading Materials Appropriate for Use in Third Grade Social Studies Program in the Schools of Dade County, Florida," *Dissertation Abstracts,* 25 (September 1964), 1660. A searching appraisal of over 80 books.

Nardelli, Robert R., "Some Aspects of Creative Reading," *Journal of Educational Research,* 50 (March 1957), 495–508. Indicates that specific training in drawing inferences and recognizing propaganda is effective with sixth-graders.

Peterson, Eleanor M., *Aspects of Readability in the Social Studies.* New York: Teachers College, 1954. Discusses readability in terms of main ideas, technical words, inferences and relationships, and details.

Preston, Ralph C., *Teaching Study Habits and Skills.* Pamphlet. New York: Holt, Rinehart and Winston, 1959. Gives practical suggestions for developing interest in learning, self-discipline in study, skill in gathering information, and mastery of content.

Robinson, H. Alan, "Reading Skills Employed in Solving Social Studies Problems," *The Reading Teacher,* 18 (January 1965), 263–269. Reports a study of fourth-graders' methods in locating and interpreting data bearing on specified problems.

Shepherd, David L., *Effective Reading in the Social Studies.* New York: Harper & Row, 1960. Though written for the secondary school teacher, contains suggestions that are equally sound for the elementary school, with illustrative sample lessons.

Socher, E. Elona, "Literal and Critical Reading in Social Studies," *Journal of Experimental Education,* 27 (September 1958), 49–56. Concludes that the fifth-grader who is competent in literal reading is not necessarily competent in critical reading.

Spache, George D., *Good Reading for Poor Readers* (5th ed.). Champaign, Ill.: Garrard, 1966. Contains an illuminating chapter on readability and lists numerous books, reporting a grade level and interest level for each.

Tooze, Ruth, *Your Children Want to Read.* Englewood Cliffs, N.J.: Prentice-Hall, 1957. Chap. 6 deals with "Books to Help Children Understand and Adjust to the Social World."

Witt, Mary, "A Study of the Effectiveness of Certain Techniques of Reading Instruction in Developing the Ability of Junior High School Students to Conceptualize Social Studies Content," *Journal of Educational Research,* **56** (December 1962), 198–204. Describes a method which improved both reading skills and social studies learning with seventh-grade pupils.

10

TEACHING ABOUT
MAPS AND GLOBES

Journey over all the universe in a map. . . .
MIGUEL DE CERVANTES

Maps are graphic drawings of the earth's surface or portions thereof. Globes are scaled-down models of the earth. Both maps and globes give definiteness to geographical names and terms. A map or a globe aids the child in a number of ways. For example, through familiarity with it, (1) he learns a region's shape, size, and boundaries; (2) he learns the meaning of various geographical terms (such as *island, isthmus, earth*); (3) he perceives relationships, such as the role of the Suez Canal in shortening shipping routes and the advantage to early settlers of establishing themselves by the mouths of rivers that afford snug harbors; and (4) he discovers correlated phenomena, such as vegetation and rainfall, through side-by-side comparison of maps (or map overlays) each of which shows the distribution of one phenomenon.

Not everything on a map or a globe is self-evident. Children while using maps and globes have revealed erroneous conceptions: that rivers flow in from the sea; that islands are somehow anchored to the bottom of the sea; and that state boundaries are barriers through which a river must cut a channel in order to traverse them. It is not enough, therefore, merely to "expose" children to maps and globes; instruction is also needed.

MAPS AND GLOBES IN THE PRIMARY GRADES

It is known that many children in the primary grades have difficulty in grasping the spatial relationships required for understanding maps.[1] But

[1] George F. Howe, "A Study of Children's Knowledge of Directions," *Journal of Geography*, **30** (October 1931), 298–304; Arthur T. Jersild, *Child Psychology* (5th ed.). Englewood Cliffs, N.J.: Prentice-Hall, 1960, P. 365; Francis E. Lord, "A Study of Spatial Orientation of Children," *Journal of Experimental Research*, **34** (March

it has also been demonstrated that steady progress can be made by most children through a carefully planned, unhurried sequence of learning activities.[2] The first map experiences should deal with the region which children can observe at firsthand without the intermediary of symbols.

At one time, the author was asked to help a group of third-grade children who had spent several fruitless weeks working with maps of the United States. It was soon discovered that one reason they were making no headway was because many of them lacked the bird's-eye-view concept. They were unable to draw, for example, a bird's-eye view of a book lying on the floor. What was needed was for some of the children to mount a chair and look down upon the book, and also to compare several sketches of books drawn from different positions before "bird's-eye view" as a concept became intelligible. In order to increase their spatial concepts, these children required trips to points at various elevations to view the neighborhood. They also needed to do some informal sketching, construction of floor plans, and construction of diagrams and models showing the routes taken by various members of the class in walking to school each day. The emphasis of their geography book upon a two-dimensional map—one of the more difficult tools a child must come to understand—was obviously introduced prematurely.

Another way to develop the bird's-eye view concept is to present a sequence of photographs of something—say, the school and schoolyard. The first photograph shows the school as seen horizontally—from across the street or from an extreme corner of the playground. The second photograph shows the school as seen from an oblique angle—from a tall building nearby. The third photograph was taken from an airplane directly above the school and is a true vertical bird's-eye view.

The prevalence of children's errors in map work and other spatial misconceptions is a good illustration of what happens when primary matters are glossed over. In addition to drawing largely upon the region which children can most readily observe, abundant opportunity should be provided for the consolidation of the kinds of geographical experiences which will be mentioned in this section.

Layouts with Blocks

A child *makes* maps before he *reads* them. He makes them as a kindergartener when, playing with blocks, boxes, and other construction play

---

1941), 481–505; Jean Piaget and Bärbel Inhelder, *The Child's Conception of Space.* London: Routledge, 1963; Ralph C. Preston, "Implications of Children's Concepts of Time and Space," *Social Studies,* **36** (May 1945), 218–219.

[2] George F. Howe, "Teaching Directions in Space," *Journal of Geography,* **31** (May 1932), 209–210; Preston; Haig A. Rushdoony, "Achievement in Map Reading: An Experimental Study," *Elementary School Journal,* **64** (November 1963), 70–75.

materials he arranges farm layouts, neighborhoods, skyscrapers, rows of stores on a street, harbors, or roads connecting home and airport or other known points. The crudity of these portrayals should not blind us to their significance: they are symbolic resemblances on a reduced scale to some spatial arrangement he has seen or heard about. In essence, that is what every map is. Blocks should be standard equipment for kindergarten and first-grade children, both large blocks for the playground and smaller ones for the classroom.[3]

By the way children build their bridges, locate their bodies of water, and arrange their buildings, the teacher can tell wherein their experience and observation are lacking. He then can aid them by planning new trips that will call their attention to arrangements as they actually exist. Pictures showing how the community is laid out also will help. Children who show insight into spatial arrangements may be asked to explain their block layouts to their classmates. The teacher can arouse their interest in reproducing observed land arrangements.

Using a Community Map

At some point in the first grade most children are ready to use a teacher-made map of the community (see Figure 5.1). This should be a large map of the community, based on a local street map from a real estate office or a vertical aerial photograph, and checked against firsthand observation. It should be large enough to show each block. Such a map is useful in many ways. For example: each child can locate his own house, those of his friends, and their distance and directional relationships to the school; the class can orient itself before and after each trip; relatively safe walking and bicycling routes can be worked out; and institutions and points of interest being studied can be located. These maps are drawn on large sheets of paper. Part of the time they should be spread out on the floor, properly oriented with respect to directions. Such maps provide a good opportunity to introduce children to map symbols, such as the conventional blue coloring of bodies of water, lines with crossbars to represent railroad tracks, and symbols that the children themselves originate, such as four-footed creatures drawn on a space to represent a cow pasture. At first, only those features are symbolized which children have seen at firsthand. In this way, the utility of map symbolism will be obvious. Children should be encouraged, when they are using a map, to be conscious of ways in which it departs from reality so that the symbolic nature of its coloring, marking, and size is thoroughly recognized. Use of teacher-made maps of the community should continue throughout the primary grades.

[3] Lucy Sprague Mitchell, *Young Geographers*. New York: Basic Books, 1963. Pp. 27, 88–89.

Children should have the experience of making their own maps, too. Their first maps generally spring from direct observation and, in addition to those constructed from blocks, are drawn, painted, or modeled from clay. The teacher's map is a good standard against which children can check their own for accuracy. They should also be encouraged to check them against their own observations. They can verify relative distances by counting their steps while walking between various points represented on their maps.

Learning Directions

Children in our present culture, with its abundant signs and guideposts, appear to have no pressing practical need to become "direction conscious" and many of them, indeed, do not become so.[4]

Children's ignorance of directions cannot be attributed solely to the absence of practical demands upon them for directional knowledge. One factor to be reckoned with is the failure of many teachers to provide them with experiences which make the language of direction meaningful. Several procedures have proven their worth:

1. Place the maps on the floor occasionally, giving the children a chance to orient them with the aid of a compass.
2. When trips are taken, diagram the route with chalk on the floor, surfaced playground, or sidewalk and make verbal reference to portions of it which correspond to any of the cardinal directions.
3. Call attention to directions by painting a north-pointing arrow on the classroom floor, on the playground, and by observing a sundial and weather vane.
4. Have the members of the class face north. Their backs will be toward the south, their right hands east, and their left west. They can remember this because the right hand is usually the more important one, and the sun rises in the east—the most important event of the day!
5. Give formal instruction. Take the class outside to observe the position of the sun and identify the cardinal directions. Hold a stick erect, one end on the ground, and observe the relation of the stick's shadow to the position of the sun. Tell about its similarity to sundials.

[4] Jersild; Ralph C. Preston, "A Comparison of Knowledge of Directions in German and in American Children," *Elementary School Journal,* 57 (December 1956), 158–160; Nathaniel Stampfer, "A Study of Map Skills Attained in Selected Middle Grades." Unpublished doctoral dissertation, Northwestern University, 1966, summarized by John R. Lee and Nathaniel Stampfer, "Two Studies in Learning Geography: Implications for the Primary Grades," *Social Education,* **330** (December 1966), 627–628.

Informal Experiences with Globes

The kindergarten child's view of the earth is likely to be a limited one, circumscribed by the horizon of his environment. However, the kindergarten year is not too early to introduce the concept of the earth as a ball. No more need be done at this level than to keep a globe in the classroom and make occasional reference to it. Later, in the primary grades, children can learn regions that are mentioned in discussion, such as the United States, Virginia, the North Pole, or the equator. With a bit of paper affixed to the globe with rubber cement, some teachers mark the approximate site of the community in which the school is located.

MAPS AND GLOBES IN THE INTERMEDIATE GRADES

Although studies have shown that concepts essential to map interpretation are imperfectly developed by intermediate grade children,[5] we should not conclude that maturational factors alone are responsible for this lag. Several investigators have found that children can be taught certain, fairly sophisticated map skills.[6] There is little question that children's potential for map learning has been underestimated.

Conditions Favorable to Map Learning

INSTRUCTION WHICH PROMOTES INQUIRY AND DISCOVERY   Studies by Arnsdorf and Possien point to the advantages of the "go-slow" discovery method in teaching map concepts.[7]

Arnsdorf's subjects were fifth-grade children who "discovered" geographical relationships through the use of color-sensitized transparent map overlays (from Technifax Corporation, Holyoke, Mass.). Each overlay depicted a different geographic feature (population density, land use, mineral resources, and so on). Lessons were conducted twice weekly.

During each lesson, the teacher attempted to develop an understanding of how the feature was distributed throughout the United States. During this part of the lesson, each child would cover the map grid with a transparency which would reveal say, the population density, and plot the infor-

[5] Daniel H. Brown, "Knowledge of Important Principles of Physical Geography Possessed by Selected Sixth-Grade Children," *Dissertation Abstracts*, 24 (June 1964), 5072; Stampfer.

[6] Val Arnsdorf, "Teaching Social Studies with Map-overlays," *California Journal of Educational Research*, 16 (March 1965), 65–74; O. L. Davis, Jr., "Children Can Learn Complex Concepts," *Educational Leadership*, 17 (December 1959), 170–175; Wilma M. Possien, "A Comparison of the Effects of Three Teaching Methodologies on the Development of the Problem Solving Skills of Sixth Grade Children," *Dissertation Abstracts*, 25 (January 1965), 4003.

[7] Val Arnsdorf, *Teaching Social Studies* . . . and "Teaching Map-reading and Geographic Understandings with Projectuals," *Journal of Geography*, 63 (February 1964), 75–81; Possien.

mation on an outline map. During each lesson, the teacher also attempted to develop an understanding of the relationship that might exist between one feature and another. In this connection, the children attempted predictions concerning relationships—for example, concerning the role of precipitation in affecting the distribution of vegetation and land use. Following the study of related overlays, the children read up on the subject from various authoritative sources in order to test the accuracy of their predictions. This pattern of instruction was continued for twelve lessons.

Before and after the experiment, the children were tested on the work-study skills section of the Iowa Tests of Basic Skills. This section contains tests of map reading, interpretation of graphs and tables, and reference skills. Arnsdorf's data showed that the children made substantial progress following the instruction.

Possien compared two "searching and self-discovery" methods with a "telling" method in map study at the sixth-grade level. Following the period of instruction, the children trained in the use of the "discovery" procedures showed no significant gains on the map-reading section of the Iowa Test of Basic Skills, but they were observed to use some characteristics of problem-solving more frequently than pupils taught by the telling method.

INSTRUCTION WHICH IS INTENSIVE   The typical daily time allotment for the teaching of map skills is undoubtedly insufficient, and it is typically not pursued with sufficient zeal. In the Arnsdorf study, instruction was intensive. His subjects devoted one hour a day for 12 days to their map study. Davis, in demonstrating that intermediate-grade pupils can learn such concepts as time zone, rotation of earth, and International Date Line, devoted 30 minutes a day to it for 14 days.[8] Rushdoony's third-grade subjects, who clearly benefited from map instruction, were taught 90 minutes weekly for 15 weeks.[9]

PRESENTATIONS WHICH ARE LUCID AND INTERESTING   It may seem paradoxical to advocate the discovery method and the presentation (telling) method as two complimentary conditions of instruction. But that is exactly what they should be—complementary. As pointed out frequently and for many years, the old issue of whether social studies should be organized deductively or inductively ". . . is pointless. . . . In the end, the important thing is that the generalization taught . . . be full of meaning and susceptible to functional use. . . . The commonly made statement that induction is *the* method of science . . . is fallacious. Scientists employ both methods. . . ."[10]

[8] Davis.
[9] Rushdoony.
[10] William A. Brownell and Gordon Hendrickson, "How Children Learn Information, Concepts, and Generalizations," in *Learning and Instruction*; Forty-ninth Yearbook of the National Society for the Study of Education. Pt. I. Chicago: University of Chicago Press, 1950. P. 123.

A presentation may be both lucid and interesting, either in an oral presentation or in writing, and on almost any map topic.[11] This can be accomplished by:

(a) Relating new concepts to familiar concepts,
(b) Showing the practical significance of a concept,
(c) Keeping the number of new terms to a minimum,
(d) Using diagrams and pictures,
(e) Occasionally proposing a pupil activity,
(f) Raising questions from time to time to stimulate inquiry.

Figure 10.1. Children study map positioned to agree with points of the compass.

Continuing Work with Directions

The abstract nature of directions prevents the primary-grade child from mastering them and calls for continuing to teach them in the intermediate grades. The practice of spreading maps on the floor and aligning them with the points of a compass may advantageously be continued occasionally throughout the intermediate grades (see Figure 10.1). When hanging maps which show north at the top, the north wall of the classroom should be used, so that the maps continue to be as nearly correct, in relation to the earth's directions, as possible. Then, when the children face the map and

[11] For an attempt to meet these criteria in a written presentation of the measurement of latitude, see Ralph C. Preston and John Tottle, *In These United States.* Boston: D. C. Heath, 1966. Pp. 16–19; and a presentation of latitude and longitude in the same authors' *In Latin American Lands,* Boston: Heath, 1967. Pp. 8–9. See also, on the same subject, the programmed text, *Latitude and Longitude,* Chicago: Coronet Instructional Films, which contains ten sets of exercises.

the north, the right side of the body is always toward the east of the earth and the map, and the left side of the body is toward the west. This practice has one obvious drawback: it causes some children to adopt a fixed notion of north as "up" and south as "down." This tendency may be offset by frequently using azimuthal projections (see Figure 10.9F) in which the stereotypes of "up north" and "down south" do not apply, and by occasionally making and posting maps in which the conventional positions are inverted. Globes which are detachable from their bases may deliberately be placed in different positions at various times. Teachers may plan a drill in which the children point to a river on a wall map and make such statements as "The Po flows down and east" and "The Nile flows down and north." Still another way to eliminate the notion of north as up is to drill children in pointing, sequentially, to the cardinal compass directions, and then up (directly overhead) and down (toward the center of the earth).

The compass can help in developing direction consciousness. Compasses are easily made with ordinary needles,[12] and constructing them will contribute to the pupil's understanding of compasses and the magnetic qualities of the earth. Because the compass needle does not point in the direction of the geographic North Pole except in a few places, a correction must be made to determine true north. *Information Please Almanac* publishes a table of "magnetic declinations" which gives the correction for many places and for the year in question, as magnetic north differs from year to year. The 1968 edition shows that for Duluth, the declination is 5° E.[13] To find true north in the Duluth area, therefore, the compass should be placed so that the needle points 5° to the east of north. In this position, the north mark on the compass points due north.

One important lesson for children to learn is that the cardinal points are fixed by nature and are not arbitrary designations. The compass, of course, shows this, but it is advisable to supplement it by demonstrating how to find directions by shadows, the pole star, and others of "nature's guideposts."[14]

Making and Using Special-Purpose Maps

A special-purpose map is a map designed to explain an explicit feature, condition, or incident. Geographers sometimes call them "thematic" maps. Most maps which appear in newspapers are special-purpose maps. For

---

[12] Carleton J. Lynde and Floyd Leib, *Science Experiences with Ten-Cent Store Equipment* (3d ed.). Princeton, N.J.: Van Nostrand, 1950.

[13] *Information Please Almanac 1968*. New York: Simon and Schuster, 1968. P. 466. Also, the topographic map covering the local area (obtainable from the U.S. Geological Survey, Washington, D.C. 20242) has a diagram in the bottom margin showing compass declination.

[14] Horace Kephart, *Camping and Woodcraft*, Vol. 2. New York: Macmillan, 1936. Chap. 4. Pp. 76–79.

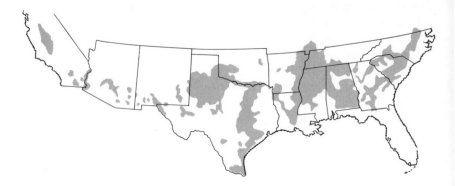

Figure 10.2. A special-purpose map showing how cotton production has spread westward.

example, the map in Figure 10.2 shows how cotton growing has spread westward in recent years. Figure 10.3 was drawn for school use. It explains why the interior of Africa was hard for explorers to enter. It emphasizes two important factors: (1) the falls and rapids along the great rivers of the interior that render them unnavigable, and (2) the extensive Sahara which cuts off the Mediterranean countries of Europe from Africa's interior. Note that this map contains no marks to indicate political boundaries, mountains, lakes, cities, oceans, or other irrelevancies; every mark on the outline is designed to contribute to one objective: an understanding of the historical inaccessibility of interior Africa to explorers.

Because of the continual need for such representations, schools should keep on hand a quantity of printed outline maps that can be used in this manner as work sheets by teachers and pupils, slate-surfaced globes (see Figure 10.4) for marking with chalk, transparent globes (see Figure 10.5) for marking with chinamarking pencils, and transparencies for use in overhead projectors which teacher or pupils can shade, label, or otherwise mark. Special-purpose maps, in addition to presenting such information as that on the maps in Figures 10.2 and 10.3, may show:

> Important routes (such as Marco Polo's travels, the around-the-world voyage of Magellan's *Vittoria*, the Santa Fe Trail).
> Distribution of resources, conditions, population (for example, location of filling stations in the community, rainfall, nonproductive land, population density, dry farming areas).
> Significant locations (such as colonial settlements at mouths of rivers, original location of Indian tribes, airports, water-power sites).

Children should also have the experience of using maps to serve their

Figure 10.3. A special-purpose map showing two reasons why Africa has been a difficult continent to explore: (1) falls and rapids along great rivers; and (2) the Sahara Desert.

own interests. A class may make a map showing the home of each of its members, or showing plans for a class excursion.

Finally, it is worthwhile for teachers and children to collect a number of different kinds of special-purpose maps: maps showing zip codes, local real estate maps, topographic maps (from the Geological Survey), harbor maps (from the Coast and Geodetic Survey), weather maps, and news maps (from the newspapers and magazine,) or *World Events* (a large map issued weekly by Silver Burdett Co., Morristown, N. J.). Such a collection can be made into an attractive and informative exhibit.

Using Standard Maps and Globes

Most maps in the atlas and in textbooks, and classroom wall maps, are storehouses of miscellaneous information and are consulted as one would consult a dictionary or encyclopedia—when in search of data. Most of these emphasize political information (boundaries, cities, and the like) or relief information (contours of the land), or combine these types of information. They should be used by the pupil in many ways.

REFERENCE WORK   They yield information such as locations, distances between locations, proximity of areas, and direction of one point with reference to another. Some reference work may be of a casual nature. Thus, if the governor is visiting town, pupils may list the points which he is scheduled to pass or visit, locate them on a map of the city, and then locate the position of the school. They can then decide where to assemble to see him. But most of a pupil's reference work is in connection with his preparation of reports, verifying his hunches and "discoveries," visualizing the location of places encountered in his reading, and checking the accuracy of his performance on map exercises.

Figure 10.4. Example of pupils using a slate-surfaced globe.

FURNISHING INFORMATION NEEDED IN MAKING "TOOL" MAPS   In studying the Lewis and Clark Expedition, pupils may list the following itinerary: St. Louis, Council Bluffs, intersection of Yellowstone and Missouri rivers, Great Falls, Three Forks, Columbia River, and the mouth of the Columbia at the Pacific Ocean. Their location is then determined from a wall map or an atlas, and the route drawn on individual outline maps of the United States or on wall maps constructed for marking with chalk.

ILLUSTRATING ORAL REPORTS   When pupils make oral reports to their classmates, they should be encouraged to use a pointer and a wall map.

LEARNING MAP SYMBOLS   Have the children learn to use a map's legend and to match map symbols with pictures of the features which the symbols portray. On a certain map, we find:

EXAMPLE OF SYMBOL	FEATURE DEPICTED
Blue	Water
Green	Elevation from sea level to 500 feet
⌒	Bend in river
〰〰	Mountain
—·—·—	National boundary

Where photographs are not available, sketches by the teacher will serve. State, provincial, and national boundaries may be arbitrary and imaginary —a fact to emphasize, since they are so prominently marked on political maps. Relief maps (discussed subsequently) play an important role in teaching map symbols. Each map symbol should eventually call vividly to mind the feature for which it stands.

LEARNING GEOGRAPHICAL LOCATIONS AND RELATIONSHIPS   Maps are studied to fix in mind names of places and their locations, shapes, approximate distances, and the like. Globes should be used freely, too, in this work. Children should learn the names and locations of the continents and the oceans and, through use of the globe, discern the relationship of these areas to each other, plus the fact that there is more than twice as much water area as land area.

ESTABLISHING LOCATION THROUGH USE OF LATITUDE AND LONGITUDE   At an early age, children observe the parallels and meridians which appear

Figure 10.5. A transparent globe. Courtesy of Farquhar Transparent Globes, Philadelphia.

on globes and maps. The possibility of using these lines for establishing locations can be introduced in the primary grades. Because of the complexity of the concept of latitude and longitude, however, it is not until later that most children will fully understand it. The concept needs to be taught and reviewed systematically throughout the intermediate grades.

The need for locating a particular cell of a grid (a network of horizontal and vertical lines) is not unfamiliar to children. Examples of gridlike arrangements which children encounter are the partitioned bookshelves in many libraries, the library's card-file cabinet, bins for holding tools, toys, and the like, lockers at bus stations and air terminals, crossword puzzles, checker boards, boxes in post office lobbies, calendars, and street maps of communities with rectangularly arranged streets. Classrooms where seats are set in rows also provide a grid-like arrangement. With a minimum of instruction, children can learn to locate a particular cell of a grid by naming the two coordinate numbers which indicate the horizontal and perpendicular rows, respectively. For example, scissors are kept in the classroom in the second bin of the top row; Johnny sits in row 4, seat 3; and the fifth of

March falls in the sixth column of the calendar and the top row (or Friday of the first week).

Once children are familiar with such elementary ideas, they can be introduced to globe and map grids. The north-south lines are called "meridians," the east-west lines are called "parallels." These are terms which children readily and conveniently can learn when they first meet with globes and maps containing them. The problem has now shifted. We are no longer concerned with locating a cell; we now wish to describe the location of a point on the earth with considerable exactness. It might be a city, a lonely island, or the spot where a plane made a forced landing. When this problem is presented to a class, some children will usually suggest that the spot be measured from the North Pole. For a start, this is satisfactory; as a result of the spinning of the earth on its axis, the two poles are indeed the natural points from which to measure—and the only such points. However, they next need to learn that the equator, midway between the poles, is the line from which measurements conventionally are made. The equator is 0° latitude; the latitude at the poles is 90°. Children with adequate background in mathematics can work out the reasoning of this—that there are 360° in a circle (such as that represented by the circumference of the earth), that the distance from the equator to a pole is one-fourth the circumference, and that, hence, the distance is 90°. Moreover, since the earth is approximately 25,000 miles in circumference, they can figure out that each degree is approximately 70 miles in length.

After the foregoing has been understood and the children have practiced using latitude in numerous map exercises, the teacher should pursue the subject further. Children can now fix the latitude of a shipwreck (see Figure 10.6). But they are apt to be stumped when faced with the necessity of determining the east-west location of the spot. After discussing the matter, however, it becomes apparent that one of the meridians of the grid must be chosen. Which one? This is the time for the children to learn of the arbitrary and conventional choice for this purpose, of the "meridian of Greenwich" (designated as 0° longitude) near London, and that the longitude of any point on earth is measured east or west from that meridian.

Working with the geographic coordinates (latitude and longitude) will be easy for children who have received instruction in the new mathematics. They will recognize the grid and the problem of describing the location of a point such as shown in Figure 10.6 as similar to the grids and "ordered pairs of numbers" worked over in math class (see Figure 10.7).[15] The need to describe the location of the point shown in Figure 10.6 will be a simple extension of their knowledge. They will describe the location of the shipwreck as longitude 15° W., latitude 30° S. The teacher should cultivate the connection between this tool of mathematics and map work.

[15] Robert L. Swain and Eugene D. Nichols, *Understanding Arithmetic* (Rev. ed.). New York: Holt, Rinehart and Winston, 1965. Chap. 14.

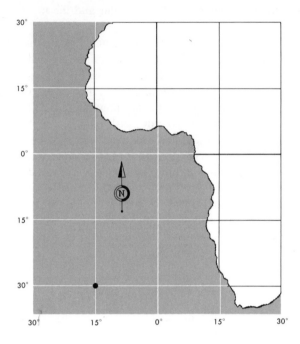

Figure 10.6. The position of the "shipwreck" in the South Atlantic Ocean is described as longitude 15° west, latitude 30° south.

ESTIMATING AND COMPUTING DISTANCES   The graphic scales on maps are studied and used in estimating and computing distances and areas. Frequent exercises of this type will prevent misconceptions of distant areas which so readily form in children's minds. Many an easterner, through casual map examination, thinks of Los Angeles and San Francisco as being more or less "twin cities," much like St. Paul and Minneapolis. By noting the graphic scale in Figure 10.8, he can easily see, even without measuring, that Los Angeles is about 350 miles from San Francisco—all day on the train, and as far as from Chicago to Minneapolis, Regina to Winnipeg, or Munich to Budapest!

Globes are useful for finding and measuring the shortest distance between places. Since the shortest distance between any two points on the earth lies along a great-circle route, the problem is to find the great circle that passes through two given points on the globe. (A great circle is any circle that cuts the globe into equal halves; the shortest distance between any two points on the earth is along a great circle.) This can be done by means of a ring cut out of cardboard with an inside circumference just barely larger than the

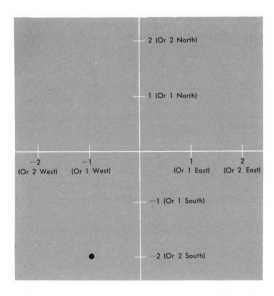

Figure 10.7. The dot corresponds to the ordered pair of numbers (-1, -2).

circumference of the globe. For this purpose the globe should be one that can be detached from its base. By slipping the ring over the globe, it can be turned to connect any two points, while at the same time dividing the globe into equal halves. The routes thus indicated, if drawn on a Mercator map, will be curved lines and will not look like the shortest distances at all. The shortest route from Tokyo to the Panama Canal will be found by the cardboard ring to pass near Pike's Peak—a fact which would never be suggested by drawing a straight line between these two places on a Mercator's map.

Understanding Map Projections

The task of map projection is to transfer the system of parallels and meridians (the "grid") from the spherical globe to a flat surface. It is desirable for a class to understand why the problem arises at all—why is the globe not sufficient? By asking the question and by directing discussion, the teacher usually will enable the class to make a few interesting discoveries: (1) There are occasions when we wish to see the earth as a whole; with a globe, we can never see more than a part of it. (2) There are occasions when we wish to see a portion of the earth in great detail; but a globe would have to be inordinately large to show the significant details of a state or a small nation. (3) There are occasions when we wish to carry a representa-

Figure 10.8. Illustration of graphic scale for estimating distance between two points.

tion of part of the earth with us, as when hiking, or on a car trip; for this purpose, a globe scarcely would be convenient.

Children's contact with globes and maps that appear in newspapers, atlases, and textbooks leads them to raise questions about the diversity in appearance of the earth and certain portions of the earth. They express wonder at the differing shape and size of a continent on different maps as they would if the familiar profile of Abraham Lincoln were to vary markedly from picture to picture. When such questions arise, it is time to introduce children to the problem of rendering a spherical surface upon a flat surface.

The concepts inherent in map projection are complex, and it is not to be expected that children of elementary school age will acquire more than a nodding acquaintance with them. The presentation should be unhurried and repeated as often as necessary. However, although there are over 200 kinds of projections, and many of the intricacies are beyond a child's grasp, he can understand the reasonableness and utility of a few common types of projection. The following exercises cover (1) an azimuthal type, (2) a cylindrical type (the Mercator), (3) an individual type (an interrupted equal-area form), and (4) a conic type. The class will learn through the exercises that all maps are necessarily distortions of the earth, that none shows everything accurately and clearly, and that each has its peculiar utility.

A preliminary exercise—one that will bring the child face-to-face with the problem of projection—consists of cutting an orange in half, removing the pulp from one half, and placing the empty hull, face down, on a flat surface (Figure 10.9A). Then push it down in an attempt to flatten it out. The result is depicted in Figure 10.9B. The difficulty of transferring a sphere to a flat surface in this manner becomes evident.

CONSTRUCTING AN AZIMUTHAL PROJECTION   To help children understand the azimuthal equidistant projection, select a ball and a circular piece of paper with a diameter equal to the circumference of the ball. Then cut the paper as shown in Figure 10.9C. Place a thumbtack or chalk mark on the ball to represent the South Pole and wrap the paper around the ball so that the points converge at the South Pole. Fasten them with masking tape and, using a globe as a model, sketch the outline of the continents roughly on the paper (Figure 10.9D). Then, open the paper (Figure 10.9E), and the continents and the South Pole will be seen to be split. Place a sheet of tracing paper above this circular map, trace the outlines, and draw the lines to connect the split portions of the continents. The result will be an approximation of one form of azimuthal projection (Figure 10.9F). The advantage of this projection is that a straight line connecting the center of the map with any other point on the map is along a great circle and gives the exact distance to that point—a projection of significance in an age of air navigation because great-circle routes can be traveled by air.

CONSTRUCTING A CYLINDRICAL PROJECTION   Tear apart the gores used in the preceding projection and arrange them as in Figure 10.9G. Again, trace the outlines and connect separated lines. The result will be similar to Figure 10.9H. Note the east-west directions, which increase as one advances from the equator to either pole, and attempt a freehand sketch which will stretch the distorted land forms as much in a north-south direction as they have already been stretched east-west. The result is an approximation of the Mercator's projection (Figure 10.9I). Despite distortions in distances, shapes are fair and directions are accurate. Any straight line is a line of constant compass-bearing, a *rhumb* line. For the ship navigator who likes to keep his ship on a constant course, even when this means a longer voyage, this has always been the favorite projection.

Some geographers do not favor the Mercator projection for use in the elementary school for several reasons. It is based on rather sophisticated geometry, and its shapes are good only for small areas. Directions over long distances (those that children are certain to notice), they point out, are distorted, and great circles are curved lines whereas, on the earth, they are straight lines. On the Mercator, lines of constant compass direction are straight lines whereas, on the earth, they are, with some exceptions, constantly curving lines. The author feels that these arguments are sufficiently compelling to justify only limited use of the Mercator projection with

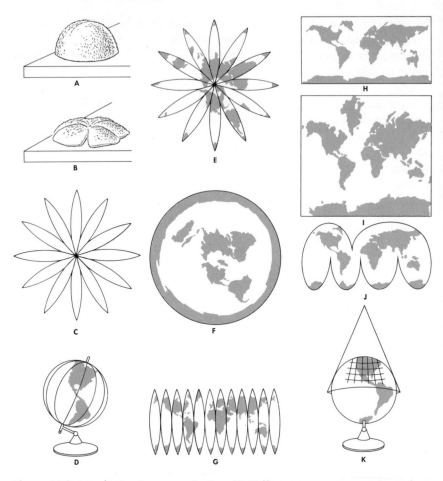

Figure 10.9. Introduction to map projection. (A) Half an orange represents hemisphere of earth. (B) Attempt to flatten orange reveals difficulty of flattening spherical surface. (C) Paper cut to fit neatly around globe. (D) Same paper wrapped around globe and with outline of continents sketched upon it. (E) Same paper flattened out again. (F) Azimuthal projection by tracing of (E) and connecting broken lines and dispersed points. (I) Approximation of Mercator's projection by revising (H) so that outlines are stretched north-south to compensate for previous east-west stretching. (J) Equal-area projection by new arrangement of gores. (K) Conic projection by tracing small area directly from globe upon transparent cone of paper.

children—just enough so that they know there is such a projection, its limitations, its areas of usefulness, and how it relates to the globe as illustrated in the exercise described in the preceding paragraph.

CONSTRUCTING AN INTERRUPTED EQUAL-AREA PROJECTION Arrange the same gores so that all contiguous land areas actually fit together without separation (Figure 10.9J). Because land areas except in the polar regions are intact, this projection is useful for showing the distribution and relative density of population, natural resources, and the like. It should be understood, however, that it only *approximates* an equal-area projection.

CONSTRUCTING A CONIC PROJECTION   Improvise a cone from a sheet of tracing paper, and invert it over a globe. Then trace the outline, meridians, and parallels of any region not too close to the equator. In Figure 10.9K, the United States has been thus drawn. It shows converging, straight meridians, curved, concentric parallels of the simple, conic projection, and minor distortion of shapes, distances, and directions for areas in temperate zones.

Other Procedures for Teaching Map Projections

A number of commercial aids are available to teach map projection which are ingenious and intriguing.[16] It is recommended that teachers try them out, either alone, or in combination with the more informal procedures described above.

TEACHING PHYSICAL GEOGRAPHY THROUGH MAPS

The Physical Environment

How important is physical environment? Some of those influenced by the strong reaction against "environmental determinism" (the belief that cultural features of a region can be accounted for by the region's physical environment) tend to minimize it. As pointed out in Chapter 5, a given environment may mean one thing to one cultural group, and is used accordingly; it may mean something quite different to another cultural group. On the other hand, as one physical geographer pointed out, given the presence of a certain culture, ". . . the nature of the physical environment may play a decisive role in human happenings."[17] Certainly, we cannot ignore the physical environment, yet in teaching physical geography in the air age, the following concepts need to be stressed.

PHYSICAL FEATURES MAKE LESS DIFFERENCE TO MAN THAN FORMERLY

[16] *Impossible Map*, a second film. New York: National Film Board of Canada; *The Map Projection Device* (Philadelphia: Farquhar Transparent Globes), and *A Map Projection Model* (Northbrook, Ill.: Hubbard Scientific Co.) include globe and projection accessories.

[17] Clyde P. Patton, "Professional Contributions to Physical Geography," in Preston E. James (Ed.), *New Viewpoints in Geography*; Twenty-ninth Yearbook. Washington, D.C.: National Council for the Social Studies. 1959. P. 20.

It is important when using the relief map as a teaching instrument to emphasize how man has grown into steadily increasing command of his physical environment, learning to overcome some of its disadvantages and to make the most of its advantages. Man ". . . plays more and more the part of cause, not of effect."[18] Modern facilities for bridge building, tunneling under rivers and through mountains, cutting through hills, and foretelling the presence of obstacles in travel reduces the potency of the physical environment. The airplane, in particular, has revolutionized geography. It overcomes the barrier formed by the impenetrable jungles of South America, for example, even providing the transportation of heavy logs and cattle. The North and South Poles are no longer the inaccessible regions of a generation ago. Man can now hop over high mountain ranges. Continued development of the airplane may create a world in which ocean, mountain, swamp, desert, jungle, and frozen waste will cease to be important barriers to man. That world is already in the making, and in consequence, physical geography is increasingly a subject that does more to explain man's past behavior than his present behavior.

This means that when relief maps are used to illustrate the following generalizations, we tend to deal to a considerable extent with history. Note how this is the case.

Some physical features invite settlement   Waterfalls were factors in the location of numerous cities such as Minneapolis, Rochester, and the fall line cities from Trenton to Macon.

Many rivers have served to attract settlement, not only because of assured access to water but also because of excellent soil built up during floods from the deposit of fertile river sediment. The soils of the valleys of the Nile, the Ganges, and the Mississippi are examples of this process.

Mouths of rivers along ocean and lake shores large enough to offer good harbor facilities have been important points of settlement. The deep waters and generous expanse of drowned river mouths that characterize the Hudson, Delaware, Sacramento, Thames, Seine, and other rivers have proved especially attractive to settlement.

Some physical features discourage settlement   The inaccessibility, eroded soil, and low temperatures of high mountains are deterrents to settlement.

Glaciated, rocky coasts with their poor soil, such as those of New England and Norway, have proved forbidding to all but the very rugged.

A smooth coast line like Australia's means few good harbors and has discouraged settlement.

Some physical features invite movement   Rivers are historic arteries of

18 Lucien Febvre, *A Geographic Introduction to History.* New York: Knopf, 1925. P. 351.

exploration; La Salle's use of the Mississippi, Lewis and Clark's use of the Missouri, and Livingstone's use of the Zambesi are well-known examples. Wide plains with their distant horizons have had a beckoning effect, as shown so well in Hamlin Garland's autobiographical writing describing the restlessness among pioneer farmers in the Middle West.

Mountain passes have played an important role in the movements of people, as seen in the historical use of the Cumberland Gap in the southern Appalachians—the "wilderness road" of pioneer days.

Some physical features discourage movement Oceans have been great isolaters. Their effect upon the social and biological uniqueness of islands is seen in Madagascar and Australia. Persecuted peoples with strong motivation and resolution, such as the Puritans and Quakers, deliberately sought spots where an adjacent ocean would make their refuge secure.

High mountains have tended to isolate regions by forming an enclosure, as in Switzerland and Tibet, or forming one in conjunction with a peninsula, as in Italy and Spain.

Some relief features affect climate Some mountains change the course of winds. For example, the Alps act as windbreaks to southern France against cold northern blasts. The Rhodope and Pindus mountains similarly protect Greece. And, of course, the elevation of mountains affects temperatures in the mountains.

Mountains with windward slopes toward a nearby sea cause the moist air to ascend, expand, cool, and lose moisture as rain descending on its windward side, and continue as a dry wind blowing from the leeward side. The Sierra Nevadas are a case in point, with the average annual rainfall at Nevada City, Calif. (on the western slope of the Sierras), over 60 inches, and at Carson City, Nev., less than 70 miles away (on the eastern slope of the Sierras), not more than 15 inches.

MAN HAS MADE INTELLIGENT ADJUSTMENTS TO UNFAVORABLE PHYSICAL FEATURES Man has constructed artificial harbors as at Madras, India; lock systems along rivers and canals; spectacular bridges across abysses in mountainous regions; and tunnels through mountains, including six along the Pennsylvania Turnpike and over 60 in the Swiss Alps.

Poor agricultural prospects in mountainous regions have been overcome through terracing, by which the Incas of Peru maintained their civilization in the Andes, and by herding.

People along rocky coasts, such as Norway's, have turned to fishing and merchant sailing to supplement their indifferent livelihood from meager soil resources.

In isolated areas of limited natural resources such as Tibet, Ecuador, and Iceland, man has developed advanced forms of democratic government made possible in part by the lack of opportunity to exploit the environment—the chief means of creating class distinctions which, in turn, make democracy difficult to practice.

OTHER PHYSICAL FACTORS INFLUENCE SETTLEMENT, MOVEMENT, AND CLIMATE Relative abundance and accessibility of natural resources is a prime factor in governing settlement and movement. Temperature and rainfall are influenced in part by latitude (distance from equator and poles), direction of prevailing winds, and direction of air-mass movement.

The Place of Three-dimensional Relief Maps

A three-dimensional relief map has a raised surface which shows the physical features of the mapped area. In the light of the preceding section, a teacher may wonder how much time need be spent on them. Relief maps are important for young children because they help build the imagery essential to understanding those problems still faced by man which are posed by the earth's uneven surface. For older children, they help in explaining climatic conditions and in building an understanding of the problems of historical movement and settlement. A variety of three-dimensional maps are available from map and specialty companies (see Fig. 10.10).[19]

Construction of Relief Maps in the Classroom

The commercially manufactured relief maps are a boon to the teacher, but they have certain limitations. They do not cover local community areas. They may not show emphatically enough a selected relief feature (such as the Cumberland Gap, Mt. Kosciusko, or Cotopaxi) to which the teacher has reason to call attention. Furthermore, children gain superior understanding of an area by mapping it themselves. The activity demands that they give attention to detail and acquire a knowledge of land forms and position which can hardly be acquired by merely looking at a map made by someone else. Map-making improves a child's ability to read published maps and interpret their symbols.

The first plastic maps should be of areas children are acquainted with at firsthand. Primary-grade children can map their communities with clay or Plasticine upon a cardboard base, modeling not only natural relief but man-made landmarks as well. If the map is modeled from putty in a water-

---

[19] Large maps and also desk-size maps are available from A. J. Nystrom and Co., Chicago. "Earth-curved" relief maps are produced by Panoramic Studios, Philadelphia, Pa. Relief molds (for making one's own three-dimensional maps) are made by Art Chemical Products, Huntington, Ind.

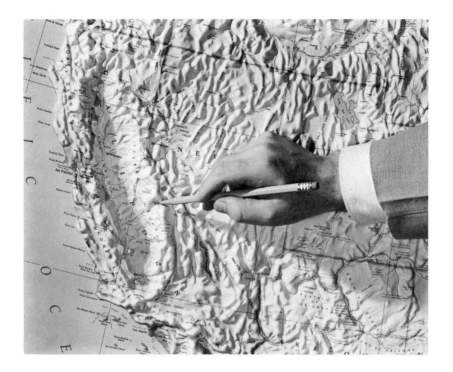

Figure 10.10 Commercially available three-dimensional map. Courtesy of Nystrom Raised Relief Map Company, Philadelphia.

proof container (a cake pan is suitable), water may be poured to fill the hollows that represent bodies of water. They should model the relief partly from memory and partly from special field trips to gather map data. The maps will, of course, be quite crude, but their rough approximations are important beginning lessons on the nature and purpose of maps. Do not plan them for exhibit—in fact, there is no reason for preserving them longer than needed to enable the child to note discrepancies between recollection, execution, and fact. Common errors in children's beginning maps include these:

1. *Omissions*—for example, of terraces or bridges,
2. *Distortion of shapes*—for example, of schoolyard or parks,
3. *Disregard of directional relationships*—for example, placing a factory on the wrong side of a river or drawing parallel streets at right angles to each other,
4. *Separation of contiguous areas*—for example, rivers built as separate entities not in contact with the shore,

5. *Disregarding natural law*—for example, having streams run a vertically undulating course or allowing vigorous streams to peter out before reaching a larger body of water or the edge of the map.

Geographic misconceptions thus indicate what "repairs" are required, and offer clues on what to emphasize on subsequent field trips, during discussion periods, and in future map-making.

The plastic maps of intermediate grade children are also to be viewed as rough, temporary productions. The teacher may invite the children to assist him in making a map. After he has made several, he is in a position to know in what ways pupils can assist, and is less apt to encourage them, in the name of "pupil activity," to start maps which they are doomed to bungle and which can be of no use to anyone. A map may possess a certain amount of amateurish crudity and naïveté without having its utility impaired. Yet fundamentally, a map should be regarded by teachers and children as a scientific tool.

Before modeling, one should become familiar with the territory to be modeled and avoid inaccuracies that easily occur when working too literally from the purely topographical data shown on a flat map. Pictures from books, periodicals, and library picture collections may be used to convey a feeling for the character of a region. If the United States is being mapped, for instance, you will need pictures to depict the contrast of the high, jagged western mountains and the low, rounded eastern mountains; the differing landscapes of the coastal plains on the Pacific, the Gulf, and the Atlantic; the appearance of the Mississippi and its valley; the Ozark Mountains; the plains; the fall line. At best, the amateur is not likely to be satisfied with his translation of the features on the plastic map, but they will be considerably closer to realistic representation if he studies the pictures carefully and keeps them in mind as he works. Posting them in the classroom for the period of map-making will promote familiarity with their features.

It is also well, before modeling, to know definitely what features are to be conspicuously portrayed. If South America is being mapped, the following features might be chosen:

1. Historically strategic areas, for example: Falkland Islands, Isthmus of Panama, Strait of Magellan,
2. Plateaus interpersing the rugged peaks of the Andes,
3. The two large lakes, Titicaca and Aullagas, in Peru and Bolivia, situated over 12,000 feet above the sea,
4. Jagged, tall Andes in contrast to rounded, low Guianan and Brazilian highlands,
5. Highest point on continent, Aconcagua, Argentina (no portion of South America is below sea level, but lowest points of other continents

can be shown by chiseling a depression in the wooden base to indicate "below sea level"),

6. Highest active volcano in the world, Cotopaxi, Ecuador,
7. Most traveled gap in the Andes, Uspallata Pass, connecting Argentina and Chile,
8. Coastal plain bordering entire continent, except for about 1,000 miles from Cape Horn north along the coast of Chile,
9. Source in Andes of many eastward-flowing rivers emptying into Atlantic Ocean,
10. At least 12 of the long tributaries of the great Amazon River.

There is no one correct list. Some teachers emphasize the highest and lowest points, since they dramatically proclaim the range of the area's topography. Other teachers, conscious that the points of extreme elevation are little different and no more significant, geographically, than other points which closely approach the elevation of the extremes, do not wish to emphasize them. Mapping allows wide latitude, and choice of details must be governed by the purpose to be served by the map and the instructional "style" of the teacher.

Some Suggested Teaching Materials: Maps and Globes

Books for Children
Brown, Lloyd A., *Map Making: The Art That Became a Science.* Boston: Little, Brown, 1960.
Epstein, Sam, and Beryl Epstein, *The First Book of Maps and Globes.* New York: F. Watts, 1959.
Rinkoff, Barbara, *A Map Is a Picture.* New York: Crowell, 1965.

Films
Introducing Globes. Hollywood: Bailey, 1963.
Maps for a Changing World. Wilmette, Ill.: Encyclopedia Britannica Films, 1960.

Filmstrips
Introduction to Maps. Valhalla, N.Y.: Stanbow, 1958.
Learning to Read Maps. New York: American Book, 1961.

Periodicals
Cartocraft Teaching Aids. Contains suggestions for teachers. Denoyer Geppert Co., Chicago, Ill.
Geographic School Bulletin. A children's weekly from National Geographic Society, Washington, D.C.

Further information about constructing three-dimensional relief maps appears in Appendix B.

FOR REVIEW AND REFLECTION

1. Compare the map and the globe as instruments in developing geographic concepts.
2. How can the teacher aid the young child in learning directions?
3. How can map symbols be taught (a) in the primary grades; (b) in the intermediate grades?
4. State how several different types of map projection can be simply explained to children.
5. What are some of the misconceptions that might be conveyed (a) through overemphasis upon the earth's relief feature; (b) through under-emphasis?

ASSIGNMENTS

1. Collect a series of special-purpose maps from the daily press, magazines, advertising folders, and other sources. Explain how each could be used in teaching the role of maps.
2. Construct a map for teaching a specified concept in a specified unit.
3. Draw up a lesson plan for teaching geographic relationships through a "discovery" procedure such as those employed by Arnsdorf and by Possien.
4. Experiment with demonstrating map projections through the informal procedures described in this chapter and through one of the commercially available devices such as Farquhar's *Map Projection Device*.

SUPPLEMENTARY READING

Arnsdorf, Val, "Teaching Social Studies with Map-overlays," *California Journal of Educational Research,* **16** (March 1965), 65–74. Fifth-grade pupils were found to benefit in map-reading and other skills following "inquiry-discovery" teaching.

Davies, Malcolm, *Geographic Dictionary.* Baltimore, Md.: Baltimore Public Schools, 1958. A list of geographical terms, each defined both verbally and through an accompanying drawing.

Davis, O. L., Jr., "Children Can Learn Complex Concepts," *Educational Leadership,* **17** (December 1959), 170–175. Presents evidence that children in Grades 4, 5, and 6 can acquire understanding of rotation of earth, International Date Line, standard time zones, and other advanced globe and map concepts.

Hanna, Paul R., *et al., Geography in the Teaching of Social Studies.* Boston: Houghton Mifflin, 1966. Contains numerous concrete suggestions for teaching map concepts and skills, arranged by grade level.

Harris, Ruby M., *The Rand McNally Handbook of Map and Globe Usage.* Skokie, Ill.: Rand McNally, 1959. Presents a wealth of ideas for use of maps and globes as tools of learning.

Kohn, Clyde F., *et al.*, "Interpreting Maps and Globes," in Helen M. Carpenter (Ed.), *Skills in Social Studies*; Twenty-fourth Yearbook. Washington, D.C.: National Council for the Social Studies, 1953. Chap. 8. Defines ability to interpret maps and globes in terms of six skills and gives suggestions for aiding their development throughout the grades.

Lobeck, Armin K., *Things Maps Don't Tell Us*. New York: Crowell-Collier and Macmillan, 1958. "Map interpretation is like the process of reading between the lines of a story. . . ." writes the author, who tells how to read between the lines of maps.

Mitchell, Lucy Sprague, *Young Geographers*. New York: Basic Books, 1963. A classic (first published in 1934) noteworthy for its spirited, imaginative approach to the study of maps by children.

Moore, W. G., *A Dictionary of Geography*. Baltimore, Md.: Penguin, 1962. A glossary of terms including those commonly used in map work.

Nurry, Bernard E., *How to Teach Map and Globe Skills*. Brookline, Pa.: School District of Haverford Township, n.d. An explicit and imaginative grade-by-grade plan for teaching map and globe concepts and skills.

Odell, Clarence B., "The Use of Maps, Globes, and Pictures in the Classroom," in Preston E. James (Ed.), *New Viewpoints in Geography*; Twenty-ninth Yearbook. Washington, D.C.: National Council for the Social Studies, 1959. Chap. 12. Gives suggestions to the teacher on map reading, map interpretation, kinds of maps, and correlated use of maps, globes, and pictures.

Piaget, Jean, and Bärbel Inhelder, *The Child's Conception of Space*. London: Routledge, 1963. Chap. 14, "Diagrammatic Layouts and the Plan of a Model Village," describes development in ability to reproduce a layout from ages 2 to 13.

Raisz, Erwin, *Principles of Cartography*. New York: McGraw-Hill, 1962. Discusses basic concepts underlying the making of maps and describes their construction.

Sabaroff, Rose, "Map Interpretation in the Primary Grades," *Elementary School Journal*, **64** (November 1963), 59–67. Suggestions for the development of ten abilities essential to map interpretation.

Strahler, Arthur N., *Physical Geography* (2d ed.). New York: Wiley, 1960. Pt. I, "The Earth as a Globe," includes a chapter on map projection—an exceptionally clear treatment.

Thralls, Zoe A., *The Teaching of Geography*. New York: Appleton, 1958. Chapter 2, "Maps and Globes Are Our Business," contains numerous learning activities.

Wagner, Louise D., "Measuring the Map-Reading Ability of Sixth-Grade Children," *Elementary School Journal*, **53** (February 1953), 338–344. Gives a comprehensive inventory of map-reading skills.

11

PLANNING CREATIVE EXPERIENCES

*Creativity is the imaginatively gifted
recombination of old elements into new.*

JOHN CIARDI

Creative expression is often thought of as an activity for the artist, to be engaged in by the nontalented only as a means of emotional release and recreation. This is too narrow a view to satisfy the present age of rapid change. In the first place, many of today's ideas and procedures will become obsolete by tomorrow. It is necessary only to contemplate how the computer will almost surely alter the role of the factory worker, the teacher (see Chap. 12), the librarian; or to appreciate the innovations in managing international affairs that are essential if our civilization is to be spared what Toynbee calls "annihilation by a knockout blow." The years ahead will call for inventive, adaptive minds.

If children are to be prepared for those years, their education cannot be confined to only the *acquisition* of knowledge. We cannot predict all the knowledge today's children will require as adults—much of it has yet to be produced. But teachers do have the opportunity to accustom children to assume creative roles. They can place them in situations where they are forced to speculate, to reason, to invent.

The reader may be thinking at this point: You have already told of ways in which this can be done. The unit method itself requires a child to think hard and, in the learning process, to contribute to decisions. The discovery method has been recommended as a means for developing creative thought. And critical reading has been advocated—a kind of reading that demands the exercise of creative judgment. What other creative experiences remain?

In this chapter, we are concerned with promoting creative habits in consolidating and summarizing what has been learned. The psychological need for such "output" exercises was succinctly stated by William James in his assertion that there can be no impression without expression.

CREATIVE ACTIVITIES IN SOCIAL STUDIES

Writing, painting, dramatizing, and other art activities in connection with social studies require the child first to collect the relevant detail, make a plan for representing or interpreting it, then execute the plan through a form of art. In taking these three steps, he organizes the relevant concepts and fixes them firmly in mind. They become a form of review or self-recitation. What an uninformed classroom visitor might regard as merely "free expression" or "play" is actually a fact-fixing and disciplining process. Art, like any medium of communication, is indeed a discipline; not only is there self-discipline in collecting and organizing the content, but the art media used in the execution impose a discipline of their own.

Creative activities, in addition to cultivating self-discipline, play a part in developing democratic citizenship. They encourage initiative, independence, and experimentation. Through the arts, the child learns respect for individuality and for the trail-blazing of others. At the same time, he learns how to cooperate—how his role in a dramatization for example, must fit in with that of others, or how his contribution to his committee's mural must harmonize with the contributions of others.

Freedom and Its Limits

Most of the suggestions in this chapter will imply that the child should have considerable freedom in selecting the form and style of his art work. It is assumed, however, that his creations will be adjuncts to his learning and hence must be authentic. If, on a mural, he plans to depict a house of the Indians of the Pacific Northwest, it is expected that he will show a plank house such as was actually built, and not a tepee. He can be as imaginative as he wishes in designing the mural, and his representation may be simple or elaborate, and it almost certainly will bear the stamp of childlike naiveté and crudity, but he must be as faithful as possible to fact. In other words, the art content should not conflict with social studies content.

ART IN THE SOCIAL STUDIES   Many art educators resist such control of art and believe it tends to stifle true creativity. They tend to favor a separation of academic content from creative activities, somewhat as occurs at Summerhill,[1] with wide latitude for pupil choice in the selection of subject matter. The author should perhaps make clear that he is not advocating that social studies "take over" art. The arts should flourish on their own in the "art" area of the curriculum. Nevertheless, the author believes the

[1] A. S. Neill, *Summerhill: A Radical Approach to Child Rearing.* New York: Hart, 1960.

teacher quite properly may channel creative activities through social studies content. The child is not less creative when he writes a story about the Pony Express and places it within Lincoln's lifetime rather than within a period that suits his fancy, or need his creativity thereby be inhibited. Magnificent historical novels, such as those by A. B. Guthrie, Jr., attest to congeniality of creative writing and authenticity.

THE MONTESSORI METHOD AND CREATIVITY   In recent years, there has been a revival of interest in Montessori's system of education. Although Montessori schools in this country are primarily preschools, the Montessori pedagogy is being vigorously advocated by its supporters for incorporation in the early school years. Many parents have been led to believe that the Montessori method leads to an ideal combination of discipline and creativity.

Anyone who has examined Mme. Montessori's writings must be impressed by her insight and her positive contributions to education. But it also becomes evident that her theory did not always jibe with her recommended practice. As Beyer points out, the Montessori method is in vogue today chiefly because of an increase in the number of Americans who see in it a means for bringing about "quick and easy learning" and not because of Mme. Montessori's belief in freedom and spontaneity.[2] Her method emphasizes such learnings as following directions and understanding spatial relationships through a specific set of materials. Beyer aptly states that creative materials (paints, big crayons, clay, and the like) ". . . just don't figure in the Montessori scheme of things." The stress is on ritualistic procedures and achievement. Children's feelings, their social interactions, and dramatic play are largely ignored. The method provides no outlet for creative thinking or performance in elementary school social studies.

The Role of the Teacher

Because creativity and conformity are opposed characteristics, it is not surprising that outstandingly creative individuals have been, at least in some respects, nonconformists.[3] To encourage creativity in children, we are compelled to abandon the ideal of the traditional schoolmaster who sought uniformity of response above all else. The description of creative thinking by Guilford and other psychologists makes this quite obvious. They show that creativity calls for traits which may often conflict with conforming

[2] Evelyn Beyer, "Let's Look at Montessori," *Journal of Nursery Education,* **18** (November 1962), 4–9; and Evelyn Beyer, "Montessori in the Space Age?" *NEA Journal,* **52** (December 1963), 35–36.
[3] Calvin W. Taylor and Frank Barron (Eds.), *Scientific Creativity: Its Recognition and Development.* New York: Wiley, 1963.

behavior—for example, the ability to see a variety of possibilities of doing something or thinking about something, the ability to furnish original ideas, and the willingness to risk failure and experience ambiguity in trying out new ideas.[4] If teachers are to promote creative thinking, they need to respect children's ideas—accept them, reward them, and urge the children to explore them.[5] There is some evidence that a factor in the release of pupil creativity is the teacher. Teachers who tend to be permissive and warm achieve this goal more fully than do aloof, controlling teachers.[6] Developing originality and fresh thinking in children is not a simple matter of the teacher's applying a technique. The teacher must see part of his role as releasing the creative impulses of his pupils. To this end, a classroom atmosphere of respect for individuality must be established.

WRITTEN WORK

Written work is commonly neglected in elementary social studies. Herman found from 1 percent to 4.5 percent of typical social studies lessons were devoted to writing activities.[7] Opportunities for written reports, summaries, and imaginative pieces in social studies are numerous and should be provided. As noted in an earlier chapter, when a child records his learning in written form, he reviews and recites it, thus fixing it in his memory for future recall and use.

Creative Writing

In the first grade, before children can write with any degree of fluency, the pupils may dictate their thoughts to the teacher, as illustrated in Chapter 9. Even in third grade much of children's creative composition should be accepted in oral form because the laboriousness of handwriting at this age for many children results in a heavy investment of time out of proportion to the meager product. On the other hand, some third-graders are enthusiastic and productive writers.

Once children reach this stage, writing assignments should be frequent and varied. Following are types of assignments which have yielded gratifying stimulation of a search for more facts, imagination, and critical thought:

[4] James J. Gallagher, "Productive Thinking," in Martin L. Hoffman and Lois Wladis Hoffman, *Review of Child Development Research.* New York: Russell Sage, 1964. Vol. 1. Pp. 349–381.

[5] E. Paul Torrance, *Creativity.* Pamphlet. Washington, D.C.: National Education Association, 1963. P. 16.

[6] Kenneth H. Wodtke and Norman E. Wallen, "The Effects of Teacher Control in the Classroom on Pupils' Creativity-Test Gains," *American Educational Research Journal,* 2 (March 1965), 75–82.

[7] Wayne L. Herman, Jr., "The Use of Language Arts in Social Studies Lessons," *American Educational Research Journal,* 4 (March 1967), 117–124.

1. Writing captions to accompany documentary pictures of places, events, personalities, and the like,

2. Writing a story of the Rip Van Winkle-type in which a person who lived in the period being studied awakes and makes comparisons and comments about the astonishing changes that have occurred between his day and ours,

3. Retelling a myth, event, or adventure—in prose or in verse,

4. Proposing a hypothesis to account for a baffling situation or problem such as the low percentage of voting turnout in the United States —lower than that in most other democracies,

5. Proposing a method for testing the hypothesis and for solving the problem,

6. Writing an imaginary editorial on civil rights, legislation adverse to billboard advertising, or some other current issue.

The teacher should be on guard lest his pupils ". . . verge toward fantasy and away from the disciplined use of the imagination."[8] The child should recognize his responsibility for acquainting himself with solid facts upon which his writing is to be based.

Notebooks

Keeping a notebook is a convenient way for a child to organize notes, pictures, reports, and impressions collected in connection with a unit. The teacher should encourage originality in its content and organization. The notebook may be the product of an individual child, of a small group of children, or of an entire class. It may be a loose-leaf notebook or a notebook especially constructed and bound for the purpose. Kindergarten notebooks may contain nothing more than pictures; sixth-grade notebooks may vie with textbooks in their systematic treatment of a subject.

The notebook has fallen into disrepute in recent years because of its long association with stereotyped content and teacher insistence on uniformity. None of these elements need be present. When individual notebooks are kept, each child should feel that he is to develop his in his own way. When group notebooks are compiled, the members of the group should meet frequently to distribute tasks and evaluate material submitted. The teacher has an obligation to inspect notebooks frequently and to regard them more as evidences of child growth or of the child's need for help than as products to be blue-penciled and rewritten.

The teacher's encouragement and suggestions concerning the notebooks will do more to raise standards of workmanship than his expression of dis-

[8] Ernest Horn, *Methods of Instruction in the Social Studies*. New York: Scribner, 1937. P. 459.

satisfaction and criticism. Children should understand clearly that a wide range of records is acceptable. Aside from their own compositions, there may be pictures, clippings, diagrams, cartoons, and graphs. Organization should be stressed so that those items which belong together will be kept together.

GRAPHIC ARTS

Painting and Drawing

When children's interest is gripped by a unit, its content may appear spontaneously in many of the pictures they will draw or paint during art periods and during odd moments of the day. Whether this spontaneity is present or not, the teacher can often encourage portrayals by suggesting that certain subjects be attempted. All the members of one second-grade class made pictures to summarize what they learned in a study of fire prevention. Pupils of a third-grade class painted pictures to illustrate activities of the American Indian. Fourth-grade pupils, in a study of the colonial period, made crayon drawings showing "then" and "now." A sixth-grade class, studying ancient Egypt, created designs in the Egyptian style. Even when all members of a class take the same subject, their pictures are bound to differ if the teacher allows each child complete freedom of expression.

Figure 11.1. Children working on a mural.

Murals

An instructive and colorful way to summarize a unit is through construction of a mural, which is done on a long strip of sturdy wrapping paper. A mural may be either a unitary layout as of a harbor, a historical event, or a panorama of a foreign culture, such as Swiss rural life (see Figure 11.1); or it may depict a miscellany such as famous inventors, locomotive engines of the past one hundred years, or aspects of medieval life. Brushes and poster paint are ordinarily used, although colored chalk and pastels also give a pleasing effect. To prevent chalk from smudging, a colorless fixative may be sprayed over the completed chalked mural.

An entire class normally is too large to work on a mural all at once. A good procedure is to have a committee of six or eight children plan and execute a mural. If the teacher plans several murals for the year, then every child can have the prized opportunity of working on one. A mural should be planned and executed cooperatively. Each child on the committee should have the opportunity to paint or draw some significant part of the study. Authentic and reasonably accurate representations usually require a good deal of research, and each child should be encouraged to visit libraries and museums with a sketchbook, in preparation for the fulfillment of his part. The successful mural becomes a social project, requiring that each child subordinate his private impulses to the larger purposes of the group.[9]

"Movies"

The misnamed "movie" is a well-known and popular device in primary grades for presenting content, reviewing a social studies trip, or summarizing a unit or parts of a unit. A committee of children makes a series of pictures which eventually are mounted on a long strip of wrapping paper. Each end of the wrapping paper is fastened to a roller and placed in a box (see Figure 11.2). As the rollers are turned, the pictures slide past the open end of the box and tell the story, picture by picture.[10]

INDUSTRIAL ARTS

Classroom industrial arts are often viewed as the least creative of the arts. For this reason, they are sometimes wrongly looked upon with disfavor. That is unfortunate. Industrial arts activities deserve a solid place in the social studies program.

---

[9] For further suggestions, see the pamphlet by Marjorie Kelley and Nicholas Ronkes, *Let's Make a Mural.* San Francisco: Fearon, n.d. See also the books by Erdt and Gaitskell, listed at the end of this chapter under "Supplementary Reading."

[10] For further details on construction, see the books by Erdt and Gaitskell listed at the end of this chapter under "Supplementary Reading."

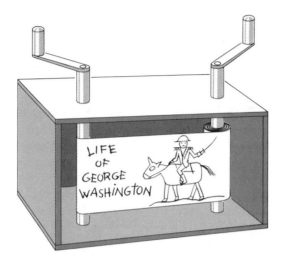

Figure 11.2. A "movie" set up for reviewing the life of George Washington. A piece of cardboard with a "window" cut in it may be taped to the front of the box to frame the succession of pictures.

Figure 11.3. Industrial arts: a second-grader at a weaving loom. Courtesy of Sioux Falls school system, Sioux Falls, South Dakota.

Industrial arts involve the reproduction of processes already worked out by others—the making of paper (see Appendix C), weaving (see Figure 11.3), tanning a hide (see Figure 11.4), and the like. On the surface, they appear non-creative. They are creative in that they enable children to make four important discoveries:

1. Discovery of the basic elements of a process which, in today's world of complex manufacture, become "lost" or at least "hidden,"
2. Discovery of the hard, muscular work, and often, the tedium required to carry out the process by hand,
3. Discovery of the emotional gratification that accompanies any successful construction of a tangible object of utility or beauty,
4. Discovery of the time-consuming nature of handcraft industry, why leisure was at a premium before the industrial revolution, the central economic role played by housewives and children in the days of handcraft, and the comparatively low standard of living of those days.

Figure 11.4. One step in tanning a hide.

The amount of *artistic* creativity called for varies from project to project. Sometimes the child can give his personal touch to the created product. For example, when weaving in connection with a study of the Indians of the Southwest, and after acquainting himself with the style of Pueblo blanket design from books or museums, the child can create his own design—but, of course, it should be in the Pueblo style and spirit. Tanning a hide, on the other hand, is a chemical process which affords little or no opportunity for the child's creative impulses.

Teachers who would like to develop industrial arts experiences, but who are hesitant because of ignorance of industrial processes or lack of skill, should consult their school's art teacher or art supervisor. The typical art specialist is both resourceful and versatile. Another possible course is to consult appropriate books, such as those by Dean, Gilbert, and Schneider who are listed under "Supplementary Reading" at the conclusion of this chapter. For example, Schneider's *Correlated Art* is divided into four parts: (1) Life in a Democracy, (2) How Civilization Developed, (3) The American Continent, and (4) World Neighbors. Part 3 deals with American history and geography; one of its subparts, devoted to Pioneer Days, contains directions for carrying out a total of 36 projects including embroidering samplers, designing quilt blocks, constructing looms, making hooked rugs, and making powder horns, dyes, and candles.

A few teachers object to industrial arts projects in social studies on the grounds that, however educational, they clutter up the classroom and make for disorder and noise. A superficial appearance of disorder is characteristic of most laboratories, especially in classrooms that are small and overcrowded; yet, social studies laboratory activities serve important ends. Some teachers arrange their rooms in such a way that these projects do not get in the way of other work, and they protect desks and floors with newspapers when the activity involves the possible spilling of liquids or other damaging materials, or scratching by tools.

MODELS

One form of model is the diorama—a "scene" arranged in a box, one side of which has been removed. It is constructed by a child who has done enough research on some phase of a unit to be able to portray it authentically and in detail—a dairy farm, a dry dock, a colonial kitchen, a street in ancient Athens, or the like. Some teachers encourage every member of the class to take a subject for special study and to construct his own diorama. Each item (person, animal, tree, chair) is made separately and then anchored in the box with thumbtacks, tape, glue, clay, or other device. Dioramas are fun to make, and the children who make them attain depth in their preliminary research. By observing the finished dioramas of classmates, they learn of details not covered by reading.

The construction of dioramas is difficult for primary-grade children because it requires such meticulous attention to detail and such fine muscular coordination. These younger children can make larger models more successfully. They can be arranged as panoramas. Needless to say, children should be provided with photographs and books to insure authentic models.

Teachers who feel unsure of their competence to direct model-making could consult a shop teacher or some of the excellent books on crafts written for teachers.[11]

DRAMATICS

Few media offer greater possibilities for summarizing a unit than creative dramatics. One investigator found a considerable gain in measurable factual learning in fifth-grade science growing out of plays. Besides a gain in factual learning, a greater improvement in cooperation, responsibility, and leadership was achieved through the use of dramatics.[12] Such values may be achieved through dramatics in the field of social studies as well.

Young children dramatize their experiences spontaneously. Prevented from actually participating in important activities of the workaday world, they participate in them in the only way they know—through play. When they assume the roles of farmers, housewives, pilots, truck drivers, knights, bulldozer operators, or railroad workers, they are identifying with the exciting work of the world—past or present—and in the process, coming into closer understanding of it.

In the primary grades, the play may be quite fragmentary. Small groups may act out stories or ideas discussed in class. An audience other than classmates is unnecessary. If costumes and property are used at all, they should be the kind that are improvised easily. Children enjoy playing certain scenes over and over again, taking turns in occupying various roles. If the teacher takes notes of what has been played and spoken, and reads them back to the class before the next drama session, the ensuing content and continuity may be improved. By the conclusion of the unit, a number of favorite scenes may be repeated for a final summary of the content.

In the intermediate grades, dramatic play becomes more formal. The desire to play before an audience in costume and with stage property increases. It is preferable to present the play to one or two other classes rather than before the entire school or before parents, since the value of dramatics as a social studies vehicle lies in the process of creating it. When a play is given before a large audience including many adults, the teacher tends to short-cut the learning process and throws his energies into supplying "finish" to the play. Excessive attention to stage property, costumes, and details of acting diverts time and energy from the educational in social studies dramatics—identifying oneself with other people. In creative

---

[11] For details of construction, see the books by Dean, Mattil, and Moore listed at the end of this chapter under "Supplementary Reading."

[12] R. A. Greene, *A Comparative Study of the Efficiency of Dramatic and Nondramatic Methods in Teaching Science to Fifth-Grade Children.* Ithaca, N.Y.: Cornell University Press, 1937.

dramatics, the teacher can discover inaccuracies and gaps in his pupils' knowledge, which they can fill in through further data-collecting and study. The dramatized story may be taken from an actual account, like that of the adventures of Marco Polo, or it may be original, such as a story of village life in Mexico. Nothing need be set down on paper at first. As already mentioned, the teacher may take notes of the children's action and lines and read them back at the beginning of the next dramatics period— or use a tape recorder. Authenticity of detail of manners, speech, property, and costumes should be checked. This requires almost constant self-scrutiny by the class. As the play grows, data-collecting increases. When a final cast is agreed upon and when the content and plot become clarified, lines may be learned, but need not necessarily be written. Property and costumes should be kept as simple as possible, so that ideas to be gained will not be lost in the mechanics of preparation. Improvisation is acceptable, and so is symbolic costuming, such as a turban worn by a boy in his regular clothes when taking the part of a Muslim.

If possible, every child should participate in every social studies play. Most children's plays created, as here suggested, contain many scenes, which makes it possible to plan a different cast for each scene, if necessary, in order to involve all members of the class. Actual participation in even a minor role gives a child the necessary opportunity to identify with other people, their work, and their problems.

A social studies play does not have to be creatively formulated as described in this section in order to be a worthwhile experience. If a teacher feels uncertain of his ability to carry forward a creative play, let him, by all means, experiment with a play that has already been written.[13]

Dramatics may also be enacted through marionettes and puppets.[14] Shy children frequently are able to participate more completely through such indirect acting than through direct acting in which they must appear before an audience in person. Their confidence may be significantly increased through working behind the scenes with puppets.

FOR REVIEW AND REFLECTION

1. What is the justification for including art projects in a social studies unit?
2. Which one of the creative activities discussed in this chapter seems to you especially valuable as an adjunct to other types of social studies experiences? Explain your choice.
3. Why is it that during the intermediate grades, the child desires a more formal type of dramatics than satisfied him previously?
4. In what respects may industrial arts activities be regarded as "creative?"

[13] Plays, Inc., 8 Arlington Street, Boston, Mass. 02116, publishes *Plays: The Drama Magazine for Young People* and other plays suitable for classroom reading.

[14] For details of puppetry, see the books by Dean, Mattil, and Gaitskell listed at the end of this chapter under "Supplementary Reading."

5. In the opening paragraph of this chapter, it is stated that the years ahead will require "inventive, adaptive minds" if the world of tomorrow is to be successfully met. Do you feel that creative art activities will really help today's children in this way, when they are adults? Why or why not?

ASSIGNMENTS

1. Become an expert at reproducing an industrial arts process. Bring the necessary materials to class, explain the process, and indicate what social studies concepts are developed through this industrial arts experience.
2. Conduct a debate on the proposition: *Resolved:* That more drill and less creative work in social studies would benefit the child and society.
3. In terms of the extent to which it reveals insight into man and society, review children's art found on the walls of the classrooms of any school you conveniently can visit.

SUPPLEMENTARY READING

Burgert, Robert H., and Elinor S. Meadows, *Eye-Appealing Bulletin Board Ideas.* Dansville, N.Y.: Owen, 1960. Includes suggestions for the display of children's creative work.

Burrows, Alvina T., *et al., They All Want to Write: Written English in the Elementary School* (3d ed.). New York: Holt, Rinehart and Winston, 1964. Offers a mine of information on writing, with many samples of children's work.

Conrad, George, *The Process of Art Education in the Elementary School.* Englewood Cliffs, N.J.: Prentice-Hall, 1964. Indicates how art experiences encourage the development of the entire process of learning.

Dale, Edgar, "Education for Creativity." *The News Letter,* **30** (December 1964), 1–4. Presents a persuasive case for emphasizing the creative aspects of learning.

Dean, Joan, *Arts and Crafts in the Elementary School.* New York: Philosophical Library, 1964. Discusses a wide range of activities including bookcraft, weaving, woodwork, and puppetry.

Dunfee, Maxine, and Helen Sagl, *Social Studies through Problem Solving.* New York: Holt, Rinehart and Winston, 1966. Chap. 9. Discusses contributions of creative activities to social sudites and gives illustrations from dramatics, music, literature, art, and crafts.

Durland, Frances Caldwell, *Creative Dramatics for Children.* Yellow Springs, Ohio: Antioch Press, 1952. Describes values of creative dramatics and tells how a sampling of scripts was created and presented.

Erdt, Margaret Hamilton, *Teaching Art in the Elementary School* (Rev. ed.). New York: Holt, Rinehart and Winston, 1962. Includes suggestions of the role of art in the social studies program, including the making of murals, dioramas, and "movies."

Fortess, Lillian F., "A Suggested Guide to the Use of Paintings as Resources in the Social Studies for the Middle Grades." Ph.D. dissertation, New York

University. Ann Arbor, Mich.: University Microfilms, 1960. A useful guide to paintings to illustrate and enrich social studies content.

Gaitskell, Charles D., *Children and Their Art*. New York: Harcourt, 1958. Has concrete suggestions in chapters on art in the academic program, displaying art, and group activities.

Gilbert, Harold G., *Children Study American Industry*. Dubuque, Iowa: Brown, 1966. Contains resource units on industries and industrial processes.

Lewis, Hilda P., *Art Education in the Elementary School*. Pamphlet. Washington, D.C.: National Education Association. Summarizes research on children's development in drawing and in art appreciation.

Lowenfeld, Viktor, and W. Lambert Brittain, *Creative and Mental Growth* (4th ed.). New York: Crowell-Collier and Macmillan, 1964. A good statement on the meaning of art education, practices which inhibit it, and its relation to growth at successive stages of development.

Mattil, Edward L., *Meaning in Crafts*. Englewood Cliffs, N.J.: Prentice-Hall, 1959. Presents step-by-step procedures for more than a hundred projects which are approached as opportunities for the creative development of children.

Moore, Frank C., *et al.*, *Handcrafts for Elementary Schools* (Rev. ed.). Boston: Heath, 1963. A how-to-do-it book with suggestions concerning grade placement and relation of crafts to academic subjects.

Neill, A. S., *Summerhill: A Radical Approach to Child Rearing*. New York: Hart, 1960. Describes techniques and outcomes of a school in which pupil freedom and creativity predominate.

Schneider, Dawn E., *Correlated Art*. Scranton, Pa.: International Textbook, 1951. Describes numerous art projects classified by categories of social studies content.

Shaftel, Fannie R., and George Shaftel, *Role-Playing for Social Values: Decision-Making in the Social Studies*. Englewood Cliffs, N.J.: Prentice-Hall, 1967. Describes how social values may be taught in social studies through analyzing concrete situations in which civic values conflict with personal interest. Contains suggestions for directing dramatic play and role-playing in the classroom.

Taylor, Calvin W. (Ed.), *Creativity: Progress and Potential*. New York: McGraw-Hill, 1964. Reports a symposium on creativity, revealing the diverse meanings it has for different experts on creativity. It provides a helpful guide to the literature on the subject.

Torrance, E. Paul, *Creativity*. Pamphlet. Washington, D.C.: National Education Association, 1963. Summarizes research on the measurement of creative thinking and on ways of promoting creative behavior and learning in the classroom.

Ward, Winifred, *Playmaking with Children* (2d ed.). New York: Appleton 1957. Helpful for suggestions on techniques.

USING AUDIO-VISUAL
MEDIA AND MATERIALS

*There is no subject that does
not require its apparatus.*
CHARLES W. ELIOT

In the previous edition of this book, the chapter on this subject was entitled, "Using Audio-Visual Aids." The substitution of "media and materials" for "aids" in its present title was not an act of caprice. It marks a significant change. It indicates rapid developments in audio-visual means of instruction. What is now wrong with the term "aids"? Teachers still use films as "aids," and properly so; but today, one can also obtain films (often of televised lessons or even full courses) and programmed materials that are so complete, systematic, and self-sufficient that it is the teacher who becomes the "aid"![1]

The term "audio-visual," if literally interpreted, would cover the entire gamut of educational experiences from raw, direct, firsthand contact with the world of people and their affairs to secondhand contact through books, television, and other media of vicarious experience. "Audio" refers to hearing and "visual" to seeing. One would be hard put to list classroom learning experiences for normal children in which either "audio" or "visual" was *not* involved. The traditional school practice to exclude printed materials from the audio-visual category seems unduly arbitrary in the light of programmed materials and instruments which are designed to include reading, on the one hand, and, on the other, the increasing use of pictures, charts, and other graphic representations in books. Perhaps the term audio-visual will disappear entirely, because it applies to the bulk of learning media. Nevertheless, the term audio-visual, as conceived in this chapter, will be quite restricted, for no attempt will be made to deal with textbooks,

---

[1] This is true of some of the films listed in the boxes, "Suggested Teaching Materials," in previous chapters.

reference books, globes, maps, models, and other media which are fully discussed in earlier chapters and in the Appendix.

MEDIA OF DIRECT EXPERIENCE

We shall begin by considering some audio-visual experiences that involve direct contact with "the real thing." Such experiences deserve to be ranked high among classroom activities. We do well when we respond to the warning of Dale that ". . . our mass media with their second-hand experiences . . ." may be ". . . cutting us off from richer acquaintance with lively, firsthand experiences."[2]

Field Trips

Field trips serve many purposes, as was shown in the examples cited and the suggestions made in earlier chapters. Mention was made of primary-grades classes taken into the neighborhood to prepare a map, to survey community institutions, to look behind the scenes of a store, to see the operations of the community's government, and to learn the cardinal directions; and of older children who were taken to see a local example of assembly-line production, to collect historical data from studying early buildings, and to observe stream action in a study of water conservation. The impressions gained through such trips help to clinch learning, and the trips normally motivate the class to dig further into the subject on their return to school.

Before making a field trip, the teacher should become generally acquainted with the proposed point of destination and make sure the trip will have educational value. The teacher should discuss with the guide the procedure for the visit and make preliminary arrangements. He should request the guide to tell the children in advance what they will see and to give them an opportunity to ask questions after the trip. If the guide knows the children's level of maturity, he may be able to key his talk to it. The teacher should also make general suggestions on what to emphasize on the tour and what to omit for the sake of brevity and clarity. He should also help the class compose a list of items of information it hopes to glean from the trip. If the list is long, subgroups may be designated to spot specific items during the tour. An understanding with the members of the class should be reached beforehand on practical details, such as time schedule, transportation, and conduct, in order to minimize confusion and discipline problems.

Whether the trip is of value to the children, or only fills their heads with

[2] Edgar Dale, "Coming to Our Senses," *The News Letter*, **31** (February 1966), 1–4.

misconceptions, depends upon how effectively the guide communicates with them. There is usually an element of chance on the first trip, but a good teacher can partly compensate for a poor leader if he is quick to note the essentials of a process and can supplement the guide's words with clarifying explanations. The children themselves often help each other by commenting and explaining what they see.

Taking a trip may be like a day off for the pupils, but it is a strenuous undertaking for the teacher. Unexpected things are apt to happen, as the writer well knows from such trips in his early teaching years. There was the boy who, on a class trip to a fish market, buried his shoes in the sand on a nearby beach and then couldn't find them. He had to go home in his stocking feet! Another time, the subway car doors closed with all the class safely in the car except one child who somehow failed to get on and was left behind on the platform! Much about field trips can be learned only through experience.

Brief discussions of the trip should be held within two or three days after it has taken place. During these early discussions, the children will usually give their immediate reactions, some of which will relate to the purposes of the trip, some not. A little later, a more formal review may be conducted, keeping strictly to the purpose of the trip, in which a summary is made by the class of the data they set out to obtain and succeeded in obtaining.

Examples of trips are scattered throughout this book in connection with other topics. One more example will be given below which deals in detail with successful procedures and values.

A Trip to a Textile Factory

I brought a few cotton bolls into the classroom. Soon several youngsters attracted by the downy softness of the bolls began to investigate them. They touched the bolls and accidentally felt the little hard knobs—seeds. Then questions came thick and fast. What are those hard things? How can thread be made from this fluffy thing? Is this made into cloth? This was just the proper motivation for a field trip.

We planned a trip to a textile factory which was located in our neighborhood. Preliminary preparations were made. The children discussed the purpose of the trip; collected information about cotton from available sources prior to the trip; and formulated the questions they were to ask at the plant. They also outlined the rules for proper and courteous conduct while on the trip. Arrangements were made with the personnel of the factory and the specific aims of the trip were mutually agreed upon.

At the factory, under the direction of the guide, the children saw the large bales of raw cotton and followed the process until they saw the finished product. They were fascinated by the carding, roving, spinning, and weaving processes. Many of the questions were answered during the tour, others remained to be answered during the discussion which would follow after they returned to school. Upon leaving, the pupils expressed their gratitude for the services rendered and returned to school with such souvenirs as samples of cotton thread, cotton, cloth, and literature. . . .

From this lesson, the children had learned that their community was an important unit in their state and in their country. They learned that raw cotton came from the South and some from Egypt and Asia. Our factory and other factories ship their products to clothing manufacturers, department stores, chain stores, auto builders, and manufacturers of furniture. Some of it is stored in the large warehouses and through the Exchange Markets finds its way to European, Asian, and other foreign countries. The children made maps showing where cotton is grown, showing important cotton markets and where most of the textile factories were located.[3]

When it is impractical for an entire class to take a trip, it may be possible for individual children to go. Sometimes, when the teacher cannot go, parents of pupils are willing to escort their children individually to the point of interest outside school hours. Or, the teacher may arrange to take a small group from the class on a Saturday. If the object to be studied is in the immediate neighborhood, children may be assigned to make the necessary observations independently on their way home. In each of these cases, those children involved can later report their findings to the class.

Museum Trips

Museums contain artifacts and other objects that often justify a class trip. Teachers should explore the resources of museums within a 50 mile radius of their schools. To give a very spare sampling of museum possibilities, the following are cited:

1. Museum of Man, San Diego, Calif., contains anthropological material useful in social studies units. It has excellent objects, for example, on the North American Indian.

2. Children's Museum, Fort Worth, Tex., has outstanding material on pioneer life.

3. National Museum, Gettysburg, Pa., contains rifles, saddle covers, and other objects used in the Civil War. It also contains an electric map which, while not an "object" in the same sense, explains the military significance of the Battle of Gettysburg. Major moves of the opposing armies are reproduced and explained in a manner that children can understand.

---

[3] The author is grateful to Sister M. Euphrosine, Bernadine Sisters, O.S.F., for this record.

4. Civic Center Museum, Philadelphia, Pa., has a working model of Whitney's cotton gin. Incidentally, it has a policy which other museums might consider adopting: it permits many of its objects to be borrowed by teachers in the state for classroom use.

5. Atwater Kent Museum, Philadelphia, Pa., depicts Philadelphia's progress from the days of Indians to the present. Its exhibits includes toys a century old and the development of shipbuilding.

6. Mercer Museum, Doylestown, Pa., has over 30,000 items, comprising a tool display with implements and machines of the days before steam power.

7. Hagley Museum, Wilmington, Del., is devoted to the industrial history of the Brandywine Valley—the diversity of its mills and the growth of the duPont Company.

Not all "museum" objects are in museums. Some may be viewed in private homes, libraries, and public buildings. They may be objects ranging from furniture to kitchen utensils. Some are heirlooms and collections from various historical periods and various parts of the earth. In one Maryland school, a boy with the help of classmates took a cannonball preserved from the War of 1812 from his cellar to their classroom.

Actual objects representing things studied bring a touch of reality to social studies units. Children in a first-grade class who had the opportunity to handle a fireman's coat gained better understanding of the term and concept "insulation." A fourth-grade class, by seeing a spinning wheel operate, understands how animals or vegetable hairs can be twisted to make thread, and the time-consuming nature of the task before the era of machine spinning.

Consultants

It may be questioned whether contact with a consultant (an expert in some field who is brought into the classroom) should be classified under "Media of Direct Experience." The author views contact with an expert who can be questioned, argued with, and pinned down as a more direct kind of experience than seeing a film, for example—no matter how authentic the film may be. The granddaughter of the pioneer oil driller, cited in Chapter 7 as consultant, brought the pupils closer to an earlier period than could a film or a book. Some of the more helpful resource people are active in an enterprise which the class is studying—advertising, the paper industry, bridge construction, or the like—and bring to the class documents, models, pieces of equipment, materials, or pictures (see Figure 12.1).

Consultants are probably most commonly invited to participate in studies of the community. Almost every community harbors one or more elderly inhabitants who are steeped in local lore. They are often glad to share their knowledge with children, some even regarding it as a privilege and feeling neglected if not called upon each year! Sometimes, the consultants are parents or relatives of pupils. One teacher enlisted the cooperation of parents, grandparents, and great-grandparents, all in the same community unit.

Figure 12.1. A specialist visits a classroom.

The consultant may be invited to the classroom or asked to receive the class at his house. Sometimes he proves a first-rate guide on a walk to significant points of interest in the community. One class was interviewing a neighbor—an old-timer in the community. They stood beside a busy thoroughfare listening to the roar of the traffic. "This was an old Indian trail known as the Allegheny Trail," said the man. His words so impressed the class that, during the ensuing weeks, the children interviewed other residents and also searched the library for more information about the history and development of their community's roads and transportation.[4]

Teachers often ask, "How can I learn enough about the unit I am teaching to give it an authoritative touch?" When a teacher feels this way, he should certainly seek out a consultant. Every school can keep a central catalog or file of experts in the community who are willing to be called upon occasionally, and of local points of interest and local establishments to which worthwhile trips may be made. Some principals send printed forms to the adult residents, explaining that the school is endeavoring to discover individuals who would be willing to give their services as consultants. If

[4] The author is grateful to Sara N. Dalton for her report of this incident.

the recipient wishes, he fills out the form, indicating the area in which he is knowledgeable and stating the approximate grade level at which he would prefer to contribute. It is a good idea for a school to designate someone—the school librarian or an interested teacher or parent—to serve as curator of the catalogue and to see that it is kept up to date.

PROJECTED MATERIALS

Films and Filmstrips

Though a film does not provide direct contact with a person, place, or event, it must be ranked high among audio-visual media for its ability to convey the detail and flavor normally reserved for the eyewitness. In fact, the better travelogues come close to competing with an actual field trip in transmitting a feeling of having "been there." Just as not all field trips are of equal educational value, neither are all films. Even a well-made film may not be suitable for a particular grade or the stage of intellectual sophistication of a given class. A teacher should certainly attempt to review every film before using it.

Some of the traditional categories of audio-visual media (such as film, television, and film strip) are disappearing. Lumsdaine points out that it matters little from an instructional standpoint where a class views a film, a television broadcast, or its recording, as far as the inherent properties of the two media are concerned; that a film may be relatively static, and a filmstrip paced even to the point of giving the appearance of motion; and that, although films, or filmstrips are traditionally regarded as media for projection to an entire class, they are now being used in connection with machine teaching for projection to individual pupils.[5]

An intriguing development is that of the single-concept 8mm film.[6] The typical 16mm instructional film runs from 20 to 30 minutes or more, and it tends to introduce many concepts at a rapid clip. The single-concept film, on the other hand, runs for less than five minutes and is designed to tie in with a specific lesson. Even the mechanical characteristic of the film recommends it: it is enclosed in a cartridge which fits into a projector without threading! Few social-studies concept films are presently available, but those on the market show their promise. Among those available are the South Asia Series single-concept films prepared by International Communications Foundation, Monterey Park, Calif. One of them, entitled "Concepts of India," runs for two minutes, presenting a series of scenes which come to

[5] A. A. Lumsdaine, "Instruments and Media of Instruction," in N. L. Gage (Ed.), Handbook of Research on Teaching. Skokie, Ill.: Rand McNally, 1963. Chap. 12. P. 588–589.

[6] Leonard W. Ingraham, "Innovation in the Social Studies: The 8mm Single Concept Film," Social Education, 30 (February 1966), 91–92.

mind when one thinks of India—snake charmers, the Taj Mahal, and the like. Another is entitled "Transportation in Developing Nations—India." In four minutes, it shows 19 different types of transportation currently used in India.

Materials for Opaque and Overhead Projection

The teacher frequently wishes to show the entire class simultaneously a map, diagram, or other part of a publication. It may contain information or ideas which he would like the class as a whole to examine and ponder. If only one copy of the publication is available, the teacher can provide for its group presentation by means of an opaque projector. The machine's versatility with regard to the type of material which it can project makes it a valuable teaching device.

The teacher may obtain 3¼ × 4-inches transparencies of maps, word lists, and so on, for throwing on a large screen in a normally lighted classroom with an *overhead* projector. Or, he may make his own transparencies on etched glass slides on which he draws or traces charts, graphs, maps, or other material. The teacher operates the projector from the front of the classroom, facing the class, while conducting a discussion of the subject, and is able, with a pencil, to call attention to various features of the projection by pointing with a pencil to the corresponding feature on the transparency.

Recordings

The possibilities of dramatic, vivid presentation of social studies content through sound give special significance to available transcriptions. Among subjects which have been dramatized through recordings are the California Gold Rush, the Louisiana Purchase, the F.B.I., and Thomas Alva Edison, all prepared by Enrichment Teaching Materials, N. Y., and based on volumes in the Landmark Books series published by Random House, N. Y. Some state departments of education have tape recordings for various social studies topics. The interested teacher may also consult the *Audio Cardalog* (3-by-5-inch cards) prepared monthly by Max V. Bildersee, Box 989, Larchmont, N. Y.; and the *National Tape Recording Catalog* issued by the Department of Audiovisual Instruction, National Education Association and National Association of Educational Broadcasters, Washington, D. C. Successful listening to recordings requires that children know *how* to listen. This cannot be assumed. Teachers may need to give attention to training children's listening habits so that they will learn to recognize main ideas, use contextual clues, and employ other analytical procedures.[7]

[7] Annabel E. Fawcett, "Training in Listening," *Elementary English*, 43 (May 1966), 473–476, 514.

PICTURES AND OTHER GRAPHIC AIDS

Pictures

Pictures on a bulletin board or wall keep before the class replicas of what they are studying—scenes, tools, work, people, or times. Pictures of contrasting ways of life are helpful to the child in making comparisons and showing relationships. In one classroom, for example, a series of pictures compared the slow, backbreaking plowing operations of colonial times with today's efficient, mechanized plowing.

A rotating committee consisting of members of the class can be given the assignment to help the teacher look for pictures of particular subjects. The committee can assume responsibility for helping the teacher in the selection, arrangement, and care of the picture exhibit.

Sometimes a much-needed large picture may be hard to find. It may be a picture of a horn book, Robert Fulton, a portion of the Chinese Wall, or the Baltic entrance to the Kiel Canal. A picture index then can be consulted profitably.[8]

In addition to having literal representations, the teacher may wish to secure prints of paintings which possess a human, feeling quality which the more literal, prosaic pictures lack. Below are listed some examples of suitable works of art which have proved of interest to children. Some depict environment and atmosphere, others emphasize dress, manners, and tempers of the times or place, while still others deal with heroic or dramatic moments.[9]

> *Modern America*
> Curry's *Tornado over Kansas*
> Ford's *No More Room at the Inn*
> Hogue's *Drought-Stricken Area*
> Kent's *America*
> Lockwood's *Corner Grocery*
> March's *Transfer of Mail from Liner to Tugboat*
> Reindel's *New England Harbor*
> Warner's *Steel, Steam, and Smoke*
> Wood's *Stone City, Iowa*

---

[8] Lucile E. Vance and Esther M. Tracey, *Illustration Index* (2d ed.). New York: Scarecrow, 1966; Jessie C. Ellis, *Travel through Pictures*. Boston: Faxon, 1935; Jessie C. Ellis (Compiler), *General Index to Illustrations*. Boston: Faxon, 1931.

[9] Replicas of the works listed here will be found in Peyton Boswell, Jr., *Modern American Painting*. New York: Dodd, Mead, 1940; Oliver W. Larkin, *Art and Life in America*. New York: Holt, Rinehart and Winston, 1949 and 1960 (see both editions); Florence W. Nichols, *et al.*, *Art for Young America*. Peoria, Ill.: Manual Arts Press, 1964; "Painting" in *World Book Encyclopedia*. Chicago: Field Enterprises.

Westward Movement
  Photograph of Baker's *The Pioneer Woman* (statue in Ponca City, Okla.)
Early American Period
  Copley's *Mr. and Mrs. Isaac Winslow*
  Peale's *The Peale Family*
  Earl's *Mrs. William Moseley and Her Son Charles*
  West's *Death of General Wolf* and *Penn's Treaty with the Indians*
Renaissance
  Dürer's *The Four Preachers*
  Rembrandt's *The Night Watch*
  Brueghel's *Return of the Hunters*
  El Greco's *Toledo in a Storm*
Medieval Period
  Photographs of Saint Michel-de-Cuxa (as reconstructed at the Cloisters, New York City) and Notre Dame Cathedral, Paris
Ancient Civilization
  Photographs of Egyptian pyramids and temples, the Parthenon ruins (and as reconstructed in Nashville, Tenn.), and Myron's sculpture, *The Discus Thrower*

If a suitable large picture of a given subject cannot be located, but a small picture is found in a book, it may be projected on a screen or a white wall with an opaque projector. A large image is thus obtained and can be left projected until accompanying explanation and discussion are finished.

Teachers and librarians frequently maintain their own picture files. Such resources are timesavers and incalculable assets.

When suitable pictures are not available to clarify a relationship, the teacher should experiment freely and boldly in drawing and diagramming on the chalkboard. He need not be "talented" in the conventional sense, and need not know how to draw the proverbial straight line in order to do this. If he wishes to clarify the concepts of wholesale and retail, he could sketch on the chalkboard, more or less realistically, several buildings to represent retail stores, with arrows pointing to each from another representation of the wholesale house.

Graphs

Children can learn to construct and interpret graphs based on data which they are studying. One school conducted a campaign to reduce carelessness of personal possessions. The principal appointed a class to collect data on all articles which had been handed in to the lost-and-found department during one week. Its members constructed a circle graph to summarize their findings (see Figure 12.2). Teachers of primary-grade children reported that the graph was understood by their pupils, and aroused interest and intelligent comment. Another circle graph, used by a class in its study of Brazil, is shown in Figure 12.3.

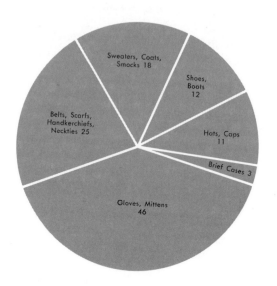

Figure 12.2. A circle graph used by primary-grade children to keep a record of articles turned in to the lost-and-found room in one week.

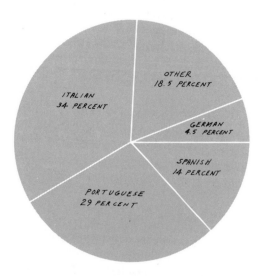

Figure 12.3. A circle graph showing nationality of immigrants to Brazil in recent years.

Bar graphs can also be read and even constructed with understanding by many primary-grade pupils, such as one showing the amount of rainfall in various parts of the nation. Older children can draw bar graphs to show the percentage of voting turnout in recent elections in selected democracies, the ratio of number of people to number of automobiles in advanced and underdeveloped nations, and similar relationships.

A line graph is a more difficult form, but should be used frequently in the intermediate grades. The one appearing in Figure 12.4 shows what numbers underlie the commonly used term "population explosion." Other line graphs of pertinence to elementary-school subject matter show major trends of the times as illustrated by the movement of women into outside-the-home employment over the past 50 years and the rise in real wages since 1900.

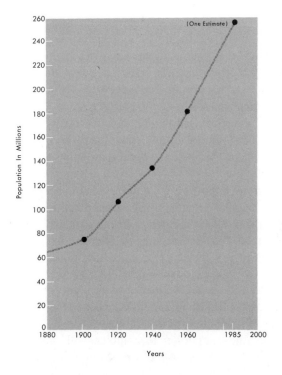

Figure 12.4. A line graph explaining the term "population explosion."

Children should be encouraged to bring in graphs from current periodicals which are pertinent to their studies. Difficult ones could be analyzed and interpreted as a class exercise. The teacher must usually take the initiative in locating tables and other statistical reports when pupils are expected to construct their own graphs. Children gain valuable experience when turned loose among almanacs, publications of the government such as the *Statistical Abstract of the United States* (U.S. Bureau of the Census), and other works which contain pertinent data for the construction of a graph.

In graph construction, pupils are faced with the necessity of making several decisions. If the time element is involved, how far back shall we go? What time intervals should be used? Can such decisions be made by children? They can, and it is the thinking they carry on during the process that is the most valuable exercise in graph-making. If their sole contact is with ready-made graphs, graphs take on a needlessly dry and forbidding appearance. After children help in constructing them, even prosaic ones will be approached with interest and understanding.

Time Lines

The place of time lines in the study of history is treated in Chapter 6, which also contains illustrations of various types of time lines (Figures 6.1, 6.2, 6.3, and 6.4). The reader is urged to review these relevant pages in connection with reading of this section which will deal largely with the construction of time lines.

A time line is a device used to give concrete quality to that abstraction, time. A line, divided into time units, is drawn on a long strip of paper. Pictures are drawn or mounted at appropriate points just above the line to represent episodes associated with the respective points.

Time lines are as important in teaching about the past as maps are in teaching about regions and cultures. They are precision instruments. Therefore, the teacher should be prepared to help his pupils in constructing them. An inaccurate time line distorts time relationships and is worthless. The following directions are offered for constructing time lines.

DEVELOP A SINGLE THEME FOR EACH TIME LINE   As a rule, it is wise at the elementary school level to depict the chronology of one subject at a time. For example, "Transportation through the Ages" is sufficient for one time line. Avoid the temptation to combine with it some other subject, such as "Shelter through the Ages" or "Architecture through the Ages." Although we want children to associate customs, events, and technologies that existed together at successive periods, the introductory time line has a different purpose to serve—to clarify the chronological relationships of a single theme. Once these relationships are learned, more complex time lines can be introduced. Bear in mind, however, that the child has difficulty with chronology.

ADOPT A SCALE APPROPRIATE TO THE PURPOSE OF THE TIME LINE   An inexperienced teacher may draw a line to a ridiculously large scale that will not fit on the walls of the classroom, but the more usual error is to make the scale too small. To be a visual display which can be read from any point in the classroom, every time line should be 15 or 20 feet long. The time lines shown in Chapter 6 were scaled small to fit the dimensions of the book (hence the scale is appropriate to the purpose), and are not intended to suggest a desirable scale for classroom time lines. Those covering vast periods of time may appropriately extend unbroken along an entire wall of a classroom, even continuing around corners, or along an unbroken hallway wall. There would be many feet of blank paper if Figure 6.3 were to be so enlarged, but these open spaces would aid in building a concept of the magnitude of time and would not be wasted. It would be a mistake to cut out these long intervals through telescoping.

USE STURDY MATERIAL   A good time line represents many hours of work. It should be made to last for years. If you use paper, make sure it is sturdy, or mount it with glue on muslin. Be sure the strip of material is continuous. The eye should be able to travel in an unbroken sweep from right to left (or from top to bottom), from the beginning to the end of the line.

SCALE THE TIME LINE ACCURATELY WITH A RULER   If one inch is chosen to represent one hour (or one week or one century), it should represent that unit of time consistently.

BRING THE TIME LINE UP TO DATE OR EVEN TAKE IT INTO THE FUTURE   A teacher who is studying the medieval period might think it necessary to show only the time between A.D. 400 and 1400. This would be a mistake. The child needs to see that period as it relates to the present, with some recent personalities and events shown in addition to ancient ones. He should be able to find his own birth date on the line. This helps tie the past in a meaningful way to the present.

KEEP THE TIME LINE SIMPLE   Keep the amount of writing or printing to a frugal minimum. Make the illustrations clear-cut and obvious. A good time line does not convey a great deal of information, but simply and unpretentiously carries the idea of development. It should lend itself to interpretation by a child at a glance and not require "figuring out."

MAKE THE TIME LINE ATTRACTIVE   Attractiveness adds to effectiveness. Each time line should be well arranged, colorful, simple, and clear. A little thought, imagination, and care in execution are the requisites.

One successful attempt to clarify and broaden time concepts is described by a teacher as follows:

> To clarify the meaning of dates and time relationships, I started a class of sixth-graders working on personal time lines of their own lives. We set up a skeleton scale on the blackboard, starting with the present and blocking out each year with its twelve months. These were copied by the children, and then filled in with birthdays, schools attended, summer vacations, trips, and any other events which were important to them. Most of the children used pictures to represent the various events. One boy drew a birthday cake, increasing the number of candles for each succeeding year. Many interesting reactions came from the discussion of these charts. The most common comment concerned the percentage of time spent in school. One child had thought that the year was divided in two equal parts—half for school and half for summer vacation; he thought the summer just went faster because he was having a good time. These charts were valuable to me as a graphic expression of the children's experiences and backgrounds.
>
> The next step was to change our scale from one year to five years, and make family time lines. These went back to the birth of the parents (in some cases, to the grandparents) and included important family events. On these time lines the child's own life became much more insignificant in the total picture, and a clearer concept of twenty or thirty years ago was developed.
>
> Then came the question of dates, what they meant, and what would happen if we kept on going back in time. So we set up still another scale on the blackboard, of 100-year intervals, and marked the time back till we came to 0. One child knew that this point represented approximately the birth of Christ, and that it was from this point that we count our years. We discussed the meaning of B.C. and A.D. A discussion of centuries followed. Most of the children thought that we lived in the nineteenth century. It was easy to correct this misconception on our B.C.–A.D. chart.
>
> The children became so interested in this graphic representation of time relationships that we made a long paper chart, and as we studied history they marked important events with pictures pinned on in their proper places. They started with dates with which they were already familiar, such as 1492 and 1620, and these became more meaningful seen in relation to a whole time picture. This was one of the most interesting and valuable projects of the year.[10]

Display of Graphic Materials

It is obvious that pictures, graphs, charts, and other graphic material need to be effectively displayed—on bulletin boards, magnetic boards, flannel boards, the chalkboard, or even the wall. Too much has already been

---

[10] The author is grateful to Barbara E. Smith for this account.

written and taught about display. It has been made into a fastidious "science." Most teachers have enough common sense to make educational displays of materials, and enough native artistry to make them attractive. Beyond this, nothing need be added. Informality is desirable, and artificial effects and clever devices that lead to fussiness are to be avoided.

EDUCATIONAL TELEVISION

Each year an increasing number of school systems are setting up closed-circuit television systems or making use of open-circuit educational broadcasts. At this writing, approximately 20 percent of American school children receive part of their instruction through television.

Some of the pioneering in this field has been ambitious. Probably the best known of the experiments are the Washington County Closed Circuit Educational Television Project, Hagerstown, Md., and the Midwest Program in Airborne Television Instruction (broadcasts from the latter were beamed from an aircraft to schools in six states). Others, less well-known, are also deserving of study, such as the Wisconsin School of the Air and the Des Moines and Polk County Schools project (in cooperation with the National Program for the Use of Television in the Public Schools).

In some instances, the broadcasts constitute entire lessons or even entire courses. Othere broadcasts are supplements to the regular classroom, as in the Des Moines project where a third-grade social studies unit, for example, such as "Beginning Map Concepts," "Clothing," or "Iowa Indians," is supplemented by six to eight telecasts of 15 minutes each.

Problems Encountered

These are still experimental years for educational television, and a host of problems have slowed its progress. Some educators have resisted television in the fear that it might eventually displace the teacher. Its image has suffered as a result of the sloganeering of some of its hard-sell promoters who, with tiresome clichés, have claimed that it is a sort of pedagogical panacea. Poor teaching has found its way into the studios, as exemplified by attempts of the teacher to be self-consciously bright and entertaining, and by patronization of the pupil audience. Certain critics have felt that too much television teaching has involved static situations, like the showing of maps, books, and pictures instead of adapting itself to what the medium is peculiarly fitted for—the presentation of motion and action. Some educators have objected to the tendency of the necessarily rigid broadcast schedule to cause school programs to become correspondingly rigid—distressingly so, they contend. Not the least of television's problems has been lack of staff and equipment.

A poll of elementary school teachers and principals reveals educational television's failure to win enthusiastic acceptance from professionals. About half of the teachers and one-third of the principals polled did not believe television instruction holds much promise for improving education.[11] In fact, most of them felt that, if it results in an increase in class size, it will be detrimental to the quality of education. Lack of confidence is not confined to school personnel. Strong lay criticism has also been expressed.[12]

Some of the problems undoubtedly will be solved in time. The quality of teaching is steadily improving through more discriminating selection of and better training of television teachers. The rigidity of scheduling will disappear once videotapes (magnetic tapes which record the sound and picture of televised broadcasts) become available for storage in the school and for use at the teacher's discretion.

Effectiveness of Educational Television

Studies of the effectiveness of educational television vary in their findings, but most reveal that it shows no striking superiority over traditional instruction. Brown reports: "The overwhelming majority (almost 90 percent) of gross comparisons between television and conventional communication conditions shows no substantial difference in achievement."[13] Defects in the research designs, however, may be one reason for the unimpressive showing. As Dale tells us, the research has been conducted almost as though television were a device in the sense that a book, a map, or a graph is a device. Television, he insists, is a *mediating* device, mediating what a classroom teacher also mediates. What we need, according to Dale, are "studies which reduce the number of variables under scrutiny. What specifically can you do with television that you can't do otherwise? And what *specific* things can you do with conventional methods that television can't do?"[14]

The Carnegie Commission on Educational Television rates educational television as disappointing in its impact on education. "With minor exceptions, the total disappearance of instructional television would leave the educational system fundamentally unchanged."[15] Yet, the Commission makes clear its position on the potential of television. "Properly used, television can bring a liveliness and an immediacy to education that no other medium can provide."[16]

---

[11] "Teaching by Television," *NEA Research Bulletin*, Research Division, National Education Association, **40** (February 1962), 7–8.

[12] Richard Franko Goldman, "The Little-Read Schoolhouse: The Videogogue and his Pedavision," *Columbia University Forum*, **5** (Winter 1961), 16–22.

[13] Roscoe C. Brown, Jr., "Evaluation of Instructional Television," in Robert M. Diamond (Ed.), *A Guide to Instructional Television.* New York: McGraw-Hill, 1964. Chap. 15, p. 163.

[14] Edgar Dale, "The Problem of Controls," *The News Letter*, **30** (May 1965), 1–4.

[15] James R. Killiam, Jr., chairman, Carnegie Commission on Educational Television, *Public Television: A Program for Action.* New York: Bantam, 1967. P. 81.

[16] Killiam. P. 83.

Television's most useful role in the schools may turn out to be in connection with programmed instruction as carried out in a computerized classroom in which a computer presents the instructional material on videotape according to the needs of the individual child.[17] Evaluation of this use of television will be awaited with interest.

PROGRAMMED INSTRUCTION

Programmed instruction is based on a "program" which is written in the form of a book or written for presentation by a teaching machine. The program contains information to be learned by the pupil. It is broken down into a series of short steps. Each step constitutes a "frame." (For an example of a frame, see Chart 12.1.) The pupil reads one frame at a time. He not only reads it; he also responds to it in one way or another, such as answering a question which it contains. The pupil is immediately informed whether or not his response is correct. This is known as "feedback." He does not proceed to a new frame until he has mastered the preceding one.

The purpose of programmed instruction is to increase the efficiency of education by providing continuous communication between the individual child and his learning materials. The "program" is, then, designed for self-instruction. It presents the subject matter in a series of small, easy steps, each of which is usually accompanied by a task for the child to perform. The child is confronted with one item of information, or one concept, at a time. He responds to the item as directed. It may call upon him to answer a multiple-choice test item by pushing a key on a machine (a minority of

---

Chart 12.1: Example of Format and Content of a Frame

You have already learned how to read a map's legend and how to find rivers on a map.

Did you know that rivers always flow *down?* They flow from high places, like mountains, to low places, like ocean shores.

You should be able to tell from a map in what direction a river is flowing.

Question:

If you want to find out in what direction one of the rivers shown on Map 6 is flowing, how can the map's legend help you?

(a) It shows how colors are used to tell about elevation.

(b) It shows how to locate waterfalls.

(c) It shows how national boundaries are marked.

Compare your answer with the correct answer on page 5.

---

[17] Patrick Suppes, "Modern Learning Theory and the Elementary School Curriculum," *American Educational Research Journal*, 1 (March 1964), 79–93.

available programs is presented by teaching machines) or by making his choice in a programmed textbook. Or, he may be directed to construct an answer.

After the child responds, he is informed of the correctness or incorrectness of his response by a light or other signal in a machine or by an answer appearing at a designated place in his programmed book. If his response is false, he is given the correct information, or information which he can advantageously utilize in making another choice. This "feedback" feature is a central element in programmed instruction: it informs the child of his progress, and it indicates his next step—whether to repeat an exercise, to respond to a similar exercise, or to go on to the next step. In any case, whatever he is directed to do next is designed to reinforce his learning— to increase his chances of responding correctly to the question or task the next time he encounters it. It is evident that the program performs two functions which a busy teacher handling an entire class cannot accomplish: (1) It presents the subject matter to each child at a rate appropriate to his needs, and (2) each child responds overtly to each presentation and receives, without delay, reinforcement for every response he makes. Thus, in programmed instruction, "taking care of individual differences," long a shibboleth, becomes a reality.

Programmed Materials for Social Studies

Fewer than ten percent of available programs are designed for social studies.[18] Some educators are skeptical about the possibilities of programmed instruction. They maintain it has only limited application and is incapable of teaching many of the things which in social studies are so important.[19] Among the matters which elude programming, they contend, are the teaching of creativity; the teaching of insight into values; the teaching how to use and evaluate various types of resources; teaching a child how to relate to others while learning; teaching which provides experience in

[18] Among those prepared for use in the elementary school are: *Map Reading* (Primary), Hughes Aircraft, Fullerton, Calif.; *The Earth in Space* (Grade 4). New York: Crowell-Collier and Macmillan; *Westward Expansion* (Grades 4–6). Chicago: Coronet Instructional Films; *Social Studies Vocabulary Development Cycles* (Grades 4–12). Chicago: Field Enterprises; *The Big City* (Grade 4 and up). Boston: Ginn; *Geography of the United States* (elementary and high school). Palo Alto, Calif.: Behavioral Research Laboratories. For indexes of programs, see the various editions of *Programmed Learning: A Bibliography of Programs and Presentation Devices* by Carl H. Hendershot, Bay City, Mich.; and of *Programmed Instruction Materials* by Center for Programmed Instruction of the Institute of Educational Technology. New York: Teachers College.

[19] Herbert A. Thelen, "Programmed Materials Today: Critique and Proposal," *Elementary School Journal*, **63** (January 1963), 189–196; Elizabeth S. Maccia, "Epistemological Considerations in Relation to the Use of Teaching Machines," *Educational Theory*, **12** (October 1962), 234–240, 246; David C. Epperson and Richard A. Schmuck, "An Experimentalist Critique of Programmed Instruction," *Educational Theory*, **12** (October 1962), 247–254.

forming hypotheses, inquiring, summarizing an argument, and the like; teaching that leads to recognition of knowledge as an open system which can be extended; teaching respect for human nature; and teaching the necessity of questioning authority—including the assumptions and conclusions of a programmer!

Doubts have also been raised regarding the adequacy of the motivating devices of programming. How adequate is feedback of knowledge of success for motivation, and the one-easy-step-at-a-time procedure? McKeachie points out ". . . that for students with basic motivation for success, motivation is highest when chances of success are moderate."[20] He expresses the view that learning should be paced ". . . so that each step offers some newness and a moderate risk of failure. One of the first steps may be to stimulate doubt about what has previously been taken for granted."[21] This is an objective which programs have not as yet sought to attain.

It would be foolish to reject programmed instruction in social studies teaching just because it has limited application. One cannot ignore the fact that children can learn from programmed materials, often more efficiently than from conventional classroom instruction,[22] and that the continuous verification it provides, plus its adaptability to the pace of the individual child, appear to contribute to the self-confidence of many children. How well it can best serve social studies, however, still has to be discovered.

The role of programmed instruction in connection with other media discussed in this chapter will undoubtedly expand. Suppes described such a coordination in individual booths in a computer-based laboratory.[23] Each booth contains a microfilm unit which presents programmed material (to which the child responds with a light probe on the face of the display), an auditory unit, and a closed-circuit television setup. The equipment is under computer control to permit presentation of the instructional material according to the needs of the individual learner.

Apart from its intrinsic merits and prospects in social studies, the concepts of programming have had an impact on textbook writing and teaching practices. Today, textbooks and teaching reflect greater attention than before the advent of programming to systematic introduction of facts and skills, and more frequent interspersion of questions, exercises, and tests to provide added opportunities for reinforcement of learning.

[20] Wilbert McKeachie, "Needed Research on Psychological Factors in Learning as Related to the Social Studies," in Roy A. Price (Ed.), Needed Research in the Teaching of the Social Studies. Washington, D.C.: National Council for the Social Studies, 1964. Pp. 79–89.

[21] McKeachie. P. 83.

[22] Delbert Barcus and Jack Pottle, "Programming the Constitution," Social Education, 29 (January 1965), 29–31; Jerry Ray Moore, "An Experiment in Programmed Instruction: Voting in Iowa, Ninth Grade Civics," Dissertation Abstracts, 25 (March 1965), 5156–5157; Lawrence M. Stolurow, Teaching by Machine. Washington, D.C.: Superintendent of Documents, 1961. Chap. 7.

[23] Patrick Suppes. P. 89.

Sources of Information about Teaching Materials

General
Education Media Index (a 14-volume index of films, maps, tapes, models, and other "nonbook" audio-visual aids). New York: McGraw-Hill, 1964.

General: Free Materials
Educators Guide to Free Social Studies Materials (6th ed.). Randolph, Wis.: Educators Progress Service, 1966.
Educators Index of Free Materials. Randolph, Wis.: Educators Progress Service. Revised annually.
Information Free. New York: Berkley, 1961.

Films and Filmstrips
American Film Review, Vol. 5. St. Davids, Pa.: American Educational and Historic Film Center, Eastern Baptist College. Prepared annually.
Critical Index of Films and Filmstrips in Conservation. New York: Audio-Visual Center of Conservation Foundation, 1965. (See also under "General" above.)

Pictures
Illustration Index (2d ed.). New York: Scarecrow, 1966. (See also Footnotes 8 and 9 in this chapter.)

Recordings
(See under "General" above.)

Programmed Materials
Programmed Learning: A Bibliography of Programs and Presentation Devices. Bay City, Mich.: Carl H. Hendershot, 1964.
Programmed Instruction Materials. New York: Center for Programmed Instruction of the Institute of Educational Technology, Teachers College, revised annually.

FOR REVIEW AND REFLECTION

1. Summarize each of the major categories of media and materials dealt with in this chapter, and state the advantages and limitations of each.
2. What criteria should govern the selection of films?
3. What procedures are required for insuring accuracy of time lines?
4. Analyze educational television's failure to have greater impact on school learning.
5. What social studies learnings would appear to lend themselves most readily to programmed instruction?

ASSIGNMENTS

1. With a specific unit topic in mind, make a collection of pictures you could present to give your class an overview of the unit during the orientation period.
2. With a specific unit topic in mind, construct a graph, a series of half a dozen etched glass slides, or a time line that would effectively present a significant concept.
3. Review a film designed for elementary school social studies. Evaluate it and explain how you would use it with a class.
4. Compare a programmed textbook with a conventional textbook covering the same content with a view to discovering what learnings each presents more effectively.

SUPPLEMENTARY READING

Brown, James W., *et al., A-V Instruction: Materials and Methods* (2d ed.). New York: McGraw-Hill, 1964. A comprehensive textbook describing ready-made materials and the creation of materials.

Brown, James W., and Richard B. Lewis, *A-V Instructional Materials Manual* (2d ed.). New York: McGraw-Hill, 1964. A how-to-do-it manual on all types of materials, experiences, and methods, ranging from chalkboard techniques to making motion pictures, from taking field trips to using flannel boards.

Bye, Edgar C., *How to Conduct a Field Trip.* Washington, D.C.: National Council for the Social Studies, 1952. A useful guide for extracting the most from a trip.

Dale, Edgar, *Audio-Visual Methods in Teaching* (Rev. ed.). New York: Holt, 1962. A basic text, expounding theory, describing materials, and explaining classroom applications.

Dale, Edgar, "Coming to Our Senses," *The News Letter,* **31** (February 1966), 1–4. Warns of overreliance upon mass media in education.

De Bernardis, Amo, *The Use of Instructional Materials.* New York: Appleton, 1960. Describes a wide variety of teaching materials and suggests ways they can be used in the classroom.

De Cecco, John P. (Ed.), *Educational Technology.* New York: Holt, Rinehart and Winston, 1964. A book of readings. Brings together research reports and theoretical discussions on programmed instruction by educators and psychologists.

Diamond, Robert M. (Ed.), *A Guide to Instructional Television.* New York: McGraw-Hill, 1964. Gives illustrations of how television has been used in various situations and for various purposes. Contains an important chapter by Roscoe C. Brown, Jr., on evaluation.

Joint Committee on Cooperation with Business and Industry of the National Council for the Social Studies, *Sponsored Resources for the Social Studies.* Washington, D.C.: National Council for the Social Studies, n.d. Deals with materials and services provided by business and industry to schools, and contains a statement of philosophy, an evaluation sheet for judging printed materials, and so forth.

Lumsdaine, A. A., "Instruments and Media of Instruction," in N. L. Gage (Ed.), *Handbook of Research on Teaching*. Skokie, Ill.: Rand McNally, 1963. Chap. 12. A penetrating review of research methodology and findings in the field of audio-visual media.

Schramm, Wilbur (Ed.), *The Science of Human Communication*. New York: Basic Books, 1963. Eleven distinguished communications specialists summarize their research on mass communication.

Stolurow, Lawrence M., *Teaching by Machine*. Cooperative Research Monograph No. 6, U.S. Office of Education. Washington, D.C.: Superintendent of Documents, 1961. A comprehensive review of the status and potentialities of the teaching machine and other devices for programmed instruction.

Suppes, Patrick, "Modern Learning Theory and the Elementary-School Curriculum," *American Educational Research Journal*, 1 (March 1964), 79–93. Part of article contains an account of computer technology and the possibilities it opens up for application of learning theory to the elementary-school curriculum.

Taylor, Calvin W., and Frank E. Williams (Eds.), *Instructional Media and Creativity*. Proceedings of Sixth Utah Creativity Research Conference. New York: Wiley, 1966. Reports the lively discussion between students of creativity and instructional media experts on how new media can be designed and how existing media may be used to promote creative thinking.

Thelen, Herbert A., "Programmed Materials Today: Critique and Proposal," *Elementary School Journal*, **63** (January 1963), 189–196. Raises thoughtful, critical questions about the concept of programmed materials as self-contained.

13

EVALUATING PUPIL ACHIEVEMENT

*He that judges without informing himself
to the utmost that he is capable, cannot
acquit himself of judging amiss.*

JOHN LOCKE

Achievement in social studies, as in other areas, should be evaluated in terms of the teaching objectives. Since the objectives of social studies are comprehensive, the teacher's appraisal of progress must also be comprehensive. The four categories of objectives, as described in Chapter 1, are these:

1. Knowledge and understanding (of the cultural heritage, man's culture in varying regions of the world, and the like),
2. Attitudes toward learning (a spirit of inquiry, curiosity, and so on),
3. Social values (respect for evidence, respect for human nature, recognition of civic responsibility, and so on),
4. Skill in handling the tools of social studies (such as classifying data and interpreting maps).

It is evident that evaluation of children's progress toward such goals will require perceptive observation and a wide range of tests.

Probably the most important source of information on pupil achievement is daily observation of the child at work. Because the teacher must divide his attention among many children, discrete episodes which are significant signs of growth for a particular child are easily forgotten or are merged with other episodes into generalizations. "John is a lazy thinker," the teacher may reflect; or "He certainly makes intelligent use of the encyclopedia"; or "I wish he would learn to stick to the subject during discussion"; or "I admire the care he gives to his assignments." And yet, the teacher may not be able to recall enough detailed instances of the child's achievements to make a convincing report of his work or to make a diagnosis. For these reasons, many teachers keep individual records of children's significant behavior and the level of their conceptual development as revealed by their writing, oral reporting, map making, and other activity. These will be useful in preparing individual conferences with parents, in entering comments on report cards or cumulative record forms, and in reviewing the child's progress with the child himself.

A convenient method for keeping such records is to use a card (5x8 inches) for each child in the class, with his name entered at the top. At the end of the day, the teacher goes through the stack of cards and enters the date and his comments about any significant achievement or behavior occurring that day. It is unlikely that the teacher will have something to write for more than a quarter of the class on any one day. As the school year advances, the cards begin to fill up, and second cards for each child may be required. Needless to say, events relating to the child's entire school program, not just social studies, are recorded on these cards; it would be unduly laborious and pointless to keep a separate card for each field of subject matter.

An example of cumulative information about a second-grade child (confined here to social studies performance) on one of these cards follows:

Oct. 3   Volunteered to get information on supersonic transport. Said his father had "lots of articles and stuff" about it.

Oct. 5   Gave a good, clear report on supersonic transport, beginning with the competition between Boeing and Lockheed for the government contract. Had information on why government is interested, its cost, seating capacity, and design. Had a picture to show the class. Remarkably well organized.

Oct. 10   I had him read a page from his textbook. Missed at least one word per sentence. The book is really difficult for him. He somehow manages to get a lot of content from it anyway.

Oct. 15   I looked through his notebook today. His spelling is poor and the pages not very neat, but the work is fairly systematic and informative. It has touches of imaginative thinking about causes of the changing picture in transportation.

TESTING THE INTENDED OUTCOMES OF INSTRUCTION

The teacher may test the outcomes of instruction through informal observation, independent assignments, or formally constructed tests. In any case, his first task is to list those changes in behavior he had intended his instruction to bring about. Here, the teacher is warned against listing vague outcomes such as "improved citizenship" or "increased understanding of our economic system." He should express the outcomes in terms of pupil behavior. Thus, "improved citizenship" might be broken down into such behaviors as "willingness to give a hearing to those holding views contrary to his own"; and "increased understanding of our economic system" might be reduced to behaviors such as "ability to give an example of how the price of a product is affected by the interplay of supply and demand." Whether informal or formal testing is contemplated, teachers will be repaid by becoming familiar with the two volumes of *Taxonomy of Educational Objectives*.[1] These volumes supply a valuable classification system of objectives. Each category corresponds to a separate type of learning situation analyzed in terms of the intended behaviors of learners. The scheme will be summarized with examples of its possibilities applied to elementary school social studies.

The Cognitive Categories

The cognitive categories are arranged in a hierarchy whereby the behaviors of a given category require, for their performance, the abilities described in the preceding categories. In other words, the six classes of behavior, summarized below, were arranged by the authors of the *Taxonomy* so that they occur in an increasing order of complexity. Thus, for a child to "comprehend" (category 2), he must have the basic relevant "knowledge" (category 1). Any social studies unit studied in appropriate depth probably makes use of the various categories, and hence, observation and test items should be spread among as many of them as practicable.

Test items covering objectives in the upper categories normally require more reading facility and writing facility than children in the primary grades possess. For this reason, many teachers prefer to introduce questions relating to those advanced categories orally to the class as a whole and to give selected children the opportunity to answer them in the setting of a classroom discussion. The examples of test items following each objective should not be thought of for use exclusively in formal tests; such items are often suitable for discussion or homework assignment.

KNOWLEDGE   This category covers such social studies material as knowledge of technical terms, dates, how maps are made, trends in urban life, generalizations about Japanese culture, theories about prehistoric man, and so on. Examples of test items:

Unit: Woodland Indians. Draw three tools that the first white settlers saw the Indians using. What were they used for?

Unit: Ancient Times. Check an invention of the Greeks and make a sketch of it below.

[1] Benjamin S. Bloom (Ed.), *Taxonomy of Educational Objectives: Handbook I: Cognitive Domain.* New York: McKay, 1956; David R. Krathwohl, *et al.* (Eds.), *Taxonomy of Educational Objectives: Handbook II: Affective Domain.* New York: McKay, 1964.

_____ Gothic spire   _____ Ionic column

_____ Roman arch   _____ Renaissance dome

COMPREHENSION   Comprehension involves the literal understanding of something ranging from simple "translation" (such as summarizing or giving an example of what has been learned) to "extrapolation" (such as drawing conclusions and predicting consequences of alternative courses of action). Examples of test items:

Unit: Growth of American Industry. Your textbook states that specialization of labor and machinery has led to lower costs of the manufactured product. Name an industry in which this has happened, tell about some of the specialized jobs which the workers do, and tell about how these jobs used to be done.

Unit: Farming. There were more farmers in the United States 100 years ago than today. How can this be explained?

_____(a)   The tractor and similar power machines had not been invented.

_____(b)   There were more people to be fed.

_____(c)   Families were larger.

_____(d)   People ate more than they do today.

_____(e)   Farm work was more fun.

Unit: U.S. Geography. Tell in your own words what the textbook means by

conterminous United States _____

roughlands _____

coastal plain _____

APPLICATION   Application is the use of a principle, skill, or other learning product to illuminate a new situation or solve a new problem. Examples of test items:

Unit: Our Community. You have learned how it pays to be safe in crossing streets. The Apex factory has a sign for its workers which reads: "It pays to be safe!" What does the sign mean? What dangers are present in a factory?

Unit: Protecting Life and Property. You have learned of ways in which fires can be prevented at home. What would help to prevent forest fires?

Unit: Geography of the Eastern Hemisphere. You have learned about the part played by mountains in the life of Switzerland. In what ways would you expect the mountains of Greece might play a similar part in the life of Greece?

ANALYSIS   Analysis consists of noting how the elements which make up the material under study are organized and interrelated. It includes the separation of statements of fact from statements of value, the spotting of interrelationships and irrelevancies in a passage, the drawing of inferences concerning purposes, biases, and so on. Examples of test items:

> Unit: Our Federal Government. Read the editorial on the cost of the "moonshot" program. Underline facts with a black pencil and opinions with a red pencil.
> Unit: Communication. How can you tell a television "commercial" from a television news report?

SYNTHESIS   This describes aspects of creative behavior, including the suggesting of how a hypothesis might be tested, the execution of a set of directions, the formulation of hypotheses, the setting up of schemes of classification, etc. Example of test items:

> Unit: The Western States. Fill in an outline map of the western states so as to illustrate the relationships between altitude, latitude, and the location of major regions of citrus and cotton crops.
> Unit: Community History. We have found many reasons why people have moved from the city to the suburbs. Some of the reasons are somewhat alike. See if you can group them under three or four main reasons.

EVALUATION   Evaluation involves the conscious use of criteria in making judgments such as detecting inconsistencies between facts presented and conclusions drawn or judging something by a set of criteria. Examples of test items:

> Unit: Scandinavia. Criticize the above map by comparing it with your textbook's list of important places and regions in Scandinavia.
> Unit: American Indians. Use the encyclopedia's definition of civilization, and decide whether or not any of the following Indian groups were civilized when first seen by America's early explorers. If so, put a "C" on the blank in front of its name. Give your reasons for marking or not marking each group.

> _____ Woodland   _____ Pueblo
> _____ Plains   _____ Northwest

The Affective Categories

The affective objectives deal with interests, attitudes, values, and other aspects of emotional behavior. The *Taxonomy* expresses these, too, in terms of pupil behavior. The hierarchy has a basis necessarily different from that of the hierarchy of the cognitive objectives. The *Taxonomy* orders affective objectives from the learner's awareness of a phenomenon (category 1) to positive response (category 2) to varying degrees of internalization—that is, to the learner's incorporation of the values into his behavior (categories 3, 4, and 5). There are thus five categories, but the fifth ("characterization by a value or value complex") deals with a highly mature, consistent system of behavior not appropriate for elementary school objectives, and hence, is omitted here.

The affective behaviors are probably more validly gauged by teacher observation than by formal tests, especially in self-contained classrooms where the teacher has the benefit of observing pupil behavior throughout the school day. For this reason, examples of test items have been replaced by examples of behavior observable by the teacher. To help bring out the relationship between the categories, the same illustrative affective goals are given for each category. The goals cited are four which are frequently mentioned in this book.

RECEIVING (ATTENDING)   The learner gives his attention to something, such as the view that there are at least two sides to controversial questions; or, he may even willingly submit himself to hearing both sides of a controversy. Examples of teacher observations:

The child becomes aware of history as a separate subject.

He becomes aware of "conservation" as the name of a process, a need, and a movement.

He becomes aware of the process of comparing sources in running down information in the social studies.

He becomes aware of the interdependence of people within a community, of a city and its suburbs, and so on.

RESPONDING   The learner does not merely give his attention, he actively responds. He may be merely acquiescent, or he may respond voluntarily and with pleasure. Examples of teacher observations:

The child performs his history homework regularly and sometimes goes beyond the letter of the assignment.

He enjoys reading from conservation magazines.

He voluntarily checks the consistency of facts under discussion in social studies class.

He voluntarily explains to his classmates how the prosperity of one key industry is related to the prosperity of other key industries.

VALUING   The learner exhibits a relatively consistent attitude toward something, such as that violence is a crude and unsatisfactory way of settling disputes. Examples of teacher observations:

The child shows commitment to history as an interesting and valuable subject through his defense of it following statements by classmates that it is dull and unimportant.

He becomes incensed over the effort of commercial interests to purchase a rare wildlife sanctuary for real estate development.

He exhibits a passion for checking facts.

His reading reflects a growing interest in international relations.

ORGANIZATION   The learner starts to build a value system. Examples of teacher observations:

Historical perspective becomes almost a way of life; the child asks in connection with almost any situation: "How did it get that way? What were the beginnings?"

He feels everyone owes something to posterity that requires all to take seriously their responsibility for the conservation of natural resources. He looks up the voting record of members of the state legislature and of Congress on conservation issues, and states that this record should be studied by voters.

He systematically checks newspaper reports of major events against other sources, and weighs conflicting information deliberately.

He attempts to integrate his patriotic feelings, his self-interest, and his conviction that the interdependence of nations requires a world view.

TEST CONSTRUCTION

At frequent intervals throughout the unit the teacher should administer informal tests of his own construction to find out to what extent pupils have acquired specified understandings, attitudes, values, and skills. A test may be of either the objective or essay form, with each question or item relating in a significant way to the basic generalizations and skills which constitute the objectives of instruction. If a teacher has clearly in mind precisely what those objectives are, he will avoid cluttering his test with questions about trivial, inconsequential information. During the course of a unit, all of the cognitive areas should be generously represented. The common tendency to overweight tests with items from the "knowledge" category should be avoided.

A good test item—whether objective or essay in form—requires time and thought for its construction. Apart from the obvious requirement of clarity, the item should be of approximately median difficulty—that is, it should be one that can be handled satisfactorily by about half of the pupils.[2] One cannot be certain ahead of time, of course, how difficult a new and untried question will be, but "median difficulty" is a standard for a teacher to have in mind.

Another criterion of a good test question or item is its tendency to discriminate between pupils who obtain the better scores on the test as a whole and those who obtain the lower scores. This characteristic, too, is not one that can be predicted ahead of the actual administration of a test.

Because of the inevitable pitfalls in item writing, teachers are urged to subject their tests to item analysis following administration.[3] The purpose of item analysis is to identify items which approximate the criteria of median difficulty and discriminability. The items which meet these criteria can then be saved for future use. Item analysis of objective items can be made with considerable precision, and it often reveals how a test item can be improved. For example, it may be discovered that a certain distractor in a multiple choice item is so implausible that it really serves no purpose and should be replaced. Item analysis also reveals which items should be rejected.

Following item analysis, the teacher is in command of detailed information concerning class performance and performance of individual pupils. He is in a position to know what material should be reviewed, what concepts should be retaught, and what content has been mastered.

After a test is corrected, the results should be recorded, and the test sheets returned to the pupils for inspection and discussion.

USING STANDARDIZED TESTS

Most schools make systematic use of standardized tests—tests which have been taken by thousands of children and whose scores become the basis of "norms." A variety of standardized social studies tests are available, and many of them have been listed and usefully annotated by Peace.[4] A more complete listing, accompanied by full-length reviews, is contained in the various volumes of the Mental Measurements Yearbooks.[5]

Standardized tests are objective in type. Their norms are usually reported in terms of grade-equivalent scores (if a child earns a grade-equivalent

[2] Frederick B. Davis, *Educational Measurements and Their Interpretation*. Belmont, Calif.: Wadsworth, 1964. P. 23.

[3] Frederick B. Davis. Pp. 281–284; and Max D. Englehart, *Improving Classroom Testing*. Pamphlet. Washington, D.C.: National Education Association, 1964. Pp. 26–28.

[4] Barbara A. Peace, "Bibliography of Social Studies Tests," in Harry D. Berg (Ed.), *Evaluation in Social Studies*; Thirty-fifth Yearbook of the National Council for the Social Studies. Washington, D.C.: The Council, 1965. Pp. 230–247.

[5] The most recent volume is: Oscar K. Buros (Ed.), *The Sixth Mental Measurements Yearbook*. Highland Park, N.J.: Gryphon Press, 1965.

score of 4.2, his performance is equal to that of the average child who is in the second month of Grade 4); percentile ranks (if a child earns a percentile score of 62, his performance is better than that of 62 percent of those upon whom the test was standardized; or a test may report results both in grade-equivalent scores and in percentiles.[6]

Certain precautions should be exercised in interpreting the results of standardized tests. (1) Social studies achievement scores of poor readers should be discounted. The chances are that the test is more a test of their reading ability than of their social studies achievement. (2) Before test results are taken too seriously, the test should be studied by the teacher to see how closely it measures content which corresponds to the content of the school's curriculum. There is wide variation in social studies programs. No matter how diligently a test author may attempt to construct an instrument that will conform to the central tendencies of curriculum practice, the instrument is certain to contain numerous items of information which pupils in a particular school never had an opportunity to learn. (3) If a child's score is signally lower than that of the average of his class, investigate his case carefully before classifying him as an underachiever in need of tutoring or other special help. Underachievers in social studies are those who perform significantly better on aptitude tests (such as intelligence tests) than on social studies tests. Statistical procedures for making the comparison are technical and beyond the province of this book. One procedure described by Davis[7] provides a refined estimate of under- and over-achievement, involving computation well worth undertaking by teachers who really wish to identify the underachievers, and who will do something of a remedial nature for them once they are identified. The older and simpler method of obtaining an accomplishment quotient—by dividing achievement age (or grade) by mental age (or grade) is frequently misleading. Not only do the two sets of scores normally correlate significantly, but the errors of measurement are magnified when the measures are divided one by the other.[8]

EXAMPLES OF STANDARDIZED TEST ITEMS

STEP Social Studies Tests

The items shown in Figure 13.1 are selected from the Cooperative Sequential Tests of Educational Progress (STEP): Social Studies, Forms

[6] These are only two of a number of derived scores in use. See Davis. Pp. 36–49.
[7] Davis. Pp. 257–259.
[8] For a fuller treatment, see Robert L. Ebel, "Using the Results of Measurement," in Harry D. Berg (Ed.), *Evaluation in Social Studies*. P. 212. Ebel even sees no justification for trying to identify the underachiever. Also see E. F. Lindquist (Ed.), *Educational Measurement*. Washington, D.C.: American Council on Education, 1951. Pp. 649–650, 715–716; P. E. Vernon, *Intelligence and Attainment Tests*. New York: Philosophical Library, 1960. Pp. 118–121, 183–184.

These Pictures Tell The Story Of Bread.
They Are Not In The Right Order.

Bread On A Store Shelf

Grain Elevator

Flour Mill

Bakery

Slice Of Bread Being Buttered

Shocks Of Wheat

20 Which picture should come first?
E The grain elevator
F The flour mill
G The bakery
H The shocks of wheat

21 Which picture should come next after the grain elevator?
A The bread on a store shelf
B The flour mill
C The bakery
D The slice of bread being buttered

22 Which picture does NOT show a step in the making of bread?
E The bakery
F The flour mill
G The grain elevator
H The bread on a store shelf

23 In which of the following states would you be most likely to see wheat growing?
A Vermont   B Florida
C Kansas   D Utah

24 Which picture shows something which would have looked most nearly the same in George Washington's time as it does today?
E The bakery
F The flour mill
G The shocks of wheat
H The grain elevator

4A and 4B. These forms are for Grades 4 to 6. Forms for junior high school, senior high school, and college are also available. The tests were produced by the Cooperative Test Division, Educational Testing Service, Princeton, N. J. The items reproduced here have been reduced in size by 45 percent. The tests are designed to measure understandings and skills that a child would learn from any social studies instruction regardless of what particular topics it might include.

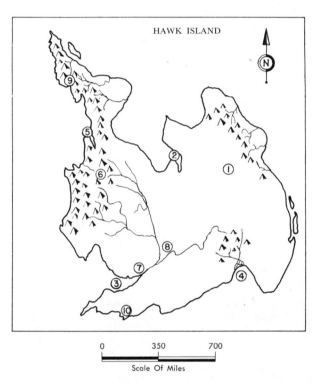

HAWK ISLAND

```
0          350          700
|_____|_____|
```

Scale Of Miles

29 About how far is it across Hawk Island from place 1 to the mouth of the river directly south of it?
 A 200 miles
 B 700 miles
 C 1400 miles
 D 2200 miles

30 Which of these places is on a peninsula?
 E 4   F 6   G 7   H 9

31 If explorers came by ship to Hawk Island, at what place would they find the safest harbor?
 A 2   B 4   C 9   D 10

Figure 13.1 (left and right). Items from a standardized test designed to measure understanding and skills. (Cooperative Sequential Tests of Educational Progress: Social Studies, Forms 4A and 4B. Reduced by 45%. Copyright 1956–1957, Cooperative Test Division, Educational Testing Service, Princeton, New Jersey.)

Primary Social Studies Test

The *Primary Social Studies Test* by Ralph C. Preston and Robert V. Duffey, designed for use in Grades 1–3, is published by Houghton Mifflin, Boston. It tests social studies content commonly taught in the primary grades. It consists of 70 items. In recognition of the uneven development of reading skills of children in the primary grades, it requires no reading by the children. The teacher reads each item aloud, and the child marks a picture in a specified group of pictures which one he thinks is the correct item (see Figure 13.2).

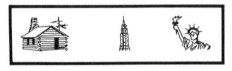

Teacher reads: "Make an X on the picture of something that was made from materials that were nearby."

Teacher reads: "Make an X on the picture of the thing that shows someone who is working for the United States government."

Teacher reads: "Make an X on the picture which shows the quickest and cheapest way to make chairs."

Figure 13.2. A sample of the *Primary Social Studies Test.* Courtesy of Houghton-Mifflin.

HELPING CHILDREN SET STANDARDS

The problem of how to help children develop a feeling for excellence exists in every classroom. The teacher may help children set standards for their work through the simple expedient of discussing standards with them. The entire class can profitably explore such questions as:

What are good ways of organizing a social studies notebook?

Why is it important not to make unnecessary disturbances during study periods and testing periods?

How can Jane's committee improve its plan for painting their mural on "Japan Today"?

How often should the bulletin board be changed and how can its appearance be improved?

How detailed should Jim make the drawing of the map of our state on the chalkboard so that it will be useful to those who have oral reports to give?

How can the lines in our play about Indians be spoken so that they sound natural?

Research studies show that when children participate in setting goals in such fashion, they tend to work more painstakingly than if standards are set for them, or are not explicitly developed. By joining the discussion and guiding it, teachers can help their pupils set standards which are realistic and challenging, that is, achievable and appropriate to their years.

Imposition of standards by the teacher may give an external appearance of being effective, yet the results may be superficial and fleeting. Forced standards may yield children's work which possesses a surface, stilted "finish" without actual pupil growth, and often, at the cost of the integrity of the pupil's expression. Standards which children help to create, which they understand and accept, and which they can meet may often seem immature, yet they represent the only sound base from which true growth can occur. The teacher's sole role is to provide the questions to be explored and guide the discussion and decisions.

REPORTING PROGRESS TO PARENTS

Parents are entitled to frank information concerning their children's schoolwork. In filling out a report card, the teacher discharges part of his obligation to the parents. Parents, however, may read more into a report card and attach greater importance to it than is justified.

One successful practice for supplementing the report card is for the teacher to invite the parents of his pupils to an evening meeting in the classroom early in the school year. A description of the units which the teacher has planned for the year offers something important to talk about. The teacher may suggest ways in which parents can help their children with the units—trips they might take, books they might read together, and clippings, pictures, and objects they could search for together.

The parents may also be told how the children's progress will be judged. The teacher may want to point out that the report card will not only tell something about the child's academic achievement, but will also reflect things not tested, such as how well he organizes and keeps a useful note-book, how well he can tell fact from opinion, how effectively he stands up before his classmates and explains concepts from a picture or graph, or how far he has broadened in his understanding of foreign peoples.

Such meetings will help, but parents will continue to regard the report card as providing the most important evaluation of their children's progress. It is highly desirable, therefore, that the teacher make the mark which he records on the card as reliable as possible. The reliability of a mark is enhanced by basing it on as many types of evidence as possible—such as evidence from the teacher's observation of the child, from teacher-made tests (which should be frequently administered), from standardized tests, from the pupil's daily work with maps and reference work, and on written and oral reports on individual projects. If the teacher is systematic about keeping records of all of these evidences of performance, he is in a position to report a reliable and defensible grade.

One limitation of a report card is its failure to indicate at what points a child may need help. It may report a low level of performance, but not a statement of factors which may be contributing to it. Many parents are frustrated by failure to know what they can do about a reported difficulty. The teacher-parent conference, a part of any good reporting system, helps such parents, as does a periodic letter from the teacher, which some schools provide, in which the teacher analyzes the child's performance and diag-noses his needs.

DELAYED EFFECTS OF INSTRUCTION

Almost every class includes pupils who seem to gain very few new ideas from a unit, whose social concepts do not seem to expand, and who seem to retain little of a tangible nature in the way of information and generalizations. Intellectual confusion or indifference may be revealed in their contributions to class discussions, their participation in dramatics, their notebooks, their drawings, and their maps.

Yet, it is not always correct to conclude that the unit has been a total loss for them. Inner development often takes place without its immediate disclosure. Perhaps not until similar materials are encountered by the child at a later period of his life will the full value of the unit be manifested. An ardent conservationist recalls having his enthusiasm for the out of doors first kindled by a lively study of conservation in a class taught by the author. An acquaintance of the author traces her ability to listen with an open mind to a teacher who stressed the need for it, often with seeming futility at the time.

Teachers never positively know which stroke of effort has the profoundest influence and *which* of their pupils have been the most deeply affected. But this should not disturb them. They are on safe ground if they consistently exercise Flanders' "indirect" categories of "communicative behavior."[9] These include the acceptance of pupil feelings, whether those feelings be positive or negative; praising and encouraging pupils; accepting, clarifying, and developing pupil ideas; and asking questions of pupils. Flanders found that pupil achievement in social studies was significantly higher in classes in which these practices frequently were employed by teachers than in classes in which teachers exercise more of the commanding, critical, authoritarian type of behavior. Teachers can normally rest assured that if they pour enthusiasm into their teaching, if their respect for their pupils is consistently expressed, and if they hold the class to high standards, every child will gain something of value and will make progress.

FOR REVIEW AND REFLECTION

1. What is the distinction between the terms "evaluation" and "measurement"?
2. What are some of the pitfalls in observation as a basis for evaluation?
3. Compare the hierarchical arrangements of the *Taxonomy*'s cognitive and affective categories.
4. Analyze the assumptions and implications of the concept that a child should achieve up to the level of his capacity.
5. Compare (a) rating card, (b) parent conference, (c) diagnostic letter as means of reporting pupil achievement to parents.

ASSIGNMENTS

1. Observe a social studies class in an elementary school, and make a list of occurrences which appear of sufficient significance to be noted in a child's individual record card.
2. Assemble specimens of one child's writing, map work, and drawing which are the products of social studies experiences. Draw conclusions concerning his probable level of conceptual thinking thus revealed.
3. Select a unit topic, and make an outline showing the relation between objectives, pupil activities, and evaluation of pupil progress.
4. Construct a social studies test and administer it (or have it administered) to a class. Subject the test to an item analysis (see Footnote 3), and show how you would rewrite the test on the basis of the analysis.

SUPPLEMENTARY READING

Black, Hillel, *They Shall Not Pass*. New York: Morrow, 1963. A popularly written attack on tests and testing.
Buros, Oscar K. (Ed.), *The Sixth Mental Measurements Yearbook*. Highland Park, N.J.: Gryphon Press, 1965. Pp. 1215–1247. Reviews social studies tests.

[9] Ned A. Flanders, *Teacher Influence, Pupil Attitudes and Achievement*. Washington, D.C.: Superintendent of Documents, 1965.

Chauncey, Henry, and John E. Dobbin, *Testing: Its Place in Education Today.* New York: Harper & Row, 1963. Describes the place and use of tests in education today, and analyzes many test items by way of illustration.

Christophel, Edna, "Checking Map-Reading Skills in the Elementary Grades," *Journal of Geography,* **60** (September 1961), 285–287. Gives examples of test items.

Davis, Frederick B., *Educational Measurements and their Interpretation.* Belmont, Calif.: Wadsworth, 1964. A clear introduction to testing, including practical suggestions for the teacher on test construction, interpretation of test results, and marking pupil progress.

Englehart, Max D., *Improving Classroom Testing.* Pamphlet. Washington, D.C.: National Education Association, 1964. A good summary of what the teacher should know about making and using tests.

Goolsby, Thomas M., Jr., "Interrelationships Among Seven Measures of Competency in Elementary School Social Studies," *Dissertation Abstracts,* **24** (May 1964), 4540. Reports rather close relationship between different aspects of social studies achievement and raises question of need to test each aspect separately.

Henson, Rosa May, "A Measurement of Social Studies Achievement in the Primary Grades," *Dissertation Abstracts,* **25** (August 1964), 934. Describes the steps in developing a test for the primary grades.

Hoffmann, Banesh, *Tyranny of Testing.* New York: Crowell-Collier and Macmillan, 1962. A critique of objective testing.

Kurfman, Dana G., "Teacher-made Tests in the Social Studies," *Educational Leadership,* **20** (October 1962), 16–19, 80. Suggests tests that will reflect understanding as well as recall.

Lyman, Howard B., *Test Scores and What They Mean.* Englewood Cliffs, N.J.: Prentice-Hall, 1963. Describes various types of tests, attributes of tests, norms, profiles, and the like.

McLaughlin, Kenneth F., *Interpretation of Test Results.* Pamphlet. U.S. Office of Education. Washington, D.C.: Superintendent of Documents, 1964. Describes development of standardized tests, explains their interpretation, and suggests how the teacher can present test results to pupils and parents.

Milor, John H., "A Superintendent Looks at Fifth-Grade Social Studies," *Childhood Education,* **41** (November 1964), 115–119. Contains a checklist for evaluating a social studies program.

Mugge, Dorothy J., "Social Studies Information of Young Children," *Childhood Education,* **42** (September 1965), 63–64. Reports finding that second-grade children responded correctly to about one-third of questions in social studies test administered before they studied the topics covered by the test. Children tended to show lack of precision, inability to handle two factors at once, difficulty in responding to key words in sentences, and poor grasp of time and place concepts.

Russell, David H., "The Dimensions of Children's Meaning Vocabularies in Grades Four through Twelve," *University of California Publications in Education.* Berkeley, Calif.: University of California Press, 1954. Vol. 11, No. 5. Reveals the problems in measuring technical vocabulary and concepts and gives examples of tests.

"Testing and the Schools," *Theory Into Practice,* **2** (October 1963), 181–245. Contains eight articles and three book reviews covering diverse aspects of testing, testing programs, and public reactions to tests.

Thorndike, Robert L., *The Concept of Over- and Underachievement.* New York: Teachers College, 1963. Explores problems in attempting to compare actual and predicted achievement.

Trimble, Clifford, "Evaluation in the Social Studies," *Education,* **86** (February 1966), 331–333. Recommends several approaches in evaluating social studies.

Wood, Dorothy, *Test Construction: Development and Construction of Achievement Tests.* Columbus, Ohio: Merrill, 1961. Concisely and clearly tells how to construct a good test.

APPENDIXES

A

DIRECTIONS FOR CONSTRUCTING
AN EROSION MODEL

SEE CHAPTER 7

The erosion model illustrates the close relationship between forests and soil. It is appropriate at any grade level. It consists of two large mounds of earth (corresponding to two adjacent hills) placed outdoors on a slight ridge where the ground tends to slope gently in opposite directions. Make the piles of earth firm with the hands and, with hands or a stick, scoop out a stream bed on each slope and continue it into the valley. The youngsters will enjoy constructing tiny bridges, houses, fences, and people to add a touch of realism. Press moss firmly to cover one of the mounds including the banks of the stream bed. Evergreen twigs may be pushed into the moss to represent trees. Holding a filled sprinkling can or the nozzle of a hose (in spray position) about three feet above the forested hillside, pour the rain upon it. The full force of the rain's descent is broken by the trees, and much of the water is soaked up by the absorbent undercover. Conse-

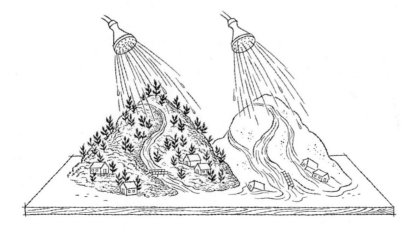

quently, the water flows down the stream bed in an orderly, leisurely manner. The water will be clear (during the second or third trial if not at first) and do no damage (see the illustration on the preceding page).

When the water is sprayed upon the exposed hill, however, the water strikes the ground with an impact that forms gullies. The water rushes down the hill with great speed, is muddy, overflows the stream banks, and is apt to dislodge the bridges and flood the lower parts of the houses.

This demonstration depicts vividly the role of vegetation in conserving water, preventing floods and dust storms, and holding topsoil in place. It can be repeated several times, with the barren mound needing repeated reconstruction.

B

DIRECTIONS FOR CONSTRUCTING
THREE-DIMENSIONAL RELIEF MAPS

SEE CHAPTER 10

Decide what dimensions the map is to be. A map four feet long and as wide as necessary to accommodate the shape of the area is satisfactory for ordinary classroom purposes. Obtain a piece of 3-ply wood of these dimensions to serve as the base upon which to build the map. Draw an outline of the map, contour lines, rivers, and lakes on the board and also on a piece of paper of the same size. These drawn lines will serve as your guide when you are modeling the plastic material on the board. (As you cover the board with the first layer of plastic material, you also cover the map sketch thereon; hence, the similarly scaled sketch on the paper becomes invaluable for checking details as you continue to build the map.)

It is not recommended that you draw the map outline freehand. Transfer the map to the board as follows. First stand the board on the chalk ledge of a chalkboard. Then project the image of a good clear map from an atlas or other source with an opaque projector upon the board. Trace the outline and contour lines upon the board. Then tack the paper to the board and repeat. In order to make the map on the large sheet of paper easy to read, crayon all water blue and color areas between contour lines a different shade for each altitude range. On the board, paint rivers and other water bodies that are at sea level with blue oil paint and then varnish them; color spaces between contour lines with crayon as on the paper.

The scale of altitude will have to be greater than the horizontal scale. The reason for this is that the roughness of the earth's surface is insignificant compared to the extent of surface area. If Mt. Everest, the highest peak in the world, were modeled to scale on a square four-foot map of India, it would be a tiny bump about an eighth of an inch high. If Mt. Kosciusko, the highest mountain in Australia, were modeled to scale on a map of Australia 3⅓x4 feet in size, it would be an imperceptible three-hundredths of an inch high, and other important elevations would

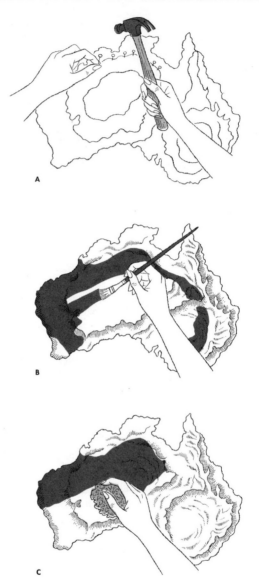

A

B

C

not show at all. It is necessary, therefore, to select a common-sense vertical scale. If the contour lines describe four different levels (let us say sea level, 100 feet, 200 feet, and 300 feet), you might assign levels on the map as follows: board level, 1 inch, 2 inches, and 3 inches. It is rarely advisable to build contours beyond 3 or 3½ inches on 4-foot maps because higher contours than these would grotesquely dwarf horizontal distances.

Hammer brads into the board every few inches along contour lines and at points where mountain peaks are to be represented (Drawing A). They should project about a quarter of an inch less than the desired height of projected contours. These are necessary guides during the modeling process and will also help to strengthen the plastic material.

Papier-mâché is probably the cheapest of plastic materials and the most generally satisfactory. However, it requires considerable work to prepare. White tissue paper (or newspaper if you are satisfied with a fairly coarse medium) is cut into squares of 1 or 2 inches, soaked in water overnight, and boiled for several hours. A quicker and equally satisfactory method is to soak the paper and then put it into an electric blender, beating it to a fine pulp. Pour off the water, and add a cup of flour and water (the consistency of heavy cream into which stir 2 tablespoons of powdered glue). Work this mixture into the paper with your fingers.

Wood putty requires no preparation, is easier to model with than papier-mâché, and produces a smoother surface. However, it is much more expensive.

Putty is easy to model with and cheap. It is good for primary grades and small maps.

Plasticene handles well in modeling, but it is expensive.

Molding sand, mixed with water, hardens in about 12 hours. It can be used repeatedly after it has set by breaking it up into small pieces with a mallet and again mixing it with water.

Sawdust when screened and mixed with wallpaper paste powder in a 4 to 1 proportion makes a strong, light map and lends itself to delicate molding.

It is best to avoid clay (which cracks easily), salt-and-flour mixtures (which are moisture collectors), and plaster of Paris (which hardens too quickly and makes a heavy map).

In applying the plastic mixture to the board, build the relief one layer at a time. Build with an eye to the brads that have been driven in as guides and with frequent reference to the map which you drew on the large paper sheet. Show the drainage systems accurately, with rivers flowing continually downhill until they reach the lowest level. Cracks and holes usually appear in papier-mâché upon drying, and these can be filled by painting a thick glue over the entire modeled portion of the map; or, if an electric blender was used in making the pulp, by filling the cracks and holes with the fuzz which forms in the blender. Varnish the map when it is dry, or apply two coats of some waterproof paint. Finally, paint the rivers and lakes with blue oil paint applied with a fine paintbrush.

The completed map may be used to demonstrate a variety of relationships. Dry regions and agricultural regions may be designated with contrasting water colors (see Drawing B), and they may later be washed off (see Drawing C) to make way for the coloring of the highlands and location of the major urban centers. It can be a products map one day and a map charting historical events another day.

C

DIRECTIONS FOR MAKING PAPER

SEE CHAPTER 11

If you wanted to make pulp and paper on a commercial scale, the first thing you would need would be a mill costing at least 10 million dollars. But you can make paper by hand in the classroom with equipment already available. You can manufacture it as it was produced for centuries before the invention of the first papermaking machine. The principle of papermaking has remained the same, but the methods, quality, volume, and variety of the products are vastly different.

This text and the photographs on papermaking were prepared by the American Paper Institute. The Institute graciously granted permission for their use in this book.

EQUIPMENT

1. A fine-meshed wire screen.
2. A metal pan, an old biscuit pan, a refrigerator tray, or an aluminum frozen food container can be used. Trim the screen to fit inside the pan. Then cut the bottom of the pan, leaving a ledge of about one-half inch wide to support the screen.
3. A forming rack or mold. This can be made from a second pan that will fit inside the first. Cut out the entire bottom, leaving only the sides.
4. A basin that will hold at least 10 quarts of water.
5. Thirty sheets of facial tissue (not "wet strength").
6. Two sheets of blotting paper, pan size.
7. Laundry starch. One tablespoon of instant starch in two cups of water will provide what commercial papermakers call "size."
8. An egg beater, or blender, and a rolling pin.
9. Household electric iron.

Step 1: Tear sheets of tissue and place in basin. Pour in starch and additional water to make about 10 quarts. Beat until thoroughly mixed.

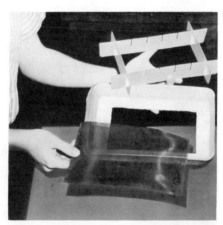

Step 2: Prepare the paper machine, consisting of pan, screen, and forming rack. This pan and rack came from an old refrigerator tray.

Step 3: Hold forming rack firmly on the screen and dip sidewise into the pulp mixture.

Step 4: Clean off the excess pulp outside forming rack. Lift out the screen on which the pulp has formed.

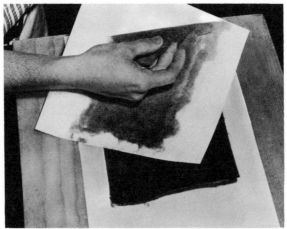

Step 5: Dry the screen and wet sheet of pulp between two pieces of blotting paper. The formed sheet will stick to them. Press out excess water with rolling pin.

Step 6: Finally, iron-dry (not too hot) the sheet still between the blotters. Trim the edges with scissors. You now have a sheet of hand-made paper.

D

PROFESSIONAL ORGANIZATIONS
AND PERIODICALS

The National Council for the Social Studies (a division of the National Education Association) welcomes to membership teachers at all levels—elementary, secondary, and college. It promotes the study of the problems of teaching social studies, encourages research, experimentation, and investigation, and seeks to integrate the efforts of all scholarly and professional groups who include among their aims the improvement of curriculum and teaching in the social sciences. The Council's national office is an invaluable clearing house for information about social programs, materials, and methods of instruction. Numerous local, state, and regional groups are affiliated with the Council. The organization offers opportunity for participation of its members at both the local and national levels. It holds a national conference annually immediately preceding and during the Thanksgiving weekend. Membership includes a subscription to the monthly, *Social Education*, and to the Council's yearbooks. Other publications are issued from time to time. Reduced dues have been established for student members. Headquarters are at 1201 Sixteenth Street, N.W., Washington, D.C. 20036.

The National Council for Geographic Education is also an organization of elementary, secondary, and college teachers. Its national conference is held annually over the Thanksgiving weekend. Membership includes a subscription to *Journal of Geography*. Other publications include a "Do It This Way" series and miscellaneous leaflets on teaching methods. The Council's headquarters are located at Room 1532, 111 W. Washington Street, Chicago, Ill. 60602.

The Joint Council on Economic Education provides consulting services to school officials and teachers, demonstrates teaching techniques in local schools, and distributes instructional material. Local councils are established in 45 states. While the Joint Council is not a membership organization, a school district may apply for a cooperative relationship for the purpose of experimenting with and developing materials and methods. Its publications are designed to assist the teacher in keeping abreast of the field of economics and in teaching economic concepts. The Joint Council's national headquarters are located at 1212 Avenue of the Americas, New York, N. Y. 10036.

The following publications contain articles which deal with the content, concepts, and scholarship in the social sciences as well as articles which treat the problems and issues faced by teachers of social studies in elementary and secondary schools.

Social Education (official organ of the National Council for the Social Studies, published in collaboration with the American Historical Association), 1201 Sixteenth Street, N.W., Washington, D.C. 20036.

The Social Studies, McKinley Publishing Company, 112 S. New Broadway, Brooklawn, N. J. 08030.

Journal of Geography (official organ of the National Council for Geographic Education), Room 1532, 111 W. Washington Street, Chicago, Ill. 60602.

Newsletter of the Joint Council on Economic Education, 1212 Avenue of the Americas, New York, N. Y. 10036.

INDEX